Frontier narratives

Frontier narratives

Liminal lives in the early modern Mediterranean

Steven Hutchinson

Manchester University Press

Copyright © Steven Hutchinson 2020

The right of Steven Hutchinson to be identified as the author of this work has been asserted by him in accordance with the Copyright, Designs and Patents Act 1988.

Published by Manchester University Press
Oxford Road, Manchester M13 9PL
www.manchesteruniversitypress.co.uk

British Library Cataloguing-in-Publication Data is available

ISBN 978 1 5261 4643 4 hardback
ISBN 978 1 5261 6707 1 paperback

First published by Manchester University Press in hardback 2020

This edition published 2022

The publisher has no responsibility for the persistence or accuracy of URLs for any external or third-party internet websites referred to in this book, and does not guarantee that any content on such websites is, or will remain, accurate or appropriate.

Typeset by Newgen Publishing UK

For Mercedes

Contents

List of figures	*viii*
Preface	*ix*
Map	*xii*

1	Introduction	1
	Outlines of the Mediterranean	1
	Genres and writers	16
	Mediterranean frontier literature	21
	Chapter overview	32
2	Slaves	35
	Modes of slavery in the Mediterranean world	36
	Becoming slaves	45
	Enslaved women	55
3	Renegades	71
	Terms, significance, sources	72
	Symmetries and asymmetries	77
	Renegade profiles	83
	Apprehending the enigma and the spectrum	121
4	Martyrs	129
	Cervantine prelude	129
	Theatres of cruelty	131
	Faces of martyrdom	139
	Martyrdom in perspective	147
5	Counternarratives	153
	Portraying the Moriscos	153
	Divergent accounts	175
	Telling other stories	181
	Conclusion	194
	Bibliography	*204*
	Index	*223*

Figures

1 Map of the Mediterranean (Courtesy of Megan Roessler, Cartography Lab, Department of Geography, University of Wisconsin–Madison)   xii
2 Agostino Veneziano, portrait of Hayreddin Barbarossa, 1535 (Metropolitan Museum of Art / Wikimedia Commons / public domain)   2
3 Image of Algiers from Braun and Hogenberg's *Civitates orbis terrarum*, 1575 (Based on a 1541 engraving by Antonio Salamanca. Historic Cities Center / Wikimedia Commons / public domain)   7
4 Seventeenth-century watercolour of the Algerian and Spanish shores of the Mediterranean (Spain. Ministerio de Cultura y Deporte. Archivo General de Simancas, MPD, 67,024)   11
5 Vicente Carducho, ink drawing of the expulsion of the Moriscos, *c.* 1627 (Museo del Prado / Wikimedia Commons / public domain)   158
6 Diego Velázquez, *Juan de Pareja*, 1650 (detail) (Metropolitan Museum of Art, New York / Wikimedia Commons / public domain)   159

Preface

Like other outsiders, I've always felt the allurement of Mediterranean cultures, literatures, geography and history from ancient times to the present, and have travelled to many of its cities and shores over the years. I've also lived in places not far from the Great Sea. The Mediterranean belongs to everyone. Mediterranean topics and themes have been integral to my research projects and teaching since long before I started writing this book, and will continue to be so even now as I've modulated to another major project, part of which overlaps geographically with this one.

Many people have accompanied me in parts or all of this Mediterranean journey.

I dedicate this book to Mercedes Alcalá Galán, soulmate, generous in spirit, intellect and talent, born on the strait that keeps the Mediterranean from drying up.

I thank Meredith Carroll of Manchester University Press for her extraordinary insight that in one stroke reshaped this book. It has been a privilege and pleasure to work with her. I am also grateful to Jen Mellor, Alun Richards, Helen Flitton and Katie Finnegan for their invaluable collaboration in the publication of this book.

For reasons that they are aware of – and sometimes many reasons or more than reasons – I want to express my profound gratitude to Luis Bernabé Pons, James Iffland, Adrienne Martín and Will Corral, Susan Friedman, Howard Mancing, Ruth Fine, Luis Avilés, María Antonia Garcés, Steven Wagschal, Kevin Ingram, Ev Hanson, Mercedes Galán Calzada, Francisco Layna, Miguel Ángel de Bunes, Enrique García Santo-Tomás, Gustavo Illades, Antonio Cortijo, Dustin Cowell, Christina Lee, Marina Brownlee, Ramón Alba, Feli Corvillo Romero, Georgina Dopico Black, Edwin Williamson, Fred de Armas, Carolyn Nadeau, Bruce Burningham, Cory Reed, David Boruchoff, Isabel Lozano Renieblas, Elizabeth Bearden, Sonia Velázquez, Hall Bjornstad, Laura Bass, Ana Laguna, Ignacio Navarrete, John Slater, Trevor Dadson, Borja Franco, Antonio Urquízar, Luís Madureira, Roy Williams, Daniel Whittington, Mario Ortiz Robles, Guillermina De Ferrari, Paola Hernández, Marcelo Pellegrini, Pablo Gómez, Barbara Fuchs, Carmen Hsu, Michael Armstrong Roche, Anne Cruz, José Manuel Lucía Mejías, José Cartagena-Calderón, José Manuel Martín Morán, Michel Moner, and – with a special kind of thanks – Félix Armadá. Those unwittingly omitted here, and there must be several, will kindly pardon my oversight.

And *in memoriam*, Carroll Johnson and Francisco Márquez Villanueva will always have my gratitude.

As adviser at the University of Wisconsin–Madison or as reader for doctoral students at other universities, I've had the privilege of working on Mediterranean themes with talented graduate students who are now colleagues in Mediterranean studies, or in early modern studies related to my own in other ways. These include Catherine Infante, Michael Gordon, Kelsey Ihinger, Ana María Rodríguez, Saylín Álvarez and Paul Michael Johnson, among others, as well as current doctoral students.

I would also like to acknowledge the generosity of Priya Ananth, whose work as research assistant has been invaluable.

I am profoundly indebted to the Institute for Research in the Humanities at the University of Wisconsin–Madison which, during my Resident Fellowship and my continuing Senior Fellowship, has provided not only time and means for ambitious projects but also a fabulous environment of weekly dialogue with fellow researchers. This book would by no means have taken the shape it has without the continual stimulus of the IRH.

A sabbatical granted by the University of Wisconsin–Madison in spring 2017 likewise offered invaluable support for this project, for which I am most grateful.

As will be noted in the book, I thank the *Journal of Levantine Studies* and *eHumanista* for permission to reuse materials in much expanded and revised versions of what are now chapters 3 (Renegades) and 4 (Martyrs), respectively, the latter translated from Spanish and rewritten. Similarly, I express gratitude to the Archivo General de Simancas for permission to use the image of the 'two shores' of the Mediterranean; and to the Cartography Lab at the University of Wisconsin–Madison – and particularly Megan Roessler – for making the Mediterranean map. Unless otherwise indicated by way of the bibliography or a note, all translations from Spanish, French, Italian and Portuguese are mine. In some cases I've consulted excellent translations from which on occasion I've incorporated a word or phrase more apt than my own rendering. These include the translations into English of *Don Quixote* by John Rutherford (Penguin, 2000) and Edith Grossman (Ecco Books, 2003), of Cervantes' *Persiles* by Celia Weller and Clark Colahan (University of California Press, 1989), and of the first treatise of Antonio de Sosa's *Topography of Algiers* edited by María Antonia Garcés and translated by Diana de Armas Wilson (University of Notre Dame Press, 2011). My translations tend towards conveying the original meaning closely as long as it remains readable and idiomatic in English.

As this book is predicated on allowing early modern writers, speakers and characters to be read and heard as much as is reasonably possible in their own words, most of the translated passages also appear in the original, particularly in footnotes. Yet for reasons of space, when a passage (in my view) offers no ambiguities, difficulties or untranslatable expressiveness – or when the translated passage appears in a footnote – the original has been omitted. Translated passages from modern scholarship are likewise not given in the original, although original words or phrases are placed in brackets whenever this seems to be called for.

Since many early modern works have multiple editions, sometimes in different languages, it would obviously be unhelpful to cite only page numbers from the particular edition I have used. More extensive works having larger units such as 'books' or 'parts' or 'treatises' and then smaller units such as chapters are cited with the largest unit in capital Roman numerals and the middle unit in Arabic numerals, generally followed by page numbers. Thus the Morisco Ricote's discourse in *Don Quixote* part II, chapter 54 would be cited as (II, 54, 1071–4), and this scheme also applies to, say, Antonio de Sosa's five-treatise work *Topografía de Argel*, which additionally has page numbers in *recto* or *verso* (r or v). I have avoided cluttering the text or notes with 'p.' or 'pp.': bearing in mind the basic three-part scheme of a number of frequently cited works, it should always be apparent if the numbers refer to pages. This format occasionally needs to be adjusted if the work has different sorts of units such as plays in verse. Works with numbered sections, such as most of Nietzsche's books, are cited by section rather than page numbers. This should enable anyone to find with ease the passages in editions other than those I use here.

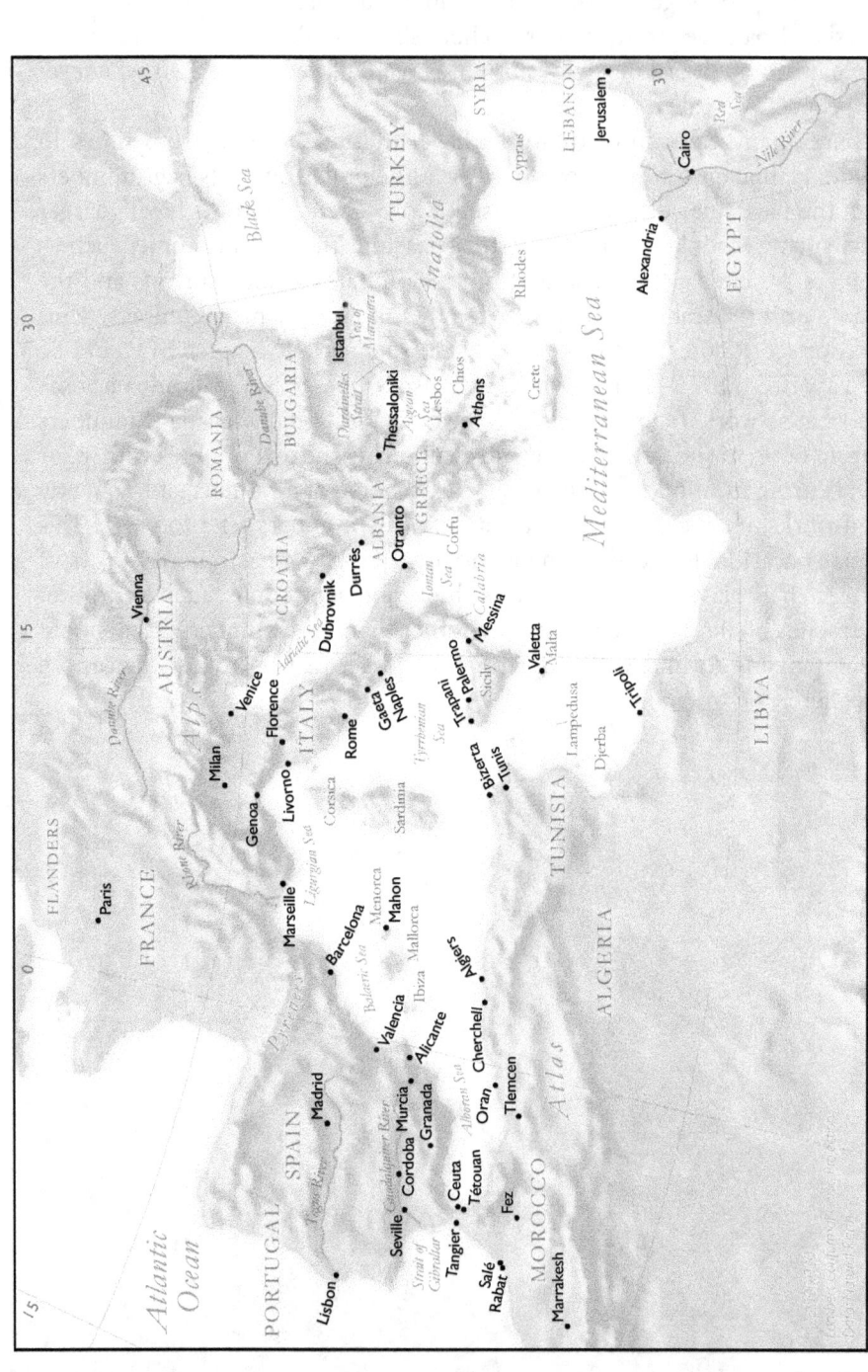

1 Map of the Mediterranean

1

Introduction

Outlines of the Mediterranean

'The Mediterranean speaks with many voices; it is a sum of individual histories', writes Fernand Braudel in his magnum opus on the Mediterranean world of the later sixteenth century (1: 13), a work that generously allows us to hear many voices. My strategy in this book consists in part of being attentive to writing and speaking in the early modern Mediterranean world, to how people characterised the modalities of relationships and communicability of that world across ethnic, religious, geographical, linguistic and racial boundaries. The texts themselves, in a wide array of discursive genres in many languages, embody writers' and narrators' voices, but also convey other voices, all of which in one way or another characterise their world and bring us into it almost as witnesses, depending on our ability to read and listen.

'Early modern' in this context begins perhaps with the Ottoman conquest of Constantinople in 1453, but mainly a half-century later with the Spanish and Portuguese conquest of enclaves on the African coast and the inception of Maghribian corsairing on the part of Aruch and Hayreddin Barbarossa, as of their arrival from Lesbos in the east. Until when? I've willingly been pulled far afield by fascinating texts of the late seventeenth century, and even the early eighteenth. Although European hegemony took hold towards the end of the eighteenth century, indeed with important precedents, the Mediterranean of corsairs, captives and slaves had prevailed almost three centuries on both sides of the religious and geopolitical divide. This was also in most respects a 'precolonial' epoch, one in which the Spanish and Ottoman Empires faced off until they signed a truce in the early 1580s. After this there were likewise no 'colonies' as such, no dominant powers in the Mediterranean, although the Ottomans continued to hold much of the eastern Mediterranean and have regencies in the western basin as well.

More problematic is the term 'Mediterranean' here. Having lived a year in Egypt and visited the Mashriq, I would have been delighted to have incorporated these lands into this study. Yet they are quite marginal because the texts I deal with rarely take us to those parts of the eastern Mediterranean, though they focus a great deal on Istanbul and other places in the east such as Cyprus and many other islands as well as the Adriatic coastline and, of course,

2 *Agostino Veneziano, portrait of Hayreddin Barbarossa, 1535*

Venice. This is to say that 'Mediterranean' here is not a geographical concept nor a historical one but rather refers to where the texts 'take' us, and this depends on what kinds of texts we're dealing with, as I'll explain further ahead. It's not my task here to define *what* the Mediterranean *is* because admittedly I won't be dealing with the whole Mediterranean: long stretches of coastline everywhere will be only vaguely invoked if not entirely left alone along with the many peoples who lived there. The same goes for whole regions, e.g. the Levant, which are by no means excluded here, but simply 'less present' owing to the internal itineraries of texts I'll be considering.

Nonetheless, the debates among historians about how to conceptualise the Mediterranean are significant here, and in turn I have my own takes on these questions, particularly as they pertain to the parameters of this study:

- What are the external boundaries of the Mediterranean, and what determines them? Does the Mediterranean include only the sea itself, or the shores contiguous with it including port cities, or all the lands surrounding it?
- Is the Mediterranean a unity, a duality or a multiplicity? Otherwise put, are there one, two, three or more Mediterraneans, and by what criteria can they be distinguished as different or, on the contrary, subsumed into a common nexus?
- What internal boundaries or frontiers of the Mediterranean can be identified, and what kinds of boundaries or frontiers are they?
- How do historical epochs, including the rise and fall of 'civilisations' and empires, affect the questions raised above?
- What aspects of the Mediterranean may be considered unique, and what aspects does it share with other regions?

Perhaps Fernand Braudel develops the broadest conception of the Mediterranean by defining the sea itself and shorelines as the core but also demarcating a 'greater Mediterranean' bordered by the Alps, the Atlantic, the desert, certain river valleys, the outer edge of the cultivation of olive trees and date palms, and so on. This enables him to take a large view and observe how peoples and regions quite distant from any of the seas of the Mediterranean connect to them by way of commerce, travel, political and military intervention. Thus, for example, considering the strong presence in the Mediterranean of Madrid, despite its distance from the sea, and of Lisbon, despite its location on the Atlantic, and of other influential places not on the shores of the *mare nostrum*, the Mediterranean can be understood within its larger context of interchange and intervention. Braudel's 'greater Mediterranean' by no means prevents him from offering a great deal of information and insight about the sea itself.[1]

In his impressive long-range history of *The Great Sea*, David Abulafia opts rather for writing 'a history of the people who crossed the sea and lived

---

[1] Braudel's concept of the greater Mediterranean has led some historians to criticise him for writing about the lands around the sea and for not being 'a maritime historian'. The accusation is unfair, for although he often does turn his attention far inland, he also devotes much attention to the sea itself, its shores, islands, ports, and all the human activities that take place there.

close by its shores in ports and on islands' (xvii). There are several valid ways to define the perimeter of the Mediterranean, each of which presupposes a different methodology. For my purposes there's no need as such to define the outer boundaries of the Mediterranean, particularly since what I'm most interested in are frontier contact zones. In any event, I don't exclude a priori the 'greater Mediterranean', not only for political or commercial reasons but also because many people from the hinterlands, among them the young Miguel de Cervantes who abandoned Madrid for Italy, *became* as Mediterranean as anyone else.

More knotty is the issue of the unity or division or plurality of the Mediterranean during the early modern epoch. Already for a millennium, Muslims and Christians had confronted each other and sometimes coexisted in different parts of the Mediterranean. The Belgian historian Henri Pirenne, in works published between the two world wars, claimed that the expansion of Islam in the seventh and eighth centuries, rather than the earlier Germanic invasions, decisively ruptured Roman history, creating a permanent barrier between western Europe and the eastern Mediterranean in particular. While Pirenne framed and nuanced the Christian-Muslim divide in novel ways, many writers from the sixteenth century till our times have insisted on situating the Muslim-Christian divide at the crux of Mediterranean history, if not world history. A different variant of this dichotomy is Samuel Huntington's 'clash of civilisations' thesis – already suggested by Bernard Lewis and echoed by a fair number of scholars today, even some who deal with Islamic Spain – which posits civilisational conflict emerging as the primary catalyst of future discord and ultimately pits Islam against non-Islamic civilisations, particularly the Christian West. I mention this because the Muslim-Christian dichotomy underlies several conceptions of the early modern Mediterranean, including Andrew Hess's *The forgotten frontier* (1978), which argues for a 'separation of the Mediterranean world into different, well-defined cultural spheres', and more specifically, a 'divergence in the internal patterns of Latin Christian and Turko-Muslim civilisations' (3). The so-called 'forgotten frontier' was most traceable in the Strait of Gibraltar, the 'Ibero-African border' separating Europe from Africa along with their respective 'civilisations' during this period.

No one denies the importance of the Christian-Muslim divide in the Mediterranean, nor am I aware that any scholars had forgotten that border or what it meant, for the first time in history, nor was it 'forgotten' during the early modern period after its inception in 1492. The frequent hostilities between Christians and Muslims at this time in the Mediterranean are not a hypothesis but a fact that has to be taken fully into account. The question is what to make of it along with much related evidence, how to characterise it and find its nuances. For example, while many scholars still frame their studies with the assumption that Islam and Christianity were at war with each other in the Mediterranean of this epoch, we'll see in subsequent chapters that there never was such a war. Hess's thesis is better articulated and, at the same time, provides insight into what was going on especially in Morocco at that time. It is also a vehement argument against Braudel's theory of the unity of the Mediterranean at this time. In Braudel's words:

> Today in 1972, six years after the second French edition, I think I can say that two major truths have remained unchallenged. The first is the unity and coherence of the Mediterranean region. I retain the firm conviction that the Turkish Mediterranean lived and breathed with the same rhythms as the Christian, that the whole sea shared a common destiny, a heavy one indeed, with identical problems and general trends if not identical consequences. And the second is the greatness of the Mediterranean, which lasted well after the age of Columbus and Vasco da Gama, until the dawn of the seventeenth century or even later. (1: 14)

In another passage, Braudel elucidates further how this 'unity' comes about: 'The Mediterranean has no unity but that created by the movements of men, the relationships they imply, and the routes they follow. Lucien Febvre wrote, "The Mediterranean is the sum of its routes, land routes and sea routes, routes along the rivers and routes along the coasts, an immense network of regular and casual connections, the life-giving bloodstream of the Mediterranean region"' (1: 276). For Braudel, then, the continual movement, contact and resultant human relations are what create a unity that might not otherwise exist. Such contact and relations might indeed be hostile, and yet this too, for Braudel, brings people together and contributes to unity. He even characterises corsairing on both sides as 'positive', correlating in its rise and fall with 'the economic health of the Mediterranean' (2: 887). He reminds us that 'two great Mediterranean civilisations, warring neighbours, were frequently drawn, by circumstances and chance encounters, into fraternization' – which he substantiates with a splendid example (2: 759) cited in the final chapter of this book.

What Hess ultimately denies in his characterisation of 'two increasingly different civilizations' (10) turning away from each other is this movement in all directions, this all-so-frequent crossing from one side to the other, this contact/conflict and interchange and sometimes mutual understanding and even friendship. Braudel's frontier is 'liquid' and porous, while for Hess it is 'a thin line', a 'rigidly delineated boundary [that] virtually eliminated the possibility of cultural experimentation' (10). Hess downplays the vivacious commerce that took place in the entire Mediterranean through every phase of hostilities, the massive trafficking of people throughout the region and thus the continuous presence of tens of thousands of captives/slaves on both sides, the vast number of renegades particularly in the Maghrib, and the displacement of the Morisco population primarily to all the lands of the Maghrib, both clandestinely before the expulsion of 1609–14 or coercively during it. He also ignores in large part the proliferation of documents, autobiographical accounts, historical and geographical treatises, not to mention fictional texts about the Maghrib during this time. A key part of Hess's argument depends on his characterisation of sixteenth-century Spanish culture, especially written works, which he has mainly learned about from secondhand sources.[2] Nor does he have a grasp on the abundant texts about Algiers or Tunis, two vibrantly metropolitan and intercultural 'corsair' cities whose intensity of contact between 'civilisations' refutes his main thesis, as would any study of Istanbul. This isn't to say that Braudel's admirable masterpiece is immune to major objections, but simply that Hess and some of Braudel's other detractors – particularly Peregrine Horden and Nicholas Purcell[3] – haven't identified what they are (e.g. his theory of 'civilisations'). In general, however, it seems to me that Braudel's conceptualisation of the sixteenth-century Mediterranean world has in important ways withstood the test of time and countertheses (see Fusaro, 'After Braudel'). What's more, many early modern texts to which he had no access, or of which he was unaware, uncannily confirm his intuitions.

For Hess there is no unity because the two civilisations politically and culturally turn inward and close the border, as it were, reducing the possibility of associative relations. This is very questionable even with regard to the Moroccan kingdoms he focuses on most, which had large numbers of Morisco exiles in the ports and palaces and in several important cities and towns, as well as captives/slaves and renegades, together with Jewish merchants (both autochthonous and immigrants/migrants), and a presence of other foreigners. Nabil Matar observes in this regard:

---

[2] For Spanish literature, Hess relies mainly on Albert Mas's work *Les Turcs dans la littérature espagnole du Siècle d'Or* (1967), as his endnotes indicate. The last two chapters of Hess's book, 'The forgotten frontier' (ch. 9) and 'The Mediterranean divided' (ch. 10) are particularly rich in ungrounded affirmations about early modern Spanish culture. I should clarify that I focus on Hess because in recent years I've heard respectable French, Spanish and American historians invoke his vision admiringly as an apt representation of the early modern Mediterranean.

[3] Perhaps under the 'anxiety of influence', Horden and Purcell do all they can to discredit Braudel and nullify his achievements, placing him as the last of 'Four men in a boat' (along with Mikhail Rostovzteff, Henri Pirenne and Shlomo Dov Goitein), who are hopelessly 'romantic', i.e. incapable of seeing the realities of the Mediterranean. Another persistent claim on their part is that Braudel's work seems 'to have marked an end rather than a beginning in Mediterranean studies' (37, 43), apparently allowing them to mark a beginning rather than an end. And implicitly, of course, they, as opposed to Braudel, are doing a 'human history' of the Mediterranean, though the humans in their work covering three millennia are largely anonymous, voiceless, faceless, unknowable, and have little if anything to tell us about themselves and their world.

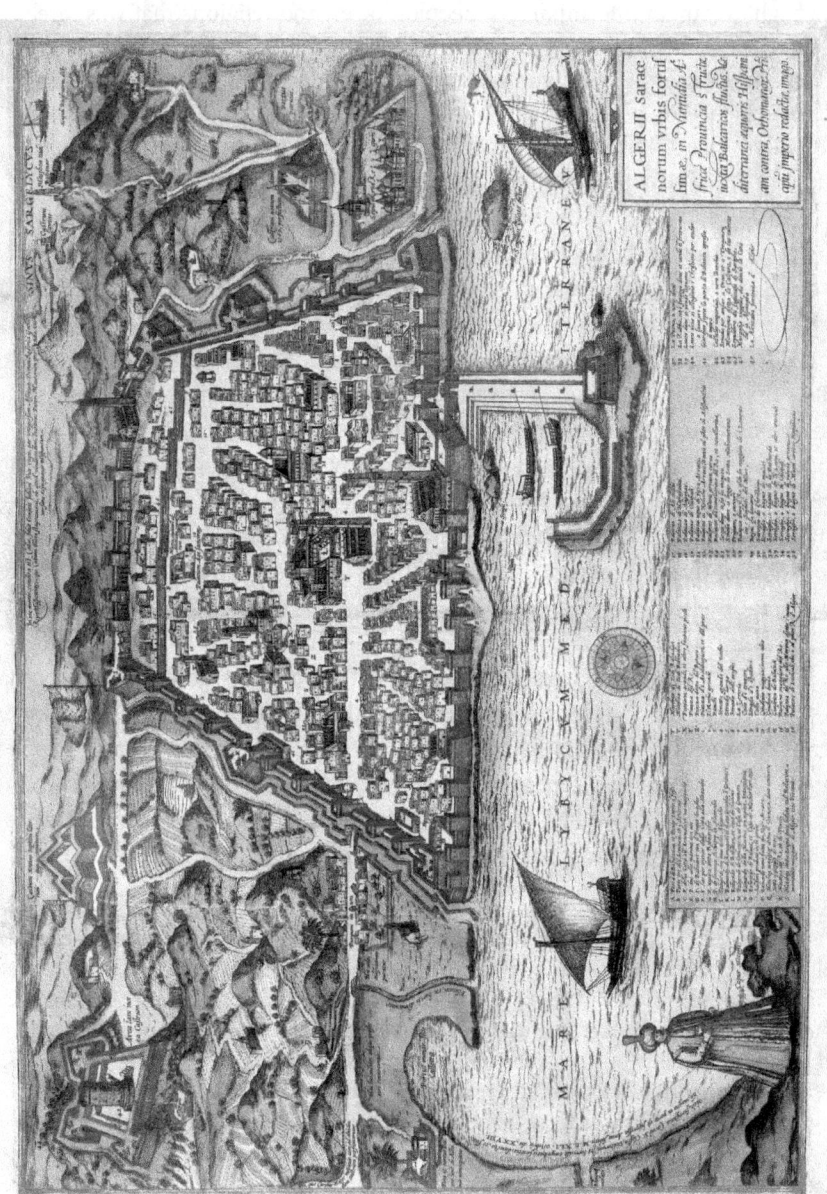

3 Image of Algiers from Braun and Hogenberg's Civitates orbis terrarum, 1575

> There were so many captives in Meknes, Ismail's capital, that the inner part of the city, al-Qunaytara, became their exclusive living quarters, with separate residences designated for the various nationalities – British, French, Portuguese, and Spanish – and for women, clergy, and the wealthy. Captivity brought about an intermixing of peoples, races, and religions that was rarely seen during this period of history. In cities such as Meknes and Marrakesh, Tunis and Algiers, captivity introduced a unique element of internationalism. The presence of peoples from outside the Mediterranean basin – Britons, Russians, Slavs, Poles, and Armenians – shows the diversity that prevailed among the captive population. ('England and Mediterranean captivity', 5–6)

For Braudel there is unity because the dominant chords of confrontation, dissonance and conflict presuppose associative contact, open lines of communication and continual large-scale crossings of the religious and geopolitical divide. His concept of unity here is close to that of Georg Simmel, for whom unity (*Einheit*) in its larger sense comprehends both harmonious and confrontational 'dualistic' relations, and in his view *depends* on conflict to bring people together and to resolve, in whatever ways, the 'dissociating factors' that gave rise to the conflict. In this generalised sense, regardless of the outcome, conflict is positive and associative.[4] We've already seen how Braudel never loses sight of the primary antagonism within the Mediterranean but sees even this antagonism as conducive to a wide range of relations and interactions. Moreover, he sees that the two sides were responsive to each other. Following the Hispano-Ottoman truce of the early 1580s, for example, he observes that both Spain and the Ottoman Empire turned their backs on the Mediterranean to concentrate on other fronts: 'This should remind us, if a reminder is needed, that the two great Mediterranean Empires beat with the same rhythm and that at least during the last twenty years of the century, the Mediterranean itself was no longer the focus of their ambitions and desires' (2: 678). If the

---

[4] In his essay on conflict, Simmel elaborates: 'This misunderstanding [regarding "unity"] probably derives from the twofold meaning of the concept of unity. We designate as "unity" the consensus and concord of interacting individuals, as against their discords, separations, and disharmonies. But we also call "unity" the total group-synthesis of persons, energies, and forms, that is, the ultimate wholeness of that group, a wholeness which covers both strictly-speaking unitary relations and dualistic relations. We thus account for the group phenomenon which we feel to be "unitary" in terms of functional components considered specifically unitary; and in so doing, we disregard the other, larger meaning of the term.' And regarding conflict in particular: 'Conflict itself resolves the tension between contrasts … This nature [of conflict] appears more clearly when it is realised that both forms of relation – the antithetical and the convergent – are fundamentally distinguished from the mere indifference of two or more individuals or groups. Whether it implies the rejection or the termination of sociation, indifference is purely negative. In contrast to such pure negativity, conflict contains something positive. Its positive and negative aspects, however, are integrated: they can be separated conceptually, but not empirically' (13–16).

choice is between one world or two, I have gravitated towards the notion of one Mediterranean world, and am averse to referring to the 'Muslim world' and the 'Christian world': it's all far too interconnected to speak of two worlds, despite the many differences and antagonisms.

It may well be that Braudel doesn't sufficiently acknowledge the socio-cultural differences among the many peoples of the Mediterranean or appreciate the importance of local spheres of trade and culture. In their extensive work on the Mediterranean, Horden and Purcell provide much evidence in support of the local nature of what took place in the Mediterranean. Given the many differences of language, ethnicity and religious affiliation, among other factors, an argument could be made that there were many Mediterraneans, at the same time as one would have to recognise that the Mediterranean as a whole had long-range trade routes, many cultural and religious similarities and that it functioned as a 'system', as it were. Unity in diversity, but above all unity: 'The Mediterranean is the sum of many seas, each with its own character, each feeding and being fed by the one "Great Sea"' (Abulafia, *The Mediterranean in history*, 15).

In *A shared world: Christians and Muslims in the early modern Mediterranean*, Molly Greene proposes a third paradigm beyond those of Braudel and Hess: 'the world of the eastern Mediterranean. This world, I argue, had a dynamic all of its own, one that is not adequately conveyed by a focus on the struggle – or absence of one – between Christianity and Islam. From the time of the Fourth Crusade in 1204 onward, the eastern Mediterranean was the point of intersection for not two, but three, enduring civilisations – namely, Latin Christianity, Eastern Orthodoxy, and Islam' (4). She focuses on the case of Crete, which was 'not only the last stop in the long contest between the Ottomans and the Venetians. It was also the site of the most enduring, and profound, interaction among Latins, Eastern Christians, and Muslims in the eastern Mediterranean' (4). Crete is indeed a fascinating case, and all the more so with the evidence she presents. Without questioning the validity of this case study as such, and admiring the richness of the three-way model, I don't see that Crete is paradigmatic of the eastern Mediterranean, or that the 'world of the eastern Mediterranean' can stand for the entire Mediterranean (as suggested in the subtitle of her book): neither synecdoche is convincing.

Most interesting for my purposes is whether the eastern and western basins of the Mediterranean can be considered distinct and separate, and indeed whether the eastern Mediterranean can synecdochically assume the characteristics of the whole Mediterranean. The eastern and western basins of the Mediterranean have indeed long been distinguished. Besides the geographical evidence for this, the eastern Mediterranean in the sixteenth century did become, as Greene asserts, 'the Muslim lake', in the sense that the Ottomans controlled nearly all of it after the conquest of the Mashriq, Rhodes, Cypress, etc., except for the coast of eastern Italy and Sicily and a number of other islands including Malta. To describe this as a 'lake' – in the wake of Greek nationalists who called the eastern Mediterranean 'the Greek lake' – seems imprecise. There are good arguments to support the idea that the eastern Mediterranean functioned rather autonomously: Ottoman control, the presence of Orthodox Christianity in many places, the reduced presence of Latin Christianity, the relative detachment of the Fertile Crescent from the concerns of the Latin Christianity of the western Mediterranean, and so on. Istanbul itself was a megalopolis unmatched in size, strategic situation and metropolitanism in the rest of the Mediterranean world.

There are also reasons to question the two-basin model of the Mediterranean. The strait of Sicily (across to the Tunisian coast) was ten times wider than the Strait of Gibraltar, for example – 90 miles wide as opposed to 9 – and was no real impediment to seafarers going from one basin to the other. This traffic was indeed constant and substantial, as evinced in countless texts of the period. For example, the soldier Cervantes was stationed in Naples, Messina, and elsewhere in the Italian west, but the naval campaigns he participated in for years took him either to the centre (Tunis) or the eastern Mediterranean. The Spanish corsair Alonso de Contreras ventured mostly into the eastern Mediterranean before returning to his base in the centre, Malta. The Ottomans themselves connected regularly with their regencies in Algiers as of 1516 and Tunis as of 1574, had fleets and corsairs patrol the islands and coastlines of the west, and even sent token support to Spanish Muslims in the 1568–70 war of Granada. A fair number of Spanish Moriscos ended up in Istanbul, as did a great many captives. Merchants also crossed back and forth continually. In sum, there is no end to evidence pointing to a large volume of traffic back and forth, by sea as well as by land, and the passage of large-scale fleets further reinforces this. The Maghrib itself stretched into the eastern Mediterranean, and Italy – such as it was – straddled west and east. I don't recall any writers of the early modern period distinguishing between the western and eastern Mediterranean. While I recognise significant differences between west and east, I don't see these as arguments for a 'world of the eastern Mediterranean': once again, there was far too much traffic, contact and interaction between both sides to warrant the autonomisation of an eastern and western Mediterranean.

That said, for nearly everyone who lived or travelled in the Mediterranean, this sea made up of different seas would seldom be conceived as a totality but instead as a relational set of places and routes that would alter according to where one was from or had been and under what circumstances. It was mostly a perception of 'here' and 'there' rather than of a cartographic image. For different people, then, the notion of what we call 'the Mediterranean' would have varied greatly according to how they were situated geographically and in every other way. Most port cities would serve in part as nuclei of specific land and sea routes connecting to other places and regions, likewise without

4 Seventeenth-century watercolour of the Algerian and Spanish shores of the Mediterranean

connecting as such to the entirety of the Mediterranean. Only a few ports (perhaps Istanbul, Algiers, Valetta, Venice, Naples) would have had the sense of connecting more or less to the whole Mediterranean, and only a minority of individuals such as heads of state, cartographers, admirals and ship captains would have had a quasi-visual awareness of the entire Mediterranean. There were of course many maps, including portulan maps, of the whole sea, enabling users to visualise it with all its contours. A mariner and corsair captain like Alonso de Contreras would have had such a totalising view, as he explored nearly all of it and, nearly twenty years since he was a young sailor, composed his pilot's descriptive guide to the whole Mediterranean with all its coastlines and islands, the *Derrotero universal* (1616).

Key to my concerns are Mediterranean frontier zones, those places where there tended to be contact and interchange of whatever kind between people of diverse socio-cultural and religious signs. These frontier zones could be on either side of the religious and geopolitical divide, which certainly wasn't a line that anyone then or now could draw in the water or on a map, but rather a sense that moving between Muslim-controlled and Christian-controlled lands and islands involved a kind of crossover that didn't occur when moving between territories controlled by people of the same religion. On either side of this diffuse, watery divide, or even on it, were spaces irregularly distributed around the Mediterranean of denser or sparser contact zones, among many other areas where there was little if any contact. Contact here refers mainly to encounters between Christians, Muslims and Jews, including between representatives of subdivisions within these categories (e.g. within Christianity, Catholic and varieties of Orthodox and Protestant), as well as adversaries within the geopolitical layout of the Mediterranean. Differences of ethnicity, language, race, gender, sexuality, and so on, would also come into play according to particular circumstances, but not all of these lines of distinction would always qualify as creating contact zones. While all port cities fell clearly on one or the other side of the most salient geopolitical and religious divide, some of them provided unusually dense contact zones, among them Algiers, Tunis, Istanbul, Thessaloniki, Valletta (Malta), Venice, Naples, Palermo, Genoa, Marseille, Valencia – and, on the Atlantic side, Lisbon. This was also the case of other cities somewhat inland such as Marrakesh, Fez, Cairo, Rome and Seville, to name a few. All of this adumbrates in different shades the frontier zones within the expanse of Mediterranean seas and lands, in some cases overlapping with the Atlantic.

I use 'frontier zone' and 'contact zone' interchangeably. The latter term was conceptualised in 1991 by Mary Louise Pratt, who defines it as 'social spaces where cultures meet, clash and grapple with each other, often in contexts of highly asymmetrical relations of power, such as colonialism, slavery, or their aftermaths as they are lived out in many parts of the world today' (34). While the first half of this definition could have some application to the early modern Mediterranean, my interest is less in power struggles and negotiations than in the range of relations that develop throughout the contact. Power is certainly a factor, yet it tends to be already decided before these encounters take place. For instance, if someone is captured and enslaved, the power factor is established from the outset and is rarely up for negotiation. Moreover, my use of 'zone' refers less to abstract social space than to an actual place such as a port city or any other identifiable heterotopia where these sorts of contact occur. In every case it's important to look into what kind of contact takes place, how the frontier zone itself acts on the relations between people and on their ways of behaving and thinking – because those who find themselves on the frontier do act and think differently from how they did or would elsewhere. They tend no longer to be who they were before; they act according to new parameters, think in ways that take into account how the 'others' think, and thereby develop a frontier consciousness. The chapters ahead will lead us to many ways in which this peculiar consciousness reveals itself.

Another critical aspect of Mediterranean frontier zones is that there tends to be a variety of 'selves' and of 'others'. The 'other' is most often plural, not because there's more than one person identified as 'other' but because the Mediterranean world as a whole offers many different *kinds* of 'others'. The city of Algiers alone displays a whole inventory of types of 'others', as Sosa's *Topografía de Argel* amply illustrates: any allusion to 'the other' as a singular concept, e.g. 'the Muslim other', is quite meaningless in that context. And within the *we/they* distinction, *we* tend to be miscellaneous as well.

Clearly, the kind of Mediterranean we find in texts of that period is historically bound. The Mediterranean I refer to is early modern, stretching from the mid- or late fifteenth century – the conquest of Constantinople in 1453 and the conquest of the kingdom of Granada in 1492 signal two transformative events – until the eighteenth century, although the texts I deal with span mainly from the 1530s to the late seventeenth century, about a century and a half. There are of course many ways to periodise Mediterranean history. Taking a long view, Abulafia distinguishes five periods, the 'Fourth Mediterranean' extending from the Black Death in 1347 to the opening of the Suez Canal in 1869, when the Mediterranean 'had to cope with increasing competition from the Atlantic, and domination by Atlantic powers' (*The Great Sea*, xvii). He subdivides this into nine sometimes overlapping periods under appropriate headings, but only a few of these bear any resemblance to the kinds of themes raised in texts examined here. The Mediterranean has undergone so many radical transformations over the centuries that, in my view, the Mediterranean of the fourteenth and the first half of the fifteenth century, as well as that of the nineteenth century, are radically different Mediterraneans from the one considered here, and can hardly be lumped together. From the sixteenth to the eighteenth centuries, on the contrary, there were many fundamental continuities, despite several highly significant shifts throughout this period.

If we turn our attention from the Mediterranean as object of study to the scholarship about it, we find several versions of the Mediterranean, some of them overlapping, contradictory, complementary or mutually exclusive. These versions spring from differences of academic discipline or approach, of epochs or regions of study within the Mediterranean, of national involvement in the Mediterranean, of languages in which the bibliographical sources are written, and so on. Networks of scholars have emerged, organising conferences and producing edited volumes, special journal issues, anthologies, introductory works by series of specialists, and the like, and these quite often ignore the research of scholars who work on different regions or issues, or from different bibliographical bases. To cite one example of exclusion or indifference, a number of top scholars from countries outside Spain have indeed been attracted to imperial Spain in the Mediterranean and especially to Sephardic or Muslim Spain through post-expulsion diasporas, and have been welcomed as fellow scholars and collaborators by an impressive group of Spanish scholars, many of them renowned Arabists and versed in other Mediterranean languages such as French, Italian or Turkish – yet this entire body of avant-garde scholarship tends to be ignored by most Anglo-American scholars of the Mediterranean. Barring these sorts of limitations, historians have in general taken the lead in Mediterranean studies while, for example, literary scholarship has most often lagged far behind. At the same time it should be noted that, with some remarkable exceptions, historians themselves have shown little interest in the 'literary Mediterranean' and less ability to understand its rhetoric and implications.

This book draws primarily on modern historiography and literary studies and explores a wide array of early modern writings including geographies, chronicles, descriptions of countries or cities, religious treatises, archival sources, autobiographical accounts, captives' tales, and all the major genres of literary works. I've worked directly with texts in Spanish, French, English, Italian and Portuguese, and in translation with texts in Arabic (of which I have basic knowledge) and Turkish. Spanish writings are most prevalent, partly because of my own specialisation and partly because they are most likely the richest source of information and literary invention in the early modern Mediterranean unless unsuspected treasures someday turn up in Turkish archives. As a comparatist I'm by no means content with sources in one language and have drawn from writings in the other languages mentioned, particularly French, which I find extraordinarily interesting. Years ago I thought that perhaps a rudimentary corpus of early modern Mediterranean texts could be identified, but abandoned that idea after finding one remarkable text after another and wondering each time how I could have been unaware of it for so long, which of course implies that there's still much I haven't found. Incompleteness is a necessary condition of this book, but I hope it's compensated for by other qualities.

This range of texts will light up the Mediterranean in many places, particularly in frontier zones, while the variety of texts and frontier zones will multiply and even reverse the notions of *self* and *other*. The proliferation of pens – 'la pluma es lengua del alma' ('the pen is the soul's tongue' [*Don Quixote* II, 16, 759]) – and voices bring people of that time closer to us: we hear them, or at least have the script of their words and can activate those voices in our imagination. This guarantees a 'human' character to what we'll be examining. In reaction to Braudel's emphasis in part I of *The Mediterranean* on slow, long-term natural changes affected by the natural environment, Horden and Purcell begin their massive work *The corrupting sea* by saying it is 'the human history of the Mediterranean Sea and its coastlines over some three millennia' (9). With some critique of *The corrupting sea*, Abulafia affirms that his own book, *The Great Sea: A human history of the Mediterranean*, 'aims to bring to the fore the human experience of crossing the Mediterranean or of living in the port towns and islands that depended for their existence on the sea. The human hand has been more important in moulding the history of the Mediterranean than Braudel was ever prepared to admit. [...] The roulette wheel spins and the outcome is unpredictable, but human hands spin the wheel' (xxx–xxxi). Admirable as this intention is, I question what 'human' means here. My impression is that it refers primarily to the often anonymous, faceless and voiceless activities of politics, war and economy, and so on. All of these are undoubtedly very 'human', but such 'human history' rarely brings us close to any humans, while that of Horden and Purcell distances us even further from human beings – unlike, say, Braudel's history, which does indeed let the Mediterranean 'speak with many voices', all the more so as his work progresses beyond that environmental first part. My aim is to intensify even further the 'human' presence of the early modern Mediterranean by focusing primarily on a wide range of often remarkable texts written by people of that epoch who gave voice to their world. As far as I'm aware, many of these texts, passages, writers or characters have never appeared in a study in English – or, in a fair number of cases, in any language – and when they have been brought up, they tend to have been dealt with quite differently from the ways in which they appear in this book.

Why such methodological insistence on texts, voices, narratives? Well, it seems to me that trying to understand the Mediterranean of the early modern era without taking into consideration what the peoples of the Mediterranean wrote and said about themselves and others – how they described, narrated, dialogised and dramatised their life and their world – would be like trying to understand, say, 'Shakespeare', without having seen or read his works, relying instead on indirect documentation to conjecture what that author was allegedly about. By no means discarding other sorts of evidence, we can learn a great deal about these peoples through their writings.

Genres and writers

If the combination of many genres raises methodological problems, more problematic, it seems to me, would be restricting investigation to only one sub-category of sources, as often happens, or excluding, say, major genres such as narrative fiction, theatre and poetry, since this would impoverish immensely our image of any particular society and of the modalities of relations that arose between foreigners and local populations. There's nothing new at all in reading a society of the past through its imaginative literature, and such literature often tells us infinitely more about that society than do texts of other discursive genres. Yet no matter how 'good' it is, imaginative literature alone can give extraordinarily distorted and unreliable representations of a historical period, as is also the case with so-called non-fiction. In fact, perhaps none of these types of writing is reliable when read naively. For me, all types of writing display the characteristics of genre, whether fictional or not, and I concur with Hayden White that historiography is saturated with rhetorical, literary and ideological tropes and that it must take advantage of these inescapable properties to be effective.

The fact that imaginative genres don't claim to be true as such, and that many other genres such as chronicles, autobiographies, geographical or ethnographic descriptions do claim to represent truth, is of course fundamentally important. This obviously doesn't mean that histories will be true, but simply that they claim to be true. As Mark Twain puts it, 'The very ink with which all history is written is merely fluid prejudice' (101). The various kinds of treatises (chronicles, descriptions, etc.) we'll be looking at tend to have a high dose of fluid prejudice, and have to be read by assessing how such prejudice feeds into writing and obfuscates what it (mis)represents. Aristotle in his *Poetics* already distinguishes between poetic truth and historical truth – a distinction highly regarded in the early modern period – without taking into account the distorting or falsifying aspects of either one of them, as Nietzsche does when referring to what we could call poetic falsity: '*The muses as liars.* – "We are capable of telling many lies" – thus the muses once sang when they revealed themselves to Hesiod. – Many vital discoveries can be made if we for once apprehend the artist as a deceiver' (*Human*, vol. 2, pt. 1, #188).

All genres are suspect with regard to their truth value, yet few if any can be discounted. In many inquisitional records, the inquisitors tirelessly tell the accused, over months and years if necessary and with the instruments of torture nearby, to tell the 'truth' until they hear what they want to hear, yet from these torturous interrogations we can glean certain kinds of knowledge about the real circumstances of the accused. Without the mulishly faithful recording of these trials we would know so much less than we do about the early modern Mediterranean. At the other extreme Cervantes, in his play *La gran sultana*, does indeed allow us to see flashes of truth by exaggerating or inverting all the common stereotypes about the Ottoman court at Topkapı palace; to get at this truth we have to work through all the playful distortions and falsifications that the play presents us with (Alcalá Galán, 'Erotics of the exotic', 27–9). Yet we can't assume that Cervantes, with all his genius and prestige, always feeds us some kind of truth: he too occasionally listens to the muses' lies, it seems. On the other hand, in recent decades historians have been deeply impressed by how much rare insight can be gained from reading Cervantes' stories about the early modern Mediterranean world. As we know, fiction can sometimes illuminate what non-fictional genres are incapable of expressing. At the same time, many of the stories of historically identifiable characters and events are 'stranger than fiction', and thus strikingly revealing, especially in the Mediterranean world. Antonio de Sosa, in his *Topografía de Argel*, provides an enormous amount of credible and highly valuable information about Algiers as long as we know how to gauge his phobias, blind spots and other limitations. These few examples show us that the best we can do is counterbalance the different genres, often reading against the grain. All of the genres, 'fictional' or 'non-fictional', steeped with more or less prejudice, provide us with the wherewithal not to construct a complete mosaic about anything but at least to contextualise different types of knowledge in relation to each other and thus get a sense of how the Mediterranean world worked. In every case we need to be cognizant of the parameters and procedures of the genre, and the writer's handling of the genre as well as the expectations and limitations of whomever the text seems intended for.

Michel Foucault opens and closes his essay 'What is an author?' by quoting a passage from one of Samuel Beckett's *Texts for nothing*: ' "What does it matter who is speaking", someone said, "what does it matter who is speaking" ' (979). The passage, uttered anonymously (not exactly by the author 'Beckett'), speaks of an unnamed person who either doubts or denies the relevance of *who* is speaking, and we as readers are at least three removes from this anonymised *who* who *is speaking*. The statement, or rhetorical question without a question mark, could readily be adapted, as Foucault does, to writing. And what does it matter that Beckett of all people is writing this, and that Foucault in particular is citing it in his own text, and that someone is reading my quotation of all this anonymity and named authority? Many of the voices invoked in early modern texts are anonymous or somehow generic, and many texts themselves could have been penned by other writers with similar characteristics. Thus there are various intensities of anonymity in the vast majority of written and spoken acts: anonymity is mutable because sometimes we know nothing at all about who is writing or speaking, and other times we know something such as what category of person (e.g. woman or man, old or young, slave or free, ruler, renegade, marabout, corsair, merchant, Turk, Arab, Jew, Christian, and so on), or what the person's name is, conferring some partial individuality on the speaker or writer beyond Beckett's 'someone'. The sheer volume of people's acts including writing and speaking, whether anonymous, semi-anonymous or fully identifiable, evidently creates patterns that lead attentive listeners and readers to decipher aspects about the life of the early modern Mediterranean's named and unnamed protagonists. The relevance or irrelevance of *who* is speaking or writing also depends on *what* is being said or written, *to* or *for whom*, *in what circumstances*, and so on. While acknowledging the near anonymity of many utterances and the frequent inconsequentiality of who is speaking or writing in such cases, in other instances we might also attach primary significance to the question of who is writing or speaking, either because of the *type* of person this is (a diplomat, a sultana, a viceroy, a ransomer of captives, a captive, etc.) or, still more important, because of the individual characteristics of, say, a writer (Rabelais, Francisco Núñez Muley, Montaigne, Aḥmad ibn Qāsim al-Ḥajarī, Cervantes, Antonio de Sosa, Lope de Vega, Evliya Çelebi, María de Zayas, Emanuel d'Aranda, etc.). No matter what 'anybody' says, none of these writers could be mistaken for anyone else, and their 'authority' far transcends the mere 'author function'. In these and other cases of writing and speaking, we need to know who is saying what to whom, how, why, and in what circumstances.

Equally compelling is the question of who *doesn't* write or speak, or who does so in inhibited ways. The vast majority of people in the early modern Mediterranean were illiterate, and another large segment would have been incapable of writing a coherent text in any language. Many would have known more than one language, but from knowing a language to being able to write in it, e.g. in Arabic, Turkish or Greek, would have been an impossible leap for most. In any of its versions the Mediterranean lingua franca, remarkable as it was as the only pan-Mediterranean language, was an unwieldy instrument stripped of most grammatical inflection, made for oral communication but unsuitable for writing other than basic communication, mockery or parody. Among those who were able to write, then, many would have chosen *not to* or would have found their writing constrained in certain ways.

In his invaluable study and anthology *Europe through Arab eyes*, Nabil Matar makes some observations regarding what kinds of texts were written by Muslims and particularly Magharibi (people of the Maghrib): 'Unlike the European corpus of captivity, the Arabic corpus produced no plays or novels, nor grand narratives interspersed with page after page of empirical (or imaginary) ethnography, fauna, or flora. The *corpus captivitis* of the Magharibi is by far smaller than its European counterpart, consisting of anecdotes, memories, letters, and miracle accounts/*karamat*, all of them rarely more than a few paragraphs' (70). Even the handling of these genres of personal experience was very different, too: Christian writers tended to write verbose accounts replete with descriptions of their humiliations and the cruelties they had to endure. Similar genres likewise followed very different conventions of style in Arabic: autobiographical writing and travel narratives often suppressed details about one's own life, quoted previous authors and inserted laudatory poems and expressions of gratitude (20, 39–41).

Despite there being a *corpus captivitis* on both sides, and despite the tempting *imitatio Christi* model available to Christian ex-captives, it is more than understandable why the vast majority of literate or semi-literate former captives/slaves did not write about this harrowing experience either during or after it. In most cases, captivity/slavery would have been profoundly degrading, with many variations of abjection. It also tended to be very repetitive, as we see in some attempts at writing about one's own slavery. And it involved a loss of agency, since, as Sebastián de Covarrubias annotates in his great lexicon, 'el esclavo no es suyo' ('the slave does not belong to himself', under *esclavo*). None of this lends itself well to writing, let alone reading. The mould that most prevails is the capture-slavery-freedom sequence, which tends to work if the slavery part is livened up, e.g. with possibilities for escape. It takes a superior story-teller and observer to turn slavery from, say, a reiterative experience of drudgery and abuse into a series of adventures or anecdotes about other interesting people in the social milieu.

The issue of who wrote, and who didn't, crosscuts with categories of gender, profession, religious affiliation, and so on. The scarcity of women writers in Mediterranean frontier zones is readily comprehensible for reasons both related and unrelated to slavery, as we're all aware, including the perpetual striving on the part of women for rights of authorship. One would have thought that the life of travelling merchants (Jews, Muslims, Christians), with its highly privileged vantage points, might have been conducive to splendid narratives, but this was rarely the case. As for soldiers constantly on the move, those who did write, whether as ex-slaves or not, have given us some of the best accounts of the Mediterranean world, but again, nearly all refrained from writing. The most silent category of all despite their enormous importance was that of the 'renegades' in Muslim lands. This will be discussed more at length in chapter 3, but for now suffice it to say that writing would have meant confessing to apostasy, for a start, and would likely have included much else such as marrying a Muslim husband or wife, as well as having children, sometimes becoming a corsair, and so on. We know about renegades not because they wrote about themselves but mainly because the Inquisition documented the loss and recovery of their souls.

One category particularly predisposed to writing were clerics from the ransoming orders, mainly Trinitarians and Mercedarians, who had a cause that induced them to anathematise Muslim cruelty towards Christian captives and alert the people back home of the dangers of Christian captives reneging, which would imply sexual depravity, the spiritual loss of a Christian, and betrayal of country and religion as renegades became the worst enemies. Some of the most virulent texts of this kind come from Pierre Dan's *Histoire de Barbarie* (1637) and Gabriel Gómez de Losada's *Escuela de trabajos* (1670), two monumental, meticulous and perversely intriguing works that spare no effort in pursuing their agenda. Here the *what for?* and *for whom?* frame the entire enterprise. Of course, all clerics were literate, and even those who didn't share the same ransoming cause were inclined to defend the faith and take on Islam single-handedly, but some were also keen observers capable of dialogue and mutual understanding. I'm referring here mainly to two extraordinary writers who were also slaves, Antonio de Sosa in Algiers and Jerónimo Gracián in Tunis, whose works will be examined in some detail.

Apart from these, there were adventurers, ex-slaves who became geographers or historians, and an educated elite who wrote in Turkish, Arabic, Italian, Spanish, French, Portuguese, and so on, including exiled Morisco writers in Tunis (Bernabé Pons, *Los moriscos*, 171–8; 'De aljamía lejana', 105–30). We'll be looking into several of their works over the course of this book. Sometimes the intended readership and purpose of the texts are patent (e.g. bolstering the faith of fellow ex-Moriscos), while at other times the texts seem to be broadly intended for anyone who might be interested, without religious or ideological concerns. Cervantes deserves special mention for how he found innovative ways to turn his experience of slavery into narrative and drama, and, far beyond this, how his eleven years in the Mediterranean enabled him to vastly expand his perspectives on 'the human', to imagine his homeland from the other shore, and ultimately create the modern novel. His presence will be important throughout this book. For his part, Antonio de Sosa and his five-treatise *Topografía de Argel* will also receive attention because of the questions it raises about genre, the limitations and remarkable achievements of Sosa as writer, the wealth of information it provides, and the representation of Algiers, a city that looms large in the early modern Mediterranean and in many of the texts considered here.

I'd like to emphasise the processual nature of other people's writing – especially far removed from us in time and place – an activity we can in some ways, no matter how remotely, engage with and reenact as we read the products of that writing, intuiting its moods, intentions and aims. If there's nothing particularly 'natural' about writing, we need to be attentive to its wilfulness, its strategies and tactics, its affinities with established writing practices including genres. 'Raw' experience may not translate easily into writing unless ways have been devised to convey it via ink on a page, and there are probably many kinds of thought and experience (e.g. of those who lived in the early modern Mediterranean) that never found their way into any kind of writing. Obviously, what we're left with is what we have, but besides viewing these texts as objects made or completed events, the methods I use advocate for striving to get glimpses into the writers' 'workshops' in order to infer – to whatever extent possible and reasonable – how these texts were composed, and try to recover the act of writing. What might these writers have been *thinking* when they wrote this or that, and why did their texts turn out as they did?

Mediterranean frontier literature

This book, then, will unapologetically draw from fictional as well as non-fictional texts as flawed but vital sources for attempting to grasp how the conflicted Mediterranean world of corsairs, captives and converts was understood in the early modern era and how it can be understood now. Yet 'fiction' is by no means a self-evident category within this context because it is fiction *configured by* this context and by no means independent of it, and because – as is perhaps also the case with non-fiction – whatever insights it may yield rarely assume the guise of plain evidence. Where fiction diverges from non-fiction is in its relative detachment from supposed facts and in its greater autonomy to explore what's imaginable and narratively interesting, to use stereotypes for a variety of purposes and occasionally to conceive of characters and plots that display paradigmatic qualities. But what kinds of invented stories are these, what do they conceal and what do they reveal?

Just after a well-known metanovelistic passage in Cervantes' *Persiles* which reflects on the difference between history and fable, truth and fiction, two characters in a village plaza unfold a canvas that represents the harbour of Algiers and the corsair Dragut's galley where they themselves allegedly figure as rowers. One of two mayors of the town, an illiterate who spent five years as a captive in Algiers, exposes them as false captives and wants to have them severely punished by the law. They explain that they decided to abandon their studies in Salamanca to see the world and go to war; as luck would have it, 'some captives passed through there, though they, too, like us now, were probably counterfeit. We bought this canvas from them and obtained information about some things having to do with Algiers we thought would be necessary and sufficient to lend credibility to our deceit' (III, 10, 535). One of them speaks so eloquently in their defence that the mayor has a change of heart and invites them to his house to give them such a lesson about Algiers that no one will catch them out again for their made-up stories (III, 10, 538).

Early modern European literature (poetry, theatre and novel) shows an abundance of such feigned stories about the Mediterranean. Few of its authors had direct knowledge of the terrain or social milieu they wrote about, and more than a few could be caught out in a lie about Algiers, Morocco, Tunisia, Turkey, or other Muslim lands. Yet oral and written sources provided so much 'common knowledge' that writers could locate their fictions there by naming the place and throwing in a few credible details, establishing chronotopic coordinates within which they could invent new stories with their own characters. As happens with these false captives, the lie is legitimated and the use of inventiveness is rewarded as an instrument to interest and entertain an audience eager to read or hear stories concerning encounters between Christians and Muslims – and sometimes Jews – in the Mediterranean world.

Elsewhere I've outlined the development and distinctive features of this kind of literature, which has a large and diverse corpus of texts ('Literatura fronteriza'). Writing stories about the Mediterranean is by no means merely thematic, since all genres that do so also share generic characteristics under the rubric of what I call Mediterranean frontier literature. Irreducible to a theme, a genre – as I understand the notion – has at its disposal an array of elements (including themes) pertaining to it and uniquely managed by it. All genres have identifiable though supple characteristics, but the close etymological relationship between *genre* and *generate* should always be borne in mind: writing according to a particular genre means producing literature that probes its limits and possibilities by way of new circumstances rather than simply conforming to the hypothetical attributes of that genre. Literary genres privilege certain ways of seeing the world, certain types of characters, certain stylistic features, and above all certain types of relationships and human experience. Fundamental to each genre is its chronotope,[5] its time-space, in which certain kinds of events tend to arise, develop and end according to the variable ideological premises and hierarchy of values of that chronotope. A genre is also defined in relation to other genres as well as aspects of life embodied in it. Mediterranean frontier literature abundantly exhibits all of these procedures and characteristics. It is not a theme within another genre but a genre that coordinates – and affects – all elements of the narrative. Moreover, any particular text may modulate from one genre to another or simultaneously take part in more than one genre. To illustrate, *Don Quixote*, as we know, is a novel that presents itself as though it were a history and, in shifting degrees, takes part in genres including the chivalric, the pastoral, the picaresque, the burlesque, and many others including Mediterranean frontier narrative.[6]

The early modern Mediterranean frontier spans a vast panorama where innumerable stories arise, set in frontier zones where human beings act in situations most often issuing from slavery, where religions are multiple, where the class and honour systems are mostly absent, and where people act in situations of great risk that require audacity and improvisation. There are already a predetermined *them* and *us*, a political and religious frontier, harsh rules of play, peculiar modes of communication and conduct, means of escape and

---

[5] Chronotope: as is well known, in a book-length essay written in 1937 (included in English translation within *The dialogical imagination*), Mikhail Bakhtin surveys an enormous range of literature in relation to this term in order to demonstrate how literary genres function with diverse configurations of time-space. It is precisely the indissoluble nexus of time-space, as opposed to the conceptual isolation of each term (time, space), that constitutes the setting within which narrative events occur and gives each genre its specific narrative (or theatrical, poetic) character. In sum, chronotopes in large part *define* literary genres and are integral to any generic taxonomy, infusing any genre with characters, interactions, plots and meanings thinkable within the modalities of that genre. As said, chronotopes often combine or shift from one to another, affecting the conditions of genre as they do so.

[6] On Mediterranean literature or philology, particularly regarding earlier periods, see also Mallette and Kinoshita.

temptations to stay. Characters can be 'borrowed' from other genres, but as soon as they pass into this chronotope they are transformed by it until they leave. This is a genre, then, that doesn't require its own kind of character – except for those sorts of characters who permanently inhabit this frontier space – but rather adapts characters to its spatial surroundings. This shouldn't be too surprising if we consider that extreme circumstances such as anarchy at sea, slavery, religious conversion and exotic eroticism turn characters into a *response* to what is happening to them. That said, it has to be acknowledged that this narrative genre favours noble characters or at least wealthy characters from the merchant class, that is, characters of social importance who can protagonise amorous or heroic episodes both within and outside the Mediterranean frontier zones.

The entire Mediterranean region – owing to its deep and complex history, its socio-cultural and religious composition, its modes of interaction and much more – displayed unique characteristics that were not found to the same degree in other regions such as the Caribbean, the northern coasts of Europe, or the seas of the Far East. Although corsairing and piracy, captivity and slavery, martyrdom, political-religious conflict, or affective relations that transcended social and religious divisions existed in many other parts of the world, such phenomena took on specific forms in the Mediterranean world that brought them together in an intensely charged ensemble out of which a great deal of narrative and drama issued. Among these, Mediterranean frontier literature has the peculiarity of adjusting to a chronotope associated with a particular region, e.g. to the chronotope of any particular city or country within the greater expanse of the Mediterranean.

The Mediterranean is not always a frontier space. Of the twenty or so Shakespearean plays set in the ancient or modern Mediterranean, only a few including *Antony and Cleopatra*, *The Merchant of Venice* and *Othello* exhibit frontier characteristics with the complex relations between Romans and Egyptians in the first of these, and the strong presence of Shylock and other Jews and the Moor Othello in the Venetian plays along with references to corsairs and the Ottoman fleet, not to mention the maritime environment, and the like. For Spanish writers, on the contrary, for over a century this frontier was a continuous obsession that found expression in the novel, among other genres. The presence of Jews in most Mediterranean cities and of Muslim corsairs or captives along Christian coastlines (both sides of Italy, southern France, eastern and southern Spain, as well as many of the islands) meant that those places were likewise saturated with frontier space.

In Spain, Mediterranean frontier literature was especially in vogue during the first half of the seventeenth century, perhaps reaching its height in the 1620s. Cervantes, Lope de Vega, Luis de Góngora, María de Zayas and Pedro Calderón de la Barca figure among the many Spanish writers who contributed to this genre with novels, plays or poems. Above all, this was not a genre independent from the rest but rather integrated with several of them, together with which it arose, flourished and declined. There's no reason to search for intrinsic reasons for its birth and decline, as though its themes and arguments were exhausted by the mid-seventeenth century. The genre's vitality depended rather on that of the other genres with which it had a symbiotic relationship. Nor does it coincide as such with the historical occurrence of corsairing, slavery, religious conversion and the like, since these were already very important long before the emergence of the literary genre and continued to be important after the genre's decline. The Barbarossa brothers were practising the *corso* in the western Mediterranean a century before Cervantes showed how to novelise and dramatise the experience of slavery in Muslim lands. Fiction took that long to appropriate this domain, and would have other models both ancient and modern (e.g. the Greek novel, frontier narratives) at its disposal. Especially worthy of consideration are more or less testimonial texts such as the five treatises of the *Topografía e historia general de Argel* (published in 1612) – attributed for decades now to Antonio de Sosa and no longer to the editor, fray Diego de Haedo – the treatises on Africa, Morocco, Tunisia and Istanbul, and the autobiographical accounts of captives and corsairs, which, if they came to be known in printed or manuscript form, provided a rich source of information, descriptions and stories. As has been shown, the *Topografía* in particular significantly inspired novelistic invention.

Moreover, since quite a few of these texts echo the classic novel *El Abencerraje* and more generally the Moorish novel, a close affinity should be acknowledged between these frontier stories situated in the Iberian Peninsula and those that take place at sea or on the other shore. In her book *Vidas fronterizas en las letras españolas*, María Soledad Carrasco Urgoiti deals with a variety of frontier stories in the peninsula *and* North Africa, demonstrating – *mutatis mutandis* – a historical, geographical and cultural continuity in the literary treatment of this mobile and multiple frontier. Important as distinctions are, it would be a mistake to differentiate too rigidly between peninsular Moors, Moriscos, North African Moors, and Turks (terms that are problematic anyway): these are all, in one way or another, embodiments of Muslim *others*, just as Jewish *others* also assume various forms. It could be objected that the texts about peninsular Moors and Moriscos are oriented towards Spain as a nation state with its cultural and religious identity, as opposed to texts that focus on North Africa and the Ottomans. Such a perspective, however, is blind to the Mediterranean and Islamic dimension of the Spanish Moors and Moriscos, as is the case in nearly all critical interpretation of the Moriscos episode in Cervantes' *Persiles* (III, 11), for example (Hutchinson, 'The Morisco problem').

By way of comparison, Mediterranean frontier literature was also much in vogue in France. Already in *Pantagruel* (1532), Rabelais has his character Panurge tell in chapter 14 how he ingeniously escaped from the Turks[7] – which

---

[7] This will be discussed in chapter 4, on martyrdom.

is in fact an exceptionally *early* and original (as well as hilarious) instance of fictional captivity and escape set in Mediterranean frontier space. Many examples of this genre in French tend to belong rather to the second half of the seventeenth century, i.e. considerably later than most of the Spanish texts. Numerous theatrical works, including Molière's *Le Bourgeois gentilhomme* (1670) and Racine's *Bajazet* (1672), draw particularly from Turkish materials. Other fictional writings take their inspiration from lands stretching from Persia to the Maghrib as well as back in time to Muslim Spain. A fascination with Granada in particular and a captivation with Spanish writings (including Cervantes) such as Ginés Pérez de Hita's *Guerras civiles de Granada*, whose first volume (1595) was translated into French in 1608, proved to be especially productive (Munari, Hautcœur), as in Madame de Lafayette's Spanish-based romance *Zayde* (1669–71).

France's idiosyncratic relations with Istanbul and the Maghrib undoubtedly nuanced the full range of discursive genres about Muslim lands, from treatises and memoirs on Algiers to captives' autobiographical accounts and a variety of fictional works that exploited a gamut of themes and motifs (corsairs, captivity, religion, the harem, baths, and much else). Albert Mas, Guy Turbet-Delof[8] and numerous other scholars point to many of the authors and writings that deal with relations with Muslim *others*. Following an Orient-Occident dichotomy, which we could translate mainly into Muslim/Christian relations and frontier chronotopes, Anne Duprat suggests that the Orient 'furnished the Occident with the multiple resources of an alternative mythology' – alternative to the classical legacies of Greece and Rome – in which 'generous sultans, corsairs and soldiers of fortune, beautiful captive women and Moorish knights turn into the essential elements of a modern poetic arsenal' that shows remarkable vitality during the early modern period. The ensemble of Maghribian stories, she continues, most aptly embodies this modernity, and powerfully contributes to the development of European narrative forms (9). The literary potential of frontier experience was not lost on early modern writers. The Mercedarian priest Antoine Quartier, captive in Tripoli (Libya) from 1660–68, remarks in his captivity narrative, *L'esclave religieux et ses aventures* (1690), on how the stories of one's experience in 'the land of the corsairs' bear a close affinity with novelistic representation: 'I tell the adventures of some Christians because they are related to my own and form an integral part of them. The reader should not be surprised if he finds that some of them sound like a novel: the land of the corsairs is the theatre of all kinds of events and novelties; the most minor capture they make of Christians

---

[8] Curiously, back in 1973, after an extensive survey of writings in French focused on the Maghrib, Turbet-Delof concludes that 'We have tried to show ... in our Second Part, that, while lacking a masterpiece, Barbaresque Africa inspired within minor but worthy writers *the sketch of an original genre*' (my emphasis, 313).

provides marvelous material capable of filling volumes.'[9] Similarly, Gabriel de Brémont begins his novel *L'heureux esclave* (1677) by affirming: 'For centuries Africa was regarded as a part of the world where people were as cruel and ferocious as the lions and tigers [sic] that it is so full of; but after amorous discoveries were made there, it appeared that love belongs to every country and that Barbary itself is only barbarous in name.'[10] Love, now that it has been found in Africa, makes Barbary essentially civil and narratable, and in this case what brings lovers together is (happy) slavery. As Christian Zonza comments in this regard, 'in *L'heureux esclave*, count Alexandre does not want the freedom that the sultan offers him because it would take him away from the sultana he loves. Slavery thus becomes an element of the novelistic dynamic because it is a factor that multiplies adventures' (156).

Indeed, with regard to Mediterranean frontier literature in general, love and sexuality also assume forms quite different from those described in contemporary treatises about the Maghrib or Turkey (e.g. those of Antonio de Sosa alias 'Haedo', Pierre Dan, Gabriel Gómez de Losada, Luis del Mármol Carvajal, Diego de Torres, Otavio Sapiencia), which convey an obsessive aversion towards homosexuality and polygamy as quintessential attributes of Islamic societies. Novels and plays, on the contrary, usually pay little attention to such practices, although they do tend to represent Muslim men and women as prone to promiscuity in a society unregulated by codes of sexually based honour. In one way or another, the amorous or erotic theme is almost indispensable in this kind of literature, and it's mostly by way of these love relationships that the array of political, cultural and religious relations is put into play. Whereas the treatises of that period never tire of belabouring the themes of political and religious confrontation, slavery, suffering, cruelty, and so on, the novel in particular shows little patience with them. The captive's tale in *Don Quixote* alludes quite briefly to a number of the most significant events and personages of the Mediterranean world, and also sketches out how the city of Algiers works, yet if the damsel Zoraida never appeared this story would go nowhere. It matters little that she lacks verisimilitude as a character and that her religiosity and love are scarcely convincing.[11] Through her

---

[9] 'Je rapporte les aventures de quelques chrétiens, parce qu'elles ont de la liaison avec les miennes, et qu'elles en composent une partie. Le lecteur ne doit point s'étonner s'il en trouve qui approchent du roman; le pays des Corsaires est le théâtre de toutes sortes d'événements et de nouveautés; la moindre capture qu'ils font sur les Chrétiens, fournit souvent des matières merveilleuses et capables de remplir des volumes' (Zonza 153).

[10] 'L'Afrique passait, depuis quelques siècles, pour une partie du monde, où les gens étaient aussi cruels et aussi farouches que les lions et les tigres dont elle est remplie: mais depuis les découvertes amoureuses qu'on y a faites, il a bien paru que l'amour est de tout pays, et que la Barbarie même n'a de barbare que le nom' (Zonza 156).

[11] See Alcalá Galán, in 'Personajes espejo' (946–7), and Hutchinson, 'Fronteras cervantinas: Zoraida en el exilio'.

and her relationship with the captive Ruy Pérez, the rest of the plot develops with characters as remarkable as the nameless 'renegade' and Zoraida's father Agi Morato and a spectrum of intercontinental, political, religious and intercultural relations.[12]

Exoticism, as a *sine qua non* of the chronotope of this type of narrative and theatre, pervades all of these stories, an exoticism whose many versions ranging from phobia to philia always display traits associated with Muslim lands of the Mediterranean. What are the characters like who belong to that exotic space, and how do they behave? To what extent do *our* characters feel attracted to or repelled by that otherness, how do they understand it, and how are they helped or harmed by it? These are some of the key questions that reveal the orientation of each story and saturate the exotic ambience in which amorous relations are played out. One way or another, the affective dimensions of human relations across religious, cultural and political barriers assume an importance rarely seen in non-fictional works, or in fictional works not set in Mediterranean frontier zones.

This kind of literature opens up a geographic, aesthetic, ethical and ideological space where human relations, thought and action take place so differently that narrators or dramatic characters often have to assume the role of translators. Many of the Christian characters are subjected to the degradation of slavery, which puts them to the test, showing who they really are, what they're worth and what they can do in a limit situation. The genre more or less obliges an author to take an ideological position regarding everything associated with Muslim *others*, their religion and ways of life. Even though the usual stereotypes are reproduced here and there ad nauseam, these works also show a variety of unusual stances. While the shift to the Mediterranean in effect gives some writers an easy way to display publicly their most orthodox credentials with regard to *Moors* and *Turks*, it also allows room for other attitudes that often downplay difference by emphasising how people from opposite sides of the divide relate to each other as fellow humans. As will be evident throughout this book and especially in the final chapter, despite the prevalent hostility between people situated in adverse relationships, there are so many credible testimonies of positive human encounters that we may be obliged to give more credence to fictional texts predisposed to emphasising such encounters than to those sorts of non-fictional works that strive to suppress them. Once again, every discursive genre and subgenre, be it fictional or non-fictional, has its means of opening itself up to – and closing itself off from – certain kinds of truths.

---

[12] Even the novel that most relies on Sosa's *Topografía de Argel*, Céspedes's *Gerardo español*, with its lengthy account of cruelties and martyrdom, is resolved by a semi-amorous relationship where an ex-lover of Gerardo, currently a wife of her Muslim master, makes possible their escape.

Regardless of the ideological projections of fictional texts and their authors, Mediterranean frontier literature offers above all a malleable chronotope in which poetic fantasy finds an abundance of options for stories in an ambience of political and religious antagonism, greater tolerance towards religious and sexual practices, vertiginous possibilities for social ascent, multilingualism, and often the defencelessness of characters (Muslims or Christians) reduced to human property in lands of *others*. Considering the ways that literary plots tend to play themselves out, this chronotope is neither a beginning nor an end for the protagonists, but rather a productive phase where new plots materialise or where plots originating elsewhere begin to be resolved. Though a good number of male and female characters become *renegades*, at least for a while, this narrative genre shows little interest in the historical reality through which most converts to Islam became integrated into their new societies without ever returning to their countries of origin. On the contrary, literary renegades, as well as literary slaves, nearly always return to their religion and country, unless those renegades are Muslim women who convert to Christianity – a common literary motif though historically rare – in which case these women leave their homelands and never return (Hutchinson, '*Renegadas*', 'Fronteras ... Zoraida en el exilio').

The case of renegade women converting in one direction or the other is particularly revealing both for how these texts misrepresent historical realities and for how they nonetheless reverberate with different kinds of truths and at the same time tell engaging tales. By having Zoraida, the beloved daughter of the rich and prominent Moor Agi Morato, choose a Christian captive as her future husband and escape from Algiers to Spain (*Don Quixote* I, 37, 39–42), Cervantes unabashedly falsifies his historical model, the anonymous daughter of the eminent Ragusan renegade Hajji Murad who married the Moroccan prince and later king 'Abd al-Malik, with whom she had a son named Ismā'īl, and who later allegedly married Hasan Pasha the Venetian, renegade beylerbey of Algiers and Cervantes' slave-master. Yet, in my view, the arrival of this exquisite Moorish lady in Spain and her integration into a noble family as well as her desire to be baptised serves to draw dramatic attention to the contrary plight of the Moriscos shortly before their expulsion from Spain. She is, after all, a devotee of the Virgin Mary, 'Lela Marién', a highly venerated figure in Islam as well as Catholicism, and this rudimentary bond with both religions facilitates her conversion. Here we see a fascinating story of novelistic fiction finding a means (unavailable to non-fictional genres) to confront the dominant ideology of the moment with regard to the ethnic and religious composition of the state. The falsification of the original model gives way to a compelling kind of truth.

Let's consider an example of a 'renegade' woman, Argelina, in Juan Pérez de Montalbán's *La desgraciada amistad* (in his collection of novellas *Sucesos y prodigios de amor*, 1624), against the backdrop of historical renegade women.

This novella steams with eroticism, rivalry, jealousy, adultery, seductions, rape and attempted rape, intended and unintended killings, suicide, attacks at sea, captivity, and a continual shifting of amorous couples, triangles and quadrangles. Although much of the novel situates us in North Africa, mainly Tunis, all of the transgressions mentioned are committed not by Muslims but by Spanish Christians in Spain, at sea, and in Tunis. We first encounter Argelina as a *dama principal* who appears to be North African and is the lover of the congenial young king of Tunis, Celín Hamete. She falls for the new captive gardener Felisardo (a noble Spaniard), confessing to him she's not an African after all but rather a Spanish noblewoman from Zaragoza, and proceeds to tell her story filled with amorous misfortunes. Interestingly, Argelina's veil of otherness inheres in her exotic dress, her intimate relationship with the king, her lax attitude towards matters of honour, her referring to herself as an *africana*, and her name, which is none other than a feminine form derived from *Argel*, i.e. Algiers: she embodies the exoticism of the Barbary coast, and has become orientalised. Clueless regarding her Spanish origins, the noble Felisardo is by no means repulsed by what would elsewhere mark her as a woman without honour. Despite its ideological constraints, Mediterranean frontier literature, as is evident in this novella, in effect betrays a fascination with orientalism and indulges in it.[13] Here as in other texts with renegade women, such fascination is intensified when one of *our* women becomes a renegade, dons sensuous garb, attracts the libido of powerful Muslim men and in other ways behaves in ways associated at that time with women in Islamic societies. Until now, Argelina's implicit conversion to Islam has not even surfaced as something worth mentioning. As happens with other literary renegade women, Argelina's sexual conduct and religious conduct seem to converge in the notion of infidelity: unchaste Christian women are prone to becoming *renegadas*, infidels. But ideology intervenes as writers of fiction are loath to allow renegade women to stay permanently in Muslim lands. While the rest of the Spaniards in this novel die at each other's hands in Tunis, Argelina alone survives and manages to return repentant to recover the religion and land of her birth, renouncing what she has become along with the pleasures and unbridled eroticism of orientalised frontier space.

---

[13] As Mercedes Alcalá Galán observes, the main themes of orientalism are present in early modern literary texts as well as testimonial writings: highly sexualised women in sensuous apparel, the slave market, the harem, the bath, the odalisque, veiled anonymity in public, and so on ('Erotics of the exotic'). Visual images of orientalism lag far behind the printed word, coming to full expression, as we know, in paintings from the late eighteenth- to the mid-twentieth-centuries – Ingres, Delacroix, Chassériau, Fortuny, Gérôme, Renoir, Matisse, among many others. Yet one can point to some pictorial images of the sixteenth and seventeenth centuries as orientalist, e.g. in a widespread vogue of portraits as of the mid-seventeenth century evoking the Ottoman Empire, including its regencies such as Algiers.

Argelina bears little resemblance to historical *renegadas*, but it's precisely in this divergence that we can grasp the workings of ideology, genre and the imagination. Although Ottoman-Venetian relations as well as idiosyncratic practices within the Ottoman court created rather different conditions for historical *renegadas* from those prevailing in the western Mediterranean,[14] the entire Muslim Mediterranean shared practices very distinct from how the Christian Mediterranean treated the women from Muslim countries who sooner or later converted to Christianity. The major differences here were that the numbers of women converts to Christianity were far smaller than those of women who converted to Islam and, more important, that Islamic societies by and large incorporated converts by offering them marriage whereas Christian societies rarely did so. Still, all too little is known about renegade women in the early modern Mediterranean. Of the few who returned to their Christian homelands, most did so against their will.[15] A reiterated complaint of clergy is that both renegade men and women came to cherish their present happiness (the pleasures of a long life, of family, etc.) without 'remembering' the homeland and religion of their past (e.g. Sosa, I, 35, 35v). What's especially wrong with such *renegadas*, then, seems to be that they formed families and became integrated, adapting extraordinarily well to societies that allowed them to do so.

---

[14] The three case studies that Eric Dursteler convincingly presents in his *Renegade women*, for example, largely depend on circumstances peculiar to Istanbul itself and its interactions with Venice.

[15] As Bartolomé and Lucile Bennassar point out in *Les Chrétiens d'Allah*, renegade women most often surface fleetingly in documents as mothers or wives of notable men. Of the 1,550 cases of renegades in their study, all of them from inquisitional records produced after the voluntary or forced return of renegades to Christian lands, only fifty-nine are women, i.e. under 4 per cent. Most of these women conveyed to the inquisitors that they had been involved in long and stable marital and family relationships. Only twenty-three returned voluntarily … Nearly all of the rest were (re)captured, quite a few of these in raids perpetrated by Christian corsairs. All but three admitted that they had foresworn Christianity. Only two expressed joy at returning to their homelands. Most surprising of all, though the Inquisition was quite lenient towards them, no fewer than thirty-one of them were resold in Sicilian slave markets (338–47)! While most men were captured as soldiers or sailors, women (and children) were captured mainly in coastal raids and on voyages, and hence there were always fewer women captives than men. Women would have made up some 10 to 20 per cent of the total number of renegades, depending on where they were and in what epoch. Unlike renegade women, renegade men disposed of a variety of means to return to their homelands if they chose to do so; but whereas men were often denied permission to convert to Islam, Christian women were actively sought after in marriage, and their conversion was encouraged. Moreover, their slave-masters rarely allowed them to be ransomed. Most seem to have adapted to a life that accepted them as concubines or spouses, and all the more so if they bore children. In Muslim countries there were no religious groups or figures dedicated to proselytising them. For more information on historical renegade women, see Hutchinson, '*Renegadas*', 529–33.

Argelina, like other literary renegade women, acts within fairly similar geopolitical coordinates and social circumstances to those in which historical renegade women found themselves, yet her story and ideological significance differ from theirs. Unlike most renegade women referred to in contemporary treatises and inquisitional records, literary *renegadas* like Argelina tend to be protagonists rather than marginal figures, partly because literature set in Mediterranean frontier space seems to require (heterosexual) love stories, quite often across the Muslim-Christian divide and in an ambience charged with eroticism. With some exceptions such as Cervantes' writings, female characters are usually more pressured than their male counterparts to renounce their religion, and do so more readily. Renegade women who adopt Islam tend to produce sultry stories full of subdued fascination, the kind of atmosphere that the writers of these texts seem to relish.

In Mediterranean frontier narrative, quite astonishingly, religion *as such* is often absent, functioning instead as a kind of marker or sign: one *is* a Christian or a Muslim or a Jew, with some internal variations. While treatises written by clerics tend to imbue with religious difference and moral judgement the kinds of space where there are Christian captives (Algiers, Tunis, 'Constantinople', etc.), literary texts for the most part reduce religion to these identifying markers of 'what' one is (e.g. Muslim or Christian) without delving into matters of ritual, belief, sin, vice, perversion, the Saviour, the Prophet, heaven and hell, the true and the false, and so on. The chronotope of the Mediterranean frontier is also a heterotopia because it is an *other* space,[16] and a space *of* the others, where characters such as renegades can even become 'others', or at least other than what they were. Such is the case with Argelina. Moreover, this time-space tends to be conveyed by means of narrative and dialogue: it's primarily a theatrical arena, a kind of stage with a cast of characters who work their way through plots conditioned not only by captivity, slavery, hostility, and a multitude of differences (linguistic, social, ethnic, religious, legal, etc.), but also by interpersonal relations that either exacerbate or transcend such differences. Unlike historical converts to Islam who mostly stayed in their adoptive lands, the idea of a fictional convert to Islam staying in the host country is almost unthinkable, especially in the case of a woman. What's interesting in these stories is not only what becomes *of* the protagonists, but what they *become*. Themes of love and sex, normally at the core of literary plots, tend to figure importantly in these transformations and grant captive and renegade women much more salient roles than they have in non-literary texts such that they often overshadow male literary characters. Nietzsche remarks: 'Christianity gave Eros poison to drink. He did not die of it but degenerated – into a vice' (*Beyond good and evil*, #168). In Muslim

---

[16] For the notion of *heterotopia* I am of course indebted to Michel Foucault's essay 'Different spaces'.

lands of the early modern Mediterranean, Eros seems not to have drunk that poison – to the chagrin of clerical writers, while literary authors willingly exploit this.

Chapter overview

Following upon the purposes, parameters and methods outlined in this introductory chapter, 'Slaves' (chapter 2) identifies the characteristics of Mediterranean frontier slavery in contrast to other types of slavery, particularly (1) the age-old trans-Saharan slavery where black slaves were taken in caravans across the Sahara desert to North Africa as well as by ship from East Africa via the Red Sea, and (2) the well-known slavery originating in West Africa and involving the massive transportation of slaves by sea to Iberia and especially the Americas. All of these as well as other kinds of slavery coexisted in the early modern Mediterranean world. My focus is on Mediterranean slavery predicated on the existence of a frontier as well as geopolitical and religious difference across spaces that were traversable and communicable: *grosso modo*, the enslavement of Muslims by Christians and Christians by Muslims, although accords between corsairing nations modified this general pattern. This kind of slavery could end in various ways ranging from ransom or escape to emancipation and, especially in Muslim lands, social integration. Race as a marker of difference was nearly absent in Mediterranean frontier slavery, while cultural and religious differences were substantial but relative, allowing for individuals to adapt themselves to one degree or another to life across the divide. I believe that this particular kind of frontier slavery was historically unique even to the Mediterranean as of the early sixteenth century. My main interest in this chapter is to focus on a range of human experience brought about by this kind of slavery, including what it meant to *become* a slave and to *live* as one, as so many writers reveal on both sides of the divide. Given the scant documentary and scholarly attention that women slaves tend to receive, part of the chapter is devoted to the ways their slavery is represented: both in fact and fiction, men and women often experienced slavery in very different ways.

'Renegades' (chapter 3) discusses the pervasive phenomenon of religious conversion, from Islam to Christianity but much more massively from Christianity to Islam, though many slaves were denied the right to convert. Keenly aware as I am of the pejorative tones of the word 'renegade', I use it in lieu of alternative, less recognisable terms to refer to converts in *either* direction. The unities and divisions of the early modern Mediterranean come into relief through the protagonism of these fascinating figures who slip through the conceptual categories most often associated with them such as syncretism, hybridity and assimilation, not to mention models of the 'divided self'. 'Popular religion' nearly always superseded notions of theological belief in the case of renegades, few of whom had any formal education, let alone religious guidance. Renegades rarely wrote about themselves, requiring us to find out about them from other kinds of sources generally hostile to them, including inquisitional records. Renegades embody the characteristics of the Mediterranean frontier and the capabilities, consciousness and versatility fomented by frontier zones. Drawing from a variety of genres, this chapter examines a range of renegade 'profiles' – women and men from many parts of the Mediterranean world who were originally Christians, Muslims or Jews. Some converted back and forth twice or more, others were crypto-Muslims escaped from Christian lands but recaptured and tried for apostasy, some became renowned corsairs who raided their native lands, some were displaced Muslim princes who emigrated and adopted Christianity, and yet others rose to the heights of power and prestige in the Ottoman Empire. The widespread phenomenon of renegades pushes the problematic of otherness to its extremes and undermines nearly every notion of 'identity'. The chapter finally turns to how to conceptualise this 'renegade' enigma in all its diversity in a highly confrontational Mediterranean that nonetheless had islands, caves and temples with shared religious practice.

'Martyrs' (chapter 4) looks into the portrayals of Christian martyrdom in Muslim lands. This was by no means reciprocal because in the early modern era there were virtually no Muslim martyrs other than those who were conventionally deemed martyrs for having been killed in battle. Rather, Christian martyrdom in Muslim territories has to be understood within the visceral rivalry between Catholics and Protestants in Europe whereby the martyrs of one side were the heretics of the other. Catholics looked especially to Muslim territories in order to produce fresh martyrs, their main strategy being to convince renegades to revert to Christianity and proclaim this loudly, thus giving Muslim authorities little choice but to execute them for apostasy. Accounts of Christian martyrdom are abundant. Some of these martyrs had no desire to be martyrs but found themselves in circumstances in which they were to be put to death and, of these, a few were able to *perform* their own martyrdom as expected. Others were executed for trying to kill their masters and escape, but were likewise considered martyrs. Of special interest are cases where a particular act of 'martyrdom' is told from radically different points of view, e.g. by a Muslim, a Catholic and a Protestant. Martyrological accounts hyperbolise the supposed cruelty of Muslims, and above all that of renegades (i.e. ex-European ex-Christians). Yet these texts show that martyrdom often involves a spiritualisation of cruelty and self-inflicted torment where martyrs suffer and simultaneously observe their own suffering.

'Counternarratives' (chapter 5) highlights and analyses the very opposite of intolerance and cruelty, namely 'exceptions to the rule': acts of kindness, generosity, love, courtesy, respect, sympathy, empathy, mutual self-interest, and so on, any of which would most likely involve tolerance and understanding.

The chapter first explores how Cervantes' narratives about Moriscos in his last two novels – the episodes of Ricote and his daughter Ana Félix in part II of *Don Quixote* and the voluntary exile of crypto-Muslims in the *Persiles* – circumvent the varieties of 'official discourse' produced by apologists of the expulsion (Jaime Bleda, Pedro Aznar Cardona, Gaspar Aguilar and Damián Fonseca, among others). The generally misunderstood episode in the *Persiles* reveals the Islamic and Mediterranean dimension in which the Moriscos are portrayed here. A variety of other counternarratives are then presented with the purpose of teasing out their situational logic as well as the ethical and emotional dimensions of each event. One such encounter involves commanders who are enemies but briefly fraternise, allowing for negotiations, agreements, courtesy, largesse, congeniality, a long conversation over a meal, and so on. Another shows people in a position of power who are generous to slaves because they themselves have relatives or friends who are victims on the other side; this is understood as reciprocity, even when the context is extremely tenuous and indirect. This also happens among members of all three religions (Judaism, Christianity, Islam). Another type of encounter arises from a solidarity between enemies and a pact to protect each other, even to exchange religions with each other. To this can be added countless instances of love or affection that arise within objectively asymmetrical relations. The series of counternarratives presented here unsettle the conventional views of the early modern Mediterranean, enquiring into the kinds of affect and logic that give rise to such apparent anomalies. In a Mediterranean in which there was no holy war on either side, where Janus-like renegades were arguably the protagonists for over a century, where commerce knew no boundaries, where cultural and even religious similarities were constantly acknowledged, spontaneous, improvised encounters of these kinds were bound to happen. In sum, this chapter explores the kinds of understanding and affect that could arise – and could *only* arise – in the generally hostile circumstances of frontier zones.

2

Slaves

O cities of the sea! In you I see your citizens, both women and men, arms and legs tightly bound with strong cords by people who will not understand your languages. And you will only be able to give vent to your pain and lost liberty with tearful complaints and sighs and laments among yourselves, for those who bind you will not understand you, nor will you understand them.

Leonardo da Vinci, *Notebook*[1]

This haunting riddle from a series of Leonardo's 'prophecies', many of them equally disturbing in their own right, gives us hints as to what the answer will turn out to be: 'Of children bound in swaddling clothes'.[2] Yet the signifiers used to set up this riddle belong to the context of captivity and slavery in Mediterranean coastal cities, where slave markets had already existed for a long time but would greatly multiply and expand over the sixteenth and seventeenth centuries before diminishing in the eighteenth and finally fading in the early nineteenth. Although Leonardo died not far into the sixteenth century (1519), this particular riddle, with its disconcerting use of the future tense, would unwittingly turn into an authentic prophecy. While slave markets and practices reached inland to major cities (Marrakesh, Fez, Madrid, Milan, Rome, Jerusalem, Cairo, etc.), their primary places were 'cities of the sea' (*città marine*). Both women and men – not to mention children and adolescents (Leonardo's language is deliberately ambivalent without reference to age: *così femmine come maschi*, both female and male) – were captured, bound and sold especially in those markets, and there are abundant testimonies regarding their suffering and loss as well as the mutual incomprehension between slavers and enslaved who didn't understand each other's languages. In this parable, even members of the same family or household or city are complete strangers

---

[1] The original reads: 'O città marine! io veggo in voi i vostri cittadini, così femmine come maschi, essere istrettamente dei forti legami colle braccia e gambe esser legati da gente che non intenderanno i vostri linguaggi, e sol vi potrete isfogare li vostri dolori e perduta libertà mediante i lagrimosi pianti e li sospiri e lamentazione infra voi medesimi, chè chi vi lega non v'intenderà, né voi loro intenderete.' The translation above is mine, construed after consulting versions in Spanish and English but holding closer to the original, where, for example, *languages* is significantly expressed in the plural (*i vostri linguaggi*), not in the singular.

[2] 'De fanciulli che stanno legati nelle fasce'.

to each other: adults and newly 'arrived' infants who don't speak the same languages. In the context of slavery there are obvious parallels, except that the 'arrival' is forced and presupposes coming from some other part of the sea.

Modes of slavery in the Mediterranean world

Slavery was widespread and integral to the early modern Mediterranean, most directly affecting many millions of slaves but also having a profound impact on the societies that lost them and on those that appropriated them. Slaves were necessarily from elsewhere, most often affiliated with a different religion and almost invariably brought up in other languages and ways of life. The massive trafficking of people, particularly from the fifteenth until the early nineteenth century, transformed the human landscapes and seascapes throughout the region, the demographics of cities, the economies of states – their labour, services, production, trade – as well as relations stretching from the interior of households to the widest enmities and alliances. Religion, culture, commerce, communities, family bonds and sexuality all underwent significant sea-changes. Actively sought and fought for, slaves assumed an enormous presence in the personal and collective life and endeavours of these societies. It was mainly slavery and the activities associated with it that brought Muslims and Christians together in vast numbers across the Mediterranean divide, and, notwithstanding prejudices, distortions and much suffering, changed how people on both sides saw the world. Understandably, it has repeatedly been suggested that Cervantes' experience of slavery was what gave rise to the modern novel.

Numerous writings over this period, including some that would figure in almost any corpus of investigation, were devoted entirely or partly to the topic of slavery. Also abundant are autobiographical accounts that frame their stories within the loss and recovery of freedom, with most of the narrative devoted to the period of slavery, a topic that readers craved to know about. Fiction, too, adopts this model and undoubtedly infiltrates into the most reliable 'true' accounts. Availing itself of books, manuscripts and archives, modern research has elucidated a great deal regarding the conditions of slavery, the means of ransom, and the like. My intention here is not to reiterate what much good scholarship has said about these topics but to reflect on what I call Mediterranean frontier slavery within the context of other kinds of slavery, drawing not only from canonical works but also texts less well known that, I believe, offer insights into slavery as it was lived and practised. Given the disproportionately scant attention that women slaves tend to receive, I'll also be using testimonial as well as fictional writings to explore representations of their various fates in Mediterranean frontier slavery. The result, I hope, will be a revealing and unusual look into this vital subject.

Regarding the term 'slave' and its degrading connotations, the many early modern authors I've consulted tend to use the terms 'captive' and 'slave' – and their direct equivalents in various languages – as interchangeable. Occasionally there are nuances that distinguish them, as in the case of the captive's tale in *Don Quixote*, a story that simply wouldn't sound right as the 'slave's tale' (though this 'captive' does refer to himself on one occasion as a 'slave'), mainly, it seems to me, because the story focuses first on how he was captured and, more importantly, on the complicated process by which he escaped, without telling hardly anything about the many years that presumably intervened between these two events. The difference in connotation would certainly not be that 'captives' and 'slaves' are different categories of people deprived of freedom, but rather that 'captive' perhaps more readily suggests the switch from being free to unfree and vice versa, whereas 'slave' is the more generic term for a state of being. In any event, this example is an exception in Cervantes' writings about captives and slaves: while in most works he uses 'captive' somewhat more often, both terms are significantly frequent and, more important, the protagonists of plays and novels are referred to indistinguishably as slaves or captives (e.g. Catalina de Oviedo in *La gran sultana*, or Leonisa and Ricardo in *El amante liberal*). Noble as they are, they have no problem in referring to themselves as slaves. Throughout the range of texts about captivity/slavery in languages including Spanish, French, Portuguese, Italian and English, the usage of these terms is nearly always quite interchangeable. Slaves are slaves from the moment they're captured until they regain their freedom – if they do so at all: 'we are your slaves' ('somos sus esclavos'), says Marcos de Obregón as soon as he and his companions are captured (Espinel II, 8, 57).

This statement by Marcos sounds so unbearably matter-of-fact to our modern ears, mindful as we are of the abhorrence of slavery, that modern scholarship tends to shy away from the term 'slave' in the context of the early modern Mediterranean frontier, sometimes even denying that Christian countries had Muslim 'slaves' or vice versa, or at least insisting on a sharp distinction between 'captives' and 'slaves' that never existed as such in the terminology of that epoch.[3] Instead, there seems to be a tendency towards

---

[3] For instance, the following assertion by Wolfgang Kaiser and Bernard Vincent regarding captives v. slaves is not borne out by any of the countless texts I have read on this and related topics: 'in the context of attaining freedom through redemption [rachat], it is important to underline the distinction between slaves and captives, *a distinction made elsewhere by the sources of the epoch*. In fact, the captive is living booty destined to be resold and returned at a price definitely higher than the price of a slave; if the redemption [rachat] fails, the captive may be sold as a slave, a less advantageous solution for his master. The captive belongs to another register: his exchange and sale, at first sight on the same market, follow at least in part other kinds of logic that lead us to talk about an economy of ransom [rançon]' (my emphasis, 138). This brief article makes other statements that are demonstrably incorrect, e.g. about aspects of Cervantes' works in relation to captivity and corsair coastal raids (140–1).

giving much more preference to 'slave' over 'captive' as the seventeenth century advances, particularly in French.[4] In any event, the key point here is that 'captive' and 'slave' were usually interchangeable terms that referred indifferently to the same people or characters. I might add that both 'captive' and 'slave' are terms that often lend themselves to amorous language during that period, and moreover are fairly interchangeable in that context too.[5]

In his *Tesoro de la lengua* (1611), Sebastián de Covarrubias begins his definition of *esclavo* by equating it with *cautivo*. He rejects the idea that *esclavo* is derived from the rebus *S* overlaid with an *I* shaped like a nail (*clavo*) that formed the symbol 'S-clavo' like a dollar sign and was sometimes branded on both cheeks of wayward slaves in Spain. Although he doesn't point out that the branded rebus is obviously derived from the word *esclavo* rather than the reverse, the enigma of the *S* plus *I* leads him to capture the essence of slavery by speculating that these letters are code for the Latin *Sine Iure* (without right) 'because the slave does not belong to himself but to his master, and thus any free act is forbidden to him' ('porque el esclavo no es suyo sino de su señor, y así le es prohibido cualquier acto libre'). Although historically there have been types of slavery that allowed for some minimal rights, this was not the case regarding the kinds of slavery prevalent in the early modern Mediterranean world. The implications of the pithy phrase 'el esclavo no es suyo', literally 'the slave is not his (or her) own', are considerable, including the following:

---

[4] Such is the case with writers such as Pierre Dan (1637), Emanuel d'Aranda (1656), Laurent d'Arvieux (1666) and, in the eighteenth century, Jacques Philippe Laugier de Tassy (1725). In fact, the diplomat d'Arvieux, who was involved in freeing French slaves in Tunis and drafting a new treatise that would exempt French nationals from captivity, uses the term *esclave* nearly 200 times, yet not once does he use the word *captif/captive*.

[5] In numerous early modern Spanish texts that narrate love stories, the lovers themselves figuratively assume the role of *esclava/esclavo* or *cautiva/cautivo*, with virtually no distinction between slave and captive because both imply a total surrender to the will of the beloved. Don Quixote considers himself Dulcinea's *cautivo*, and likewise in the classic work *El Abencerraje* Abindarráez calls himself Xarifa's *cautivo* while she also declares herself a *cautiva* of love. The concept replicates itself when there are real captives, so that enamored masters can be *cautivos* of their *cautivas*, and enamored ladies can be *cautivas* of their *cautivos*. Cervantes, among others, plays repeatedly with this paradox, e.g. in his play *El trato de Argel*, where the slave-master Yzuf tells his slave Silvia that Love 'has made me a slave to my slave, / a slave who is my lady' (vv. 1085–6). Thus the language of love interiorises the eroticism inherent in the absolute imbalance of power and rights that exists in captivity and slavery, often inverting it. As I've explored elsewhere, María de Zayas would take such amorous slavery to an extreme complexity in *La esclava de su Amante* (*The slave of her Lover*) in the collection *Desegaños amorosos* (1647), where a Moorish slave named Zelima, who looks like 'a princess of Algiers, a queen of Fez or Morocco, or a sultana of Constantinople', is really a noble Spanish woman who arranges to be sold as a Moorish slave to her rapist ex-lover, and only begins to take control of her destiny once she has been bought.

- the slave belonged to the master and was subject to his will, without there being any other person or entity that could intervene in case of abuse or cruelty;
- legally and to some extent socially, the slave was *nobody*, or as the Mooress Arlaxa puts it in Cervantes' play *El gallardo español*, 'Ya no es nadie el que es esclavo' ('Whoever is a slave is nobody' [v. 2672]);
- the slave's value is a function of what he or she is worth to the owner as 'use value' or within a market of potential buyers or ransomers (exchange value).

How such powerlessness and disenfranchisement actually play themselves out according to different writers of the period will be looked into ahead.

Numerous kinds of slavery were widely practised in the early modern Mediterranean world, each of them drawing countless slaves into its vortex. The Ottomans themselves developed a complex system of slavery from multiple sources and for many purposes, in some cases involving intermediaries as diverse as Muslim slave traders from the East African ports (traders who had their own networks inland), Ethiopian Christians, North African Arabs, Coptic Christians and, perhaps above all, Crimean Tatar raiders with their vast scope of slave expeditions over Eastern Europe, Russia, Circassia and elsewhere in western Asia. The Ottomans also engaged directly in the capturing of slaves in the Balkans and everywhere else their military campaigns allowed them to take non-Muslim slaves. To this should also be added the capture of slaves by corsairs from the Ottoman regencies. Very different but in one respect analogous to slavery was the *devşirme* system of taking Christian boys from their families within the confines of the Ottoman Empire, mainly the Balkans and Anatolia, converting them to Islam and enlisting them as janissaries. These men, women, adolescents and children, some of them emancipated sooner or later, were destined for rigorous education and government service, for military service, for rural and urban labour, for domestic service, for sexuality, for concubinage or marriage, or for ransom or exchange for other people or goods, among other purposes. Such an astonishing array of different origins and functions of slaves was in some respects peripheral to the Mediterranean world, but in other regards not only coincided with the dominant forms of slavery in the region but also had an impact on many lives and activities throughout the *mare nostrum*. The expanse of writings about the Ottoman Empire abounds in references to sub-Saharan African slaves, to Christian slaves from Christian lands of the Mediterranean as well as from Eastern Europe, Russia and elsewhere, to black and white eunuchs, to harems, to elite young captives sent to the palace for education or for concubinage, to sultanas, janissaries and powerful renegades, etc., all of them correlated with practices of slavery.

Besides these kinds of slavery, yet also in conjunction with them, three major types were practised in the early modern Mediterranean:[6]

(1) the age-old trans-Saharan slavery where black slaves were taken mainly in caravans across the Sahara desert to North Africa, from Marrakesh to Cairo, as well as by ship from East Africa via the Red Sea;[7]
(2) slavery originating in the hinterlands and coasts of West Africa and other major stretches of the Afican coastline and involving the massive transportation of slaves by sea to the Americas, sometimes by way of Europe (especially Iberia);
(3) and what I call 'Mediterranean frontier slavery' involving, *grosso modo*, the enslavement of Muslims by Christians and Christians by Muslims within the Mediterranean region.

While the second of these had by far the greatest global impact and has been widely researched, and the first, more poorly documented, had already drained much life from sub-Saharan Africa for centuries, it's the third of these that I intend to discuss here, explicitly or implicitly against the backdrop of the others with which it coexisted in many places.

Unreliable as many demographic estimates necessarily are, they ought to be taken into account to provide us with some idea of the relative scale of populations and slave trafficking. Not without caveats, Braudel guesses that there were some 60 million people in the Mediterranean region by the end of the sixteenth century, 38 million of them corresponding to Christian lands (Portugal 1 million, Spain 8 million, France 16 million, Italy 13 million) and 22 million to Islamic lands (the European part of Turkey 8 million, the Asian part another 8 million, Egypt 2–3 million and the rest of North Africa roughly the same) (394–6). While the population of cities was drastically affected by plagues among other factors, Istanbul, the largest city, seems to have maintained a population of at least a half million, Cairo had nearly 300,000, Naples perhaps around 250,000 on average, while Rome, Seville and Algiers would have ranged between 100,000 and 150,000 people.

Regarding the influx of slaves, Fatiha Loualich surmises that perhaps two million black slaves were brought into the Maghribian countries via the trans-Saharan caravans in the sixteenth century and as many more in the seventeenth, with a decline in the eighteenth and nineteenth centuries ('Emancipated', 202).[8] Considering Braudel's modest population figure for

---

[6] See Michel Fontenay, 'Routes', for a predominantly economic overview of three types of slavery: the trans-Saharan, Tatar-Ottoman and Mediterranean corsair modalities.

[7] For caravan routes, see for example the map by Vitorino Magalhães Godinho reproduced in Braudel 1: 183.

[8] Michel Fontenay discusses several estimates for the numbers of trans-Saharan slaves over the centuries, some of which coincide with those of Loualich ('Routes', 816–17, n12).

the Maghribian countries, this would suggest that a disproportionately high number of sub-Saharan slaves were brought in during this period, not to mention ever since the ninth century. Early modern testimonies such as Sosa's *Topografía de Argel* render this disproportion credible: 'When they go out, ladies usually take slave women with them, both black, of which they generally have many ..., and white, of which there also tend to be many. The number they take varies because each one goes accompanied according to her status and means. Some take eight or ten, others six, four or two. But normally they take no more than one or two' (I, 32, 28r–v). In this kind of slavery, women were more sought after than men, mainly as domestic workers but also as concubines (Loualich, 'Emancipated', 203).

The trans-Atlantic slave trade is estimated to have involved around 12 million African slaves.⁹ As the Mediterranean world was at times on the fringes of this trade, the influx of these slaves primarily affected Portugal and Spain, from Lisbon to Valencia, east of which slavery became 'whiter' on the northern shores of the Mediterranean. 'Today', writes Bernard Vincent, 'we know that more than a million people, perhaps close to two million in Portugal and Spain belonged to others between the mid-fifteenth and mid-nineteenth centuries. The vast majority of them had to do hard labour in absolute moral solitude' ('L'Esclavage', 445). As Vincent explains, two radically different types of slavery, trans-Atlantic and 'Mediterranean', compatibly coincided over this territory and are comprised in this figure. The estimate is useful, and the means by which these slaves were acquired are well known as are the purposes they served, yet, given the figures supplied by the Trans-Atlantic Slave Trade Database (see note 9), it would seem that the 'Mediterranean' slaves would have been proportionately much higher than those of the trans-Atlantic trade.

Elsewhere, Vincent affirms that the number of Muslim slaves in Portugal, Spain and Italy during the early modern period undoubtedly amounted to more than a million. He also recalls Bartolomé and Lucille Bennassar's estimate of at least 300,000 converts to Islam on the other side, a figure that must have been somewhat larger, as he convincingly argues (introduction to Martínez Torres 16). Most estimates put the total number of Christian slaves (renegades or not) at more than a million, a figure that would roughly counterbalance the estimated number of Muslim slaves in Christian lands. No matter what the numbers might have been, there's no doubt that Mediterranean frontier slavery profoundly affected both sides of the Mediterranean and the millions of people who were forced into it.¹⁰ Scholarship has very often disregarded the

---

⁹ Pablo F. Gómez has kindly provided me with the estimate along with this most impressive database: www.slavevoyages.org/assessment/estimates.

¹⁰ Salvatore Bono, a scholar highly aware of slavery on both sides of the Mediterranean, says that in an oral presentation he attempted a 'comprehensive, approximate and risky first evaluation of the total number of individuals involved in [frontier] slavery in the entire Mediterranean basin, from the Middle Ages to the elimination of slavery, say, in

practice of Mediterranean frontier slavery in Christian lands, and in its most visceral forms – even today – has concentrated instead on the terror struck by 'Barbary pirates', the cruel treatment of Christians at the hands of supposedly non-white Muslim masters, and the like. Of course it's almost impossible not to focus more on slavery in Muslim lands because the existing documentation is so overwhelmingly lopsided in that direction. Yet we have enough material about Christian corsairs, the enslavement of Muslim populations and defeated armies, the raids into the Maghribian interior from the presidios, the aggressions committed by Malta, the presence of slave markets in virtually every sizeable Christian port, and so on, to remember that slavery in both Muslim and Christian lands was an integral part of Mediterranean life and economy, as Braudel reminds us (886–90).

The issue of race requires some clarification here. In many Spanish texts including those of Cervantes we find references to white slaves (*esclavos/as blancos/as*) and black slaves (*esclavos/as negros/as*), and other languages express this in predictably similar ways. The distinction is very clear. Black slaves were from sub-Saharan Africa or the Canaries, whereas white slaves were generally Muslims from North Africa, the Levant and Ottoman Turkey, as well as Spanish Moriscos enslaved in Spain especially during armed conflicts (e.g. the war of the Alpujarras in 1568–70). More simply put, white slaves were usually Muslims from the Mediterranean world – or alternatively, Christian slaves in Muslim lands. We know from numerous testimonies that Moriscos were as 'white' as other Spaniards. Like other writers after him, Antonio de Sosa takes a keen interest in the skin colours of Moors in the Maghrib as well as those from European and Asian Turkey, and finds most of them (particularly the women) white, while others have complexions in different shades of tan (e.g. *trigueño*, wheat-coloured), but all slaves from these regions and ethnicities are considered 'white'. Many scholars have mistakenly assumed that North African Muslims were considered, as it were, 'non-white', and have read racial differences into ethnic, cultural, civilisational, religious and continental oppositions.[11] Mediterranean frontier slavery had virtually nothing to do with race as such.

1830 … It seemed to me that an order of magnitude could be indicated between 4–5 and 8–10 million individuals involved' (*Il Mediterraneo*, 99–101). The expression 'individuals involved in slavery' seems ambiguous. More helpfully, Felicia Roșu reports Bono as estimating 'that there were about twenty thousand Muslim slaves around 1600 in Naples alone, and four to five hundred thousand between 1500 and 1800 on the Italian peninsula'.

[11] To single out one example among others, Robert C. Davis's 2003 book *Christian Slaves, Muslim masters: White slavery in the Mediterranean, the Barbary coast, and Italy, 1500–1800*, while attempting to set up 'Barbary' slavery as a mirrored inversion of American (trans-Atlantic) black slavery, entirely misconceives its object of study as of the very title, which implies that Christians were white and Muslims were not, and that, 'in the Mediterranean', Christians were the victims of these non-white Muslim slave-masters whose cruelty is highlighted in the introduction. Davis gives only the slightest nods to

As opposed to trans-Atlantic and trans-Saharan slavery, whose enslaved victims were taken over immense expanses of land, sand or water and, if they survived the journey, had no possibility of ever returning and were forced to live and work in utterly strange places, Mediterranean slavery emerged from the circumstance of religious difference and political opposition across a porous and diffuse frontier that, as we know, united as much as it divided. This kind of slavery resembled slaveries in other epochs or regions of the world similarly articulated along a frontier but differentiated itself by the cultures, religions and geopolitical formations specific to the early modern Mediterranean. It was hence a frontier slavery rendered unique by Mediterranean geographical, historical and cultural configurations. The frontier within this context meant that people from either side could be enslaved and commodified by those of the other, primarily for economic reasons, and that many intermediaries including religious orders, Jewish merchants, diplomats and other officials would be involved in the operations. In general, owing in part to Catholic religious orders, ransoming operations from the Christian side were better organised than from the Muslim side, with the result that the slavery of Muslims would on average have lasted longer.

Negotiations on both sides would sometimes begin as soon as a battle or raid was over as the victors hoisted a flag of truce to discuss ransom and conclude the transactions. Everybody understood how this worked. The nature of the frontier was such that, while military campaigns or corsair attacks on other ships at sea or on coastal populations often resulted in pillage and capture, the soldiers or corsairs sometimes ended up being slaves of those they were trying to enslave. Uprisings within the boundaries of Spain and Turkey, both of which practised internal colonialism, resulted in the enslavement of rebels – of Moriscos in the case of Spain. Yet in the Mediterranean in general there were no relations of colonisers and colonised as such on opposite sides of the frontier, no uncontested aggressor that would bleed dry the human resources of lands across the water. Another source of slaves came from the constant incursions from the presidios into the Maghribian interior, the *cabalgadas* (cavalry raids), that captured substantial numbers of men, women and children who were sold back or sent away to Spain. Military clashes on sea and land resulted in the enslavement of many of the defeated soldiers,

---

a 'counter-enslavement' that 'some Christian states' practised, he believes, as a reaction to Barbary slavery (xxvi), because any due acknowledgement of Christian masters and Muslim slaves would undo his model, as would any questioning of this racially conceived opposition. He furthermore injects into Muslim slavery practice 'an element of revenge – almost of *jihad* – for the wrongs of 1492', when, '[b]y expelling the Moors from southern Spain, Ferdinand and Isabella created an implacable enemy for their resurgent kingdom' (xxv). That said, this book does include useful lists of information about the estimated numbers of slaves in Algiers, Tunis and Tripoli over three centuries according to many early modern authors.

occasionally many thousands at a time (e.g. with the resounding defeat of the Portuguese in the Battle of Alcazarquivir – or Wādī al-Makhāzin, or the Three Kings – in 1578). But once peace was established between the Spanish and Ottoman Empires in 1581, the big wars once again gave way to corsair activities that had been taking slaves and other goods all along but now intensified their offensives.

Distances were traversable in Mediterranean frontier space, alterity was relative rather than absolute, the other religions were different but in certain ways recognisable, some languages were more understandable than others, and the new *modus vivendi* as well as natural environment, foreign as it no doubt felt, would always bear at least some familiarity to what people knew elsewhere in the Mediterranean world before they became slaves. Moreover, slaves would associate with others from their own lands, be they other slaves, renegades, religious figures or merchants. Although more for some than for others, the possibility of return by a variety of means (ransom, exchange, escape, etc.) was often conceivable. There were also possibilities, unevenly distributed, of integration into the enslaving society: most dramatic in this regard were the meteoric careers of numerous corsairs and political figures in the Ottoman Empire, as well as the rise of powerful women as wives or concubines.

All of this contrasts sharply with trans-Atlantic and trans-Saharan slavery, even if there were common elements in all three kinds of slavery. The bilateralism of Mediterranean frontier slavery often created the need, even in hostile circumstances, to come to an understanding and to agreements. At the risk of retaliation for any breach of expected conduct, mutually recognised procedures ensured that negotiations and exchanges could take place. If, for some, slavery would turn out to be perpetual, for others it would end or evolve into something else, through escape, ransom, exchange of slaves, emancipation, conversion, social integration, marriage, and so on. Some of these possibilities were also open, say, to slave women brought from the other side of the Sahara, yet their chances of return were virtually nil; as we know all too well, slaves from the trans-Atlantic trade had even fewer alternatives open to them.

Other rules, too, constrained the practices of enslavement, creating exceptions with regard to who could be enslaved according to nationality. Despite references to *pirates* in texts of that period, there were few pirates in the early modern Mediterranean, and those few had no support from any governing authority. In any event, whenever writers wanted to speak ill of corsairs they called them 'pirates', which was a derogatory term and referred to a different category of seafarer. However, 'corsair' was by far the more common term (e.g. in Spanish, *corsario* or *cosario*), derived of course from the Italian *corsaro* and *corso*, the maritime 'course' that corsairs voyaged in search of slaves and other bounty at sea and along the coasts. Given the anarchy that often prevailed in the Middle Sea, scholars have sometimes questioned whether corsairs weren't really pirates. In spite of violations on the part of corsairs, there were vital distinctions between them because corsairs – state-sponsored pirates if you will – were in many ways responsible to those political entities that sponsored them and were obliged to honour the non-aggression treaties they had with other governments, as well as the rules for distributing plunder, and so on. The diplomat Laurent d'Arvieux, whose express mission in Tunis in 1666 was to free illicitly taken French slaves and renew a pre-existing agreement, writes that the military leaders in Tunis didn't want peace with France, and that the Portuguese renegade Cuchuk-Murad declared 'that if all the French slaves were given back, [Tunisian] ships would lack rowers because, as Tunis was already at peace with the English and Dutch, the only ones left to steal from and enslave were the Spanish and Italians, and that such a shortage could doom the Republic' (27). His concern is understandable. The corsairs' patent restricted their options in this and other ways, but also legitimised their exploits not only in the eyes of their own government and allies but also to some extent in those of their enemies. The young Spanish corsair Alonso de Contreras, warranted with a corsairing patent 'signed and sealed by the Grand Master' of Malta (I, 3, 25), recounts that when the people of Estampalia (an island east of the Cyclades now called Astypalea) complained to him that a Christian frigate had abducted their priest and asked for ransom, he pursued it poised for battle 'because it was necessary to fight even though they were Christians, as they are people who go armed without a license, and all of them are hoodlums and steal from Moors and from Christians' (I, 5, 41). When he reached the boat, the captain told him he had a patent from Messina. Contreras recognised it as false and abandoned the captain on a small island 'naked, without any food, so he could pay for his sin by dying of hunger'.[12]

Becoming slaves

João Carvalho Mascarenhas, a slave in Algiers from 1621 to 1626, barely alludes to himself when narrating the events of his captivity. Only much later do we find out more about him: that he has travelled much of the world, coming to know parts of Asia, East Africa, Brazil and the Mediterranean both as an official in Portuguese Asian endeavours and as a galley slave for Algerian corsairs. In his captivity account he focuses on two families of superiors whom he has accompanied for months from Goa via the Cape of Good Hope and St. Helena to Lisbon. Some of the voyagers have been away for twenty years and are much looking forward to seeing their families and friends again.

---

[12] 'desembarqué al capitán en el islote, desnudo, sin sustento ninguno, para que allí pagase su pecado muriendo de hambre' (I, 5, 41).

But when they arrive in sight of the port of Lisbon, at the mouth of the river Tajo, their ship Conceição, laden with untold riches acquired in the East, is attacked by seventeen 'Turkish' corsair vessels from Algiers and set on fire, leaving the passengers to drown or swim: 'One can imagine the plight of our people between these three cruel enemies: fire, water, and Turks'.[13]

The first of these two families is that of the wounded captain dom Luís de Sousa, who requests that his beautiful, beloved young wife dona Antonia and some servants be brought to him from other ships. 'The wailing and tears of this lady, when she saw her husband in such a lamentable state – wounded, poor, enslaved – moved the Turks themselves to pity.' The sentences that follow enumerate the immense riches he has lost, including vast quantities of money, the most beautiful artefacts and jewels that have ever been seen in China, India, and Persia, and 'Chinese and Japanese women slaves in incredible numbers. And he saw himself suddenly in such great wretchedness … And his wife was as poor and as much a slave as her black women slaves'.[14] Owing to his wounded leg and his deep melancholy at seeing himself and his wife in this desolate state, says Mascarenhas, God snatched him out of this life and sent him to rest in the other. What's so striking here is the sense of extreme loss. The almost infinite wealth he has acquired in colonies abroad is seen as great merit on his part, and his wife completes what would otherwise be the picture of the ideal colonial couple in sight of home. Husband and wife now see each other as the embodiment of utter misfortune, as slaves no better than their own slaves that are no longer theirs, as former owners who are now owned by others. Their adversity is seen as a much graver and more painful loss than that of others who have lost less, and those who have lost the least are the slaves who change owners without losing anything because they have nothing to lose in a material or legal sense. From a broader perspective, we could say that global colonialism with its own forms of slavery, regarded as legitimate and desirable, is disrupted by Mediterranean frontier slavery, which by this time has already been active in the Atlantic for a quarter of a century with different kinds of ships modelled after those of the 'northern invaders' (as Braudel calls them), the English and Dutch.

If this portrait is meant to evoke pity, Mascarenhas's account of another family, particularly dona Maria Ribeira, 'one of the greatest ladies in India', goes much further. Like dom Luís de Sousa, the rich noble Pêro Mendes de Vasconcelos, her husband, who was a high officer in India, dies of his gunshot

---

[13] 'Os nossos bem se deyxã ver, que taes estariam metidos entre tres tam crueis inimigos, como era o fogo, a agoa, & os Turcos' (I, 7, 19).

[14] 'as escravas chinas & japoas não havia mais que pintar, & verse logo em tanta miseria … & sua mulher igual com suas negras tam pobre & tão escrava como ellas' (I, 8, 22).

wound in her presence. The divan of Algiers claims her along with her beautiful blind daughter with luminous eyes and two handsome, well-educated boys of eleven and twelve years. The younger of the boys dies in her arms of the plague, and the elder is sent as a present to the Grand Turk in Istanbul for an elite education. Accompanying this elder son are many handsome youths including a boy of the same age, the son of a Portuguese noble and of 'the most noble and virtuous wife there ever was' in India, who had been sent across the world to the Portuguese Court for his education but is now redirected to be educated at the court of the Grand Turk (I, 12, 28). This dramatic reorientation of the boy's fate involves a change of destination and destiny. The simplicity of the narrative, however, doesn't conceal the utter grief suffered by dona Maria:

> This lady was the most unfortunate woman in the world, and she still is. Coming from India with great riches after having left her relatives there, she embarked on a ship and, the day she saw the land where she would live comfortably with her husband, he was killed by gunshot, her elder son was taken to Constantinople to be turned Turk, the younger died of the plague in her arms, she became a slave, and, adding to her servitude and travails, she saw her beautiful blind daughter in the power of barbarians. I know of no other woman who has suffered so many misfortunes. And this is still so today because she and her daughter are slaves of the divan. (I, 13, 28)

This is about as much loss as one can imagine, exemplifying what slavery is: total loss, ultimately a loss not only of all one has but of oneself, which now belongs to someone else, and of all one's family. These two examples, focused on formerly privileged families who have fallen into utter misfortune, show the extreme reversal of fortune that results from the event of becoming a slave. This in effect stands for all slavery, and regardless of Mascarenhas's blind reverence towards the colonially privileged, his representation of the absolute loss suffered by those who had been the most fortunate does indeed stand for his own loss of freedom and fortune as well as that of all others, no matter who they are, who likewise suffer a loss of everything including themselves.

Mascarenhas goes on to tell how the other captives (himself included, though he tends to erase himself) were taken to the Batistan in Algiers – the market for slaves and other captured goods. Chance would dictate each person's fate,

> good or bad depending on whether the master was good or bad. For indeed there is no worse adversity in life than when a captive waits to find out who his master will be, because a man cannot come to greater woe nor, for his

sins, to such misery than to be a slave, but if his bad fortune leads him to be a slave of a vile master, he can no longer expect anything good from his stars and must regard himself as entirely forlorn, because there is no worse hell in this life.[15]

Unlike the nineteenth-century orientalist painters who would portray the slave market from the viewpoint of the buyers of naked young women, Mascarenhas dramatises the supreme anxiety felt by slaves during that brief juncture when their fate, already sunk into the abjection of slavery itself, still depends on the new master's character, which will make their hell better or worse. Emmanuel d'Aranda narrates in detail how he and his companions were captured, and how a renegade responds to him in Flemish: 'Have patience, brother, it's the fortune of war, today for you, tomorrow for me.'[16] This signals the reversibility of fortune in Mediterranean frontier slavery, especially when uttered by someone who is apparently a countryman of his who has reneged. D'Aranda nonetheless says their worst experience was the process of being inspected and auctioned off as slaves after they were taken off the boat in Algiers: 'This is where our tragedy began' (33). And he too, as we'll see, had a variety of luck with different masters, some of whom he was able to choose himself.

As a variant, let's consider the captivity of padre Jerónimo Gracián, Teresa of Ávila's beloved last confessor and himself a mystic, who, en route from Sicily to Rome via Gaeta, was captured by a 'Turkish' galley: 'I found myself a prisoner, naked, robbed of what I held most dear, which were the papers of a spiritual doctrine that I had exerted much effort in writing and that I was taking to Rome to publish, and, as you will understand, I was vexed that the Turks were cleaning their rifles with them.'[17] The debasement of *Armonía mística*, an irreplaceable mystic manuscript, into disposable paper for cleaning the Turks' gun barrels, runs parallel to the degradation of this Carmelite theologian into a slave in the possession of Tunisian renegades. Gracián is by no

---

[15] 'Daqui cada hum seguio sua ventura, tendoa boa ou má conforme o patram bom ou mào, com que deu, que certo na vida não ha pior transe do que he esperar o cativo nesta hora o amo que terá, porque um homem não pòde chegar a mayor desgraça, nem seus peccados o podem trazer a mayor miseria que a ser escravo, mas se sua mà fortuna o trouxe a ser escravo de roim patrão, nam tem, que aguardar cousa boa de sua estrela, se nam terse por desgraciadissimo, porque não ha pior inferno nesta vida.' (I, 13, 28–9)

[16] 'Patience, frère, c'est la fortune de guerre, aujourd'hui pour vous, et demain pour moi' (31).

[17] 'Y en un punto me vi desnudo, aprisionado y despojado de lo que más pudiera tener codicia, que eran unos papeles de doctrina de espíritu que había escrito con mucho trabajo y llevaba para imprimir en Roma, sintiendo, como era razón, ver que los turcos limpiaban con ellos sus escopetas' (68–9).

means blind to the ironies of this situation, and in fact recounts many other aspects of his slavery with this acute self-awareness and sense of humour. Bad weather forces the Turks to brand the cross on the soles of his feet, because when there was bad weather the Turks, if there was a captive priest on board, would brand a sign of the cross on the bottom of his feet, 'and if the weather didn't change they would burn me alive' (69). During his year and a half as a slave, Gracián does indeed run the risk of being burned alive for encouraging a renegade to renounce Islam with loud public gestures – which the sceptical pasha doesn't take seriously – but otherwise negotiates a privileged position among Christian captives, visits renegade women and men, and enters into intriguing exchanges with Jews and Muslims.

Little has been said about how some slaves, both men and women, were able to negotiate the conditions of their slavery, which is to say that Mediterranean frontier slavery allowed a certain leeway as to what kinds of master-slave relations could emerge. To take a rather extreme example, Emanuel d'Aranda tells of his relations with perhaps his most beloved master:

> As for me, I stayed with my new master Cataborne Mostafa. And though he was but a poor soldier, I enjoyed my time with him because he would often say to me: 'Emanuel, don't be sad, imagine that you are my master and I am your slave.' I would eat with him from the same plate as we were seated together with our legs crossed in the Turkish way.[18]

Much to d'Aranda's chagrin, his master falls into disgrace, and d'Aranda has to find another master, a friend of Cataborne Mostafa's named Mahomet Çelibi Oiga, who d'Aranda has reason to believe is jealous because a fellow captive has spoken too 'familiarly' with Mahomet's wife; Mahomet at first says he has no room for another slave, but finally gives in to admit d'Aranda into his household as a slave. Here we have a slave-master finally allowing someone to be a slave in his household, and we see the kinds of sentiments such as jealousy that can arise from relations between a master's wife and another slave. Ultimately the hierarchy is flattened, and what we're left with is a household with volatile interpersonal relationships that the slave-master is unable to control.

It is the (Christian) religious writers who for centuries have dominated the discourse about Christian slavery in the Maghrib. Some, like Pierre Dan and Gabriel Gómez de Losada, were militant spokesmen for their ransoming

---

[18] 'Quant à moi je demeurai chez mon nouveau patron Cataborne Mostafa. Et encore qu'il ne fût qu'un pauvre soldat, j'avais du bon temps avec lui, car il me disait souvent: "Emanuel, ne soyez pas mélancolique, pensez en vous-même que vous êtes mon patron et moi votre esclave." Je mangeais avec lui et du même plat, étant assis à ses côtés les jambes croisées à la mode turquesque' (69).

religious order – in their case the Trinitarians – while others belonged to the Mercedarians, all of whom had every interest in condemning Barbary slavery as the worst kind of slavery that the world had ever known, much more cruel than the treatment of Muslim slaves in Christian lands. Other religious writers included Antonio de Sosa, who didn't belong to either of these orders but, as a captive, spews forth the most hateful diatribes in his *Dialogue on captivity* (*Topografía* III) along with Jerónimo Gracián, who in his *Treatise on the redemption of captives* wilfully forgets all the kindnesses he was shown during his captivity, as well as the complex mediation roles he performed in Tunis, and launches into a systematic attack very much along the lines that would later be followed by the likes of Dan and Gómez de Losada. All of these religious writers were highly erudite and could trace a biased history of slavery from the earliest times of Antiquity to the present in order to show that there had never been anything like the cruelty of slavery on the Barbary coast. Easy as it would be, there's no reason for us to delve into the very predictable forms of demagogic discourse produced and reproduced by such writers. Gracián says that in contrast to the noise, stench and insect-infested 'dungeons' of Christians in Barbary, any jail for Muslims in Christian lands is a 'delightful garden' (100). All of these religious ideologues do in effect capture the deep despair of enslaved Christians in cities such as Algiers, Tunis and Tripoli (Libya), and yet are contradicted by practically every testimony regarding slavery in the Mediterranean. Effective as their propaganda was, not only did they pay no attention to how Muslim slaves fared in Christian lands, but they were also blind to the many variations of slavery of Christians in Muslim lands such as those we've just seen in the case of d'Aranda. For his part, Jerónimo Gracián ignores much of his own experience as a slave, such as when the pasha of Tunis reportedly scoffed at those who wanted to burn Gracián for his apostasy in turning a renegade back to Christianity, saying: 'What does it matter to you if he turns Christian? We'll have one more oar in our galleys' (74). All such instances – and they're the norm – undo the false argumental threads sustaining that Islam was competing with Christianity over the souls of Christians, forcing them to convert, and so on.

Any description or narrative based on experience rather than religious ideology would find it hard to sustain any morally negative invective against all those who were called 'Turks' (or 'renegades', 'Barbary pirates', 'Moors', etc.). We've seen how Mascarenhas underscores the cruelty of Turks in the sea battle and as slave-masters, yet he devotes much more attention to their remarkably humane treatment of the captives, moved as they are by the suffering of these people, and he concedes that some slave-masters are much better than others. His emphasis on the empathy felt by Turks could be seen as a rhetorical means of dramatising dona Antonia's plight, yet he insists beyond all doubt on this humaneness:

The Turks' treatment of the people in their ships was very good, and not what one would have expected from Barbary corsairs ... They came to tell [the captives below deck] not to let themselves be stripped or despoiled of anything, and if any Moor tried to do so, they should cry out and he would be well punished. They separated the women from the men, warning the captives not to approach one other, and if they did so they would be thoroughly whipped and thrown into the sea. And to avoid this, there were twelve lanterns lit all night long in each vessel, with Turks on guard. They regard as very grave any sin of the flesh committed at sea, and any ship on which this happens cannot be saved and will sink right away. They gave us what they themselves ate: they made for everyone a large cauldron of boiled rice or wheat, with abundant biscuit, olives and cheese ... Many of them commiserated with us about our hardships and were astonished to learn that we had been at sea for so many months, and they brought us raisins and grains, which for them are a delicacy.[19]

If it's the luck of some to be captors and of others to be captured, the 'Turks' ('Barbary corsairs') are exemplary in the way they talk to their captives, sympathise with them, share with them and treat them the way they treat themselves. Indeed, Mascarenhas in no way individualises any of the Turks in these passages, yet the collective representation in effect commutes master-slave relations into relations of hospitality as long as the journey to Algiers lasts. The fleet enters triumphantly into the port of Algiers 'to celebrate what for our captives was only misery, anguish and misfortune' (I, 11, 26). Nonetheless it is significant that the women captives are protected – from the thievery of 'Moors' and the lust of other Christians. Despite suppositions to the contrary in contemporary scholarship, we shouldn't presume that Christian captive women were necessarily subjected to sexual violence by their captors or slavemasters: at times they were, other times they weren't, and it's worth looking into the circumstances and whatever indications there might be regarding the kinds of pressures or violence they might have been subjected to – or

---

[19] 'A ordem que os turcos tiveraõ com a gente que coube a cada nao foy muyto boa, & não como de barbaros cossairos ... Depois de os terem debayxo, lhe vinhaõ dizer que nenhum se deyxasse despir nem tomar nada, & se algum mouro o quizesse fazer que gritassem, & que logo o castigariaõ muy bem. Puzeraõ as mulheres apartadas dos homens, requerendo aos cativos que naõ chegassem huns aos outros, & que se o faziaõ lhe dariaõ muyto açoute & o botariam ao mar. & para evitar isto, estavaõ toda a noyte em cada navio mais de doze alampadas acezas, com turcos de guarda. Porque tem elles por gravissimo peccado cualquier peccado da carne que se comete no mar, & a embarcaçam em que se fez nam pòde salvar & se irá logo ao fundo. Davaõ ao comer o que elles comiam, que para todos se fazia huma grande caldeyra ou de arroz ou de trigo cozido, biscoyto em muyta abundancia, azeytonas & queyjo ... & muytos se compadeciam de nossos trabalhos & se espantavaõ de haver tantos mezes que andavamos pelo mar, & nos traziaõ algumas paças & grãos, que he regalo entre elles' (I, 10, 24–5).

not. A woman's ability to resist or negotiate likewise varied according to her circumstances.

Religious Christian writers diverge a great deal as to how willing they are to recognise any positive attributes in the 'Turks' and 'Moors'. The theologian Antonio de Sosa does indeed express deep admiration for a number of people he writes about, especially in his *History* (part II of the *Topografía*). However, his treatment of the virtues of Muslims in Algiers follows upon a long chapter on their vices – they incarnate the seven deadly sins – and introduces the topic in a backhanded way: 'God created nothing that ... he did not endow with some good quality and virtue, even if it is hidden to men, because we see that even the adder, with all its poison, is useful to the earth, and that most excellent remedies are made from venom. I say this because the Moors and Turks of Algiers are not altogether deprived of goodness and virtues'.[20] As it turns out, these good qualities are precisely what Christians are often lacking in Sosa's view: unlike many Christians as well as renegades who brought their bad habits with them from Europe, these Turks and Moors don't swear or blaspheme but instead praise God, they don't gamble, they are obedient to their superiors, they withstand hunger, they never quarrel or deceive each other, they are clean, religiously devout, and so on. Compared to the inventory of vices, however, this quick list of virtues is scant praise, and in any case mainly serves as a mirror in reverse of the vices of Christians. As we've seen, autobiographical writers such as Mascarenhas and d'Aranda, to name only two, or Cervantes in his fictions, have no qualms about acknowledging good qualities when they see them in Moors and Turks, and these testimonies no doubt offer us a more credible view.

In consonance with such representations, some writers go further to openly criticise as misguided the accounts of religious writers and their followers. Laurent d'Arvieux writes in his diary:

> People imagine that Christians who have the misfortune of being slaves in Barbary are tormented there in the most cruel and inhumane way. There are people who, to stir up the charity of the faithful, self-assuredly produce these pious lies. Their intention, although good, is still a lie ... Like many others, I thought this was true and would perhaps still believe this error despite what I had seen in the other parts of the Ottoman Empire where I've been. But what I saw in Tunis set me straight. It's true that there are masters with bad humour, harsh, disagreeable and even cruel; we see masters in

---

[20] 'Ninguna cosa crio Dios a la cual ... no dotase de alguna propiedad y virtud buena, aunque a los hombres sea oculta, porque vemos que hasta la víbora, siendo de tanta ponzoña, aprovecha en la tierra, y que de venenos se hacen excelentísimos remedios. Digo esto porque no dexan de tener los moros y turcos de Argel algo de bueno y virtudes' (I, 37, 39r).

Europe who are no more reasonable and who would perhaps be more barbarous than those in Tunis if they had slaves. (44)

The logic, he explains, is essentially commercial, where the Turks aim to buy cheaply and sell for as much as possible, and to do that they have to take good care of their merchandise as one would a horse. Rarely, he says, is any Christian forced to convert to Islam, though they are sometimes subjected to attempts at persuasion. Above all, widows commonly offer what they have to their slaves if they adopt Islam and marry them.

But far beyond the economic facts, d'Arvieux says, 'What I've seen in Tunis has convinced me that these people are humane [ces peuples sont humains]'. He goes on to enumerate the many generous and affectionate relations he has seen, e.g. how the freed slaves themselves would ask to stay with their former masters rather than wait on board for the day of departure, how their masters would have them eat with them, give them tobacco, and 'look at them as their children', embracing them when they departed and assuring them they would be most welcome if they ever returned. Moreover, he says that slaves often bring bad treatment upon themselves, particularly since many become expert thieves, and – if they're allowed with their guards' complicity to roam the streets at night – they break down shop doors and loot everything, often making malicious accusations against Jews if they're caught (45).

Even if we assume that the experience of slavery in the Maghrib may have become less onerous over many decades, it's worth seeing how Laugier de Tassy in effect echoes d'Arvieux's account half a century later. Laugier de Tassy is aware that some categories of slaves are very vulnerable to abuse in Algiers: those of higher rank who are bought by slave-trafficking descendants of Moriscos; lower-class women who, unlike other women, aren't protected in safe-houses of the divan but are rather subject to the violence of their owners; and 'young boys' likewise 'strongly exposed to the violence of certain masters, who buy them with that intent' (279). Yet he asserts more generally: 'There are two types of slaves: those of the divan or the republic, and those of private owners. Neither of these is by any means as miserable as is alleged in the fabricated accounts made by monks or by former slaves, who have their own reasons for swaying the public in this way' (275). He mocks the solemn ceremonies of returning slaves conducted by religious orders in Spain, in which ex-slaves parade two by two with their waist-length beards still uncut, dressed in Moorish garb and 'weighed down by chains they never wore' (285). The experience of slavery depends not only on the character of the masters but also on the *naturel* of the slaves themselves, and even if some slaves have ended up with bad masters, all masters have to humour and indulge their slaves for fear of losing them. Many slaves, says Laugier de Tassy, have as much or more domestic power than their masters, sleep in the same bedroom, eat with them and 'are cared for and beloved like children' (277–8). Some slaves, he says, have the privilege of operating taverns, and 'earn money by every sort of iniquity, and could buy their freedom in a year; but most of them give in to debauchery and libertinism, and they'd rather be in Algiers than in a Christian country' (277). Moreover, 'there are slaves who are so habituated to Algiers, owing to their profits and their lasciviousness, that they buy the right to be slaves for a long time or their whole lives' – and he goes on to explain how these deals are made with their masters (281). Laugier's remarks are very revealing and can by no means be dismissed as anticlerical discourse: I recall nothing in earlier accounts that hints at such practices of voluntary (though nominal) slavery in the Mediterranean region.

This is the kind of slavery in which significant numbers of Christian slaves in Muslim countries *could* want to stay even as slaves, and while conversion did not *ipso facto* presuppose emancipation, much higher numbers converted to Islam, only a small percentage of whom returned to their homelands. We have of course testimonies of many who suffered slavery, and the example of Cervantes who eloquently expressed the hardships of his slavery[21] and staged four perilous and unsuccessful escape attempts. Very often, however, we can observe slaves settling into a routine and an attitude of relative acquiescence. After all, everyone travelling in the Mediterranean region or living along the coastlines understood that enslavement could happen to anyone. Thus, Mascarenhas comes to accept that he and his companions were (who knows why?) condemned by divine justice to be slaves (I, 11, 25). Cervantes ventriloquises about his five years of captivity during which he 'learned to have patience in adversity.'[22] 'I gradually became accustomed to this life,'[23] writes d'Aranda, who even appreciates what this unwanted life of necessity had to teach him and fellow slaves: 'there is no better university than an Algerian prison to teach people how to live.'[24]

I've deliberately avoided the most canonical sources for information about captivity and slavery in the Mediterranean. Mascarenhas, Jerónimo Gracián, d'Aranda, d'Arvieux and Laugier de Tassy provide materials and insights seldom seen in studies of slavery. I believe they provide rare but valid viewpoints that go against the grain of most early modern texts about slavery, and in so doing help to characterise Mediterranean frontier slavery with different paradigms. Many aspects of slavery will go mostly unexplored here,

---

[21] He does so most notably in an autobiographical poem entitled 'Epístola a Mateo Vázquez', now recognised as his after much debate, written during his captivity in 1577.

[22] 'aprendió a tener paciencia en las adversidades' (*Novelas ejemplares*, prologue, 51).

[23] 'Je m'étais peu à peu accoutumé à cette vie' (40).

[24] 'il n'est point de meilleure université que le bain d'Alger pour apprendre le monde à vivre' (152).

including ransoming procedures and other means of attaining freedom, the experience of slavery in a variety of those 'cities of the sea', the ways in which slaves figured in the economy of enslaving societies, and so on. We've already glimpsed at several differences between men's and women's slavery. The next section will explore themes barely covered, if at all, in most slavery studies, namely women's slavery, the experience of Muslim women on the other side, and the relations of women's slavery to sexuality. We'll again see these through a variety of fairly unknown texts, this time with a mix of testimonial and fictive literature.

Enslaved women

Among the millions of Muslim and Christian slaves in the Mediterranean world of the sixteenth and seventeenth centuries, a substantial number of them were women and girls, victims of war and corsair expeditions. For different reasons, and unlike the case of male slaves (although not so different from that of male children and adolescents), not many of these women returned to their countries of origin. Women, in fact, were generally rather more valued than men both in Muslim and Christian countries. Curiously, Maghribian and especially Turkish slave girls, adolescents and women were the most valued in the Iberian Peninsula, while male Muslim slaves – above all the Turks – were the least valued, well below other categories such as blacks, mulattoes, etc.: for the Christian owner, it was not the same to have a 'white' female slave in the house as a 'white' male Turkish or Maghribian enemy (Stella 102–5). Also, on the Muslim side, many women of Christian origin, as well as (male or female) children and adolescents, were not ransomable because their owners refused to put them on the market: often the owners – mainly renegades – sought to marry slave women and encouraged them to convert to Islam. A large proportion of the slave women ended up integrating through marriage into Maghribian or Turkish society. Much of what has been said thus far about Mediterranean frontier slavery applies to both women and men, yet both historical testimonies and literary texts lead us to understand that women and men experienced slavery very differently. Although many factors must be taken into account, including the domestic labour that women were required to do, sources often stress the erotic attraction of women for their buyers or male owners, which would have played an important role in these differences. Together with gender, the modality of slavery also had important consequences, as Fatiha Loualich affirms when saying that white slaves could be ransomed, but not black slaves. Women, she says, were much more often emancipated than men (80 per cent of cases v. 20 per cent in her archival searches), and she makes a strong argument in favour of the integration of emancipated women, as opposed to other historical accounts that refer to emancipated women's poverty, prostitution or continued servitude.[25]

When it comes to talking about female slaves, both literary and non-literary texts of the period are likely to focus on young, beautiful women. The mere mention of a female captive/slave tends to evoke, unless otherwise specified, the image of a sexually appealing woman endowed with an exoticism that intensifies her seductive power for free men around her. According to very diverse texts, the fact of slavery and, therefore, the prospect of possessing a woman tends to intensify desire among those who can acquire her by force or money. Nonetheless, the historical realities would often have been different, at least in Muslim countries, since this 'instrument with a voice' (as Aristotle defined slaves) had, besides her voice, a will of her own that could prevent the owner from forcibly taking her. Early modern writings narrate a variety of encounters between Christian slave women and free Muslim men without providing us with any set pattern as to how they ended up. Muslim men were frequently held back by their own principles of restraint – moral, superstitious, economic – and indeed many, without resorting to prostitution, had multiple sexual options available to them, depending on their means and inclinations – wives, concubines, black and white slave women, adolescent boys. We've also seen comments to the effect that if a slave woman did not want to yield to the owner's requests, there was little she could do and no legal restraint on him. In Christian lands, however, there were far fewer opportunities for marriage and integration into the social domain, and it seems that the owners of Muslim slave women were subject to little restraint. Numerous studies on slavery affirm that the various functions performed by slave women often included sexual relations with the master.[26]

The recurrent scenes of gifts, purchases and possession of slave women going back to ancient literature attest to a marked eroticisation of the enslaved female body. The offering of slave women to great warriors or military leaders is a supreme gift on the part of the donors and an opportunity to glimpse the

---

[25] She goes on to explain: 'In Islam, emancipation is a pious act and believers are strongly encouraged to free their slaves. As their lives neared their end, masters sometimes emancipated all their slaves … There were also specific Islamic injunctions regarding female slaves. A concubine with children had to be emancipated upon the death of her master. In fact, in accordance with the Quran and Sunna, she was no longer a slave as soon as her pregnancy was confirmed. Her children were also emancipated and, as soon as their paternity was established, the children of slave women acquired the same rights as the father's heirs from marriages with free women' ('Emancipation', 203–4).

[26] Such studies include those of Alessandro Stella, Françoise Orsoni-Avila and Bernard Vincent ('L'esclavage moderne'). See also María Soledad Carrasco Urgoiti (*Vidas fronterizas*) and Emilio Sola ('Historia de la frontera') about women captives. Irvin Schick, for his part, offers a fascinating analysis of the relations between alterity and eroticism throughout *The erotic margin*, especially as of the eighteenth century.

character and temperament of those who receive the present. On the other hand, the auctioning of slave women in the market can excite great passions among those who wish to buy them, reaching exorbitant prices. Such is the case of the sale of Leonisa, the female protagonist of Cervantes' *El amante liberal* (*The generous lover*), but other texts of the period also represent this erotic-mercantile drama. We could also turn to earlier texts such as a letter sent by the Andalusi writer Abū Bakr al-Barḍaʾī (thirteenth century) to his friend Abū l-Baqāʾ al-Rundī, in which he tells how he went to the slave market and was rapt with desire when contemplating a slave of extraordinary sensual beauty whom he describes in poetic and palpably physical detail. Then comes the auction: 'The people strained their necks to see her and offered great sums for her. The rich were eager to value her highly, and her price kept going up. Everybody placed bets to attain the object of his desires until a young man sincere in his love came and had no qualms about squandering his fortune to save his heart' (Granja 163). The author is beside himself and begs his friend: 'Find a cure before you see your friend fallen, killed by love, and buy him a slave woman before you have to repent for having let him die.' While this letter is a kind of joke that gives the author the opportunity to exercise his literary prowess in describing a voluptuous woman – and the friend responds in an equally jocular tone with a similar description of another young woman who can serve him – the epistolary exchange is attuned to a tradition that maximises the erotic aura of a slave woman being sold.

In the Christian-European imaginary of the time, slave women opened up a space of eroticism and sexuality different from those of marriage, prostitution and adultery, among others. As the soaring prices of Muslim slave women confirm, the presence of a beautiful young slave woman, moderately exotic in body and attire and Muslim in religion and land of origin, created the ideal conditions for that erotic-sexual space from the perspective of male slave buyers. Possessing a woman as property, acquired as merchandise or booty or a gift, already implies power over that slave woman who, when captured, 'lost freedom of body and her country', in the words of Miguel de Castro.[27] This erotic-sexual space seems to favour a rather attenuated alterity, as is more generally the case of Christian-Muslim relations in the Mediterranean: recognisably related but distinct peoples, contrasted but by no means opposed cultures, a backdrop of religions and geopolitical configurations often contrary but not antithetical. For European Christians, 'white' slave women brought together all of these desired characteristics. Besides, the fact that they were Muslim justified their being treated as slaves, as eroticised exotic property, without applying the norms of other types of sexual relations in force in Christian countries. Slave women provided an *extra*ordinary erotic-sexual space.

---

[27] 'perdía en aquel día libertad de cuerpo y la patria' (35).

The soldier Miguel de Castro's autobiographical *Vida* (written *c.* 1612, revised *c.* 1617) presents us with rare insights into how this played out, particularly with regard to a woman named Mina. In a text whose main thread is a series of romantic and sexual adventures, the ongoing episode of Mina is perhaps the most singular and significant of all, even though Castro dedicates two-thirds of his book to his dull nocturnal escapades with the Spanish courtesan Luisa de Sandoval in Naples. This young soldier in fact tells us very little about his military campaigns, although he does narrate in great detail a raid that his fleet of fourteen galleys makes in the Albanian port of Durazzo (now Durrës). What's unusual about this passage is that it tells with horror how women leap from the castle to their death, how the soldiers kill them together with their children and how Castro himself saves a child that a companion was going to kill, and other things 'worthy of abomination'. Although this expedition would count as a military success, Castro doesn't hesitate to condemn the atrocities of his companions and express deep sympathy towards the victims. It turns out that on his ship 'eleven male slaves and twenty-six women came aboard, along with some children. Among the women there were two: one called Fatima, with a lovely body and beautiful face, white as alabaster, and two carnations on each cheek'.[28] He gives a meticulous description of this beautiful, exotic slave, whom Castro tries to protect against the painful and degrading abuses of another soldier. But Fatima disappears almost immediately: 'The slave woman was later requested by don Diego and don Gerónimo Pimentel, and she had to be given over to them [fue fuerza dárselas]' – which allows us to see how the highest authorities appropriated the most desirable captive women (as also occurred with Christian women captured by Muslims). Castro, who is usually attracted to wayward women, censures Fatima as wanton even as he bemoans her fate: 'Truly this grieved me, though she showed herself to be too licentious, and to such extent that, having been a slave for so short a time, and outside her own land, she did not acknowledge any of us, and showed herself to be too free and easy going, and not of good demeanour.'[29]

Everything told about the razzia and Fatima sets the scene for introducing Mina, as beautiful as Fatima but more demure, and this modesty increases her charms for Castro:

---

[28] 'Venían once esclavos varones y veinte y seis mugeres entre chiquillos y grandes, que había algunas criaturas. Entre las mugeres había dos: la una llamada Fátima, de buen cuerpo y bello rostro, blanca como un alabastro, y dos claveles en cada mejilla' (34–5).

[29] 'Verdaderamente me pesó, aunque mostraba ser algo demasiado desenvuelta, y en tal medida, que habiendo tan poco que era esclava, y fuera de su tierra, y que no conocía a neguno de los nuestros, denotaba y daba indicios de muger desenvuelta y libre demasiado, y no de buena congetura' (36).

The other of the two beautiful women I mentioned was not as white as Fatima. She was a little more bronzed, not much, neither white nor brown, with black hair and dark eyes, and she was well-proportioned. Her features were finer than Fatima's, and above all she showed a modesty and bashfulness together with a dignified and discreet look that alone was enough to reveal her to be a person of quality, which she was. Her name was Mina, and I confess my weakness because my will yielded to her so much that I still have feelings for her, even six years later, and not so forgotten or so few that they might not last many more.[30]

The relationship between Mina and Miguel develops while she's transferred from house to house and owner to owner, and is characterised by ingredients of condolence, affection, love, friendship and eroticism, although they never have sexual relations, not because they don't want to but because they can't. This results in a sustained erotic tension throughout their relations, which last from the summer of 1606 until more or less the following summer. According to the text, Miguel is about 16 years old[31] and Mina 22, always accompanied by her five-year-old daughter, which is no problem for Miguel or any of the owners: nobody seems to be interested or bothered by her family life or her sexual relations before captivity since they now see her as a sexual slave transferable to new owners. In the only passage of the *Vida* in which the author is interested in the genealogy of a lover, other slaves say Mina is the granddaughter of the vizier of Albanian sultan Amet Agá and daughter of Viquir Agá, 'a deputy who was governor of that province in the time of the vizier Agá Mahamut' (36) and lord of Durazzo, among other posts he held. Though she belongs to an influential family, at no point is there any mention of a possible ransom or negotiations with her family: while she's transferable among Christian owners, we might surmise that she isn't ransomable because she's worth much more than a market price, no matter how high. In fact, not so

---

[30] 'La otra que he dicho de las dos hermosas no era tan blanca como esta; era un poco trigueña, no mucho, de suerte que no era muy blanca ni era morena; cabos negros y ojos negros y de buen tamaño. Las faciones mejores que la otra, y sobre todo una modestia y humildad acompañado con una vista grave y vergonzosa que sola bastaba a dar a entender ser persona de calidad, como lo era. Esta se llamaba Mina, y confieso mi flaqueza, que me rindió la voluntad de suerte que aun hay reliquias, con haber pasado seis años, y no tan olvidadas ni tan pocas que no basten a durar muchos' (36).

[31] Antonio Paz y Meliá, editor of the original 1900 edition, discusses the evident chronological anomalies that arise from the fact that the author says he was born in 1593: 'Can we accept that an 11-year-old boy [when he arrives as a soldier in Italy in 1604] can carry out such amazing deeds?' He considers other possibilities, e.g. that Castro was born in 1583 or perhaps 1590. Randolph Pope and Margarita Levisi, for their part, believe that Castro was most likely born in 1590.

much is paid for her those times when she is sold, but it seems that only a few are allowed to buy her: she can't be acquired by any buyer, regardless of how rich he may be.

Miguel de Castro can have this love/friendship with Mina precisely because she is a *slave* but *not his* slave. Of course, Castro doesn't allude to sexual relations between Mina and her successive owners, though it's highly unlikely that they don't occur. In fact, the itinerary of Mina as a transferable slave is well documented. There is first the capture in Durazzo by a soldier: 'She was captured by an ordinary soldier of the company' – but Castro writes in the margin, probably years later in 1617 when he adds other notes, 'by my hands' (36). Did he capture her, then? If that's the case, why not say it in the text of his book, written in 1612? Taking into account the massacre described in Durazzo, capturing her could save her life, but it would also have meant taking away 'freedom of body and her country', i.e. condemning her to a life of slavery, which might be hard for Castro to acknowledge, given his sentiments for her.

In any event, the first one to lay claim to buying this female slave was Antonio de la Haya, captain of Castro's company, the night after they left Durazzo (36). But he had it very difficult because of both his superiors and other competitors, as indicated in this revealing passage about the acquisition of slave women:

> We arrived at Messina, where by order of the general all male and female slaves were taken to the commander's ship, some one hundred and seventy in all. There they were put up for sale after the marquis [of Santa Cruz] and the two brothers [don Diego and don Gerónimo Pimentel] had taken their pick. And they did not overlook the one I hoped would be taken someplace where I could be in contact with her, for the marquis wanted her right away for himself, and the captain asked him to do him the favour of leaving her for him, as he would pay for her and, besides, she was one of those taken by his company. The marquis did not persist though I know he was most unhappy about it, as was don Diego Pimentel ... After the marquis let go of her, many cast their eyes on her with the intention of paying whatever they could for her. Captain Antonio de la Haya, seeing that everyone was eyeing her and that it was already hard for him to wrest the large hawks from her by pleading, and that the other captains were pursuing her, stood in the middle of the stern and loudly declared in the presence of the marquis and all the lords and captains: 'Gentlemen, this slave was taken by my company, and I have already borne the shame of asking the marquis to leave her to me. There is no use in going after her to buy her because even if she were to cost me two thousand escudos, no one else would take her.' All were silent and refrained from bidding, and the captain bought her and a five-year-old girl, her daughter, for ninety escudos. I received no little joy in this, and

straightaway took her and her little one to the galley, and once on land to the palace, to the room where the captain lodged.³²

During his absences the captain leaves her in the custody of one lord and then another – and their wives – always with other slave women. But when the captain dies of a war wound, Mina and her daughter are inherited by a brother, Juan de la Haya, who lives in Valladolid and asks a cousin of his who acts as an auditor in Italy to put them up for sale, which he does right away. Castro goes to visit her and gives us a glimpse of how she feels when being auctioned: 'I was despondent over her being sold, and as she was a new arrival and wouldn't be aware of my meagre means, asked me to buy her, as if I were some prince or mighty merchant. I disabused her of that idea if she had it. She implored me to do all I could to see her, no matter where she might be.'³³

The sale of Mina ends up separating her from her daughter and precipitates a series of transfers that are none other than gifts among nobles:

> They told me she was in the house of don Juan de Benavides, who had bought them for two hundred and eighty escudos. I went to don Juan's house to see her, but she was not there, as he had sent them as gifts, the little one to the marquis of Santa Cruz, general of the galleys, and the big one to the count of Benavente, who in turn gave her over to don Juan de Zúñiga,

---

³² 'Llegamos a Mesina, a donde por orden del General se llevaron todos los esclavos y esclavas a la capitana, que serían todos ciento y setenta. Allí se pusieron en compra, después de haber escogido el marqués y los señores dos hermanos los que les pareció. Y no se les olvidó en el tintero la que yo deseaba que fuese a parte donde estuviese comunicable, que el Marqués la quiso luego para sí, y el Capitán le pidió que le hiciese merced de dejársela para él, pues la pagaría, y que era de las que su compañía había tomado. El Marqués no porfió, aunque sé yo que le pesó harto, y al Señor Don Diego Pimentel ... Muchos echaron el ojo a ella después que el Marqués la dejó con propósito de dar por ella lo que fuese posible. El capitán Antonio del Haya, viendo que todos echaban el ojo a ella y que le costaba ya el quitársela de las uñas a los gavilanes grandes por vía de súplica, y que los otros capitanes la perseguían, dijo en medio la popa de la capitana en presencia del marqués y de todos los señores y capitanes en alta voz: "Señores, esta esclava la tomó mi compañía, y ya me cuesta mi vergüenza el pedir al señor marqués que me la deje. No tienen que andar tras ella para compralla, que si supiese que me ha de costar dos mil escudos, no la ha de llevar nadie." Todos callaron y se eximieron de la compra, y ansí el capitán la compró a ella y otra niña de cinco años, su hija, en noventa escudos. No recibí yo poco gozo en ello y luego la hize llevar a galera y de allí a tierra a palacio, al aposento donde posaba el Capitán, a ella y a la chiquilla' (37).

³³ 'Sentía que la vendiesen, y como era bozal y no debía conocer mi poca posibilidad, me decía que la comprase yo, como si fuera mercader muy grueso o algún príncipe. Yo la desengañé de aquella dubda, si es que la tenía. Pidiome encarescidamente que en todas maneras do quiera que fuese procurase vella' (72).

who was most happy with the present, and he loved her very much, because she was, as I said, very beautiful.[34]

Mina receives lessons in housework, lodges in the viceregal palace of the count and countess of Benavente in Naples and, when she becomes ill, converts to Christianity with the name of Inés. An unexpected marginal note at the end of Castro's *Vida* indicates that Mina/Inés would later live in Spain and would be sold again: 'From Benavente, she and others, because of excesses [desmanes] they carried out in the count's house, were sold in Granada' (231). In sum, Mina is captured in Durazzo, bought by the captain and inherited by a brother of his, who puts her up for sale; she is bought by don Juan de Benavides, who gives her to the count of Benavente, who in turn gives her to don Juan de Zúñiga, although it seems that she stays with the count and countess and is resold much later in Granada. Unlike what happens with perhaps most Christian slave women in Muslim lands, nobody talks about marriage, and there appears to be no means of incorporating her into this society closed to slaves, even after religious conversion. Mina's case illustrates how Muslim slave women passed as luxurious sexual property from one owner to another – noble and wealthy, including the highest nobility – above all through sales and gifts.

There are moments when the narrative gives us some sense of what Mina might be going through. Castro tells how she weeps at the death of the captain, but since his death has significant consequences for her, it may not be clear why she's weeping. In a certain sense, the itinerary of houses and masters is little more than a backdrop for the erotic-amorous relationship that Miguel de Castro has with her, a relationship founded – as one gathers from his *Vida* – on an intimate understanding between the two, on mutual affection, on the situation of weakness on the part of both of them, and on reciprocal esteem, among other qualities. Even their mutual inability to communicate unites them: 'she knew nothing of our language and I knew nothing of hers.'[35] By his account, their relationship brimming with eroticism is frustrated by the surveillance of the whole world and finally undone by Mina's inaccessibility. He narrates in detail several of their blissful moments of reunion, 'the progress of our love' (38, 59, 71–2). Powerful men possess Mina as a slave and many others covet her, but it seems that the only one who has her heart

---

[34] 'Dijéronme estaba en casa de don Juan de Benavides que las había comprado todas dos en ducientos y ochenta escudos. Fui a casa de don Juan por vella, y no estaba allí, que las había enviado ya presentadas, la una al Marqués de Santa Cruz, general de las galeras, la chica, y la grande en casa del Conde de Benavente, que la presentó al Sr. don Juan de Zúñiga, que se holgó muchísimo del presente, y la quería muchísimo, porque era, como digo, muy hermosa' (72–3).

[35] 'ella era bozal y yo también en su lengua' (36).

is Miguel, an ordinary soldier, or so at least he would have his readers believe. It's a love of soul and body accentuated by the exoticism of Mina, sublimated by her modesty and the vigilance of others, and exacerbated by the pathos of its inviability, since ultimately both lovers lack control over their present and future precisely because she's a slave. There are undoubtedly distortions and misunderstandings (and probably fictitious aspects) in this episode as there are in all autobiography – and even more in this case because of linguistic and cultural barriers. Even so, Castro's *Vida*, through the empathy of the author-protagonist, offers us a vivid portrait of this slave woman in her tragic circumstances. If I'm not mistaken, it thus provides us with a unique document of a Muslim *esclava* in those 'cities of the sea', a coming together of the contrary identities of Mina and the author Miguel.

The story of Leonisa in Cervantes' *El amante liberal*, published within the *Novelas ejemplares* the year after Miguel de Castro composed his memoirs in Malta, provides an interesting fictional counterpoint to the story of Mina. Leonisa, a Sicilian Christian noblewoman, is captured in a raid by 'Turks', particularly the Greek renegade Yzuf, who is obliged to participate in negotiations to exchange her for a lot of money but is ultimately unwilling to do so. In the distribution of slaves he insists on keeping her 'with the intention of turning her into a Moor [volverla mora] and marrying her' (149). Yzuf dies in a shipwreck, and she remains on an island with seven surviving Turks who give her 'the same respect as if she were their sister' (171), but when they are picked up by a Turkish ship they sell her to a rich Jewish merchant, who tries to seduce her, and when he fails, opts for selling her. And so Leonisa appears in Cyprus for sale before the powerful qadi (judge) and two pashas, spectacularly dressed 'in Berber apparel, so well adorned and fitted that she could not be equalled by the richest Mooress of Fez or Marrakesh, who in dress surpass all Africans including the Algerian women with their many pearls' (157) – and we're told the details of her sumptuous attire. As readers of this novel are well aware, 'the singular beauty of the Christian woman' subdues the hearts of the three buyers, who hope 'to possess and enjoy her' (158). The ingenious outcome manoeuvred by the qadi distributes the expenses among the three, leaving Leonisa in the house of the qadi under the pretext of sending her as a present to the Grand Turk in the name of the pashas Ali and Hazán and thus reserving 'the use of her' (*el uso della*) to Sultan Selim (159).[36]

Thus Leonisa arrives in Cyprus as a virgin (*entera*), although seduction attempts and the threat of rape by the qadi still await her, as do abduction attempts by the three Muslim competitors. With one minor exception – the desires of the *renegada* Halima for Ricardo – the whole vortex of passions and desires of this sexless but sultry novel revolves around her. Although

---

[36] For an extended analysis of this scene, and of the entire *novela*, see Hutchinson, *Economía ética en Cervantes*, 81–93.

her itinerary until her sale in Cyprus coincides more or less with that of documented cases of male and female captives, as of her arrival in Cyprus in luxurious Berber garb the novel takes narrative routes mapped by pure fantasy. Most unrealistic of all, it seems to me, is the behaviour of the high Muslim authorities. Much has been written about the concupiscence and ebullient sexuality of the sultans or figures like Hayreddin Barbarossa, Dragut, Uluç Ali ('Ulūj 'Alī, Uchalí) or the Venetian Hasan Pasha, but this wouldn't necessarily justify any compulsion on their part to 'possess' and 'enjoy' a Christian captive woman for sale, no matter how spectacular she might be. All of them had at their disposal multiple resources for sex, and all were politically astute. It should be noted that the two pashas of *El amante liberal* correspond at least in name to Uluç Ali and the Venetian Ḥasan Pasha, both of them Italian renegades. However, apart from their name and rank, the pashas share practically nothing with these historical figures as they're portrayed by the captive Ruy Pérez in *Don Quixote* I, 40 or the chroniclers of the time. Uluç Ali (Uchalí), in particular, was highly respected and admired, not only by Muslims but also by Christians, whom he treated with great humanity, whereas Ali Baxá (another title of Uluç Ali) in this *novela*, like Hazán Baxá, is not even a shadow of his historical model: a grotesque caricature, an incarnation of lust fixated on a captive. It would serve little purpose to take into account either of these historical pashas, since there's no similarity between their historical profile and that of the pashas of this novel, and the qadi is just as bizarre. These characters may not be quintessentially 'Muslim' but rather a mirror image of buyers of slave women in Christian lands. Trapani itself, where the protagonists of this novel are from, had a large slave market, as did many other cities on the coasts such as Messina and Naples, where Cervantes spent many months.

Commenting on the transfer of power between the two pashas that's taking place outside Nicosia at the time that Leonisa appears, Carroll Johnson says that it corresponds not so much to Ottoman customs as to the 'residence' practised by outgoing and incoming Christian governors, and adds: 'The semiotic value of Ottoman society is destabilized. It can stand either for what our society is and should not be, or the reverse, what ours should be but is not' (*Cervantes and the material world*, 125). If the transfer of power that unfolds within the large tent alludes more to the Christian 'residence' than to Ottoman practices, it would not be implausible to conjecture that the auction of Leonisa in that same tent might be more reminiscent of a slave woman in Christian than in Muslim lands. The possible consequences for her – sexual submission to the master, abduction, rape – and the violence between competitors don't match up with the most common practices towards captive women in Ottoman lands, where the tendency towards conversion to Islam and marriage to the master prevails, without interference from rivals.

There's a play of mirrors in this text, an example of which is the strange symmetry between Leonisa dressed in Berber attire before her concupiscent buyers and a Tunisian captive woman offered to Charles V in his tent during his invasion of La Goletta and Tunis, as Ricardo remembers a story his father told him: 'they presented to him a Mooress of rare beauty, and when they offered her to him, some rays of the sun shone into the tent and illuminated her hair, that in its golden colour competed with the sun itself – something unique in Mooresses, who always pride themselves for their black hair.'[37] In her perceptive analysis of cultural transvestism, Barbara Fuchs comments on the 'porosity between Christianity and Islam in the Eastern Mediterranean', the 'voyeuristic delight' and the 'structural equivalence of the Spaniards to the Turks of the main narrative' (*Passing for Spain*, 68–70). The anecdote tells of the excited reaction of the gentlemen present, especially an Andalusian and a Catalan poet, the first of whom improvises a five-line stanza (*quintilla*) with 'difficult rhymes', lacking the 'necessary rhymes' to finish the poem, but the Catalan poet completes it with another *quintilla* 'with the same rhymes' that likens the face of the Mooress Axa with a precious stone and with a spear of Muhammad that pierces his entrails. So much emphasis on rhymes should put us on the alert: unwittingly the Andalusian has chosen the strange rhymes -*oma* and -*axa* because, in effect, they have to resonate with Mah*oma* and A*xa*, i.e. the prophet Muhammad and 'Ā'isha, the name of this captive and also of Muhammad's favourite wife, which the Catalan poet has immediately intuited. The custom on the part of all modern editors of suppressing the Arabic *shīn* (ش), transcribed as *x* in early modern texts (the sound *sh*, which also existed in the Spanish of that time, especially with words of Arabic and Mexican origin), in favour of the modern Spanish *j* makes this playful poem almost incomprehensible, besides corrupting the meaning of the Arabic name ('Ā'ishah = 'she who is lively, has vitality', far from the ugly name *Aja*, as it's always transcribed now). The poem, with its rhymes restored according to the first edition, is as follows:

> Como cuando el sol asoma
> por una montaña baxa,
> y de súpito nos toma
> y con su vista nos doma
> nuestra vista y la relaxa;
>   como la piedra balaxa,
>   que no consiente carcoma,

---

[37] 'le trujeron a presentar una mora por cosa singular en belleza, y que al tiempo que se la presentaron entraban algunos rayos del sol por unas partes de la tienda y daban en los cabellos de la mora, que con los mismos del sol en ser rubios competían, cosa nueva en las moras que siempre se precian de tenerlos negros' (164).

> tal es el tu rostro, Axa,
> dura lanza de Mahoma,
> que las mis entrañas raxa.[38]

The rhymes, says the Sicilian renegade Mahamut, 'sound good to my ears', and they could only sound good in this way. Even words of Latin origin with rhyme in *-axa* enter into the Arabising and Islamising orbit of the language of this poem, all as acknowledgement of the charms of the sensational captive Axa with blonde hair. We can only imagine how Charles V receives his 'present' since the anecdote says nothing in this regard. But this interesting digression in the text obliges us to see the two beautiful captive women as ambivalent (each displaying attributes, dress or hair, associated with cultures they don't belong to) and comparable to each other from different sides of the ethnic-religious frontier. It also shows us the emperor Charles V as a Christian counterpart of the Muslim competitors in Cyprus, even if as emperor he doesn't have to compete for the most beautiful captive woman: ultimately these top commanders aren't very different from each other, nor is what happens in their tents very different either. While the enslaved women have no control over their destiny, their presence 'captivates' their masters, who are pierced with the spear of Muhammad, to cite the jocose amorous language of the poem. Yet Leonisa, like various other Cervantine slave women – Nísida in *La Galatea*, Silvia in *El trato de Argel*, Costanza in *Los baños de Argel*, and above all doña Catalina de Oviedo in *La gran sultana* – will overcome her slavery and belong to herself again (*ser suya*). Doña Catalina in particular is integrated into the peak of the Ottoman Empire as wife and future mother of sultans while persisting as a Christian – and it should be noted that the Ottoman sultan, contrary to custom, insists that she remain Christian and dress in Spanish mode, all of which he finds more interesting and desirably exotic than the usual women converts to Islam who dress in Ottoman style.

Indeed, Spanish literary texts are likely to accentuate the eroticism of slave women and their precarious sexual situation, but then free them from slavery and isolate them from conversion. Such literature tends to distort the slavery of Christian women by representing Muslim owners or competitors, often renegades, as incurably libidinous and prone to amorous fixation, losing their minds in the presence of beautiful Christian slave women. Unlike the vast majority of Christian slave women of that era, who end up converting to Islam, marrying and having children, literary slave women most often resist the double

---

[38] Roughly: 'As when the sun rises / over a low mountain, / and suddenly possesses us / and with the sight of it tames / our sight and calms it; / like the ruby stone / that is incorruptible, / such is your face, Axa, / a harsh spear of Muhammad / that tears my entrails' (1: 165). The same lines appear as a kind of joke in Cervantes' *Los baños de Argel* (vv. 2144–53), pronounced by a sportive sacristan, thus provoking the ire of the corsair captain Caurali: 'is this Christian a clown?'

danger of religious and sexual seduction and eventually return home. Many variants exist, but politico-religious ideology often favours such an argument.

An outlandish novella by Francisco de Lugo y Dávila, *Premiado el amor constante* (*Constant love rewarded*) (1622), serves to illustrate how this ideologically motivated kind of plot guides the story. I focus here on the female protagonist Zara/Leonora. In a corsair attack, Hayreddin Barbarossa captures Zara's mother, who is pregnant with her, while her father dies in the battle. Soon after the birth, Barbarossa exchanges the mother for ransom, leading her to believe that her baby daughter is dead. Zara herself tells her story:

> They gave me over to be raised as Barbarossa's daughter born of one of his wives, whose child was the creature that, in the barter, my unfortunate mother received. I grew along with the fame of my beauty and no less the love of my feigned father, who raised me in his rites and law, spreading and confirming the opinion that I was his daughter. He came to wield the scepter of Tunis and to promise me the inheritance of the kingdom (such was the heartfelt love he bore me). And to oblige me all the more, he told me many times about my birth, entrusting to me this secret as vital as life itself.[39]

With Charles V's invasion of Tunis, she's captured by German soldiers, freed by her lover Celimo/Carlos and recaptured by the imperial troops:

> Word quickly spread to faraway places until it reached his Caesarean majesty himself [Charles V], who was obliged by this rumour to command that they bring before him the prisoner taken by those soldiers who, triumphant, and in particular the brave Spaniard Benavides, presented themselves to their prince and presented Zara, so beautiful, amid tears and afflictions, that she could have been seen as an example and second act of Scipio and the maiden of Cartagena; and Charles V as having greater value, virtue and largesse than the Roman.[40]

---

[39] 'Diéronme a criar por hija de Barbarroja, habida en una de sus mujeres, cuya fue la criatura que, en mi trueco, recibió mi mal afortunada madre. Crecí y creció la opinión de mi hermosura y no menos el amor de mi fingido padre, que me crió en sus ritos y ley, esparciendo y confirmando la opinión de que yo era su hija. Llegó a regir el cetro de Túnez y llegó a prometerme la sucesión del reino (tal era el verdadero amor que me tenía), y tal que para representarme mayores obligaciones me refirió muchas veces mi nacimiento, encargándome el secreto de él, igual con el vivir' (86–7).

[40] 'Corrió la voz en corta distancia de tiempo larga distancia de lugares, sin parar hasta la misma persona de la majestad Cesárea, a quien obligó el rumor a mandar que trajesen ante sí la presa que hicieron aquellos soldados, los cuales, gloriosos, y en particular Benavides, valiente español, se presentaron a su príncipe y presentaron a Zara, tan hermosa, entre llantos y aflicciones, que pudo verse ejemplo y acto segundo de Scipión y la doncella carginesa; y en Carlos Quinto mayor valor, mayor virtud y mayor largueza que en el romano' (85).

The allusion to Scipio refers to the presentation in Cartagena of a beautiful and illustrious captive woman, engaged to a Celtiberian prince; the young Roman commander returns her 'as much a virgin [tan entera] as she was before' (*Floresta española*, 358) and thus gains enormous respect among the vanquished. Performing a 'second act of Scipio' and even surpassing it, the virtuous Carlos V, seeing that she can be brought over to 'the true faith', takes interest only in the beautiful maiden's soul and entrusts her to the marquis of Aguilar to have her baptised and taken to Spain. Nonetheless, Zara/Leonora, now free of 'the abominable and perverse Mohammedan sect', is again captured, changing sides for the fifth time, and is taken along the 'infidel coasts' to the sultan in Constantinople:

> where I was once free, I am a slave; now they sell me; passing from one hand to another I am introduced to the Grand Turk; now to my misfortune he falls in love with me, now he presses me to return to the errors of my early years; now he flatters me, now he oppresses me with terrors and omens. He has me imagine myself occupying a position as one of his wives, but then he conveys the power of a passionate slave-master; now he is harsh, then gentle and affectionate, and I a frail woman. (96)

Thanks to the sultana's jealousy and the skills of a double spy, she manages to escape from Istanbul and reunite with her lover Celimo/Carlos, who by this time is a great Christian corsair. The two protagonists connect the three most imposing figures of that historical moment in the Mediterranean world: Hayreddin Barbarossa, Charles V and Suleiman the Magnificent. For Zara/Leonora, the first is like a father who is 'feigned' and 'barbarous' but loves her like a daughter, the second as a great Christian prince who transcends all carnal desire, and the third as a stereotype of the lustful sultan incapable of resisting the charms of a captive woman and insistent on her turning Turk, yielding to his desires and marrying him. Although Charles V and Suleiman are in the same situation with respect to the beautiful *cautiva* presented to them, their behaviour is entirely different owing to the novel's ideological orientation within an arena of politico-religious adversaries. Even so, and despite the sultan's insufferable persistence within this fiction, his intentions seem to be 'honourable' within the context of marriage and social inclusion, thus reflecting a manifest historical difference between Muslims and Christians in the treatment of slave women. Even this literary Barbarossa, by in effect adopting a child he stole and treating her as his beloved heir, demonstrates a much more open attitude, for example, than those attitudes towards captured girls we see in Christian Europe (e.g. the case of Mina's daughter in Miguel de Castro's *Vida*). The fact that Zara/Leonora escapes, although it conforms to the literary pattern, constitutes an exception to the rule, since in reality very few captive women returned home. Yet, as will be seen in the next chapter, several historical renegade women organised spectacular escapes.

Undoubtedly there were countless slave women whose experience diverged considerably from that of those considered here. But literary and non-literary sources about slave women are obviously guided to a large extent by masculine fantasy, focusing above all on beautiful women who are portrayed as extremely erotic when they're perceived as moderately exotic. There are coincidences and disparities between literary fiction and historical documentation since literature exploits the sexualisation inherent in widespread attitudes towards female slavery but departs from historical truths when these are ideologically troublesome. Treatise writers from that period such as Jerónimo Gracián, Antonio de Sosa, Pierre Dan and numerous others rarely do any better on this score, as their 'histories' tend to be equally saturated with distorting ideologies that likewise diverge from historical truths of the kind that tend to appear in studies of the past several decades. Of course the historical documentation itself, beginning with the careful records of the Inquisition, is similarly biased and misleading, but truths can be extracted from it, as they can from all the kinds of sources mentioned here, including works of fiction.

Yet literary representations, above all through the pen of Cervantes, not only distort historical truths but also reveal otherwise unsaid truths by pointing out the parallels between slavery in Muslim and Christian lands. On one side and the other there is a traffic not only of men but also of women, a constant movement of buying and selling, gifts and the exercise of rights. From our modern perspective there can be few heroes among the slave traders and slave owners, but it's important to acknowledge that there were significant differences in the practice of female slavery between the Muslim and Christian countries. Specifically, the inclusion, however imperfect, of Christian (or renegade) slave women within Maghrib, Mashriq and Turkish societies through marriage contrasts with the treatment of slave women as unassimilable sexual property in Christian societies. On both sides, however, the slave herself occupies a space of her own outside of guilt and morality: sexualised to a maximum, slave women – unlike prostitutes or courtesans, for example – remain innocent. Such a set of contradictions and paradoxes is only possible in a fantasy forged in the waters and coasts of a simultaneously nearby and exotic Mediterranean.

Every instance of slavery we've seen in this chapter, whether factual or fictive, would be improbable if not impossible in the context of either the trans-Saharan or trans-Atlantic slave trades. Taken together, all of these instances flesh out a profile of this quite peculiar form of slavery that was predicated on the existence of a frontier as well as geopolitical and religious difference across spaces that were traversable and communicable. Slavery ranged from temporary to permanent, but always with the sense that it could end in distinct ways varying from ransom or escape to emancipation and, especially in Muslim lands, incorporation into what were once strange societies. Cultural and religious differences were substantial but relative, allowing for individuals to adapt themselves to one degree or another, or 'be adapted', to life across the divide. Language differences too were often extremely marked, yet ways were most often found to surmount those communicative breaches. Slavery on each side of the frontier was widely practised at the expense of the other, and, barring some discrepancies we've seen, more or less in similar ways. Although various kinds of slavery formed part of the landscapes and seascapes of the Mediterranean since ancient times, I sense that this particular kind of frontier slavery was historically unique even to the Mediterranean, taking a quantum leap into its early modern form especially as of the early sixteenth century. Although this might have presupposed a long sequence of events and circumstances going back even to the expansion of Islam in the seventh and eighth centuries, as well as the crusades, the growing Aragonese presence in the Mediterranean, among other factors, it arose much more immediately from such events and processes as the Ottoman conquest of Constantinople and later expansion into the Mashriq and its reach into the Maghrib, along with the rise of Portugal and what would become a united and aggressive Spain. This is to name only some of the most important. Mediterranean frontier slavery in its early modern form resulted from the confluence of such circumstances, along with new maritime technologies and emergent economies that, to one extent or another, involved trafficking in people. My primary interest in this chapter has been to focus on a gamut of human experience brought about by this kind of slavery, including what it meant to become a slave and to live as one, as Leonardo's riddle so poignantly conveys and as so many writers reveal. Renegades, to whom we now turn, were a product of this new system, often former victims who would later figure among its protagonists and its most paradigmatic representatives.

3

Renegades

Perhaps no human category is more representative of the unities and divisions of the early modern Mediterranean than the so-called renegades, whose protagonism stands out as much as their enigmatic character masks them. Even to gather them into the same category might be questionable, since it could be said that the only thing that all renegades had in common is that they were Christians – or occasionally Jews – who converted to Islam, for many reasons and in many different circumstances. Yet certain modes of thinking and acting are discernible to one degree or another across the spectrum of renegades, providing some of the keys to comprehending the workings of a Mediterranean world configured not only by political and religious parameters but also by ubiquitous liquid frontiers and perpetual movement. Given the near absence of texts written by renegades, and hence their virtual lack of self-representation except when under interrogation by the Inquisition, we have to rely on texts that were often very hostile towards them. Precisely because of this, I strive to take into account the full range of sources available – rather than just one or another sector of them, as has nearly always been done – calibrating the means of distortion and defamation, the ideological biases, so as to approximate some kind of historical and literary truth. I intend to work through this range of texts to discover insights into who the renegades were, how they thought, and how and why they acted as they did within their adopted societies. Standard conceptual terms such as syncretism, hybridity, assimilation and the like fall short of helping us understand these remarkably versatile and capable frontier figures who assumed a new name, attire, allegiance, language, conduct and religion, all of these perceived as contrary to what the renegades were prior to conversion.

Although I delve into some texts that focus on interesting theological differences between Christianity and Islam as perceived by authors of that period, relatively few renegades show any sign of having converted to Islam out of religious conviction, which of course by no means denies that religious concerns genuinely motivated some converts to Islam and, more importantly, that the vast majority of them probably ended up practising Islam. What is often called 'popular religion' nearly always prevailed over notions of theological belief in the case of renegades, few of whom had any educational training, let alone theological guidance in spiritual matters. With this in mind, I'll briefly discuss methodological problems arising from the kinds of texts that represent renegades, present a geohistorical overview and contextualisation of the renegades, consider a number of individual profiles of renegades including – to stretch the term even further as has sometimes been done – profiles of converts from Islam to Christianity, and reflect on who the renegades were and what roles they played in the Mediterranean world.

Terms, significance, sources

The term *renegade* and its equivalents in the European languages (Spanish and Portuguese *renegado/a*, Italian *rinnegato/a*, French *renégat/e*, etc.) are by no means impartial. The Latin etymology of the word, *renegare*, is transparent and denotes emphatic denial: what renegades denied – or were said to deny – was, of course, Christianity. Occasionally dictionaries claim the term's neutrality with reference to an apostate from *any* religion before conceding that it primarily refers to converts from Christianity to Islam. Muslims who became Christians were known as converts, not renegades, just as the main Arabic term for a convert to Islam was *muhtadin* (مهتد), one who is 'rightly guided', and certainly not a 'renegade'. In Christian Europe, then, the term 'renegade' emphasised an unjustifiable act of renunciation and betrayal of religion and country rather than a more or less voluntary adoption of Islam and Muslim society. Other available terms occasionally used in early modern texts and revived by a few modern scholars include the medieval word *muladí*, of Andalusi origin,[1] and the Spanish and Portuguese word *elche*, borrowed from the Arabic *'ilj* back in the times of the kingdom of Granada.[2] Another term for renegades, widely used throughout Europe, was 'Turk': those who had 'turned Turk' and were anything but Turks. The feared Barbary corsairs in the Mediterranean between the sixteenth and eighteenth centuries were mainly 'Turks' of this kind. The term 'Moor' often served the same purpose, designating converts to Islam who were by no means Moors. Despite its drawbacks, the term 'renegade' remains more recognisable than any of the alternatives.

The early modern Mediterranean world would in fact be incomprehensible without taking into account the key roles of the converts to Islam both

---

[1] Emilio Sola, as is evident in the title of his book *Uchalí ... el mito del corsario muladí en la frontera*, and Miguel Ángel de Bunes Ibarra (who introduces this book), are among those who favour the term *muladí*. The *Diccionario de la Real Academia Española* (20th ed.) defines *muladí* as an adjective referring to 'a Christian Spaniard who, during the epoch of Arab rule in Spain, embraced Islam and lived among Muslims'. The term comes from the Arabic *muwalladín*, a plural form of *muwallad* used in parts of Andalusia, with various interpretations including 'born of a non-Arab mother', 'raised as an Arab'.

[2] The term *elche* is used, among other places, in Rodríguez Mediano 173–92; Harvey, *Muslims in Spain 1500 to 1614*, 27–33; Epalza, *Los moriscos*; Sola, 'Francos o libertos', 91–9.

in the east and the west.³ Owing in part to the *devşirme* system, the majority of the grand viziers of the Ottoman Empire during the 170-year period from 1453–1623 were converts of Christian origin, therefore renegades,⁴ mainly from the Balkans (Temimi, 'L'impact', 513). Nearly all of the concubines, wives and mothers of sultans were also of Christian origin, converts to Islam. A good number of the 'kings' of Algiers – as most European texts call them (i.e. *beylerbeys*, viceroys, governors) – during the sixteenth century were renegades or sons of renegades, and many renegade women married men with wealth and power. More generally, the hundreds of thousands of anonymous renegades, even those who remained slaves, undoubtedly helped shape their adopted societies in countless ways. These societies were extraordinarily willing to integrate renegade men and women and offered them possibilities unimaginable, especially for people of humble birth, in their countries of origin.

Antonio de Sosa,⁵ who for a half-century now has been credited with having written the monumental treatise on Algiers entitled *Topografía de Argel*, says there were more renegades in Algiers than Moors, Turks and Jews combined, and that renegades in Algiers represented nearly all Christian nations on earth. He provides an impressive list of national and regional origins, starting in northeastern Europe, moving across and down the map to the Mediterranean (including Syria and Egypt), and ending with 'the Abyssinians of Prester John and the Indians of the Portuguese Indies, Brazil and New Spain'.⁶ He goes on to explain why Christian slaves would abandon the true path: some wanted to be treated less cruelly by their masters, others were attracted to the carnal vices of the Turks, adolescents were subjected to the 'villainy of sodomy' and took a liking to it as the Turks lavished more attention on them than on

---

³ See the introductory chapter regarding relations between the eastern and western basins of the Mediterranean.

⁴ Some of these would have been 'converted' at a very young age. Standard early modern usage in Spanish, particularly with regard to Christian children or adolescents taken captive and converted to Islam, includes all 'Christian-born' converts to Islam – regardless of the age at which they were captured – under the rubric 'renegade'. The Ottoman *devşirme* system in the eastern Mediterranean does of course stretch the term 'renegade'.

⁵ In addition to what she writes about Sosa in *Cervantes in Algiers* (66–90), María Antonia Garcés has published illuminating information about Sosa in her English edition of the first part of the *Topografía*, entitled *An early modern dialogue with Islam* (1–78).

⁶ *Topografía* I, 13, 9v. The full list includes some fifty countries or provinces of origin, nearly all European, beginning with Muscovy in the northeast and moving systematically down to the Mediterranean, as though the author were exercising his geographical knowledge without giving a sense of the authentic demographic composition of the renegades. Yet he seems to suggest that renegades come from all Christian nations on earth. This would interestingly convert Algiers into a kind of 'everywhere', a 'pantopia', as it is also represented by Muslims and Jews from many lands, as well as sub-Saharan slaves.

their wives, and so on. It was inconceivable to Sosa or any other Christian treatise writer that there might also be an array of other sound reasons for converting to Islam. Sosa concludes by saying that – except for Moriscos – these renegades are the worst enemies that Christianity has, and that almost all the power and wealth of Algiers is in their hands. In all fairness, however, it should be noted that in part II of the *Topografía*, the *History of the Kings of Algiers*, the author displays an impressive equanimity and sometimes uncontainable admiration for several of the renegade viceroys of the sixteenth century starting with the Barbarossa brothers Aruch and Hayreddin, whom he believes to be renegades.

In general, however, the very thought of renegades tended to arouse deep antipathy on the part of Christian writers, especially the clergy, for whom renegades were far more dangerous and detestable than other Muslims. What's more, unlike returning adventurers or ex-captives, the renegades rarely spoke or wrote about themselves unless, like Giorgio del Giglio Pannilini or Joseph Pitts,[7] they wanted to clear their names of apostasy and reconnect with their homelands after returning there, or if they were interrogated by the Inquisition, which is the source of most knowledge about renegades. Apart from texts focusing on the Ottoman court, Turkish and Arabic sources about converts to Islam are scarce.[8] A classic exception would be Fray Anselm Turmeda, alias 'Abdullāh al-Tarjumān, who went to Tunis to convert to Islam, and decades later in 1420 wrote his autobiography and anti-Christian polemic in Arabic.[9] Two early modern exceptions are Adam Neuser and Thomas d'Arcos. The former (*c.* 1530–76) was a popular unitarian pastor from Heidelberg who, after suffering imprisonment for allegedly denying the divinity of Jesus, escaped, converted to Islam and travelled to Istanbul; a letter of his to the sultan recounting his conversion and offering his services has been preserved (Courcelles). Thomas d'Arcos (b. 1568), a well-educated Frenchman with much curiosity about the peoples of North Africa, was captured by Tunisian corsairs when he was about sixty and spent two years as a captive, after which he converted to Islam, took on the name Osman and lived for the rest of his life in Tunis, where he maintained correspondence with friends including cardinal Nicolas-Claude Fabri de Peiresc, who, in letters dating 1631–37, came

---

[7] Pannilini's two manuscripts, written between 1564 and 1579, are summarised, analysed and cited at length by Florence Buttay (59–75). Joseph Pitts' *A true and faithful account …*, first published in 1704, is included in Daniel Vitkus's anthology *Piracy, slavery and redemption*, 218–340.

[8] This is also the case with captives' autobiographical narratives, which are very rare in Arabic sources. Both Hind Loukili (39) and Matar (*Europe through Arab eyes*, 38–41, 45–7, 57, 63, 70, 89–91) reflect on why this is so, pointing – among other things – to the shame associated with captivity and to the inhibited use of autobiography in Arabic during this period.

[9] See Míquel de Epalza's edition of this work, *Fray Anselm Turmeda*.

to accept his conversion and wanted d'Arcos to convey to him historical and scientific knowledge about Tunisia (Matar, *Europe*, 68, 186–7). Aside from such exceptions, if we take into consideration factors such as education, language, audience and content, it's not hard to see why renegades wrote so few autobiographical accounts. Many were almost if not entirely illiterate. Those who could read and write might not have been sufficiently literate in the most appropriate language for such an account. If the readers were Christian, the very fact of having renounced Christianity would already involve a scandal that was hard to justify. The fact is that renegades almost never recorded their own stories and were rarely written about neutrally or sympathetically. Most of the sources focusing on renegades are filled with hate: almost the only way to get to know the renegades is by way of toxic texts.

Because of the peculiar nature of the sources about renegades, the bibliography merits some scrutiny and could be roughly divided into several categories. One of these would be treatises written primarily by former captives or ransomers who wrote descriptions or chronicles of Muslim cities or kingdoms, and the conditions of captivity within them. Istanbul, Algiers, Tunis and Morocco figure prominently, as does Africa itself (or what was known of it) in the wake of Leo Africanus's *Description of Africa*. Other chroniclers focus on historical figures admired by both Muslims and Christians such as the Barbarossa brothers. Renegades appear in all of these works, especially in the enormously engaging works of clergy (e.g. Antonio de Sosa, Jerónimo Gracián, Pierre Dan and Gabriel Gómez de Losada) who tended to portray renegades as viciously as possible. Sosa's *Topografía*, mostly written during his captivity (1577–81) but not published until 1612 under the name of the editor fray Diego de Haedo, influenced all subsequent writing by Christians about the Maghrib and the Ottomans, and also provided many narratives that novelists and playwrights would later rework.

Of major interest are two other categories: the autobiographical narratives of travellers, corsairs, ex-captives and exiles, and the fictional reconfiguration of the Mediterranean in the works of many writers (including Cervantes, who spent six years as a soldier in Italy and the wider Mediterranean and five years as a captive in Algiers). It's in these two groups of texts that one finds not only wild exaggerations and pure stereotypes but also highly instructive tales of renegades. Cervantes' Mediterranean stories, including those of his plays and longer novels, are all populated by renegades portrayed with a variety and subtlety of nuance rarely seen elsewhere.

In the 1980s and 1990s there was a burst of interest by researchers in delving into archives of the Inquisition, located everywhere from the Canary Islands to Venice; the most important of these investigations, the Bennassars' magnificent work *Les Chrétiens d'Allah*, was based on 1,550 cases. When renegades returned to Christian lands, whether voluntarily or by recapture, they were required to present themselves to the Inquisition, which was usually lenient towards them unless they refused to renounce Islam or had been proven to have harmed Christians. The standard line of interrogation was by no means designed to find out what the reality of the renegades' experience as Muslims had been. Instead, they were asked whether as renegades they drank wine or ate pork (points in their favour); washed themselves, recited the *shahāda* (the Muslim creed); went to the mosque and prayed (and understood what they were saying); and whether they had married, had children or Christian slaves, or had captured Christians. The returning renegades, a minute percentage of the total, had to explain their circumcision if they were men, but generally knew the script of questions and expected answers, claiming of course that no matter what they had or hadn't done they had always remained Christians in their hearts. The Bennassars and others working with these sources – among them Lucia Rostagno, Anita Gonzalez-Raymond, Lucetta Scaraffia and Isabel Braga – are keenly aware of the epistemological problems involved in gathering information about renegades in general by studying this atypical group via the records of the Inquisition. Still, they relate some fascinating life stories and many examples indicating that renegades often had theologically aberrant and uninformed notions about belief in Christianity and Islam.

Numerous other studies have explored slavery, captivity and religious conversion in the Mediterranean world from diverse perspectives and by the use of different criteria. These studies have almost always confined themselves to a subsection of the larger bibliography by using, for example, texts in one or two languages but not others; historical but not literary sources (or vice versa); major literary authors like Cervantes but not lesser ones; archival records but not published works (or the reverse); modern studies but not early modern treatises, and so on. While indebted to all such studies, I strive to work with as many disciplines, genres and languages as possible, looking for narratives, descriptions and ideologies across the whole range of sources. This chapter presents an overview, as well as selected examples, of such a broad endeavour.

Key to this approach is the notion that, within the geopolitical layout of the Mediterranean and particularly with regard to the relations between Muslim and Christian territories, the entire Mediterranean was frontier space (though with varying characteristics and degrees of intensity). Indeed, many of its islands, coastlines and major ports were populated by frontier figures, among them Jews (including Conversos and Marranos), exiled Spanish Muslims (Moriscos), captives, slaves, and, of course, renegades. Apart from the many slaves brought from south of the Sahara to both Muslim and Christian countries, race was rarely perceived as a distinguishing factor in the relations among Mediterranean peoples,[10] and this, too, facilitated the crossover for renegades.

---

[10] Of course, this question is complex, since Christian Spain, for example, held onto notions of *caste* (*casta* in Portuguese and Spanish), a term originally used for breeds of animals such as horses and later extended as a hybrid concept referring to both ethnicity

Symmetries and asymmetries

Although most bibliographical sources from the sixteenth century to the present tend to portray the early modern Mediterranean as being infested with Muslim corsairs who captured countless Christians and took them into slavery in cities stretching from Istanbul to Marrakesh, a more accurate picture – as many scholars now acknowledge – would show rough symmetries between the numbers of captives taken, whether by Christian or Muslim corsairs. As Fernand Braudel points out, there were substantial slave markets both in the Christian and the Muslim port cities where corsairs were based. These tended to be among the strategic cities of the western and central Mediterranean:

> in Christendom, Valetta, Leghorn and Pisa, Naples, Messina, Palermo and Trapani, Malta, Palma de Majorca, Almeria, Valencia, Segna and Fiume; on the Moslem side, Valona, Durazzo, Tripoli in Barbary, Tunis-La Goletta, Bizerta, Algiers, Tetouan, Larache, Salé. From this list, three new towns stand out: Valetta, founded by the Knights of Malta in 1566; Leghorn, re-founded in a sense by Cosimo de' Medici; finally and above all the astonishing city of Algiers, the apotheosis of them all. (2: 870)

Referring to a study of ships plundered near Venice between 1592 and 1609, Braudel concludes that Christian (which by this time included English and Dutch 'northern intruders') and Muslim corsairing 'roughly balances out', and he infers that this would have been the pattern for the entire Mediterranean (2: 886–7). Many sources indicate that Christian corsairs did about as much damage in coastal raids and maritime attacks as Muslim corsairs. If notorious Algiers was reviled as the haven of thieves and kidnappers, prestigious Malta, with its Knights of St. John and licensed corsairs, reciprocated with similar plundering, raids and captive-taking. Just as Algiers was subject to famine and dire hardship when the corsairs had a bad season, Malta's economy depended heavily on the *corso* (the Italian term referring to corsair activity, 'corsairing'), and all of the cities mentioned above relied to one extent or another on the traffic of captives and stolen goods. Maligned as it was and had to be, corsairing played an essential role in much of the Mediterranean world – economically, politically, socially and culturally – unequally distributing life's fortunes and disasters and bringing millions of strangers into contact through slavery.

---

and religious affiliation: the three castes were Christians, Jews and Moors. Medieval Spanish is also notorious for providing the world with the term *race* (*raça*), which referred to blemishes and imperfections in cloth and was used to describe people who had some – or had no – *raça* of Jew or Moor.

While the aggregates of corsairs, captives and slave markets were quite comparable on both sides, other factors betrayed profound differences. Significantly, the number of converts to Christianity was only a tiny fraction of the number of converts to Islam, which amounted to at least three hundred thousand between 1550 and 1700.[11] These were the renegades. Studies of conversion in the opposite direction tend to claim that historians have unjustly neglected this topic but end up revealing how remarkably few Muslims converted to Christianity, despite the enormous numbers of Muslim captives in Christian lands and, in certain times and places, the assiduous attempts to proselytise them.[12] For Naples, Livorno, Rome and Civitavecchia, Salvatore Bono estimates just over two thousand converts to Christianity during the early modern period, and more than 90 per cent of these would have been slaves.[13] While not negligible, this is barely a trickle compared to the torrent of conversion to Islam. In his survey of Muslim communities in seventeenth-century Spain, Bernard Vincent provides an overview of converts to Christianity and recounts the lavish ceremonies choreographed in large public squares. What stands out in his account is the coherence and tenacity of these communities of post-expulsion Muslims – comprised of Moriscos who never left Spain or who returned, immigrants from the Moroccan coast, slaves brought from the presidios in North Africa, merchants and others – and the frustration of the religious orders that ultimately had little to show for all their proselytising efforts ('Musulmans et conversion', 193–205).

Indeed, there were reasons why so few Muslims converted to Christianity. While slave-masters were not required to free their converted slaves, the idea of Christians owning Christians went against the legitimising rationale of slavery. Unless piety or social pressure prevailed, it was more in the interests of slave owners to have their slaves remain Muslims. Most important, Christian countries were too closed in every respect to allow even the most talented ex-slave to assume any significant role; a rare exception would be Leo Africanus – alias Ḥasan al-Wazzān al-Fāsī – who in any event is believed to have gone

---

[11] Bennassar and Bennassar 168. For Bernard Vincent this figure is a minimum estimate (in his introduction to Martínez Torres, 16).

[12] Bono, 'Conversioni di musulmani al cristianesimo', 429–30, 437–8; Bono, 'Slave histories', 100; Belhamissi, *Les Captifs algériens*, 35–7, 53–63; Barrio Gozalo 183, 206–8; Scaraffia 11–12, 45–6. In *Europe through Arab eyes*, 69, Nabil Matar recounts some fascinating instances of 'new Christians'.

[13] Bartolomé Bennassar, 'En guise de conclusions', 541. Basing his analysis on baptismal records in Naples from the late sixteenth through the eighteenth centuries, and particularly a brief surge at the start of the seventeenth century when there would have been some twenty thousand captives, Salvatore Bono calculates one to three per thousand of the annual number of Muslim captives in the city converted to Christianity ('Conversioni', 437–8).

back to the Maghrib and reverted to Islam.[14] Except in the case of Moriscos who remained in Spain or returned there, marriage of former Muslims to Christians of any class was virtually proscribed. Women were destined either for domestic labour or for being passed along as sexualised gifts among the nobility, as we've seen in the previous chapter, and men likewise found themselves in adverse and quite hopeless circumstances. In contrast, the prospects for both women and men who lived in Muslim lands and converted to Islam were far more open.

Some Muslim captives would no doubt have seen it as advantageous to switch religions since they might be treated better or at least minimally accepted, but many more would have seen their captivity as a *miḥna*, an ordeal and test of faith (Loukili 39). Whereas Christianity, and particularly Catholicism, viewed Islam as a heretical sect founded by a false prophet and thus excluded it from the realm of religious truth, Islam incorporated Christianity as a revered but misguided religion of the book. For Muslims, Christianity was a necessary stage towards the perfection of Islam, and from this inclusionary viewpoint it would have made no sense to backslide into what was often seen as an obsolete religion. Although official Christian views of Islam were obviously ignored by many Christians who converted to Islam, certain identifiably Islamic attitudes towards Christianity do seem to have been quite generally held by Muslims. To name just a few of the more objectionable aspects of Christianity voiced by Muslims of the early modern period (including crypto-Muslim Moriscos in Spain), the Trinity and the divinity of Christ were considered unacceptable, while the practice of the Eucharist and the doctrines of original sin and redemption aroused aversion. There's of course nothing historically significant in such attitudes, and they only begin to explain the enigma as to why so few Muslims converted to Christianity.

By most accounts, converts to Islam were quite uninterested in questions of dogma and rarely saw themselves as seekers of any religious truth, other matters being much more important to them. Let me stress here that while standard theological approaches to belief among the peoples of the early modern Mediterranean can be helpful in distinguishing religious profiles and prototypes, especially among the intellectual elites, they yield only limited insights into why people converted from one religion to another.

Yet it's instructive to learn what theologically minded writers have to say, even if they aren't representative of more general 'popular' attitudes. The learned ex-Morisco Aḥmad Ibn Qāsim al-Ḥajarī – who as a young man had helped with the translation of the lead books in Granada, escaped from Spain in 1599 and joined the Moroccan court in Marrakesh – tells the story of a former monk named Ramadan who, before converting to Islam, answered a

---

[14] See Natalie Zemon Davis's superb study of Leo Africanus, *Trickster travels*.

question put to him by the Moroccan sultan Moulay Ahmad by saying that Jesus was one of the three persons of the divinity and that he 'died to save the world from the original sin committed by our father Adam'. According to al-Ḥajarī, the sultan responded with a parable:

> 'Suppose I ordered whoever enters this garden, which is part of our felicitous residence, to be killed. And suppose that someone who knew about the prohibition disobeyed me and entered the garden. I found out about this and ordered the servants to bring my son, and when they had brought him I told them: "Kill him because so-and-so entered the garden, although I forbade the people to do so."'
>
> He then said to the monk: 'This is the same as what you are doing when you claim that Jesus is the son of God and that he was killed [for the sins of others]. Would any intelligent man say such a thing?' The monk was dumbfounded and could not find an answer. (105)

Al-Ḥajarī recounts other occasions when he refutes Christian arguments, especially during his time in France and the Netherlands where he went as the sultan's emissary (1611–13). In a similar vein, the French Arabist Étienne Hubert relates to al-Ḥajarī the proof that a monk, also present, has devised of how Jesus could be 'God's son and also God':

> [Hubert] said: 'When the blessed and exalted God saw that it was good that everything came forth and gave birth in accordance with its nature and form, He wanted to have a son like Himself!' He asked: 'What do you say now?'
>
> I answered him: 'Following this analogy, our lord Jesus would have wanted to have a son like himself also, and his son another son, with the result that the number of gods would now be infinite.' I then asked him: 'What do *you* say now?'
>
> He was perplexed and stood there with his piece of paper as his error was evident. (117)

In learned disputes the burden was mostly on Christians to explain the mysteries of their faith, and Muslims were rarely convinced. Al-Ḥajarī begins his book by affirming:

> One of the blessings the exalted God bestowed upon me was that He made me a Muslim in the land of the infidels, ever since I was aware of myself, through my blessed parents ... God had created in my heart a longing to leave the lands of Al-Andalus in order to emigrate to the exalted God and His messenger and to enter the land of the Muslims. God realized this purpose and fulfilled this wish and brought me to the city of Marrakesh in Morocco [in 1007/1599]. (61–2)

Al-Ḥajarī wasn't the only Muslim writer who would praise God for *releasing* the Muslims of Al-Andalus by having Philip III expel them (see chapter 5). Such attitudes of superiority, widespread beyond the intellectual elite, were often mixed with a dose of repugnance on the part of Muslims towards Christianity, and would have inhibited conversion. Compared to the fair number of Catholic clergy who opted to cross over to Muslim lands and convert, the Muslims who went to convert to Christianity were fewer by far. Whereas doctrinal differences were by no means the primary factor in the vast majority of conversions, since the Abrahamic religions in the Mediterranean were characterised far more by their distinct modalities of praxis than by their disparities in belief, the attitudes deriving from such differences no doubt did figure into the resistance to conversion, particularly on the part of Muslims. In contrast to the countless Christians disposed to renounce the religion of their upbringing, even though their motives for converting might not have been religious at all, the few Muslims who did so can be readily counted in baptismal records and documents of the period. At the same time, despite the insistence of religious authorities such as Catholic inquisitors who emphasised differences in belief as the key to salvation and damnation, many Muslims and Christians – and Jews, too, of course – recognised vital affinities between their religions.

Especially among Christians, the distance between Orthodox theology and popular perception could be immense. How could one tell the difference between a Christian and a Muslim? In his autobiography, the Spanish corsair captain Alonso de Contreras recalls how, as a young man in 1601, he took part in a deadly battle with a 'Turkish' ship that was finally subdued somewhere near the North African coast. He and his companions took the enemies captive and found 250 dead men whose bodies they threw into the sea. He remarks:

> That day I saw something that shows what it is to be a Christian. Among the many dead that were thrown into the sea, there was one face up, which is quite the opposite of Moors and Turks who, when thrown dead into the sea, turn face down right away, while Christians turn face up. We asked the Turks we'd taken as slaves how that one was face up, and they said they'd always suspected him of being a Christian: he was a baptised renegade from France, and was already a man when he reneged.[15]

---

[15] 'vi aquel día cosa que para que se vea lo que es ser cristiano; digo que entre los muchos que se echaron a la mar muertos, hubo uno que quedó boca arriba, cosa muy contrario a los moros y turcos, que en echándolos muertos a la mar, al punto meten la cara y cuerpo hacia abajo y los cristianos hacia arriba; preguntamos a los turcos que teníamos esclavos que cómo aquel estaba boca arriba y dijeron que siempre lo habían tenido en sospecha de cristiano y que era renegado bautizado, y cuando renegó era ya hombre, de nación francesa' (ch. 3).

This anecdote tells us that even when dead, or perhaps especially when dead and floating face up or face down, it was possible to tell the difference between Christians and Muslims. According to Contreras's account, even the Muslim captives confirm the rule by explaining the anomaly.

Yet it was not always so easy to distinguish between Christians and Muslims in the early modern Mediterranean world: it is precisely in the chameleonic, crossover figure of the renegade, in its many guises, that the question of religious and cultural belonging becomes most problematised. Rather than face up or face down, renegades are sometimes faceless and sometimes two-faced, but always miscellaneous beings, shoring within themselves knowledge and habits of the culture and society of their upbringing while assuming new habits and capabilities in their adopted culture and religion.

It's unlikely that Contreras attaches much, if any, symbolic importance to being face up or face down. One might think of Christians looking heavenward as they're often depicted in religious paintings of the period – and Muslims bowing to the ground in submission to God. Muslims, including renegades, were an integral part of the Mediterranean seascape traversed by Contreras for so many years. While there is never any doubt about his loyalty as a Christian corsair in the service of Spain or Malta, he shows no signs of being involved in a religious war against Islam in general or of harbouring resentment towards renegades in particular. He is quite capable of punishing Christians and rewarding Muslims, and almost nothing scandalises him. He carries out a daring raid on the island of Chios to steal the lover of an Italian renegade, Soliman de Catania, who rules the island:

> We went inside the house, and without any resistance we took the Turkish renegade woman, of Hungarian origin, the most beautiful I ever saw. We also took two *putillos* [sexual slave boys], a renegade and two slaves, one of them Corsican and the other Albanian ... We embarked and sailed as fast as we could out of the Archipelago, as God gave us good weather. The Hungarian woman wasn't his wife but his lover. I regaled her lavishly as she deserved ... I learned that Soliman de Catania had sworn to find me, and when he caught me he'd have six blacks take their pleasure with my buttocks, because he thought I was sharing his lover's bed, and then he'd have me impaled. He wasn't so lucky as to catch me.[16]

---

[16] 'Entramos dentro y sin ninguna resistencia cogimos la turca renegada, húngara de nación, la más hermosa que vi. Cogimos dos putillos y un renegado y dos cristianos esclavos, de nación corso el uno y el otro albanés ... Embarcámonos y caminamos a más no poder hasta salir del Archipiélago, que Dios nos dio buen tiempo. La húngara no era mujer, sino amiga; regalela con extremo, que lo merecía ... supe que Solimán de Catania había jurado que me había de buscar y, en cogiéndome, había de hacer a seis negros que se holgasen con mis asentaderas, pareciéndole que yo me había amancebado con su amiga, y luego me había de empalar. No tuvo tanta dicha en cogerme' (ch. 5).

The woman and the two boys were soon ransomed from Malta – all three of them were renegades, as was the ransomer himself, who was en route to his new post as beylerbey of Algiers. Although the Inquisition in Malta interfered with the commerce (especially the ransom trade) of the Knights of St. John by taking renegades out of the slave market and trying them for apostasy, business as usual prevailed there. This kind of commerce – between Christians and Muslims – often eclipsed religion at the same time as its very functioning depended on the politico-religious divide. Contreras' lively account of this episode diverges radically from the viewpoints of religious treatise writers, yet undoubtedly immerses us more authentically in a frontier sensibility.

Renegade profiles

Despite centuries of misrepresentation, the profiles of a good number of renegades have come into focus. Some renegades were already well known in their own times while others, such as the women who crossed over from one side or the other of the Venetian-Ottoman divide (as Eric Dursteler recounts in *Renegade women*), have only recently come to light.[17] Given the many novelties that resourceful scholarship has produced even in the past decade, many more will undoubtedly appear in the larger mosaic of early modern converts in the Mediterranean world. Since any discussion of renegades is likely to crosscut them into countless fragments, a series of biographical (or fictional) vignettes is presented here in the hopes of inviting reflexion about the wider spectrum covered by the rubric 'renegade' and of providing some flashes of insight into individual cases. There's of course nothing original in this approach since other studies have used it to superb advantage, revealing a great deal about the Mediterranean by narrating frontier lives. My intention is to draw particularly interesting examples from the breadth of sources I work with, summarising but also picking up on curious particularities, convinced as I am that 'la vérité se trouve dans les détails' (truth is found in the details). These vignettes and accompanying remarks will necessarily be sketchy, pointing to their sources for fuller accounts. An attentive consideration of such thoroughly Mediterranean stories and histories, I believe, can help dispel many misconceptions about renegades that continue to circulate in our own present.

---

[17] See also Tijana Krstić's study *Contested Conversions to Islam* focusing on conversion narratives mainly in the 'lands of Rum', i.e. Turkey itself together with lands west and north of it (Greece, the Balkans and other eastern European lands, all within the Ottoman Empire).

1. Uluç Ali

Let's begin with perhaps the most famous renegade of all, Giovan Dionigi Galeni alias Uluç Ali (nicknames, variants and new titles would include Uchalí Fartax, 'Ulūj 'Alī, Ochali, Euldj Ali, Occhiali, Kılıç Ali Paşa, etc.), about whom there is ample documentation that tends to tell us more about how the authors of these texts regarded him than who he actually was.[18] Extracting his personality from all he is reported to have done has always been something of a Rorschach test. Antonio de Sosa starts his substantive account of him with this appraisal: 'One of the men of our times on whom Fortune chose to indulge herself … showing the powers of her caprices, was Aluch Alí.'[19] In modern times, Braudel and others have seen his stunning career as the zenith of what a renegade could aspire to (e.g. Bono, *Corsari*, 350, 358). Captured in 1536 when he was about eighteen in a raid on the Calabrian coast by none other than Hayreddin Barbarossa, this son of a fisherman (or, in other sources, a shepherd or swineherd) toiled for years as a galley slave. He converted to Islam to avenge an affront by a Turkish soldier, assumed the name Ali (to which so many epithets would be attached), gained his freedom, and married the daughter of Jafer, his former master.

He thus began to take advantage of a kind of patronage system within the networks of corsairs where an established corsair would – for familial, sexual or strategic purposes, or any combination of these – 'adopt' one or more promising renegade slaves or corsairs.[20] Hayreddin Barbarossa, for example, had brought the flamboyant young Dragut (Turgut Reis) into his circle of intimacy and would later go to great lengths to ransom his protégé from captivity. Uluç Ali served and enjoyed the support of Dragut (based on the island of Djerba off the Tunisian coast), who recommended him to the admiral of the Ottoman fleet, Piali Pasha, who in turn recommended him to the sultan to replace Dragut (who died during the siege of Malta in 1565) as beylerbey of Tunis, and soon after to govern Algiers, and finally to be admiral of the Turkish fleet. For his part, Uluç Ali recruited his own group of young renegade protégés and especially favoured his *garzón* Hasan Veneciano, who, despite the hatred his cruelty provoked on the part of Christians and Muslims alike, would follow the same route as corsair captain, beylerbey of Algiers and admiral of the fleet, thanks to Uluç Ali's almost unwavering support.

---

[18] Emilio Sola's *Uchalí* anthologises not only the well-known sources but also many archival records related to 'Ulūj 'Alī. I draw from numerous other sources here including Cervantes' *Don Quixote* (I, 40), Sosa's *Topografía* (II, 18) and other references in the *Topografía*, Salvatore Bono's *I corsari barbareschi* (350–8), Tobias Graf's *The Sultan's Renegades* (127–30), and Emilio Sola and José de la Peña's *Cervantes y la Berbería*. See also Orhan Koloğlu, 'Renegades and the Case Uluç/Kiliç Ali'.

[19] 'Uno de los hombres en los cuales en nuestros tiempos la Fortuna quiso burlarse … mostrando lo que pueden sus antojos, fue el Aluch Alí' (II, 18.1, 77r).

[20] These practices are commented on from various angles by, among others, Sola and Peña 210, 224–7; Carroll Johnson, *Cervantes*, 122; Garcés, *Cervantes in Algiers*, 112–14.

These patronage links enabled the enormously capable Uluç Ali to rise quickly through the ranks. He earned fame as a corsair captain who performed daring raids on the Italian coasts (including those of his native Calabria), was appointed viceroy of Tunis and then Algiers, distinguished himself as the only Ottoman admiral to do well in the massive naval battle at Lepanto, became admiral of the Ottoman fleet, which he modernised, and he definitively reconquered Tunis in 1574 after don Juan de Austria had taken it the year before. In the meantime he acquired thousands of slaves and reportedly kept in contact with his family back home. A couple of times spies and diplomats tried to tempt him back to Italy with a title of nobility, but he allegedly wanted the title of prince of Salerno, and the negotiations broke down. Though historians take these reports at face value, it seems very unlikely that the supremely astute Uluç Ali, curious as he might have been, would have consented to any such arrangement, not least of all because he, like every returning renegade, would have had to present himself to the Inquisition – how could he have survived? – and besides, no offer could come close to matching all that he would have had to renounce. In fact, none of the important renegades was ever seduced by any such offer.

Judgements of Uluç Ali's character on the part of Christian writers often depend on perceptions regarding his attitudes towards Christianity and his treatment of Christian captives. Cervantes' narrator and first-person protagonist of the captive's tale, Ruy Pérez de Viedma (*Don Quixote* I, 39–41), who was captured by Uluç Ali during the battle of Lepanto, says of his former slave-master that 'he was morally a good man and treated his captives with great humanity' (I, 40), in sharp contrast to his cruel protégé Hasan Veneciano, whose slaves included the historical Cervantes and his fictional character Ruy Pérez de Viedma. Many contemporaries likewise comment on Uluç Ali's kind demeanour towards his slaves (Bono, *Corsari*, 357). As an exception, Cervantes' friend Antonio de Sosa at times portrays 'that dirty renegade Ochali' (*Topografía* III, 118r) in a sinister light, telling, for instance, how he angrily condemned a repentant renegade – i.e. an apostate – to be executed on a gigantic iron hook, or how he had many janissaries beheaded or impaled in punishment for their killing the beylerbey of Cyprus, or how, in bouts of drunkenness – and explicitly likened to Caligula – he would order a captured knight of Malta to be given hundreds of blows naked, laughing with delight as he heard the man's cries of pain (Sosa, *Topografía* IV, 171r; II, 18.5, 80r). The most truculent of these anecdotes appear in Sosa's *Dialogues*, which are patently propagandistic against everything Algerian and Muslim: this last example is especially suspect for its sordid manipulation of Uluç Ali's image, contrary to a character who even Sosa sometimes shows to be merciful and indeed admirable.[21]

---

[21] E.g. in the *Diálogo de los mártires* (*Topografía* IV, 178v [story 22]), he refuses to allow vengeance to be taken on Christians who had mutinied in an attempt to gain their freedom.

Similarly, Uluç Ali's contemporaries often speculate about his being favourably inclined towards Christianity and even suspect him of secretly harbouring the religion of his youth (Sola and Peña 80–1). This could have been wishful thinking on their part since there is much evidence to suggest that his conduct accorded with what a Muslim ruler was expected to do. Yet his religiosity seems to have been double, encompassing both his adopted Islam and the religious praxis of his native Calabria, as Bono recounts:

> he was respectful towards [his slaves'] devotion; in particular, he was generous with his slaves who were priests, asking them to pray for him. On the occasion of a fearful plague that raged in the imperial capital, he ordered five hundred Christian slaves to form a procession in honour of San Rocco invoked by the people of Calabria as protector against the plague. (*Corsari*, 357)

Assuming this actually occurred, it shouldn't be read as a sign of crypto-Catholicism, since the public invocation of San Rocco during a plague in Istanbul is neither *crypto* nor indicative of any dogmatic belief, but rather a hedging of bets and a spontaneous call for help in the most desperate circumstances.

Until his death in 1587, the last 15 years of his life were centred in Istanbul. On the shores of the Bosphorus outside the city, he built – with the help of thousands of his slaves – a palace to live in and a sumptuous mosque to be buried in. 'He had a custom', writes Sosa: 'he wore black on the days he was melancholy and didn't want to be spoken to about business matters; and when he wore colours it was a sign that anyone could approach him and freely discuss things with him' (*Topografía* II, 18.6, 80v). But he remained an essential political and military figure throughout this time, taking the imperial fleet out on missions now and again and engaging in the games of power and influence. In 1579, in a war between the Ottoman Empire and Persia, he went on a frustrated expedition to the Black Sea, receiving some support from the Grand Khan (*Topografía* II, 18.6, 80v). Two years later, he arrived in Algiers with sixty ships with the intention of conquering the kingdom of Fez and perhaps of uniting the entire Maghrib under the Ottoman Empire, but this met with stiff internal opposition from the janissaries and Sultan Murad himself once he was informed of his subordinate's overreaching (*Topografía* II, 22.3, 88r). These two expeditions of his, stretching northeast into Asia and southwest to the Atlantic coast of Africa outside the bounds of the Ottoman Empire, together with his protagonism in the strategic confrontations between Christian countries and the Ottoman Empire, cast him as a figure of intercontinental – even global – importance in the sixteenth century. Like other frontier figures of the Mediterranean world, both named and anonymous, he could also be considered a synchronising agent, i.e. one who helped bring the disparate allochronic cultural and political entities into the same geohistorical time zone, a peripheral peasant offshoot of late Renaissance Italy who would become third in command within the Ottoman Empire.

Much about him belongs to legend, even his death: some said a Christian slave poisoned him, others that he was killed by a barber while being shaved, and yet others said he died 'in the arms of a Greek woman of rare beauty after declaring his love for her'.[22] In 1989 a monument with an impressive bust of him was erected in his hometown of Le Castella, on the Calabrian coast he so often raided to capture his own people. The inscription alternates between Italian and Turkish, giving his names in each, his place of birth and death, the century in which he lived without concrete dates, and in Turkish the major positions he held. Straddling languages, cultures, religions and antagonistic powers, the crossover Giovan Dionigi Galeni / Kılıç Ali Paşa looks outwards with a commanding gaze, recognised as a local and transnational hero four centuries after his death. The large family that survived him was not genetic but generic, a community of renegades: 'He had no son or daughter, but in his household he had more than five hundred renegades whom he provided for and called his children' (Sosa, *Topografía* II, 18.6, 80v).

2. Cali / Nurbanu Sultan

A female counterpart to Uluç Ali and others who ascended to high positions within the Ottoman Empire would have been the Christian slave girl who converted and became 'wife' or favourite consort (Walide Sultana) to a sultan or was mother to a sultan. (There are numerous variants of this in fact and fiction, including Cervantes' play *La gran sultana*.) A remarkable letter of 1566, written in Greek and translated into Turkish, reveals the travails of a woman from the island of Corfu who, having returned free after twenty-seven years as a slave of the Turks, discovers that her daughter Cali, captured by corsairs along with the whole family when she was seven, is the 'wife' of Sultan Selim II and mother of the future Murad III:

> My dear lady and daughter,
>
> It has now been twenty-nine years that I have been thinking only about you, if you are alive or dead ... And finally, having heard that you are the wife of Sultan Selim, with whom you have had a son named Sultan Murad, I have given thanks to the majesty of God. In your earliest years there were signs that you would rise to greatness, and I hope that you attain even more happiness than this.

---

[22] I quote Bono here (*Corsari*, 357), who in turn draws from the biography by Gustavo Valente, *Vita di Occhialì* (Milan, 1960).

My dear daughter, since I, your poor mother, was captured, I spent twenty-seven years as a slave, during which time I suffered many fatigues and tribulations. But finally, by the will of God, I was freed two years ago and I returned to our place in Corfu, to our old home where, having heard about you, I have written this letter and am sending it with your uncle.

My name is Righina, your father's name is Nicola, yours is Cali. You had two brothers named Jorgi and Manoli and a sister named Fatmi. When we were captured you were seven years old. Your father died on the galleys. Your brothers and sister have vanished, I have heard no news of them. If you don't believe me, you can call on your uncle and verify everything [...]

The village where you were captured is called Assumetto, near Corfu ...

You used to say: 'Mother, mother, the Turks will come and take me away. Cairadin bassa [Hayreddin Pasha (Barbarossa)] will take me away.' And we would say: 'This daughter of ours, she's going to end up being a Muslim.' And before long, by God's will, everything you said came true.

O my daughter, if you feel the obligation one has towards a mother, send someone to find me and I'll come to you. If you're ashamed to say that I'm your mother, I can do nothing about it; but we'll find each other in the other world.[23]

The girl Cali (or Kalē, Kali) would presumably become Nurbanu Sultan, about whom there is a conflicting version of her geographical and ethnic origin. The most thorough and convincing study of Nurbanu's origins that I'm aware of is that of Benjamin Arbel, who examines both traditions dating back to Nurbanu's lifetime. By one tradition, Nurbanu would have been Cecilia Venier Baffo, illegitimate daughter of the Venetian patrician Nicolò Venier, governor of the island of Paros in the Aegean Archipelago, and of the Venetian patrician woman Violante Baffo, and would have been captured by Barbarossa on Paros during the period 1537–40 when she was about twelve years old. By the other tradition, of which the letter above is one of several supporting documents, she was Kalē Kartánou (with spelling variations), a Greek girl from Corfu who was captured there in 1537 when she was perhaps seven along with her parents Nicholas Kartánou and Basilikē and their other children George, Emmanuel and Phōteinē. Assessing the differing 'degree of unsoundness' of the two versions, Arbel concludes that the Greek Corfiote origin is more plausible. Apart from the specific question of origins, the

---

[23] I've translated most of the only extant version, in Italian (Arbel 257–8), which, as Benjamin Arbel indicates, was itself – according to Righina's (Regina's) brother Michales Papadopoulos – translated from a Greek translation of a Turkish original. In doing so I've consulted Emilio Sola's translation of this Italian version into Spanish ('Historias de la frontera', 347–8) as well as the mostly complete English version that Arbel provides (250–1) with mainly Greek transcriptions of names (Cali = Kalē, Righina Quartana/o/i = Regina (Basilikē) Kartánou, etc.).

storylines of the two versions do nonetheless coincide: a young girl of socially significant parentage is captured, quite possibly by Barbarossa, and eventually becomes Selim II's Walide Sultan and mother to Murad III, wielding substantial political influence.[24]

In any event, I'm more interested here in story than history, and (if it's valid to draw from the letter) this is an almost paradigmatic story of a family on that diffuse Mediterranean frontier, exposed to the greatest uncertainties and the widest range of destinies from the death of the father and slavery of the mother to the unknown fates of brothers and sister, and to the immense wealth and power of the sultana. The beauty and simplicity of this potential anagnorisis between mother and daughter after twenty-nine years bridges the two religions: by God's will, says the Christian mother, the daughter has become a Muslim, and the mother thanks God for her daughter's astonishing fortune. And should the daughter be too ashamed to acknowledge her mother, they'll still see each other in the other world which no doubt will be the same place for both. Doctrinal differences between the two religions dissolve as this ex-slave reaches out to her daughter sultana. A mother's primordial bonds of flesh and blood transcend all religious, political, social and cultural boundaries that have come between her and her daughter. Although there's no further information, a reencounter in Istanbul seems very likely, and it could hardly be coincidental that the bearer of the letter, the Corfiote merchant Michales Papadopoulos, Regina's brother, is subsequently given a mandate by the sultana (specified as mother of Sultan Murad) authorising him to free Corfiote slaves wherever he might find them.[25]

3. The renegade of Tarifa/Tetuan (and an anecdote about Cigala/Sinan Pasha)

Germain Moüette's captivity narrative (1683) includes a story which he says he heard from one French and six Spanish captives, although Guy Turbet-Delof

---

[24] Lucetta Scaraffia (153) follows the Venetian tradition concerning Nurbanu's origins, but her characterisation of Nurbanu's historical role coincides with other accounts: 'Cecilia Baffa, illegitimate daughter of Nicolò Venier ... captured at twelve years of age by Barbarossa, enamored Sultan Selim II (1566–74) and became his wife, with the name Nur Banu, and was mother of the heir Murad III (1574–95). Both as wife and as mother of a sultan, she exercised considerable political influence in favour of Venice, and was honoured by the Republic. After her death in 1583 she left an enduring memory among the Venetians, who were both amazed and disconcerted by the incredible rise of a girl whom the custom of noble families would have destined for the convent or a modest marriage.' Caroline Finkel, one of the few historians aware of both traditions, is inclined towards the Greek Corfiote origin of the sultana: 'Long thought to have been born to a noble Venetian family, captured when a child by the grand admiral Barbarossa and consigned to the imperial *harem*, it seems, rather, that she was a Greek from Corfu' (166).

[25] This second letter is quoted in Sola, *Uchalí*, 127.

questions Moüette's account and persuasively argues that the story is a complex interweaving of Muslim and Christian narratives.[26] The events would have taken place much earlier around the middle of the century. In bold outline, two Spaniards, exiled for their crimes and obliged to serve in a presidio on the Moroccan coast near Tetuan, get fed up with the harsh life there, desert one night and head for Tetuan with the intention of converting to Islam. Before they arrive they're captured and taken to the governor, who asks them why they've come. One of them brashly says he denies God and wants to follow the law of Muhammad, for which the good governor, scandalised by his atheism, has him burned. The other, more prudent, is admitted as a convert, treated kindly and freed when his master dies. He prospers as a corsair making raids on the Spanish coast and wants to marry a woman described as extraordinarily beautiful but very wilful. She tells him she'll only marry him if he captures his own father, mother and sisters and brings them as slaves to serve the two of them when they're married. Without thinking twice about it he arms his ship and sails across the Straits of Gibraltar to his hometown of Tarifa, where he's greeted with the utmost joy by his family. He almost succeeds in deceiving his family into coming with him to the boat, but the plan fails. He is imprisoned and given every chance to repent by the inquisitors, but he 'loudly protested that he was a Mohammedan and that as such he wanted to die for the love of one of most beautiful ladies of Africa'. So they burn him at the stake. We're told that the lady profoundly laments having made such a demand of this worthy man.

This story, with obvious layers of fiction, has the Muslim-Christian frontier inscribed within it. Despite being intercontinental, its geography is all very local. As Turbet-Delof points out, nearly all the details about this unnamed renegade in the first half of the story are surprisingly pro-Muslim – e.g. the integrity of the governor of Tetuan, the matter-of-fact mention of the renegade's circumcision and approving depiction of the renegade's rise to prominence as a corsair – while the second half of the story turns anti-Muslim, depicting him as a monster and an apostate. Renegades were always accused of being traitors to their homeland and religion – and in fact many renegade corsairs actually led attacks on their homeland because they knew the terrain – but this story formulates the betrayal in the most quintessential way: our renegade, for the love of an African Muslim woman, has no qualms about enslaving his own family. Curiously, unlike his godless companion who was burned by the Muslims, he becomes a good Muslim yet ends up being burned by the Inquisition on the other side as a martyr for his love and his

---

[26] Guy Turbet-Delof, *L'Afrique barbaresque*, 274–7, where the story is reproduced with annotations in an appendix, 319–25. The story is told in chapter 16 of Germain Moüette's *Relation de la captivité*.

creed. One shouldn't be fooled by this story: relatively few renegades tried by the Inquisition were burned.

Regarding the enslavement of one's own family, earlier texts in Spanish come close to the formulation of Moüette's story. Cervantes' play *Los baños de Argel* begins with a corsair raid on the Spanish coast, guided by the renegade Yzuf who scandalises his fellow (repentant) renegade Hazén for having plundered his hometown and seized his own uncle and nephews into captivity (vv. 10–12, 652–4, 797–804). Even closer is Sosa's characterisation of renegades who act as guides on raids and embark full of laughter, 'bringing along, with their hands tied, their own parents, brothers and sisters and relatives, whom they sell or turn Moors or Turks, without anyone getting in their way or saying a word' (*Topografía* III, 10, 116r–v). Gómez de Losada echoes this almost exactly: 'And sometimes they capture their own parents, brothers and sisters and relatives, whom they sell' (I, 12, 34). It seems that this notion of capturing and selling into slavery one's immediate family had turned into a standardised perception, infiltrating the very essence of the renegade as the epitome of betrayal. Although some corsairs were known for raiding the coastlines they knew best, the notion that they intended to capture and enslave their own families bears the signs of misrepresentation, especially among those writers who claim to be telling the truth. On the contrary, many renegades maintained relations with their people back home, sending them letters or money, or collaborating with them in various ways. If renegades were seen as betrayers of their religion and homelands, then, portraying them as enslavers of their own families metonymically falsifies this perceived betrayal. What distinguishes Moüette's story from the others here is that love, not greed or power, motivates the renegade, and that, rather than selling his family, he would have them be his slaves and his wife's slaves, an ideal household setup for a young married couple.

The well-documented story of the renegade Cigala's reunion with his mother and other family members provides a paradigmatic counterexample to this sort of fabrication. Cigala, alias Cığalazade (Cağaloğlu) Yusuf Sinan Pasha, born Scipione Cicala, was the eldest son of a Sicilian viscount-corsair who had married a beautiful 'Turkish' captive of his from Castelnuovo (present-day Herceg Novi, Montenegro), and many years later was himself captured in 1561 by Dragut with this seventeen-year-old lad destined to be educated in the sultan's Topkapı Palace for imperial service. Cigala would turn out to be the last of the greatest renegades of the century: he took on key roles in the Ottoman war with Persia, was admiral of the Turkish fleet for two extended periods, and was briefly the Ottoman grand vizier. As admiral in September of 1598, while his fleet once again menaced the coasts of his native Sicily, he wrote to the viceroy of Sicily requesting permission to have his beloved ageing mother come aboard to see him. His letter and the viceroy's response express extreme courtesy at the same time as the viceroy takes into account Cigala's offer to ransom captives and refrain from attacking Messina, and lays out the conditions for the visit, among them holding Cigala's son as a hostage in the port. Cigala's letter to his mother, from whom he has been separated 'for thirty or forty years', overflows with filial affection: 'My dearest mother, I have no other desire in this world than to see you, and I trust in God that you will come with my honourable brothers and sisters ... Once I have seen you I will send you back without any harm, and will continue on my way.' Replete with embraces, conversation and gifts, this visit unfolded as planned, with other family members also present.[27]

4. Giuseppe

In May of 1581 Montaigne, in his travels through Italy, came to a place called Bagno alla Villa where he was told about a soldier from there named Giuseppe who was captured at sea by the 'Turks'. 'To be freed', writes Montaigne, 'he turned Turk (there are a good number who have done so, and especially from the hills nearby, still alive), was circumcised, got married there'.[28] While raiding the coast nearby, he and 'other Turks' strayed too far from their ship and were caught by the local people, but Giuseppe opportunely declared that he was a Christian and had surrendered on purpose.

> He was freed a few days later, came to this place and to the house opposite the one I'm lodging in. He comes in and meets his mother. She asks him gruffly who he was, what he wanted, as he was still dressed as a sailor and was strange to see there. He finally makes himself known since he'd been lost for ten or twelve years, embraces his mother.[29]

She fell into a deep swoon, finally came to but died soon after,

> everyone believing that this jolt brought her life to an end. Our Giuseppe was celebrated by everyone, received in the church to abjure his error, given the eucharist by the bishop of Lucca, among other ceremonies. But it was

---

[27] Sources consulted include Sola, 'Carta', 219–29; Kaiser 256–7; Scaraffia 121–3; Galán 187–9; Finkel 172, 187; Graf 119–26. See especially Türkçelik's book-length study. Cigala's capture, education in the imperial palace and subsequent career in the Ottoman Empire would later be paralleled by another outstanding renegade, the Segovian *hidalgo* Gutierre Pantoja, whose biography is admirably reconstructed from inquisitorial records by Bartolomé and Lucile Bennassar (141–63).

[28] 'Pour se mettre en liberté, il se fit Turc (et de ceste condition il y en a plusieurs, et notammant des montaignes voisines de ce lieu, encore vivans), fut circuncis, se maria là' (*Journal de voyage en Italie*, 1268).

[29] '[il] fut mis en liberté quelques jours après, vint en ce lieu, et en la maison qui est vis-à-vis de cele où je loge: il entre, et rancontre sa mere. Elle lui demande rudement qui il étoit, ce qu'il vouloit, car il avoit encore ses vestemans de matelot, et estoit estrange de le voir là. Enfin il se faict conêtre, car il estoit perdu despuis dix à douze ans, ambrasse sa mere' (1268–9).

all a hoax: in his heart he was a Turk, and to go back there he steals away from here, goes to Venice, joins the Turks and takes up his journey again. There he is fallen into our hands again, and since he's such a strong man and so expert a seafarer, the Genoese still keep him and make use of him, well fastened and garrotted.[30]

This story is at least as interesting for Montaigne's wry narration as for the portrait in motion it provides of Giuseppe. Quite uniquely for his time, Montaigne blithely recounts the story without scandal – or sympathy for that matter. Instead of dwelling on questions of conscience, he jots down three actions in just a few words denoting Giuseppe's conversion, circumcision and marriage. To palliate Giuseppe's turning Turk, Montaigne notes that many in the hills nearby have done the same and are still alive, and this also gives a sense that renegades, even when absent, form part of the frontier culture of coastal Italy (as was also the case with other Christian lands): renegades are *us*. Yet renegades such as Giuseppe are also *them*, 'Turks', and are 'Turks' in their hearts. Hence 'our' Giuseppe escapes back to wherever he lives, presumably somewhere on the Barbary coast, but he again falls into 'our' hands. This modulation in the use of the possessive concords with the play of time and space in this anecdote: the story's tenses switch back and forth between a more distant past and an immediate present (when he comes to see his mother as well as his defection and recapture), and the space alternates between the *here*, 'the house opposite the one I'm lodging in', and remote places that blur beyond the horizon.

Apart from the single sentence mentioning Giuseppe's conversion, circumcision and marriage, we learn practically nothing more about his experience as a renegade except that as a corsair he raids the coast of his own people, is a 'Turk' in his heart (whatever that might mean in the case of someone who ostensibly converted not out of religious conviction but in order to be freed from slavery), and would rather be *there* (wherever that is) than *here* in his native village or elsewhere such as Venice. *There* he has a wife and a life; *here* he has a mother who, according to the perception of the local people, dies as a consequence of the joyful shock of reuniting with him once he tells her who he is, thus leaving him orphaned but perhaps blamable for her death. *Here* he's wholeheartedly reintegrated by everybody back into the community and the Christian fold, but his act of reentry is a bluff from the moment he's captured.

---

[30] 'jugeant chacun que ceste secousse lui accoursit la vie. Nostre Giuseppe fut festoïé d'un checun, receu en l'église à abjurer son erreur, reçeut le sacrament de l'evesque de Lucques, et plusieurs autres serimonies: mais ce n'estoit que baïes. Il estoit Turc dans son cueur, et pour s'y en retourner, se desrobe d'ici, va à Venise, se remesle aus Turcs, reprenant son voïage. Le voilà retumbé entre nos meins, & parce que c'est un home de force inusitée et soldat fort entandu en la marine, les Genevois le gardent encore, et s'en servent, bien ataché & garroté' (1269).

Regardless of what his motives might be, we can surmise that he's no longer at home *here* to be who he was, and that he thinks he belongs *there* where he can be who he has become.

The quick succession of events between here and there allows little room for moral indignation or religious censure. One could easily imagine how some of Montaigne's contemporaries might tell the story, laying emphasis on Giuseppe's apostasy whose emblematic act is circumcision, his marrying a Muslim woman, the betrayal of his own people in corsair raids, his blameworthiness in the death of his mother, his ingratitude and deceitfulness towards all those who welcomed him back, his persistent apostasy and perfidious escape to the lands of the 'Turks', and the justice of his punishment upon recapture. Montaigne, on the contrary, infuses the story with his boundless curiosity, equanimity and wit, letting the details he has chosen elicit interest and amusement. He lends it a peculiar economy, weighting it not on the renegade's interiority but rather on moments such as the odd anagnorisis and the fatal consequences for the mother, whose death is followed immediately in the narrative with celebrations of Giuseppe's return such that we don't know whether it was mourned by her renegade son.

There's nothing particularly remarkable about Giuseppe *as* a renegade. He reneges as one would expect, submits to circumcision, marries and gets employment doing what he knows how to do as a soldier and mariner. When captured he pulls out his ace in the hole, saying he's Christian and that he meant to be caught. He takes advantage of the unique opportunity to revisit his village and see his mother, plays along with all the festivities and rituals done on his behalf and then furtively defects. Everything he does is entirely reasonable under the circumstances, and countless renegades did or would have done just the same. What *is* remarkable is the phenomenon of renegades that Giuseppe so adeptly exemplifies. He has become double, duplicitous, able to use his face as a mask and dissimulate as one of *us* when he's really one of *them* – and *we* and *they* may not be so far apart. We still know next to nothing about him since Montaigne has had to rely on the local oral tradition as his only source, and the local people know they've been duped by this renegade of theirs.

5. Giorgio del Giglio Pannilini

Some of these characteristics are evident in Giorgio del Giglio Pannilini (*c.* 1507–80), who could be considered almost as an archetype of low-profile renegades. Hailing from the island of Giglio in the Tyrrhenian Sea near the west coast of Italy, he was captured by Ottoman corsairs at least four times, reneged twice – first around 1549–50 in Algiers, and later in 1560 in Istanbul – spent up to ten years in the Ottoman Empire, and was twice reconciled with the Inquisition. In some of his letters he vaunts being a 'perpetual slave'. He escaped or was rescued as many times as he was captured, and apparently did not return voluntarily to Ottoman lands, though his conversions to Islam were voluntary. He says he was slave of Hayreddin Barbarossa, and claims to have captured the young swineherd who would become 'Occhiali' (Uluç Ali). He also claims that his sister was none other than the sultana Roxana, implying in his letters that he had direct influence with the Sublime Porte.

Thanks primarily to the study of this figure by Florence Buttay, we know him mainly through two autobiographical manuscripts written between 1564 and 1579 in which he constantly reinvents himself in the most self-aggrandising ways and justifies his repeated apostasy in unorthodox terms as he seeks to find points of congruence between Christianity and Islam. As Buttay demonstrates, his contacts with several of the important political leaders of his time led to efforts to find out whether his promises and influence peddling were reliable, resulting in the conclusion that he was a liar and impostor. Yet he did act as a key intermediary in several ransoming operations from both the Christian and Turkish sides, often with a view to personal profit. Informed letters written about him offset many of the exaggerated claims he makes about himself, yet also confirm the broad lines of his captivities and conversions. He did indeed have a sister in the imperial palace, not Roxane but a slave, though he was never able to meet with her. The Florentine *bailo* Albertaccio Alberti discovered much of this but took an interest in him nonetheless, offering to take him back to Italy at his own expense when he saw him vacillating towards Islam: 'He is a very weak man and, judging from what he tells me, I fear that before you answer this letter he will have turned Turk.' Pannilini visited Alberti three weeks later with a turban on his head, calling himself Mahomet Bey (69). The disgruntled *bailo* of Florence remarks in a new letter: 'just as he's been a bad Christian, he'll be an even worse Turk' (71). Buttay comments on this:

> On the contrary, ten years later Pannilini characterised his captivity as martyrdom and his years of captivity in Muslim lands as a unique experience that enabled him to better discern the true religion: "I am inclined to believe that my faith is the most valid of all because it was conquered with the sweat of blood ... Few know this holy faith because to have it one has to be patient and catch the world against the current and attribute both bad and good to heaven."

As Buttay mentions, Pannilini also repeatedly resorts in his manuscripts to the topos of Islam being a garden of delights for the body but harmful for the soul, quite the opposite of Christianity (71). After being rescued by Ragusans in 1564 he returned definitively to Italy: 'non piu volsi vedere mare' ('I no longer wanted to see the sea'), he writes in the Sienna manuscript (63). He took a job as a gardener and worked on his autobiographical writings, both of which in their titles encapsulate his entire life from the year he was born to the present as a *viaggio* (journey) undertaken by him, Giorgio Pannilini (an adopted surname), from Sienna, 'through Asia and Africa and Europe by sea and by land' (60). He did indeed travel extensively at least on the fringes of all three of these continents, yet the word *viaggio* and particularly the metaphor of life as a journey camouflage his life as boundless adventure whereas his kind of travels were those of a captive or corsair, Christian or Muslim, almost entirely in the Mediterranean.

What primarily distinguishes Pannilini from nearly all other renegades is that he narrates his own accounts about himself. Letters by other people about him serve as a corrective to his most outlandish fabrications. Yet this inclination to patently fictionalise himself forms an integral part of who he was. His capacity to assume roles, invent his genealogy, dissimulate, shift religious allegiance again and again, hyperbolise his importance and virtues, intercede in high-level negotiations even when both sides knew he was a fraud, pose as an authority on Christianity and Islam: all of this defines the character who became his own author after long experience in multiple captivities, religious and cultural switchovers, corsairing on both sides, and practical knowledge in the art of living and thriving in a divided Mediterranean. He was a kind of nobody who for that reason had a virtual monopoly to construe himself in the image of his fantasies, and besides he was gifted in rhetoric and storytelling. This is a renegade we can get to know via his own words, contorted and distorted as they may be.

6. The *valenciana*

Captive women, who rarely had the chance to return to their homelands, were highly sought after in marriage and often converted to Islam and married Muslims, many of whom were renegades themselves, frequently from the same homeland as their spouses (Bennassar and Bennassar 327), so that cultural bonds were reconstituted on the other side of the religious divide. Historical and literary sources, nonetheless, occasionally offer us spectacular instances of escapes organised or abetted by renegade women. Braudel mentions an escape that took place in 1595: a prominent lady, together with all her household slaves and many others (thirty-two in all), embarked near Algiers and sailed to Valencia (2: 874).[31] A similar escape in 1586 was

---

[31] This may well have been the inspiration for the episode recounted here, which makes explicit reference to 'another escape like this one' that happened in Algiers. This story also invites some comparison with the real-life story of Marquesa Dezcano, a married woman from Sardinia who spends a few years as a captive in Algiers, but in 1595, seeing that her husband has no interest in ransoming her nor her master in selling her, decides to renege in order to find a way back home, without truly abandoning Christianity, she says. She takes on the name Fatima, dresses as a Mooress, marries a new husband – an Italian renegade – with whom she has a child, and in 1603 somehow finds her way to the Spanish coast. This story is summarised in an appendix of Martínez Torres (125–6).

organised by Drusiana, a Greek renegade woman who arranged for a boat to come from Naples and take her, her renegade Catalan husband, their daughter, and twenty-two others, from Algiers to Mallorca and then Rome (Gonzalez-Raymond 135; Bennassar and Bennassar 341). Such feats, exceptional as they were, lend an aura of credibility to a fictional account in Vicente Espinel's 1618 novel *Marcos de Obregón* (II, 13, 103–9). This remarkable story is told by a nameless Morisco renegade to his captive Marcos, protagonist and fictive author of the novel.

Mami Reis, a renegade corsair from Algiers – powerfully rich, successful at sea, noble-minded, handsome, generous and well-liked – goes about his business along the Valencian coast. In a mill, he captures a young woman who has been too frightened to run away. She's so beautiful that her captors say that 'such a jewel in form and face had never been seen in Algiers', and Mami Reis 'said he valued this capture more than if he had sacked all of Valencia' (II, 13, 103). As they return by night, the beauty and grave elegance of her face 'gave light to the whole galley, and everyone bowed in reverence as though to something divine, amazed that Valencia could bring forth such sovereign gems' (II, 13,104). He consoles her on the journey back to Algiers, offering to make her not his slave but his wife and lady of his household. The story continues:

> To be brief, he went to disembark not in the city but by a recreational property of his with vineyards and sumptuous gardens. She found herself so obeyed by slaves and friends of the Turk that it seems she began to soften and leave behind the sadness brought on by her captivity. In time she came to love her master and marry him, abandoning her true religion for her husband's, in which she lived blissfully for six or seven years, loved, served, regaled, full of jewels and pearls, and oblivious to having been a Christian.[32]

Lavish feasts are constantly made in her honour, and she dwells 'in all this idolatry, her pleasure being the rule by which everybody lived' (II, 13, 104).

But events take an abrupt turn. After a slave from Menorca is ransomed, she sends him a letter asking him to return with a boat on a certain night during the season when her husband is away corsairing. Courageously, and with religious fervour, she rallies her slaves 'bought with the blood of Christ' to join her, assumes the role of captain and gets her household and portable wealth into the boat, during which time a black slave woman and two little

---

[32] 'Para abreviar, fuese a desembarcar no a la ciudad, sino a una heredad suya, de grande recreación de viñas y jardines muy regalados. Ella, que se vio tan obedecida de esclavos y amigos del turco, parece que se fue ablandando y dejando la tristeza que le había causado el cautiverio. Vino, andando el tiempo, a querer bien a su amo y a casarse con él, dejando su religión verdadera por la del marido, en que vivió con grandísimo gusto seis años o siete, querida, servida, regalada, llena de joyas y perlas, y muy olvidada de haber sido cristiana' (II, 13, 104).

'Turks' (*turquillos*) are stabbed to death for crying out. For her this is a journey of salvation: 'He who put this in my heart will guide me to safety. And if this does not happen, I'd rather be food for horrible sea monsters in the deep abyss of the caverns of the sea, dying as a Christian, than be queen of Algiers against the religion professed by our ancestors' (II,13, 106). Hunted by dozens of Algerian ships, her boat finds itself in the morning in the (Balearic) islands between the two galleys of her husband Mami Reis, whose men – disguised as Spaniards – are poised to raid the coast. She shrewdly tells her boat companions to dress as Turks and pretends to flee, thus outwitting her husband, who is delighted that his disguise has worked, 'and with great laughter they celebrated the brigantine's flight'. She thus makes it back to Spain, 'where she is very rich and content, giving generous alms from her husband's wealth; and although in Algiers there was another escape like this one, it was with more power and fewer circumstances' (II, 13, 107).

The renegade narrator explains that his purpose in telling this episode is to prove that 'there is no one who doesn't have his or her first religion stamped on the heart', particularly among the baptised like himself (II, 13, 107). Still, he's perplexed as to why the Valencian woman didn't have the courage to run from the mill where she was captured, and yet was able to embark on such a daring exploit. Marcos resolves the mystery: 'When the lady was a virgin', he says, 'with the natural coldness that virgins have, fear obstructed the limbs and veins of her body so that she couldn't flee or even move; but after she married and absorbed the force of her husband's heat, her nature improved and she gathered the strength to take on such a difficult feat' (II, 13, 108). The dialogue concludes with Marcos explaining that none of the women mentioned in Antiquity could have been virgins, including the fighting Amazon women, but that no Amazon woman ever performed a feat so great as this *valenciana* did.

This story obviously doesn't offer us a piece of raw life. Vicente Espinel's novel, presented as the autobiographical narrative of Marcos de Obregón, continually points to its own Orthodox Catholicism, and at times Marcos alludes to his true identity as a fictional Espinel. Despite Marcos's extended captivity in Algiers, there's no sign of Espinel having had first-hand knowledge of the city or its people: as Cervantes' 'false captives' in the *Persiles* (III, 10) demonstrate, anyone can tell stories about captivity in Algiers though it's advisable to get at least a little information from someone who has been there. The Morisco renegade narrator of the story is already an ideological pro-Christian creation of Espinel filtered through the fictional narrative of Marcos, and hence this Valencian woman and her husband appear through yet another highly suspect filter of ideology.

For her, becoming a Muslim – judging from what we're told – involves no adoption of new beliefs or practices contrary to Christianity, and we never hear of Mami Reis doing or saying anything distinctively Islamic. Nor is there any reference to mosques or prayers or the 'false sect of Muhammad', let alone the leitmotifs of polygamy or sodomy. For her, becoming a Muslim essentially means falling into oblivion, forgetting that she's a Christian. It also involves a life of carefree luxury with feasts, jewels, slaves, a doting husband and enjoyment of the spectacular gardens for which Algiers was so renowned. This blissful life as a renegade is paradisiacal, even hedonistic. Her return to Christianity involves an awakening, a remembering who she is and who her ancestors were, and with this comes her resolve, her fiery speech bordering on the rhetoric of martyrdom.

This *valenciana*, whose Christian and Muslim names are withheld from us, demonstrates remarkable adaptability to her Algerian life and her renegade husband.[33] There seem to be no language barriers, sensations of estrangement or hostility, problems of social integration, marital difficulties or religious concerns. Nor does she seem to have any qualms about her husband's *modus vivendi* or the source of her own wealth. All of this is quite unusual in fact and fiction, and all the more so because there's no attempt to manipulate readers against Islam, Algiers, corsairs or renegades, with all of which this enchanting woman is identified. Her beauty and deserved happiness excuse everything and put everybody on her side, readers and characters alike, through the quick narration of six or seven years as a renegade.

The story recounts switches in fidelity, and every such turnabout is also an act of infidelity. Primarily, of course, this is a story about a woman being captured, becoming a renegade, marrying her Muslim captor, and years later acting on a *prise de conscience* to return to her home and religion while abandoning and fooling her husband, who now belongs to the other side, the other religion. While she is an infidel (from a Christian vantage point) she is faithful to her husband, but when she returns to her original faith she breaks with her husband and, in a quick-witted act of self-defence, deceives her deceiving husband at his own game of corsairing. This escape and *burla* give comic closure to the story that began with her victimisation as a captive, and the final detail adds an amusing touch as she lives 'very rich and content, giving generous alms from her husband's wealth' (II, 13,107) – in

---

[33] The text doesn't say that this fictional Mami Reis is a renegade, but judging from his behaviour, his profession and his name it would be hard to imagine him not being one. Sosa's *Topografía* (I, 22, 18r) gives a list of thirty-five corsair captains active in Algiers in 1581, ten Turkish and twenty-five renegades – or sons of renegades in some cases – from lands stretching from Hungary and Greece to Spain; seven have the name Mami, all of them renegades, and one (a Venetian) is called Mami Raez, which is identical to Mami Reis since these are two ways of transcribing the Arabic and Turkish words for 'captain'. In part II of the *Topografía* (8.2, 70v), Sosa mentions other renegade corsairs named Mami Raez, one of them Neapolitan and the other Corsican, and in part IV (*Diálogo de los mártires*) repeatedly mentions the Neapolitan and the Venetian Mami Raez, also adding a Greek by this name.

effect laundering an illicit wealth acquired through robbing and capturing Christians like herself and returning it to its place of origin.

The cultural cross-dressing reveals not only that Turks can pass for Spaniards and Christians for Turks, but that the Turks passing for Spaniards don't realise that they've been recognised as Turks or that the Christians passing for Turks are really Christians. The fact that they can pass for each other, or at least try to do so, reveals that the differences aren't as pronounced as they're often made out to be and that everybody was more or less skilled in the arts of deception. In this game of recognition and misrecognition, the *valenciana* outmanoeuvres her husband, which she probably wouldn't have managed to do had she not become a renegade herself and married a corsair, absorbing his 'heat'. Ultimately this story seems to be setting up a series of oppositions between raided Christian Valencia and raiding renegade Algiers. It might not be out of place to recall, besides, that Valencia had recently been emptied of its crypto-Muslims, its Moriscos, and that Algiers had been the destination of a great many of them before and during the expulsion, including the narrator of this story. Perhaps this woman– referred to as 'maiden', 'lady', 'she', 'this *valenciana*' … – has no name because she is so identified with Valencia, which alone can produce beauties the likes of which Algiers has never seen. Valencia wins out over Algiers, Christianity over renegade 'idolatry', beauty over the seizure of beauty, restolen wealth over stolen wealth – and yes, wife over husband, woman over man, although our male commentators do their best to qualify this, saying in effect that she breaks the bounds of gender, acting with manly courage (literally 'pecho varonil'), which is as high a compliment as any that can be paid to a woman's character. But this winning can only happen through a process of becoming or joining with the other, initiated and concluded by the violence of capture and abduction from here to there and escape back again from there to here.

7. Alicax, Francisco Pérez/Alí, Diego Díaz, Arabia/Margarita: renegade Moriscos and Turks

The term 'renegade' enters into an absurd terrain when applied – as it often was – to Moriscos, or to captured Muslim slaves, particularly because many of these 'renegades' never considered themselves Christians to start with. Since Moriscos were expelled for being seen as enemies of the state and crypto-Muslims – *tan moros como los de Argel* (as Moorish as the Moors of Algiers) – their reentry into Christian dominions through capture or clandestine return exposed them to being judged and punished for the same apostasy for which they were expelled, a contradiction that inquisitors did not find troubling because Moriscos were baptised, hence Christians, and baptism provided the baseline from which to condemn any traces of Islam.

A very different question raised by modern historians is whether exiled Moriscos and converts to Islam (renegades) were almost indistinguishable in certain Maghribian cities. Although attempts have been made to conflate the two categories by arguing that Moriscos and renegades were engaged in similar activities ('piracy', military service, translation), occupied a similar social position, were regarded as suspect Muslims, etc.,[34] much more evidence points to the divergences between renegades and the 'Andalusians',[35] revealing them as unmistakably distinct social groups in their new societies: their economic and political roles were by no means the same, they were perceived in very different ways and likewise saw themselves as very unlike each other, etc.[36] In any event, it's not surprising that Moriscos would on this account too be associated by their European contemporaries with renegades and even be called renegades or 'Turks'.

---

[34] Most notably in Wiegers, 'European converts'. Mercedes García-Arenal introduces this article by Wiegers with the following assertions: 'The culminating stage in the history of the renegades coincides with the expulsion of the Spanish Moriscos (1609–14) and their settling in the Maghrib. In 17th-century Tunis and Algiers, Moriscos and renegades constituted groups that were hard to distinguish. They lived in the same quarters and had the same professions, worked together in corsairing and the militias but were also translators, interpreters and secretaries. Their social position in a closed and separate space was also similar, and the political power of the regencies used them in the same way. The sincerity of the Moriscos' commitment to Islam was similarly questioned' (*Conversions islamiques*, 13).

[35] When referring to former Moriscos (from *anywhere* in the Iberian Peninsula, not only 'Andalusia') living in North Africa, early modern Spanish writers with knowledge of the Maghrib – including Luis del Mármol Carvajal, Antonio de Sosa and Francisco Ximénez – often call them *andaluces*. In his history of viceroys or 'kings' of Algiers (*Topografía* II), Sosa refers again and again to the 'andaluces o moros de España' ('*andaluces* or Moors from Spain'), 'genízaros, turcos, renegados y andaluces o moriscos de España' ('janissaries, Turks, renegades and *andaluces* or Moriscos from Spain'). This early modern meaning of *andaluces* as 'Moors/Moriscos from Spain' is often translated into English as 'Andalusians', e.g. in the translation of al-Ḥajarī's book. I mention this so as to clarify my occasional use of 'Andalusians' or the italicised *andaluces*. North Africans used the Arabic word *al-andalusī* (from which the early modern Spanish *andaluces* is derived) to refer to any (ex-)Morisco from the Iberian Peninsula, which they continued to call al-Andalus, and even today Moroccans prefer this term to the neologism *al-muriskiyyūn* with regard to the descendants of Moriscos (as Luis Bernabé Pons has kindly informed me). In English, 'Andalusi' (pl. 'Andalusis') can also refer to former Moriscos living in the Maghrib, or (as an adjective) to the historical and geographical al-Andalus.

[36] Such evidence is widely distributed over the bibliography, but it would suffice, say, to compare Bartolomé and Lucile Bennassar's *Les Chrétiens d'Allah* with Míkel de Epalza's *Los moriscos antes y después de la expulsión* to appreciate the profound differences between renegades and Moriscos in the Maghrib. Epalza, for instance, quotes a seventeenth-century European ambassador as saying that 'Moors and Jews are considered subjects and vassals; the Granadans are included among the Moors. Only the Turks and renegades rule'. He also cites the Morisco Al-Ḥajarī as saying that in Tunis 'there are two plagues: one is the renegades and the other is the [rural nomadic] Arabs, and this is also the case in Algiers and Tlemcen'; the Moriscos, Epalza says, suffered at the hands of these two social groups, but got along well with the urban-dwelling Moors (234–5).

Moriscos in exile were called by many names, many of them exogenous, including 'Morisco', 'Moor', 'renegade' and 'Turk'. The unnamed Morisco (see chapter 5) who tells the story of the *valenciana* in Espinel's novel, and who is a major and quite likeable character over seven chapters, is – according to the language of the text – a Morisco, a Christian, a Moor, a renegade, a Turk, a Spaniard and an Algerian, but most insistently a renegade. From both sides he is both one of *us* and one of *them*. The terms 'Morisco', 'Moor', 'renegade' and 'Turk' are saturated with a dense history, alien perspectives and ambivalent semantics.

One 'Morisco renegade' who became particularly famous – especially after he was burned by the Inquisition – was Alicax, whose story is told in connection with the martyrdom of a Valencian friar named Miguel de Aranda in 1577, when both Sosa and Cervantes were captives in Algiers. The main source is Sosa's *Diálogo de los mártires* (*Topografía* IV, 179r–83r), although the story with some variations also figures in two hundred lines of an early propagandistic play that Cervantes never published, *El trato de Argel*, which Lope de Vega would draw from in his own play *Los cautivos de Argel*.[37] Besides these sources, considerably more can be learned about Alicax's background from the inquisitional records of his trial in 1576, in which the main narrative voice is his own, however much it may be mediated by interrogation and transcription.[38] Following Sosa's account, which is more detailed and nuanced than the one in Cervantes' play, the fisherman Alicax and his brother Caxetta escaped from the Valencian coast and settled with their families and relatives in the Morisco-populated port city of Cherchell west of Algiers. Alicax armed a modestly-sized corsair boat

> with which he captured along that entire coast a large number of Christians whom he sold in Algiers, and also brought with him many Moriscos from that kingdom, transporting them across to Barbary. With his successes Alicax became so proud that, to show everyone how fortunate he was, he painted his brigantine all green and put many flags and banners on it, which was quite a sight.

---

[37] This is story 23 (162–73) in the edition by Emilio Sola y José María Parreño of the *Diálogo*. It is also told in Cervantes' play by the character Sebastián in a lengthy monologue in act 1, vv. 489–686.

[38] In his edition of Lope's play *Los cautivos de Argel*, Natalio Ohanna gives an account of the inquisitorial records related to Alicax's trial (17–21) and, as an appendix, provides a full transcription of this valuable document. I am grateful to Ohanna for sending me a digital version of the original document. As he points out, the spelling of Alicax's name varies widely in the document, as also occurs with his first name. In modern Arabic-English transcription, his name would most likely be 'Abdallāh 'Alīkashīt. The most consistent form of the name in the document appears to be Alicaxet. I've settled for 'Alicax' because that's how it appears in the texts of Sosa and Cervantes, and also because it often appears in the document more or less as such.

But after some time he suffered misfortune because, when certain Spanish galleys found him on the Valencian coast, they caught him with his brigantine. Taken thus and put to the oar, which is usually what they do to those sorts of people, the lord count of Oliva, whose vassal he had been, heard about this and tried to get hold of him to punish him because in his lands – more than in others, since in them he was born and was knowledgeable – [Alicax] had inflicted great damage and in particular had taken away to Barbary a large number of Moriscos, his vassals.

But the inquisitors of that kingdom of Valencia, informed of this and considering the crimes of this Moor to be so enormous and their punishment to be within the scope of the Holy Office, had him taken to the jails of the Inquisition. (IV, 179r–v)

While the double story of Alicax and fray Miguel de Aranda is just beginning, the story of Alicax is almost over. He refuses to back down in any way, and is condemned to death by the Inquisition:

in the month of April of 1577, the Moor Caxetta, his sister-in-law [Alicax's wife] and nephews heard the certain news given by some Moors who fled from Valencia – as they do every day – that Alicax, after being a prisoner of the Holy Office for some time, was finally condemned for his great guilt and crimes, for having been pertinacious in all the hearings he was given, without ever acknowledging his guilt, but rather very obstinately saying he was a Moor and wanted to die a Moor, and finally, at the beginning of November 1576, having been handed over to secular justice, he was publicly burned in the city of Valencia. (IV, 180r)

The document of his trial coincides with this trajectory but offers a much broader picture of him. Alicax informs the tribunal of the names of his entire family over three generations, including when he married each of his two wives and when they died, and what children they and a slave woman bore him. He says that since his family lived in the countryside, his parents said he was never baptised. He spent his youth labouring in the orchards and fishing. When he was twenty, presumably around 1556, his father took him and a dozen others – mainly Moriscos and captive Moors from North Africa – to the town of Cherchell west of Algiers. He then worked in the fields and at sea, first as a soldier and later as a boat captain, and participated in large-scale activities including the sieges of Oran/Mazalquivir and Malta. In time he became an accomplished corsair captain, transporting Moriscos including family members and former neighbours to North Africa, seizing ships and their goods, and engaging in a few raids in which he captured Christians in Spain and sold them in Algiers, but finally was captured by Spanish galleys. Witnesses corroborate the main outline but testify that he must have been baptised because nobody escaped baptism, and that his Christian name was

Francisco, which, as Ohanna observes, is the name that Lope gives the Alicax figure in his play, thus implying that Lope didn't rely on Cervantes' play alone for information about Alicax (282–92).

Alicax's life and death serve in Sosa's *Topografía* as background information for the story of fray Miguel de Aranda's martyrdom. Were it not for the fate of fray Miguel, Alicax's story would have been relegated to the annals of the Inquisition without finding its way into Sosa's and Cervantes' texts. What happened to fray Miguel de Aranda was very much the doing of Alicax's family and other Moriscos from Cherchell and Algiers within the dynamics of relations between Spain and the Maghrib. This priest is captured with other Christians in a corsair raid on the Catalan coast. When the boat arrives in Cherchell, Caxetta enters to ask for news about his brother, who he knows is a prisoner in Valencia though no one dares to tell him that Alicax is a prisoner of the Inquisition.

What characterises the Moriscos in both texts is their deep anger, their resentment against Spain and especially the Inquisition, their collective power in doing harm, their nasty treatment of Christians and their thirst for blood and vengeance, qualities that are all hyperbolised to validate this tale of Christian martyrdom. Caxetta proposes to Alicax's wife and children that they buy a Christian to offer him in exchange for Alicax. At the slave market in Algiers he buys the priest Miguel de Aranda as a promising pawn for bargaining. For many months Alicax's family treats fray Miguel as cruelly as possible to try to force an exchange, but in April of 1577 they finally get word from escaping Moriscos that Alicax was burned by the Inquisition half a year earlier. Outraged, they decide that the best revenge would be 'for them to do the same to Fray Miguel and publicly burn him alive' (*Topografía* IV, 180v).

Central to the story is the changing logic of *quid pro quo*. These Moriscos, regardless of whatever else they may be, are masters in the art of making deals. The whole Mediterranean functioned by this logic, and the frontier protagonists (renegades, Moriscos, Jews, merchants, captives, ransomers, spies, etc.) all worked according to these principles. The only institution immune to this logic was the intransigent Inquisition, with which it was impossible to make a deal. The Moriscos in this story don't find out until too late that their adversary is none other than the Holy Office, and thus they persist in proposing the even exchange of a Morisco corsair for a Christian priest. Once they find out about the burning, the *quid pro quo* changes from a live man for a live man – where both sides stand to gain – to blood for blood and fire for fire, all as an act of public catharsis matching loss for loss, death for death. Curiously, Alicax anticipates this kind of *quid pro quo* in his testimony before the Inquisition, although he sees his counterpart in this equation as a corsair captain rather than a priest: 'He said that if he were to live, he would live as a Moor, and if he were to die, he would die as a Moor, and if they were to condemn him, the same would be done to others in Barbary, and to a captain they are holding there, and that he had nothing more to say' (293 [51r]). The avenging Moriscos believe they respond to the Inquisition in its own language. The Christians in the story as well as the Christian authors Sosa and Cervantes (or his mouthpiece in the play, Sebastián) deny any *quid pro quo*, seeing rather the just punishment of a guilty apostate corsair disproportionately linked with the unjust sacrifice of an innocent priest, a perfect scenario for martyrdom. We'll resume the story of fray Miguel de Aranda when considering martyrs in the next chapter.

As far as I'm aware, there's no Muslim account of Alicax that might give transcendent meaning to his life and death, but Sosa's account tells us clearly enough that he was burned not for his 'crimes' as a corsair but rather for his 'pertinacious' adherence to Islam. His guilt consists in his being an apostate, a renegade. In the same text, *Diálogo de los mártires* (*Topografía* IV, 150r), Sosa tells the story of a renowned Castilian corsair named Juan Cañete who caused enormous harm and was greatly feared in Algiers until he was caught in 1550. After nine years in prison, a Greek renegade named Caur Ali killed him in a way that showed none of the characteristics of how martyrs die, yet this story figures within the series of edifying narratives associated with martyrdom, even if Sosa himself doesn't insist that all the protagonists are strictly martyrs. What's more, Gonzalo de Céspedes y Meneses would pick up on this character and hyperbolise his heroic and 'martyrly' qualities in the novel *Poema trágico del español Gerardo*. By Sosa's criteria, the Morisco corsair Alicax would be much more of a martyr than the Christian martyr Cañete, since he in effect died for his religious faith, except that he was an apostate who deserved to die.

Despite Sosa's unmasked antipathy towards the Moriscos, the details of his narrative provide interesting glimpses into their position and roles in Valencia and Algeria. The clandestine migration of Moriscos from the Spanish to the Barbary coast happens 'every day', and Moriscos such as those in Cherchell facilitate these escapes, making for sizeable communities of Moriscos in many cities of the Maghrib already decades before the expulsion, communities that control ports like Cherchell and already have a voice in a city like Algiers. In Algiers itself we see how the politics plays out between the Moriscos, the beylerbey, renegades, ransoming clergy, and so on. We're also given a quick look into the quasi-feudal internal colonialism practised in the kingdom of Valencia, where the lord (count of Oliva) still regards the long-escaped Alicax as a vassal and wants to give him exemplary punishment for taking away so many other Morisco vassals, his labour force. Once Alicax is caught, the issue of jurisdiction arises precisely because he's a Morisco. Whereas the text leads us to understand that any other Muslim corsair would be 'put to the oar' when caught, the feudal lord claims his right to punish his vassal but is in turn overridden by the Inquisition, which regards Alicax as falling entirely within its domain (*Topografía* IV, 179v). Of course, the Inquisition required all renegades to submit to its authority, but its treatment would generally be much harsher in the case of Morisco renegades.

The case of Francisco Pérez alias Alí reveals the same inquisitorial logic in its starkest contradiction (Benítez Sánchez-Blanco 190–1). Deported from Granada to La Mancha in 1570 when he was nine years old, he and his family were expelled in the general expulsion when he was fifty. After they were rejected in France, their first destination, they settled in Algiers. A few years later, in 1615, when fishing on the Algerian coast, he was captured by a Mallorcan corsair and processed by the Mallorcan Inquisition. Alí firmly argued that since Philip III had expelled him for being a Moor (Muslim), he *was* one and wanted to remain one. As Rafael Benítez argues, this put the inquisitor in a bind, exposing the fact that Moriscos were punished not for putting the security of the State in danger, nor for being apostates as such, but rather for belonging to the 'Morisco nation'. By clinging to the incoherent 'apostasy' argument, the Holy Office in effect condemned him to be burned at the stake for the same reason that he (as a Morisco) was expelled in the first place.

Another case, well known thanks to the investigations of Mercedes García-Arenal and several others,[39] is that of the Morisco Diego Díaz, twice expelled from Spain and twice returned. At the time of the expulsion in 1611, when he would have been twenty-six years old,[40] he went briefly to France, and soon after his clandestine return he was caught and deported to Algiers – 'Even though I was expelled from Spain as a Moor, I did not arrive in Algiers as one' (Kagan and Dyer 162) – where he says he spent some months before escaping back to Spain on a fishing boat and swimming to shore. Significantly, he belonged to those 'old' Moriscos whose ancestors had settled in Castile centuries earlier and converted to Christianity before the royal edict of 1502, and he was from Daimiel in La Mancha, one of the five *Villas del Campo de Calatrava* where, as Trevor

---

[39] *Inquisición y moriscos*, 140–50; also included in her anthology *Los moriscos*, 271–84. Diego Díaz is the subject of an extensive chapter of *Inquisitorial Inquiries*, ed. Kagan and Dyer, 147–78, and of commentary by Trevor Dadson, *Los moriscos de Villarrubia*, 459–64.

[40] Dadson (*Los moriscos de Villarrubia*, 460) notes that Diego Díaz was baptised in May of 1585, and would have been twenty-six at the time of the expulsion in 1611. Whereas Díaz testifies that he was then '16 or 17, maybe 20', Dadson – citing Rafael Benítez – argues that it would have been in Díaz's interests to claim he was a decade younger than he was, since an adolescent couldn't be held as responsible as a grown man. Dadson specifies that Diego Díaz was actually expelled twice to France (before his third expulsion to Algiers) because he first returned but was caught *en route* in Haro, imprisoned for three months and brought back to France. Dadson also certifies the date of Díaz's confession of his circumcision: 12 July 1618 (in Avignon), i.e. more than five years after he escaped back to Christian lands – a delay that the prosecutor found suspicious and prodded him to explain.

Dadson has amply demonstrated, assimilated Moriscos survived the expulsion and reintegrated (Dadson, *Los moriscos de Villarrubia*). He was tried by the Inquisition in 1632–34,[41] two decades after the expulsion officially concluded, at a time when the remaining Moriscos were of course no longer viewed as an internal threat. Besides some of the usual accusations levelled at religiously aberrant Moriscos (not eating pork, eating meat during Lent, changing clothes on Friday, etc.), the main question was whether his circumcision had been forced or voluntary. The inquisitors believed that Muslims didn't force anyone to be circumcised, and if they did one could always opt for death instead (García-Arenal, *Los moriscos*, 275). The prosecutor, taking into account that 'the offender is of the caste of Moors who indubitably belonged to the sect of Muhammad and for that reason were thrown out of Spain', repeatedly uses the verb *renegar* when surmising what Diego Díaz did when he was circumcised: he must have reneged (García-Arenal, *Los moriscos*, 275–8). Inquisitorial trials of Moriscos before the expulsion generally focused on signs of apostasy but not on acts or ceremonies of reneging, which were in the province of renegades. To simplify a complex and fascinating case: Diego Díaz insisted that he was forcibly circumcised, he skilfully answered all questions, and after a former captive named don Bernardino Medrano testified that he had seen Moriscos customarily taken by force and circumcised in Algiers, Diego was let off with the light sentence of a reprimand in the courtroom and public penitence.

With Alicax, Francisco Pérez (Alí) and Diego Díaz, we see Mediterranean mutations of the apostasy trials of Moriscos. Whereas previously the question was usually whether Moriscos were *still Moors* despite their baptism, the question now is whether their contact with Maghribian Muslims has reconfirmed or renewed or reinitiated them in Islam and turned them into renegades. No longer is the prime evidence located within the sovereignty of Christian countries but is rather to be imagined in Muslim lands, most particularly Algiers in these three cases, and the religio-political hostilities between Christian and Muslim lands infiltrate into the Inquisition's handling of apostasy. The prosecutor in Diego Díaz's trial wants to know all about his exile in Algiers, including who he associated with, what he wore, what he said about his religion, and so on (Kagan and Dyer 157–8). The inquisitors found themselves in a troublesome vacuum since there were no personal witnesses

---

[41] Kagan and Dyer (*Inquisitorial Inquiries*, 149–62) give a reliable chronology of the trial, which would have begun sometime in 1632. An attorney apparently hired by Díaz requested his release from the jails of the Inquisition in Cuenca in November 1632, as well as the release of his wife, Magdalena del Castillo, who was ill and 'about to give birth'. She was released, and he was too, it seems, but he was again imprisoned on 25 August 1633, and had his first hearing the following day. The sentence was delivered on 18 January 1634, whereupon he was released from prison.

to inform them: only the accused could answer these questions about himself concerning this crossover phase in which he denies having converted to Islam. By inquisitorial criteria, Moriscos were no ordinary renegades. Most male renegades were circumcised and had some explaining to do, but if they insisted on their practice of crypto-Christianity they were more or less let off the hook, as it were. The problem for Morisco renegades was that, when interrogated about their supposed conversion to Islam, they were suspected of harbouring crypto-Islamic beliefs and practices now masked as crypto-Christian beliefs and practices. Or to put it simply, they were systematically under suspicion of being Muslims no matter what they did, and their contact with Muslims would have revived the Islamic proclivity they were seen as always having within them. A returned Morisco comes to embody Algiers (or anywhere else in Muslim lands) and Islam itself.

Was Diego Díaz a Muslim? The list of accusations points to a number of practices associated with Islam. He claims that certain things about life in Algiers repel him such as how men urinate or engage in sodomy with slave boys.[42] Moreover, he impresses the judges with how well he knows the Christian prayers. Ultimately his argument is this: 'If I had followed and kept the law of Muhammad I could be in Algiers right now, since it is a land of plenty and full of vice. When I got there, they wanted to marry me off, but because I follow the law of Our Lord Jesus Christ I returned to Spain in a fishing boat' (Kagan and Dyer 161). He seems to be more Christian than Muslim, not only because he's defending himself in an inquisitorial trial but also because he shows himself to be more at home in Spain than in Algiers. And he understands the Spanish-Catholic system of values and beliefs so well that he can manipulate it to the judges' satisfaction, in excellent Castilian, procuring about as light a sentence as the Inquisition would allow without losing face, even though the prosecutor had recommended in vain that he be tortured (García-Arenal, *Los moriscos*, 278). The question is probably not whether Diego Díaz *was* a Muslim or a Christian, since religious doctrines don't seem to be of prime interest to him, but rather what strategies would allow him to get back to his life: 'I beg your lordship … to make the inquiries quickly, so that I may see my wife and children and return to live as a married man. In all my life I've never known Moorish ceremonies or anything about them' (Kagan and Dyer 163). For a 'normal' renegade, the Inquisition would have dispatched such a

---

[42] 'I went into a building where there were two or three hundred young Turkish men … I saw that when they needed to urinate they lowered their trousers and pulled their skirts up and squatted like women. Then they took their shameful parts and hit them several times against the walls to clean the urine off. They say that if even one drop of urine gets on their shirt, they will go to hell … These Moors bought slave boys to sleep with them. Look, my lord, this is depraved! Why would anyone want to be a Moor?' (Kagan and Dyer 162–3).

clear-cut case in a reasonably short time, yet here even Diego's pregnant wife was incarcerated for some time, and he himself languished in prison for most of the two-year trial period, twenty years after he returned to Spain. This is because he was seen as a *Morisco* renegade, and a Morisco *renegade*, and was thus worse off than either a Morisco who wasn't a renegade or a renegade who wasn't a Morisco.

Unlike the case of Diego Díaz, records of the Inquisition provide us with the trials of numerous other Moriscos or 'Turkish' slaves, both men and women, who were accused and often condemned for apostasy for reverting to a religion – Islam – they probably had never abandoned, regardless of their having been baptised. Those seen as apostatised converts to Christianity were often condemned to death. Let the following example suffice for many. A woman named Arabia – recorded as being from Peligrat, Turkey – was enslaved in Palermo in 1603 when she was about thirty, baptised as Margarita in 1606, tried for apostasy in 1615–17 and condemned to death for *pertinacia*. Over the months of her trial she was asked the same questions time and again, and most often insisted that she had never intended to be a Christian and that she wanted to die a 'Turk'. One can only imagine what she was going through as she made the following kinds of declarations (in the scribe's style), some just days apart (AHN 1748, no. 25):

> She said she would rather be a dead Turk [turca] than a live Christian. (10v)
>
> She said that if she consented to be baptised, she did so with her tongue and not her heart, and that the ill treatment [la fuerza y malos tratamientos] of her master forced her to do so, and she wants to be a Turk and not a Christian. (12v)
>
> She said … that if they wanted to burn her, let them burn her. (16v)
>
> She said that she had been touched in her heart by our Lord God from now on to leave the sect of Muhammad [la seta de Mahoma] entirely, because she has understood the warnings she has been given that she strayed, and thus she was converting to our holy Catholic faith in which she promised to live always, submitting to whatever the tribunal might command, like a baby bird to its mother [como un polluelo a su madre]. (16v–17r)
>
> She asked why they had her as a prisoner, for she doesn't want to be a Christian or a Turk. (18r)
>
> [Reminded of her recent confession,] she responded with arrogance and laughter, calling the two interpreters Lutherans, saying they were beasts, and that she hadn't said such words … She said that just as she entered these prisons as a Turk, she wants to leave as a Turk, and she repeated this twice and said she doesn't want to be a Christian. (18r)
>
> The said Margarita responded that since she entered these prisons she lost her baptism and all the other Christian things, and that she doesn't want any religion [no quiere ninguna ley]. (21r)

> The said Margarita said that they were all asses, and that she doesn't want her advocate or the interpreters or anyone. (21v)
>
> She said she wanted to go to hell, and that Christians go to hell and Moors to heaven, responding to everything with great haughtiness and pertinacity. (22r)

Days after these last statements the inquisitional tribunal of Sicily condemned Arabia/Margarita to the stake for apostasy. Conditioned by the interrogation techniques and her imprisonment, and filtered through two interpreters (who grossly misrepresent her, they say she says) as well as a scribe, her testimony is at several removes from us. As was customary, the scribe duly records not only what they say she said but also, more directly, her defiant and scornful attitude so contrary to a bearing of submissive contrition that might win her some leniency. Ultimately, judging her as an apostate whose apparently forced baptism is deemed valid, the tribunal views her religious itinerary as a double crossover, from there to here and back, whereas she mostly insists that she never veered from Islam at all. Most unusual, perhaps, are those declarations to the effect that she allegedly wants to have nothing to do with *either* religion, seemingly uttered in moments of exasperation unless these statements are misrepresented. In any event, though she was a captured Turkish slave, she was trapped in the same logical bind that Alicax and many other Moriscos were.[43] Though they were crypto-Muslims, the Inquisition's legal criteria

---

[43] These folders of documents from the Sicilian Inquisition (AHN 1747–8) show comparable cases, and other instances have been found in archives elsewhere. For example, Míquel de Epalza comments on the absurd, merciless fate of Zara / Catalina de Barón (AHN 1747, no. 22): 'The case of Catalina Barón, from Bellús near Xátiva [Valencia], is paradigmatic, as studied by Cardaillac. Expelled from the port of Cartagena towards Orán with her husband, she was abducted before reaching Algerian territory by the galley captain who was transporting them. Sometime later the captain gave her to another ship captain who took her to Palermo, where he had her as a slave. She was given over to the marquis de la Mora, who freed her and procured a passport for her to go to Tunis. Denounced by a cousin of hers, a slave, as a *conversa* and *renegada*, she had to suffer a long and degrading trial by the Inquisition, which had no scruples regarding the contradiction of accusing her of having reneged the Christian faith, which had been imposed on Muslims who were expelled from Spain for being Muslims' (*Los moriscos antes y después*, 221–2). Following up on research done in the Torre do Tombo in Lisbon, Saylín Álvarez (24–61) documents and analyses a fascinating case of nineteen Moriscos from several families – mostly women and children, because seven men had fled to the coast – who were captured in 1599 near Tangiers as they attempted to escape to the Maghrib and later taken to Lisbon and tried by the Inquisition from 1600–05 for trying to leave Spain illegally, just a few years before the expulsion of the Moriscos (1609–14) would make it illegal for them *not* to leave. This boatload of crypto-Muslims was essentially accused of apostasy. In particular, Álvarez shows how the highly resourceful strategies of three Moriscas – Lucía de Guzmán, Isabel Herrera and Inés López – evolved over the course of their lengthy trial, beginning with inventions of false genealogies.

turned them into renegades. On the other side of the spectrum was Diego Díaz, who apparently was not a crypto-Muslim but was nonetheless tried for apostasy, and acquitted.

8. Illustrious *conversos* from Muslim lands: Ḥasan al-Wazzān al-Fāsī/Leo Africanus, Mawlāy Shaykh/Felipe de África, Mehmed Cheleby/ don Felipe, etc.

A highly significant yet numerically minute category of renegades is made up of eminent Muslims who settled in Christian lands and converted to Christianity, whether temporarily or permanently.[44] Some were exiles, some diplomats, others captives. Some stayed, others left. The most renowned of these could perhaps be counted on two hands, yet the conversion of each one of them was celebrated as a triumph of Christianity over Islam. Popes, cardinals, kings and grandees were involved in their conversion as baptisers and/or patrons, typically conferring their names on the converts.[45] Pope Leo X, whose baptismal name was Giovanni de' Medici, bestowed his names on Ḥasan al-Wazzān al-Fāsī (i.e. from Fez) when he baptised him as Ioannes Leo Africanus, a name that Ḥasan al-Wazzān rendered into Arabic during his remaining years in Italy as Yuḥannā al-Asad al-Gharnāṭī (John the Lion the Granadan). Captured by a Spanish corsair in 1518 and baptised by the pope in 1520, he spent the next seven years devoted to projects including the *Descrittione dell'Africa* until he apparently stole away in 1527 to settle in Tunis. As Natalie Zemon Davis points out, his return as a high-profile apostate to Muslim lands would have put him in a precarious situation and given him limited options as a traveller, husband and father, diplomat, writer and scholar (249–57). Commenting on a fable about a trickster bird (which Davis

---

[44] There have been several studies of converts of this category, the most wide-ranging and authoritative to date being that of Beatriz Alonso Acero, *Sultanes de Berbería en tierras de la cristiandad* (2006). Alonso Acero also co-authors with Miguel Ángel de Bunes the very substantive 'Estudio preliminar' of *Felipe de África*, which I draw from below. Natalie Zemon Davis's classic study *Trickster travels* is of course an inspired enquiry into Leo Africanus, whose own *Descrittione dell'Africa* remains the primary source of knowledge about him.

[45] Miguel Ángel de Bunes and Beatriz Alonso Acero elaborate on this: 'the practice of bestowing on neophytes the Christian name of their patrons was very common: don Felipe Gaspar Alonso, grandson of the Sa'di Muley Cidan, who was captured in 1635 by the governor of Mamora, managed to escape from his prison and get to Spain, where he would show his desire for conversion and was baptised in the royal chapel, receiving the names of Felipe (in honour of his patron Philip IV), Gaspar (in reference to the count-duke of Olivares), and Alonso (for the patriarch of the Indies, brother of the duke of Medina Sidonia, who baptised him). For his part, Gaspar de Benimerín received his name from don Gaspar de Andrada, governor of the islands of Cabo Verde, where the Moroccan was converted'. Bunes and Alonso go on to relate the conversion of three illustrious Persian emissaries who converted to Christianity in Spain and were integrated into the court of Philip III ('Estudio preliminar', lv–lvi).

uses as a leitmotif in her book), he concludes that 'when a man sees his advantage, he always follows it ... I will do like the trickster bird ... If the Africans are being vituperated, [this writer] will use as a clear excuse that he was not born in Africa, but in Granada. And if the Granadans are being railed against, he will find the excuse that he was not brought up in Granada' (110).

The Sa'di prince and contender to the throne of Morocco Mawlāy Shaykh (in Spanish, Muley Xeque) was baptised at the monastery of El Escorial by the Cardinal Archbishop of Toledo – in the presence of the papal nuncio, the future pope Pius V – as Philip II and his daughter the princess Isabel Clara Eugenia, at Mawlāy Shaykh's request, patronised the ceremony. Now named Felipe de África and even Felipe de Austria, the new *converso* was declared a grandee of Spain, was given titles and generous sources of income, was treated well in every respect and in no way disappointed those who had pledged their prestige on him. His life could be subdivided into four stages: (1) 1566–78, from his birth to the battle of Alcazarquivir, after which the victor Aḥmad al-Mansūr claimed the throne; (2) 1578–93, his exile for eleven years in Portugal and then several more in Andalusia, culminating in his conversion; (3) 1593–1609, from his conversion to his departure for Milan just before the expulsion of the Moriscos; and (4) 1609–21, his final years in northern Italy.

As Miguel Ángel de Bunes and Beatriz Alonso observe, there is nothing in the prince's behaviour until his sudden conversion at twenty-seven that suggests that he might convert to Christianity. On the contrary, he was notorious for his youthful unruliness, for having Moriscos plot to liberate him from his de facto captivity in Spain, for ransoming Morisco slaves, for keeping an entourage of up to fifty-seven people far beyond his means, and for continually pestering Philip II with requests for everything from money to political and military aid to overthrow Aḥmad al-Mansūr. Quite simply, he must have realised that his options on the other side of the Strait of Gibraltar were reduced to almost nil and that his virtual detention and dependence on Philip II augured a dim future. In contrast, as a prince of Africa he would have the gateways of privilege, status and wealth opened up to him if he were to renege Islam and embrace Christianity. He saw his advantage and followed it. It was a logical choice, even though it would scandalise his entourage and a great many Muslims in Morocco.

There is also an entirely different explanation of his conversion, or at least one that perhaps explains what triggered it: shortly after being transferred to the city of Andújar, Jaén, he experienced a *coup de foudre* upon seeing the image of the famous Virgen de la Cabeza in a hermitage the night before the start of the annual procession and pilgrimage dedicated to her.[46] The

---

[46] Catherine Infante explores how images of the Virgin were instrumental in the conversion of several illustrious Muslims in Europe, and focuses on the case of Mawlāy Shaykh as represented in Lope's play *Tragedia del rey don Sebastián y bautismo del príncipe de Marruecos* (101–30).

image of the Virgen de la Cabeza and the pilgrimage so impressed him that he suddenly wanted to convert, and let this be known. It is significant that in Mawlāy Shaykh's case, as in that of other comparable conversions, the conversion itself appears to have nothing to do with questions of doctrine (e.g. the Trinity, Christ's divinity, redemption from sin, etc.) and everything to do with a figure common to Islam and Christianity – Maryam/Mary – except that Catholicism multiplies the attributes of Mary into many distinct Virgins and represents them in images often capable of captivating the emotions. Although Lope de Vega's play *Tragedia del rey don Sebastián y bautismo del príncipe de Marruecos* explains the prince's conversion entirely in relation to this event, without regard for his life circumstances – and Mawlāy Shaykh's biographer Jaime Oliver Asín takes Lope's play as the primary *historical* document elucidating the prince's conversion and baptism – the event itself rings authentic, much as it fills a vacuum of convenience. Moreover, everything from here on confirms that Mawlāy Shaykh *became* what was regarded as an exemplary Christian, and that he practised this in many ways, returning twice to Andújar to thank the Virgin for his conversion, and particularly in Italy (Milan and Vigevano), where he devoted himself to masses, fasts and even flagellation (Bunes and Alonso, 'Estudio preliminar', xlvi). In his will he named his natural daughter Josefa de África, a nun in Zamora, as his heiress.

Beatriz Alonso Acero documents a few dozen cases of members of Maghribian royal families in exile in Europe, demonstrating the strategies of displaced dynasties or displaced branches of dynasties in taking refuge especially in Spain and Italy during the sixteenth and seventeenth centuries. Among others, supplanted Wattāsids and Sa'dīs from Morocco, Zayyānids from the kingdom of Tlemcen and Ḥafṣids from Tunis went into exile and tried to make their worth known either as converts or as potential political allies. A good number of these men and women, then, did in fact convert to Christianity. What we don't know is exactly why they did so. To say that they freely embraced Christianity indicates that there was generally no coercion as such to convert, yet in most instances the converts understood that there was little chance of their returning to their homelands and that conversion would make their life in exile more accepted. They also knew that their income and financial security, often drawn from the royal coffers, would most likely be increased if they converted. These elites were generally well-received and awarded generous pensions. While circumstances thus tended to favour conversion, there is little evidence as to how religious considerations came into play regarding sentiment and belief, and the motivational ingredients of this religious 'embrace' are thus hard to disentangle. In any event, the relative frequency of these conversions among exiled royalty may have removed some of the scandal and stigma that tended to accompany the abandonment of Islam.

Within this group of 'renegades' I'd like to consider the story of another renowned apostate, Mehmed Cheleby, as recounted by the French envoy to Tunis in 1666, Laurent d'Arvieux – a superb connoisseur of cultures and languages of the Mediterranean – who came to know him well through many hours of conversation, and also discussed Mehmed at length with others who knew him. Yet even d'Arvieux would not have been able to foresee some of the dramatic final twists in the story. In broad outline, d'Arvieux portrays Mehmed, son of the Tunisian dey Aḥmad Khuja, as cordial, full of *esprit*, strikingly handsome, prone to indulge in pleasures and enamoured of European arts from a young age:

> Mehmed Cheleby loved music, comedy and the other kinds of entertainment practiced among Christians, which his slaves had given him a taste for. He had them stage performances that gave him infinite pleasure. The desire to see Europe, which had been so delightfully portrayed for him, made him want to take refuge there; by this means he would distance himself from his wife, whom he was unable to love, and from his father, whom he feared.[47]

He gathered all the portable wealth he could and arranged for a boat to take him and his slaves to Sicily, where the viceroy had him taken with all honours to Palermo and then instructed in 'our religion'. Duly informed of this, Philip IV ordered that he be treated like a prince and baptised with his name. In the company of the viceroy Pedro Fajardo and vicereine, who acted in the name of the king and queen of Spain, the archbishop of Palermo baptised him (in 1646, under the age of twenty) as don Felipe – in fact, as Inocencio Felipe Pedro Fernando Ignacio, though he too would become known as don Felipe de África. He later went to Rome and was ceremoniously received by Pope Innocent X, who gave him a Greek-style crucifix 'that he still has today'. From Rome he went to Spain, where the king accorded him a generous pension and conferred on him the title of knight of Santiago. He chose to live in Málaga, where he soon fell in love with a young woman who 'played the lute flawlessly, had a profound knowledge of music and sang marvelously' (63). Back in Tunis his choleric father, Ahmed Dey, disinherited him and had his wife and servants strangled, believing that they had known his plans. Ahmed Dey died not long afterward. Meanwhile, don Felipe incurred debts, exhausted his credit and ruined his reputation as he gave himself over to pleasure and scandal. D'Arvieux observes: 'Besides, the libertine life he was leading was not

---

[47] 'Mehmed Cheleby aimait la musique, la comédie et les autres divertissements usités chez les Chrétiens, dont ses esclaves lui avaient donné le goût; il les faisait exercer à des représentations et s'y plaisait infiniment. L'envie de voir l'Europe, dont on lui avait fait des peintures fort agréables, lui fit prendre l'envie de s'y retirer; par ce moyen, il s'éloignait de sa femme qu'il ne pouvait aimer, et de son père, qu'il craignait' (d'Arvieux 62).

to the liking of a nation so religious as Spain' (64). He in turn was now weary of his life there.

It was at this low point that don Felipe's mother contacted an English pilot and former slave of his to have him brought back to Tunis. His justification for leaving Spain was that he was going to spend the holy year of 1650 in Rome. The pope offered to grant him the title of knight of Malta. Under this pretext, don Felipe guilefully had his household, including his presumed wife the musician and her mother, board a ship purportedly bound for Italy that was conveniently blown off course into the harbour of La Goletta. Dressed in Spanish style with his hair grown out, Mehmed was escorted in Tunis to the dey and the divan, which decided unanimously to have him burned as an apostate.

> The dey, who was a creature of his father and wanted at least to save his life, spoke in his favour, arguing that his youth and the fear of the harsh disposition of his father had brought this misfortune upon him; that he deserved to be given some leeway, since he had come back of his own accord without being forced to do so, and could have remained among the Christians with honour; that his view was that he should be promenaded throughout the city dressed as he was, to be exposed to the cries and insults of the people, and then delivered to his mother. (66)

He had not only insults but also eggs and ordure hurled at him – telling d'Arvieux years later that death would have been less agonising than these affronts – but was handed over to his mother, who welcomed him with a flood of joyful tears, had him shaved, dressed in Turkish attire and sent the next day back to the dey, who received him well and urged him to live as an exemplary Muslim.

> His mother's financial largesse to him proved to be insufficient as he reverted to his lavish way of life:
>
> In Turkish dress he led the same life as he had in Christian dress: he would go from one garden to another, spend his days and nights in the debauchery of wine, women and *garçons* – he had picked up a large number of these sorts of people. [...] But the continual scandals he provoked prevented his being given employment in the Republic ... He was always regarded as a Christian, and it was to no avail that he called himself Mehmed Cheleby since the children always taunted him by shouting 'don Felipe'.[48]

---

[48] 'Il menait sous l'habit turc la même vie qu'il avait menée sous celui de Chrétien: il courait d'un jardin à l'autre, passait les jours et les nuits dans la débauche du vin, des femmes et des jeunes garçons; il avait ramassé un grand nombre de ces sortes de gens. [...] Mais les scandales continuels qu'il donnait empêchèrent qu'on lui donnât aucun emploi dans la République ... On le regardait toujours comme Chrétien, et il avait beau se nommer Mehmed Cheleby, les enfants lui criaient toujours "Don Philippe"' (67).

In spite of renewed attempts at demonstrating he was a devout Muslim, he was unable to dissuade people from believing that he was a Christian 'in his soul'. As d'Arvieux remarks:

> What would people have thought if they knew as I did that he wore the golden crucifix that the pope had given him? For although he wore it disgracefully, being as he was an apostate and an extravagant debaucher, nothing more would have been required to have him burned. […] Though he loved music, the symphony, ballets, comedies and other European divertimenti, he was much more discreet after his return from [the hajj in] Mecca. (67)

He even settled a dispute between Murad and Mehmed Beigs, each accompanied by an army of 'fifteen or twenty thousand men ready to cut each others' throats over this quarrel', and the pasha rewarded him publicly for this. According to d'Arvieux, Mehmed Cheleby would often meet secretly with Le Vacher, the apostolic vicar in Carthage and consul in Tunis, about 'the state of his conscience. But what he had to do to return to the bosom of the Church was so difficult, since it would require having himself burned, that until Mr. Le Vacher's departure they were unable to resolve anything' (68).

This is about as far as d'Arvieux gets with the story. Sources gathered by Beatriz Alonso Acero confirm Mehmed Cheleby's clandestine return to Christianity at least as of 1656, when he proposed handing Tunis over to Philip IV and thus creating a Spanish protectorate on the ruins of ancient Carthage. The king paid no attention to this offer, which was made much later in 1670 to Louis XIV, who likewise declined. Having received no support from Christian rulers, don Felipe privately reverted once again to Islam. After participating in a government crisis in Tunis he was imprisoned, but the governor of Algiers intervened to send him on a diplomatic mission to Istanbul where he was named the new pasha of Algiers in 1672; death by plague prevented him from assuming his new position (Alonso Acero, *Sultanes en Berbería*, 155). These sources differ from d'Arvieux's account in that they ignore his cultural interests in Europe and personal problems in Tunis, stressing instead his desire for power and personal gain as the key to each of the four times that he as a recurrent renegade switched between Islam and Christianity. We don't know which if either of the two religions he was more inclined towards during these later years in Tunis and, what's more, d'Arvieux seems to minimise the impact of the hajj that Mehmed undertook. If the statement about secret conversations with Le Vacher is true, it certainly makes sense that this *bon vivant* would want to avoid being burned at the stake as a martyr for his beliefs. There is in fact nothing martyrly about him, nor are his two most fateful decisions – going to Europe and returning to Tunis – motivated by religious concerns.

Yet religion on both sides lays claims on him. As a voluntary exile from Tunis and an African prince to boot, he seems to be given no choice but to convert to Christianity, and from his vantage point this would suit his purposes since high prestige and income would accompany it. Besides his not getting along with his father or the wife his father picked for him, and thus wanting to get away from them, one might think of him as a cultural and artistic adventurer drawn to European art forms and culture, particularly as seen through d'Arvieux's early modern cosmopolitanism. Conversion would have been a necessary means for him to live in exile and act upon this strong sense of attraction, and even for him to live as a libertine beyond paternal control. In spite of his capriciousness and scandalous behaviour, he was indeed cultured and, among other skills and talents, was fluent in spoken and written Arabic, Turkish, Spanish and Italian. His return to Tunis likewise seems to have no religious motive, yet the stakes were now very high since he essentially arrived as a returning fugitive whose apostasy was manifest in his appearance, and in fact all too well known long before he arrived. Almost burned for this, he was later urged, according to d'Arvieux, to declare his Christianity openly and be burned for it as an Islamic apostate and Christian martyr. Yet, at least in his first two conversions, what he seems to want is to actualise his hedonism, a hedonism with a broad spectrum extending from sexual pleasures to the arts, and to be at least minimally tolerated despite these perceived excesses. He loves Europe but not enough to stay there permanently; Tunis draws him back, but he never seems to be entirely accepted or quite at home there. As a culturally versatile, multiple apostate, Mehmed Cheleby belongs to both sides and perhaps to neither.

9. Alcaide Mahamet the Jew

I conclude these renegade sketches with a depiction of the *alcaide* Mahamet, Sosa's master, because he shifted through a series of religious affiliations from Judaism to Islam to Christianity and back to Islam, thus encompassing all three of the major Abrahamic religions of the Mediterranean. To distinguish him from others named Mahamet (as transcribed into Spanish), Sosa adds his title *caide* or *alcaide* – one who governed lands and towns under the jurisdiction of Ottoman Algiers, or who held a prominent important position in the city – and an epithet indicating his Jewish origin, 'el judío'. Sosa also lists him among the thirty-five owners of corsair ships and names him among those who have the most sumptuous houses in Algiers (*Topografía* I, 14, 11r; I, 22, 18r; I, 39, 42r; Garcés, *Cervantes in Algiers*, 73–7).[49]

---

[49] As mentioned earlier, María Antonia Garcés, in her Introduction to the English translation of the first part of the *Topografía*, provides a revealing account of Sosa largely derived from her discoveries of new documentation. Among much else, she casts light on his captivity as well as on his singular slave-master Mahamet (41–65).

Alcaide Mahamet was also powerful and audacious. When Hasan Veneciano came to govern Algiers in 1577 'with the most rapacious greed for money the world had seen', he took possession of all the captives for ransom belonging to corsair captains, Turks and Moors. Not even his predecessor Rabadan Pasha dared to oppose him. The only one who did so was 'alcaide Mahamet the Jew, who never allowed him to take a knight of Malta and two clerics, all three of them his slaves. This cost them four and a half years of the most terrible captivity there has been in all of Algiers and Barbary' (*Topografía* II, 21.3, 84r). Though it's not made clear exactly how and why this resulted in such an abysmal slavery for these men, one of whom was Sosa, Mahamet's unique defiance towards the formidable Hasan signals a fearless character with political clout, especially remarkable in view of the low status of ethnic Jews in Algiers including those who converted to Islam (Sosa, *Topografía* I, 28, 23r–v).

The circumstances of Sosa's indirect portrait of him are highly conducive to misrepresentation, since Sosa by all indications suffered over four years of extremely harsh treatment at the hands of his master, being chained to a rock (as he puts it), confined several times in a dungeon cell, and subjected to hunger and cold, among other hardships. In addition to cruel master-slave relations, the fact that Mahamet was a serial renegade no doubt transferred to him the antipathy that Sosa felt towards renegades in general, a leitmotif throughout the *Topografía*. Mahamet's Jewish origins, deceitful Christianity and repeated espousal of Islam would be unlikely to arouse any sympathy from Sosa. Rather than portraying his own master, Sosa adroitly has his friend and visitor Antonio González de Torres do so as interlocutor in the *Diálogo de la captividad de Argel* (i.e. *Topografía* III, 1, 96r–7r).[50] The more González de Torres characterises Mahamet as a tyrannical, despicable atheist, the more Sosa can distance himself and express pious gratitude that such a cruel instrument of God's wrath should punish him for his own unspecified sins. Not only is the account of Mahamet in Sosa's text unreliable, it perhaps tells us next to nothing about who Mahamet was. We never hear directly from alcaide Mahamet the Jew. Rather, González de Torres invokes public knowledge and what 'everybody says': in his account we don't hear what Mahamet says but what González de Torres says he says. It's also evident that González de Torres scarcely knows him personally, if at all, and thus relies on hearsay as he tells his interlocutor Sosa what Sosa the writer is probably ventriloquising through González de Torres. While there may be little truth in this account,

---

[50] Fray Antonio González de Torres was a Portuguese noble, a knight of Malta captured with Sosa in April 1577. His captor and slave-master was none other than the Spanish renegade Morat Raez Maltrapillo to whom Cervantes voluntarily handed himself over after the failure of one of his escape attempts, which suggests that he would have served as a vital intermediary between Cervantes and Hasan Veneciano. Besides, there are puzzling clues indicating that González de Torres might have been involved in the authorship of the *Topografía*.

its value lies precisely in what the act of representation reveals about Sosa and González de Torres and their attitude towards this professional renegade.

After bemoaning Sosa's fate, González de Torres depicts Mahamet in a poignant passage that's worth quoting at length:

> I now see what I've so often heard Moors and Turks say publicly around Algiers, that this *alcaide* Mahamet the Jew, your master, does not recognise or fear or adore any God. He is neither a Moor or Turk, nor a Jew, nor a Christian. No doubt this is so because, as is publicly known, he himself says that when he was a Jew in Animay – a village twelve leagues from Marrakesh – already a young man, he chose to become a Moor, and to spite his own people and affront all the more the Jews who denied him the favour that he sought (as he says), he would become a Moor in Jerusalem, home of the Jews. Later, captured by a galley over here near Metafuz ... by the famous Cigala, from Genoa,[51] he was baptised after a few days and lived for fifteen years as a Christian with so much hypocrisy and dissimulation that (as he tells it with great laughter) they took him for a saint. And later taking as much as he could steal of his master's silver, which had been entrusted to him, he fled with it to Venice and from there to Constantinople, not to turn Moor or Turk again but only to dress himself in the skin and semblance of a Moor, because no one has ever seen him enter a mosque or say prayers or carry out a ceremony of Moors or smell of anything that is Moorish. And now I also see what they say of his life and his more than gentile customs, that he does nothing other than busy himself day and night delighting in money, counting money, weighing money, trafficking in money, hoarding money, melting gold and silver, practicing alchemy and secretly making counterfeit money.[52] Finally, it must be a great truth that, just as this monster bargains and speaks with such cunning, deception and lies, the proverb says: 'malicious and cunning like alcaide Mahamet the Jew'. He is so contrary to everyone that ... he approves of no religion or sect, regarding none as good or even necessary, but in everything he is an ungodly atheist, like Epicurus or Protagoras ... or Lucian and others, undoubtedly believing that neither in heaven nor on earth nor in hell or anywhere else is there any deity that cares for us and rules or is concerned about human affairs.[53]

---

[51] Genoese corsair, father of the renegade Cigala (Cığalazade Sinan Pasha).

[52] Garcés deduces that he 'was in charge of the mint, and he apparently made counterfeit currency on the side' (*Cervantes in Algiers*, 73).

[53] 'agora acabo de creer lo que muchas veces he oído decir públicamente y platicar a muchos moros y turcos por todo ese Argel, que este alcaide Mahamet el judío, su patrón, a ningún Dios reconoce, ni teme, ni adora; ni es moro o turco, ni judío, ni cristiano; y sin duda ansí debe de ser, porque demás de ser público, él mismo dice que siendo de nación judío, en Animay, lugar distante de Marruecos doce leguas, de su propia voluntad, y siendo ya hombre, se hizo moro, y por despecho de los suyos y para afrentar más los judíos que no le daban el favor que quería (como él dice) no se quiso hacer moro sino dentro de Hierusalem, común patria de los judíos, y después cautivado en una galeota,

This diatribe is about something much worse than embracing the enemy's religion. Like many other renegades in Sosa's view, Mahamet follows the logic of being neither one thing nor another, religiously speaking, but it goes much further. The narrative begins with a wilful rejection of his native religion and of his coreligionists, whom he wants to offend by converting to Islam in the symbolic home of Judaism. He is already defiant and willing to go to great lengths to carry out this supreme insult, even if it means sailing across the entire Mediterranean. Later, falling prey to a famous Christian corsair, he inaugurates a fifteen-year hiatus as a Christian, starting with his readiness to be baptised right away and culminating in his being taken for a saint, much to his sarcastic amusement. This phase is marked by religious hypocrisy and betrayal of the trust his master has put in him, ending in theft and abandonment. While one can imagine González de Torres and Sosa to be especially irked by his feigned Christianity, Mahamet doesn't seem to be chagrined by the waste of so much of his early manhood. The narrator carefully specifies that Mahamet did not become a Muslim again, but only assumed the guise of doing so. Thus Mahamet is neither a Jew nor a Christian nor a Muslim, but rather a 'godless atheist' who despises all religions but apparently switches one religion for another for purposes of wealth or power. Much worse than having a contrary religion is having none at all. What fills the godless void is money, Mammon, taking the place of all three religions, and he himself is 'inhuman', a 'monster' in all he says and does. In a city where, according to Sosa, about half of its free residents were *turcos de profesión*, i.e. renegades – dwelling in no fewer than 6,000 of the city's 12,200 houses – *alcaide* Mahamet the Jew would be perceived as an emblematic figure: cruel, corrupt, devoid of any religious

---

aquí cerca de Metafuz ... del famoso Cigala, ginovés, se baptizó luego a pocos días y vivió quince años cristiano con tanta hipocresía y disimulación que (como él mismo lo cuenta con grande risa) le tenían por un santo. Y cogiendo después lo más que pudo robar de la plata de su patrón (que le era encomendada), huyó con ella a la ciudad de Venecia, y de allí a Constantinopla, no a volverse otra vez moro o turco, mas a vestirse solamente del pellejo y semejanza de moro, porque jamás hombre le ha visto entrar en mezquita de moros, ni hacer oración o cerimonias de moros, o oler algo que sea de moro. Y también creo ahora lo que todos dicen de su vida y costumbres más que gentílicas, porque dicen comúnmente que no es otra sino ocuparse días y noches en revolver moneda, contar moneda, pesar moneda, trafagar moneda, atesorar moneda y hundir oro, plata, alquimia y hacer a ascondidas falsa moneda. Y, finalmente, debe ser también muy gran verdad que ansí como es este monstruo en todas sus acciones y costumbres, en tratar, conversar y platicar con tantas astucias, engaños y mentiras, que anda por proverbio: malicioso y astuto como el alcaide Mahamet, el judío. Es tan al contrario de todos, que ... ninguna ley o secta aprueba, ninguna tiene por buena ni aun por necesaria; mas en todo es un impío ateo, cual Epicuro, o Protágoras ... o Luciano y otros; persuadiéndose, sin duda, que ni en el cielo, ni en la tierra, ni en el infierno o otra alguna parte del mundo, hay alguna deidad que tenga cuidado de nosotros y gobierne o se cure de las cosas de los hombres' (*Topografía* III, 1, 96v–7r).

or civil allegiance but capable of passing for whatever suits him, devoted in body and soul to money and to what money can do.

Apprehending the enigma and the spectrum

Although many other renegades could be profiled, this series shows both wide diversity and 'family resemblances' among them. Numerous others, including historical as well as literary women renegades, appear elsewhere in this book because, particularly on the Muslim side from Istanbul to Marrakesh, converts took on an extraordinary protagonism in many spheres of life, e.g. in government, society, warfare, the economy, and undoubtedly culture and religious practice too. To a fair extent the early modern Mediterranean was a Mediterranean *of* the renegades, and along with them, of other frontier categories, all of which, whether by commerce, conflict or other means, kept the Mediterranean substantially interlinked despite distances, borders and divisions. Like other frontier figures, the renegades literally embodied this dense network of interconnection, including the conflictual nature of the *mare nostrum*, and kept the lands and islands of the Mediterranean more or less in the same historical time zone.

Whether by force or choice, crossing over to the other side of the geopolitical and religious divide meant interrupting one *modus vivendi* and initiating another, for better or for worse, even if many who did so continued to be slaves. To the extent that the vast majority of conversions were voluntary, no matter how conditioned by circumstances, the decision to convert would have had to factor in the consequences of doing so, including how this might affect their possible return, what loyalties might be broken, what new bonds might be created or reinforced, and, generally, whether it was in their interests to convert. Leo Africanus speaks for many – both men and women – when he says: 'when a man sees his advantage, he always follows it' (Natalie Zemon Davis 110). They may or may not 'do like the trickster bird', as he puts it, but those converting had to consider the probability of this being a lifelong change, aware that the currents of life could carry them in unforeseen directions, regardless of their initial intentions.

Christian writers, both lay and clerical, tend to characterise the act of 'reneging' as a moment of great weakness in someone who succumbs to temptations of whatever kind, false promises, invalid excuses, and so on.[54] Nearly all writers focus on inclinations towards sodomy among renegades

---

[54] In contrast with Christian clerical writers' obsession regarding conversions to Islam, 'Ottoman writers and bureaucrats', as Marc Baer remarks, 'were not concerned with the motivation of the convert and rarely recorded any of his or her intentions in changing religion, let alone the former religion or name' (Graf 3).

or on captives' affairs with women, which, if they were caught *in flagrante*, allegedly forced them to choose between death by drowning (along with the woman) or converting to Islam, in which case both lovers would be spared. There are many variations on this theme.[55] But regardless of the motive, reneging is *the* act of supreme betrayal to Church and country, of disloyalty to one's own people, of breaking emotional bonds and becoming a traitor politically, socially and religiously, thus turning into a kind of monster who nonetheless can be reconciled and uneasily taken back in the event of returning to the homeland. Ransomers and fellow captives often express anxiety in seeing the massive numbers of former captives who crossed over. What the texts don't say is that captives tempted to renege must have been impressed by the sheer numbers of renegades and the good fortune that had befallen many of them.

At the very least, renegades would embrace the other religion or appear to do so, adapt to their new social and cultural environment, become familiar with new languages, interact with a dazzling array of human types, adopt new modes of behaviour, acquire skills or hone those they already possessed (e.g. translation *sensu lato*, mediation, survival techniques), relativise their notions of what's true and real, become adept at switching roles, and quite often learn to dissemble. Even for their contemporaries they tended to be enigmatic, uncanny, *unheimlich*. Many would have the chance to make themselves 'worth more' and become more versatile and capable people than they were before, which the quite open Muslim societies of the time generally enabled them to do.

One of the biggest fallacies about the early modern Mediterranean still in evidence is that it was a space in which Christianity and Islam were at war with each other. Of course there were countless attacks and counterattacks, battles, raids, threats, and even (from the Iberian side) failed attempts to colonise the Maghrib, but grand religio-imperialistic schemes such as that of Cardinal Cisneros in the early sixteenth century were abandoned. The successes of the Ottomans and North African corsairs, Charles V's disastrous campaign against Algiers in 1541, and the death of Portugal's King Sebastian at the Battle of the Three Kings (Alcazarquivir, Wādī 'l-Makhāzin) in Morocco in 1578, put an end to such plans. With much more of a political than a religious agenda, the Ottomans extended and consolidated their power in the eastern and southern Mediterranean throughout much of the sixteenth century, but after 1580 they directed their energies elsewhere. There obviously would have

---

[55] In his captive's tale, João Carvalho Mascarenhas tells a curious story of a Portuguese captive in Algiers who has a passionate affair with his master's niece, and, at her behest so that he can later marry her, he reneges but immediately gets the plague. Three days after reneging, in the midst of his agony, his ransom arrives along with a letter from his wife back home, enclosing a lock of his newly born son's hair. Mascarenhas concludes: 'and thus at once he lost his wife, his son and his freedom by heaven's just punishment, and above all his soul' (III, 7, 84).

been no captives or renegades without a religiously divided Mediterranean, but the interests and motives of those involved most often had little to do with proselytism. The goal was not to conquer or subjugate the other side but to take the fullest possible advantage of it.

One might think that each conversion to Islam would have been welcomed and celebrated, but few were (apart from special cases such as priests or nobles who converted). Many Christians were refused permission to become Muslims and were even beaten for daring to try (Jerónimo Gracián, *Peregrinación de Anastasio*, in *Tratado*, 113; Gonzalez-Raymond 135; Gómez de Losada 255; Barrio Gozalo 184–7). With characteristic wit, the Belgian former captive Emanuel d'Aranda tells of a French captive named Jean 'who wanted to turn Turk and remained Christian' *malgré lui* (165). Weary of rowing as a galley slave, Jean asks his master Ali Piccinino (Picenino, Pegelin, Bitchin, Bitchnin) – a renegade and corsair of Italian origin, owner of thousands of slaves and immensely powerful in Algiers from the 1620s until his death in 1645 – for permission to turn Turk. Piccinino flatly refuses 'because renegade slaves are worth much less than Christian ones since the Turks don't use renegades as rowers, but only Christians' (165). Jean gets dressed and shaved as a 'Turk', takes on the name Mustafa, and goes to one of his master's pleasure gardens. The 'refined' Piccinino, having heard what was going on, appears on his horse and calls out 'Jean!' When the captive tells him his name is Mustafa, not Jean, Piccinino has four slaves beat him until he screams: '"My name is Jean, not Mustafa, I'm a Christian and not a Turk, and I'll put my Christian clothes back on!" He did this so well that Piccinino could say that he brought a Christian back to Christianity by the blows of a club.'[56]

A letter dated 1550 talks about the desperation felt by captives after three years in Algiers without anyone being ransomed; this led to mass conversions of hundreds of them, and the unfulfilled desire of many more to do the same.

> Those who went to turn Moor were so many that the king didn't know what to do, and was advised not to give any more licenses because he wouldn't have any Christians left. The first thing they did in the king's house was make a cross on the ground and spit on it and stamp on it and shout that they were Moors, denying the true Jesus Christ as God.[57]

---

[56] '"Je m'appelle Jean et non pas Mostafa. Je suis chrétien et non pas turc, et je remettrai mes habits chrétiens." Ce qu'il fit si bien que Pégelin pouvait dire avoir remis un chrétien dans le christianisme à grands coups de bâton' (165).

[57] This letter is published as an appendix (with no commentary) in José Antonio Martínez Torres, *Prisioneros de los infieles*, 170–5. 'Eran tantos los que se yban a tornar moros que el Rey no sabía qué haçerse, y fuéle aconsejado que no diese más liçençias porque no le quedaría más cristianos. Lo primero que haçían en casa del Rey era una cruz en tierra y escupirla y pisarla y a grandes bozes dezir que heran moros, negando al verdadero Jesucristo por Dios' (172). See also Turbet-Delof, *L'Afrique barbaresque* (143), for comparable instances.

These actions, however, were to no avail. When large numbers of captives were not even allowed to become renegades, it's difficult to talk about a war of religions in the early modern Mediterranean, or of rigidified geopolitical blocks. But this letter points to so much more: how desperation, survival, collective hysteria and anger could be determining factors in the will to change religions. Like so many other texts recounting similar episodes, it also points to the fact that adult male Christian captives were generally worth much more to their masters as Christian slaves than as Muslim slaves, since the exchange value of renegades was greatly reduced, and (as noted above) even their value as labour diminished because they were spared the toil of rowing. An added irony is that those who refused them permission to become renegades were often, like Ali Piccinino, renegades themselves.

Religious belief rarely seems to have been the prime motive of converts in this geohistorical setting. What one sees again and again is that while the question of belief was transcendent for Christianity and Islam, it was not always so important for the people who practised Christianity and Islam. Whereas Christian authorities in particular stressed only doctrinal and ritualistic differences with Islam (the divinity of Christ, the Trinity, washing, and so on), many renegades under interrogation by the Inquisition had no problem in recognising fundamental similarities between these two Abrahamic religions. Being a Jew, a Muslim, or a Christian (other than Protestant) in early modern times often had more to do with what one did than what one thought.[58] The clerical writer Gabriel Gómez de Losada remarks: 'And it's very noteworthy that if a Jew wants to renege, he first has to become a Christian, hearing mass from a priest and eating bacon, which is what Turks think our religion mainly consists of, so that the shift from his own religion is not immediate'[59] (237–8). Pierre Dan describes quite similarly how a Jew becomes a Muslim, initially pointing out that childhood circumcision exempts him from circumcision *à la Turque*: 'But he is first obliged to become a Christian, which he does by eating pork and loudly pronouncing the words *Issahac*, which means "I confess that Jesus is the true Messiah." He then raises his finger to heaven, and by the words *La illah Allah etc.*, which he declaims before everyone, he declares himself a Muslim.'[60] This sequence, he explains, is the result of Muslims' absurd

---

[58] This notion concurs with Stephen Prothero's discussion in *God is not one* of *orthopraxy* and the limited importance of belief in many religions.

[59] 'Y es cosa muy singular, que si quiere renegar un judío, ha de hazer primero professión de christiano, oyendo missa de un papaz y comiendo tocino, que es en lo que entienden los turcos que consiste principalmente nuestra ley, de modo que de la suya no ha de ser inmediato el tránsito' (237–8).

[60] 'Mais il est obligé aussi de se faire premièrement chrétien, ce qu'il fait en mangeant de la chair de porc, & en prononçant hautement ces paroles, *Issahac*, qui signifie, "je confesse que Jésus est le véritable Messie." Ensuite de quoi, il lève le doigt vers le Ciel, & par ces mots, *La illah Allah &c.* qu'il profère devant tous, il se déclare Mahométan' (*Histoire de Barbarie*, 354–5).

(*folle*) belief that Muhammad's religion (*loi*) 'is the perfection and consummation of the two religions established by God: that of Moses and that of Jesus Christ' (305). Quite simply, it was impossible to deny the family resemblances and genealogy of these religions, or the fact that the Mediterranean peoples were generally more concerned with religious praxis than belief.

Some historical renegades were able to move back and forth, living as Muslims in Muslim lands and as Christians in their native Christian lands, which meant that they were simultaneously Muslims and Christians, or at least alternated between the two religions. One common perception among renegades, very troubling to Christian clergy who liked to say that renegades were neither Moors nor Christians, was the relativistic idea that, in the words of a Catalan renegade, 'Good Moors are saved in their religion and good Christians in theirs; bad Christians and bad Moors go to hell' (Bennassar and Bennassar 494). Even Muslim authorities sometimes worried about what sort of Muslims renegades would be, since they brought all their bad habits with them (drunkenness, blasphemy, fighting, and so on). A Portuguese writer surmises with regard to renegades that 'there is a difference between their outward aspect and their deep conviction; ... the Moors regard them as Christians, and the Christians regard them as Moors. Neither the Christians nor the Moors are right because they are neither one nor the other' (Rodríguez Mediano 189). 'What man is there in the world', asks the Trinitarian Gómez de Losada, 'who, having been nurtured with the milk of our Catholic faith, can deny this as true and necessary for eternal health, its mysteries being so manifestly believable? ... What renegade lives in Algiers who doesn't know this ...? What renegade doesn't know the doctrine of Muhammad to be false, so contrary to reason?' (256). However, it should also be taken into consideration that since more than 90 per cent of them never returned to the lands of their birth, most renegades must have lived religiously as Muslims, and culturally as Turks or Maghribians or citizens of other Muslim lands of the Great Sea.

What Gómez de Losada and others of similar disposition refuse to acknowledge is that captives and renegades often developed their own religious and moral irenicism on the margins of doctrinal teachings, and that belief itself allowed for a great deal of latitude and in any event was malleable private property that could be manifested in whatever ways that circumstances might require. What's more, many renegades seem to have been clueless about doctrine, yet had their own notions of what was good and bad. One renegade, asked by inquisitors whether he knew what the Muslim creed meant – in these documents the *shahāda* tends to be deformed beyond recognition – said he had asked around until another renegade told him it meant 'Alleluia' (Rostagno 63). Domenico Battagerin, having been reconciled for apostasy in 1686, was brought back in 1690 for asserting, for example, that good Jews, Turks and heretics are rewarded by an afterlife in heaven, and that circumcision is worth the same as baptism and guarantees salvation. Asked about Muhammad, he says: 'I believed and held that Muhammad was the son of God as the others believed because that's what the other Turks called him, but I didn't know if he was the son of God or a prophet or saint and now I take him for a devil.'[61] Giovanni Ermani della Moldavia testified in 1695: 'I lived at that time as a Turk, eating meat on Friday and Saturday, without knowing or even thinking about what religion [*legge*] I was living under' (Rostagno 70). We see such latitude of belief also in contexts that have nothing to do with renegades during the early modern period, e.g. in *Don Quixote*, where the congenial Morisco Ricote tells Sancho Panza: 'I know very well that my daughter Ricota and Francisca Ricota my wife are Catholic Christians, and though I'm not as Christian as they are, I'm still more Christian than Moor, and I always beseech God to open the eyes of my understanding and let me know how I ought to serve Him.'[62] This notion of being *both* Christian and Muslim but *more* one than the other had no place in Christian dogma. Similarly, but removed from any religious context, don Quixote fondly says of Sancho that 'he doubts everything and believes everything' ('duda de todo y créelo todo', II, 32, 900): generalised doubt and belief coincide without any sense of contradiction or internal rift.

For most renegades, religion formed part of the much broader set of life circumstances. The pull towards their homelands that many must have felt undoubtedly included memories of religious practice, but with little sense of the theological doctrines that might have stood behind them. Captives often said they became renegades with every intention of fleeing from Muslim lands, but many ended up staying – out of love for their Muslim wives and children (Gómez de Losada 257). Obviously, deeper affective loyalties were often felt towards the communities in which the renegades lived than towards those they had left behind.

Several models thus appear for what or who these enigmatic renegades were. They could be crossover figures, *becoming* the cultural and religious 'other'. They could be neither Christians nor Muslims, or both at the same time. They might be outwardly one of them and inwardly the other. They could be Christians in the eyes of Muslims and Muslims in the eyes of Christians. Or it might not matter which religion they professed as long as they were good Christians or good Muslims rather than bad ones. Modern scholars often pick up on such views by considering renegades as split or contradictory

---

[61] 'Io ho creduto et tenuto che Mahometto era figlio de Dio come lo credevano li altri perché cossì lo chiamavano li altri turchi però io non sapeva si era figlio di Dio o profeta o santo et hora lo tengo per diavolo' (Rostagno 68).

[62] 'yo sé cierto que la Ricota mi hija y Francisca Ricota mi mujer son católicas cristianas, y aunque yo no lo soy tanto, todavía tengo más de cristiano que de moro, y ruego siempre a Dios me abra los ojos del entendimiento y me dé a conocer cómo le tengo de servir' (II, 54, 1073–4).

subjects, as simultaneously victims and victimisers, or as personalities with dual or multiple identities. In my view, the notion of 'identity', necessary as it is, has for several decades prevented scholarship from getting a grasp on how frontier figures such as renegades thought and acted. Sometimes there's 'no there there', or not much 'there'. Rather than asking whether such people *were* X or Y, or how much they had of either identity at any given moment, or how their identities conflicted with each other – as if we knew more or less *what* those identities consisted of – I prefer to ask how frontier figures performed in frontier zones and how they are represented there. Uses of the term 'hybridity' tend to share some of the problems inherent in discussions of 'identity', explaining very little until we ask not just what the hypothetical ingredients of that hybridity are but what its particular dynamics may be, how they function together. As suggested at the outset of this chapter, terms such as 'assimilation', 'hybridity' and 'syncretism' could have some limited usefulness in conceptualising the kinds of processes that renegades underwent, but also carry with them unwanted baggage that ineptly construes identity and, moreover, fail to capture this fundamental aspect of variable and shifting agency that renegades developed.

We can rarely know what renegades 'really' believed, and although many were undoubtedly sincere in their beliefs or disbeliefs, the renegades' behaviours were pragmatic and strategic. It was only the Inquisition that insisted on 'sincerity' in this regard, so at the very least the notion of sincerity should be bracketed. Renegades answering to the Inquisition had learned the lesson to 'always be sincere, even when you don't mean it', and they led the authorities to believe that they had always been Christians in their hearts. Beyond this, there seems to be no way to map out a split identity of renegades. Despite the insistence – in nearly all scholarship about renegades – on this notion of a split identity and conflictive personalities, this model is questionable at the very least. What evidence points to renegades as split or fragmented, 'divided against themselves'? If pressed, I would suggest that they functioned something like the Portuguese poet Fernando Pessoa's heteronyms, having at least two different names (Pessoa had around seventy-five), two past histories, two ways of seeing the world, and so on, but with an ability to modulate between the heteronyms when they needed to. Many texts reveal a remarkable ability on the part of renegades to operate on both sides of the divide, to know how things worked both 'here' and 'there', to understand the languages and the lingua franca common to all, and to translate linguistically, culturally and religiously while looking out for their own interests. Perhaps the adage *traduttore, traditore* – the translator is a traitor – is more aptly applied to them than to anyone else.

In the captive's tale in *Don Quixote* (I, 39–41), a repentant Spanish renegade in Algiers – described by the captive as a great friend – translates all the letters between the beautiful Zoraida and the captive, finds out who she is, single-handedly devises the plan for escape, buys the boat, makes all the important decisions, interprets spoken Arabic, intercedes between Zoraida and her father, and does all that needs to be done to finally bring the group to the Spanish shore, causing alarm when he's seen dressed as a Turk. Without him there would be no plot. He is the omnipresent facilitator and intermediary, the one who understands languages, knows how things work and makes everything happen. Yet at the end we still know almost nothing about him. He is pure instrumentality, pure capacity, pure mediation. And he remains nameless throughout: it's enough to call him the renegade, or *our* renegade. As far as I'm aware, none of the hundreds of illustrations of this story over the past centuries shows his face. Cervantes may have come closer to reality than anyone else in his conception of the nature of a renegade.

In the geographic centre of the Mediterranean, between Tunisia and Sicily, is an island called Lampedusa (a destination for refugees in recent times). Alonso de Contreras passed by in 1601 and said that in a cave near the harbour there was an altar with a painting of the Virgin Mary on one side, and on the other the sepulchre of a Muslim holy man. Each of them was surrounded by gifts of food for Christian and Muslim captives who might take refuge there: 'It is true that these alms are left by Christians and Muslims so that when escaped slaves get there they have food to eat until a Christian or Muslim ship comes by.'[63] Local legends talk of a hermit, possibly a renegade or ex-renegade, named Andrea Anfosso, who looked after the sanctuary for years until he escaped with the painting of the Virgin Mary to his hometown on the Ligurian coast. In Sicily the popular expression 'fare il romito di Lampedusa' – to do like the hermit of Lampedusa – means to be a person of double religion (Arnaldi 13–47). Lampedusa in fact came to symbolise a shared space, belonging to both sides and both religions and to neither, and it still retains some of that aura. I would like to suggest that renegades most characteristically correspond not only to the hermit who took care of the place but also to a desacralised version of the sanctuary itself.

---

[63] 'Es cosa cierta que esta limosna de comida la dejan los cristianos y turcos porque cuando llegan allí, si se huye algún esclavo, tenga con qué comer hasta que venga bajel de su nación y le lleve, si es cristiano o turco' (ch. 3).

4

Martyrs

Cervantine prelude

Perhaps Sancho Panza is one of the world's literary characters least inclined to martyrdom. This may be why the duke and duchess and their household submit him to what the narrator, Altisidora, don Quixote and Sancho himself call martyrdom, which consists of slaps, pinches and pinpricks in order to resurrect Altisidora (*Don Quixote* II, 69–71). And if martyrdom is the word that characterises this torment – just as the lashes to disenchant Dulcinea belong to the semantic field of penitence – the sufferer will be a kind of martyr. Once again don Quixote marvels at the virtues of Sancho's body, whose pain, it seems, can disenchant and resurrect maidens; and once again Sancho questions this logic, since he sees no link between cause and effect, that is, between his own pain and the resurrection of others, and he doesn't understand why he has to suffer for matters that are extraneous to him. This scene also unfolds intermittently like an auto-da-fé and an infernal ceremony: the kings/judges Minos and Rhadamanthus rule, the beautiful body of a dead girl lies in display, and Sancho is dressed in inquisitorial garments of the *sambenito* cloak whose painted flames don't burn and the *coroza* whose painted devils don't carry him off (as he calmly observes). Among so much solemnity and suspense, this costume of the penitents provokes don Quixote's laughter, and will be worn by Sancho's donkey when they arrive at their village. We're presented, then, with a mixed theatrical model, parodic-satirical in every aspect.

What there is of martyrdom in this episode is of course far from the religious martyrdom that in that era aggravated the conflict between Catholicism and Protestantism and claimed victims in the Nordic countries, in the Mediterranean and even in Japan. A geo-religious map would indicate the distribution of martyrs in certain areas, but wouldn't show a ducal pleasure mansion in the interior of Aragon: martyrdom had its own geography. Our martyr Sancho doesn't die, he defends no religious dogma, he won't be taken directly to heaven for his martyrdom, he provides no edifying model for others. But his martyrdom – expressed in singular and plural, as *martirio* and *martirios* – is not merely understood as 'pain or suffering, physical or moral, of great intensity', to cite one of the meanings of the term in the dictionary of the Real Academia Española. For everyone other than Sancho and don Quixote it is instead a jocular martyrdom that evokes a hell both classical and popularly Christian, with playful devils, situated on the boundary between life and death. It's a martyrdom in which the martyr, through persuasions of others, lets himself be martyred against his will and common sense, and in which the benefits for the martyr are nil but are transferred to another person, the woman brought back to life. Don Quixote doesn't doubt that this strange martyrdom is a gift granted by heaven, as he says to Sancho: 'Be patient, my friend, and oblige these gentlemen, and give many thanks to heaven for having placed such virtue in your person that through its martyrdom you can disenchant the enchanted and resuscitate the dead.'[1] Sancho as a martyr suffers unjust persecution, the 'infernal ministers' torture him as they please and the authorities supervise. Martyrdom becomes something laughable where the cruelties of others, however malicious, are carried out within a playful framework. In fact, this episode reveals certain aspects of the logic of martyrdom, transforming into mockery one of the most sacred themes: above all, the causality, according to which the martyr pays with his or her pain and death the most direct passage to heaven, is subverted. Instead of killing the martyr, this martyrdom of Sancho's consists of making him suffer to restore life to a 'maiden more capricious than wise' who has no special relationship with the martyr but does have one with his master. This is perhaps the last word on the part of Cervantes about martyrdom.

It seems that the diverse treatment of the topic of martyrdom depends not only on geo-religious considerations but also on literary genre, and to some extent also on a hypothetical evolution of Cervantes' handling of Moorish and Turkish themes. Martyrdom appears very little in his long and short novels, coming into view here and there with a few brushstrokes. In *El amante liberal*, the repentant renegade Mahamut declares to his friend and compatriot Ricardo: 'you are not unaware of the burning desire I have of not dying in this religion which I seem to profess, for when I can go on no longer, I will confess and loudly proclaim my faith in Jesus Christ, from whom my young age and lesser understanding parted me, even though I know that such a confession will cost me my life, for in exchange for not losing my soul, it will be well for me to sacrifice my body' (1: 139–40). He thus confirms who he is and where his loyalty lies, and the subject does not reappear in the rest of the novel. In *La española inglesa* Clotaldo's Catholic family is alarmed when Queen Elizabeth (Isabel) asks that the captive of Cádiz, Isabela, be brought before her, and Clotaldo begs the girl to 'use every possible means to prevent them from being condemned as Catholics, for although in spirit they were prepared to receive martyrdom, the weak flesh still refused such a bitter fate' (*Novelas*

---

[1] 'Ten paciencia, hijo, y da gusto a estos señores, y muchas gracias al cielo por haber puesto tal virtud en tu persona, que con el martirio della desencantes los encantados y resucites los muertos' (II, 69, 1188). Cf. don Quixote's remark to Sancho further ahead: 'And although your virtue is *gratis data* and has not cost you any study at all, suffering torments [*martirios*] on your person is more than study' (II, 71, 1199).

ejemplares, 1: 247). This terror of martyrdom turns out to have no bearing on the novel's plot, although in its historical context such fear was justified.

Cervantes' theatre, in contrast, represents martyrdom more crudely and insistently, particularly in three of the five extant works whose action takes place in Muslim lands in the Mediterranean: *El trato de Argel, Los baños de Argel* and *La gran sultana*, although not in the frontier *comedia* of *El gallardo español* or in the contested lands of *La conquista de Jerusalén*. The first two, set in the Algiers that Cervantes knew, devote very long and vehement passages to martyrdom, unlike, say, the captive's tale in *Don Quixote* (I, 37, 39–42), likewise set in Algiers, where martyrdom is practically absent as such, although there is talk of cruelties to Christian captives, and both Zoraida and the renegade risk their lives for their adherence to Christianity. In sum, martyrdom in the works of Cervantes is found almost exclusively in the theatrical works set in Algiers. The Istanbul ('Constantinopla') of *La gran sultana* also raises the issue of martyrdom, but doña Catalina de Oviedo's desire for martyrdom is ironically frustrated.

Theatres of cruelty

Before discussing these works, we should broaden our perspective by contextualising the strategic deployment of martyrdom in the religious struggles of that epoch. This will let us see not only the consonances and dissonances of Cervantes' treatment of the subject concerning the representations of martyrdom in his time but also his apprehension of this peculiar and by no means universal phenomenon. It's necessary to analyse the functions and forms that martyrdom assumes in that era and to reconceptualise it according to some rather unusual criteria since the conventional definitions of martyrdom usually diverge from many of the cases that appear in early modern texts. Specifically, it seems to me essential to situate the cruelty of others and oneself in the axis of martyrdom and examine the motivations of all who participate in these complex events considered 'martyrdom'. It's also necessary to question the verbal or visual representation of martyrdom to investigate its techniques, its aims, its meaning and its public.

While Muslim lands were highly suitable for fomenting martyrdom – and many Christian writers dealing with relations with Muslims refer to Catholic martyrs – Islam paradoxically remained quite peripheral to the rationale of martyrdom: to cite the title of an anti-Protestant work published in Antwerp,[2] 'the theatre of cruelty of the heretics of our time' played itself out not so much in the Maghrib or Turkey but in countries in direct conflict between Catholics and Protestants. However, although martyrdom was practically unilateral

---

[2] Richard Verstegan, *Theatrum crudelitatum haereticorum nostri temporis*, 1587.

(Christian) in the Muslim Mediterranean, a more local circuit was created where martyrdom did serve more specific interests.

From the middle of the sixteenth century until well into the seventeenth century, Protestants and Catholics rivalled each other to determine who the true modern martyrs were, victims of Protestants or victims of Catholics: our victims were martyrs, theirs were heretics. In 1563 the Englishman John Foxe published his intractable book entitled *Acts and monuments* ..., popularly known as *The book of martyrs*, asserting that the true martyrs were Luther, Calvin, and all other leading figures of Protestants, even Henry VIII, and arguing that the cause, rather than the resulting death, was the determining factor of martyrdom (*non poena sed causa*) (Monta 5), thus echoing the etymology of the word *martyr*, which means 'witness'. However, this book, like almost all works of the genre published by Protestants and Catholics, is filled with frightful deaths well illustrated to show the unbridled cruelty of the persecutors and the glorious deaths of the martyrs. Its illustrations were perhaps a response to other representations, published a few years earlier, of the martyrdom of Carthusian monks in London under Henry VIII, and in turn would be countered by other series of illustrations in a continuous propagandistic struggle. In 1564, French and Swiss Calvinists published a work on their own martyrs, especially those massacred in Paris (*Histoire des martyrs persécutés et mis a mort pour la vérité de l'Évangile*), also abundantly illustrated. The obsessive production of illustrated texts, in addition to paintings – especially from the Catholic side – would continue in the early decades of the seventeenth century. These works included the *Theatrum crudelitatum haereticorum* (1587) written by an Anglo-Dutch Catholic who fled from Elizabethan England, and Antonio Gallonio's *Trattato degli instrumenti di martirio* ... (1591). In sum, although martyrdom had always been important since the beginning of Christianity, the massive corpus of works published precisely during this period may mark the historical peak of the production of martyrology, and much of it focused on contemporary martyrdom.[3]

In the illustrations one sees that the acts of cruelty are very similar, except that roles are constantly reversed between Catholics and Protestants: both can be persecutors or victims, but the depictions of cruelties are almost identical. (Also similar are the illustrations of the cruelties of the Muslims of Algiers, belonging to the same genre and signalling by way of clothes and turbans who the perpetrators of such atrocities are.) Apart from this, those who inflict the most ingenious and horrendous tortures tend to do their job like skilful workers, insensible to the unbearable pain of others, while others calmly

---

[3] In this regard, see Alfonso Rodríguez G. de Ceballos; the previously cited book by Susannah Brietz Monta; and the introductions of José María Parreño and Emilio Sosa to their edition of Antonio de Sosa's *Diálogo de los mártires de Argel* (13–20 and 27–32).

watch the spectacle. Cruelty in the context of religious struggles correlates with gender: those who inflict pain, supervise and watch the spectacle are almost always men, while the victims are men and women, sometimes even children.[4] Undoubtedly these illustrations, together with their verbal explanations, are meant to provoke both wrath against unspeakably cruel heretics and empathy for the victims who suffer the utmost pain in the name of their faith. These two powerful emotions, formulated along the *we/they* dividing line, are integrally united and simultaneously experienced. A few touches in the engravings and woodcuts mark which figures are Protestants and Catholics, and hence which ones are good and bad, but the figures themselves are entirely reversible in this war of martyrs, whose representational techniques for conveying torture and martyrdom are quite constant. In contrast, there is no such symmetry in the representation of Catholic martyrdom in Muslim lands.

The Jesuits were especially ready to combat Protestant heresies, having founded seminaries designed to train missionaries for regions with specific languages such as Germany or the British Isles. Of the 450 Jesuit priests sent from seminaries in Flanders or France to Elizabethan England over a period of thirty years, ninety (i.e. one-fifth) were executed and therefore martyred (Rodríguez G. de Ceballos 219). These priests were in effect trained to be martyrs. In Spain, Rome and elsewhere, the seminaries were filled with paintings depicting scenes of Catholic martyrs in Protestant countries. But the Jesuits of course had a global mission, sending missionaries to America and the Far East, and along with Franciscans suffered martyrdom in Japan in 1597. Inspired by the Jesuits but independent of religious orders, the famous noble Luisa de Carvajal made a vow of martyrdom in 1598[5] and in 1605 went to London, where she lived until her death in 1614, doing everything possible to be martyred while preaching openly and filling her house with pieces of the corpses of executed Catholics,[6] but in vain: to quote Luis de Granada, 'it is

---

[4] An exception would be the episode in the Alpujarras war when Morisco men tie a priest to a tree and hand him over to women armed with knives to do whatever they please (Pérez de Hita 2: 17).

[5] See the text of this vow in the bilingual edition of the anthology of works by Luisa de Carvajal y Mendoza, 118–20. It expresses a strong desire to unite with Christ and a promise to 'seek all those occasions of martyrdom that are not repugnant to the law of God'. She also says that 'it has given me great pleasure and contentment to have made this vow'. See in this respect Antonio Cortijo Ocaña and Adelaida Cortijo Ocaña, 17–19.

[6] See, for example, Camilo Mª Abad: 'They dug bravely and with great haste. They threw out sixteen bodies of thieves lying on top of the quartered martyrs; and finally they took out that treasure, which they put in sacks made with sheets that doña Luisa had given them. Having seen where the martyrs were buried, her faithful servant Lemeteliel guided them … In a coach rented for twenty reales the holy relics finally arrived at the house of doña Luisa, who received them with a devout procession. It was in the new house in the Spitalfields district, larger than the one in Barbican. She and her companions formed

one thing for the heart to fail martyrdom, and another for martyrdom to fail the heart' (423).

While Catholic martyrdom in the Maghrib responded to the same need to produce new martyrs vis-à-vis Protestantism and to represent them verbally and visually, the dynamics of martyrdom were very different (Vincent, 'Les Jésuites', 519–27). There was no longer an approximate symmetry according to which 'our martyrs are your heretics', and vice versa, since Islam at this time in the Maghrib and in the Ottoman Empire generally took little interest in martyrdom. In fact, even in texts written by Muslims in writings of the sixteenth and seventeenth centuries, I have not found anyone considered a martyr by Muslims, apart from those who were called martyrs because they died fighting against Christians.[7] Luis Bernabé Pons points out regarding what has often been referred to as *taqiyya* – whereby Muslims were counselled by their religious authorities to publicly conform to Christian practices while privately holding fast to the tenets of Islam – that during this period, 'Islam desires no martyrs; life is the supreme gift that God has given to man, and must be preserved at all costs' (*El cántico islámico*, 38). It should also be remembered that Muhammad, unlike Christ, was not a martyr. Similarly, there is no recognition on the part of Muslims that the Christians who were deemed martyrs were anything other than delinquents, criminals, or at most apostates. As far as I know, the Muslims of this time did not produce martyrologies or encourage their people to actively seek martyrdom. In religious conflicts between Catholicism and Islam, then, there were only martyrs on one side, and the resulting martyrologies served Catholicism and its religious

---

two rows, all with two candles in their hands. The pathway from the door to the prayer room was covered with roses and other flowers, while branches decked the walls. They placed the holy bodies on a carpet in front of the altar, covered them with crimson taffeta on which they strewed many fragrant flowers and, kneeling, they prayed for a while. All day long heretics known to the household kept coming by, preventing the bodies from being properly cared for by Luisa's hands until the night, when she cleaned them with dry cloths and little drops from her mouth and anointed them with spices and strong aromatic substances before having them well enclosed in boxes of lead' (283).

[7] David Cook studies the evolution of various types of martyrdom in Islam from its beginnings to present times. He points to no Muslim martyrs in the early modern Mediterranean. In the case of the Moriscos, he concludes that, despite the wars of Granada and the expulsion in 1609–14, it seems that they did not produce any martyrs. It was the opposite of what had happened in the middle of the ninth century in Cordoba when Christian monks created a movement of martyrdom (85–6). This last episode is more broadly summarised in Chejne, *Muslim Spain*, 71–2. In a qasidah by an anonymous Morisco addressed to the Otttoman sultan Bayazid II in 1501 shortly after the Morisco uprising, the poet mentions a series of massacres in places where Muslims refused to renounce Islam – and hence died *for* their religion – yet these torments are communal and there's no reference to martyrdom as such (García Arenal, *Los moriscos*, 33–41).

orders not only in their struggle against Islam but also in their more general strategies towards martyrdom.

Martyrdom is no doubt a limited and peculiar genre within the broader theatre of cruelty, but it can also be considered its most paradigmatic expression. Although unevenly distributed, examples of cruelty can be found in almost all texts and visual illustrations of the sixteenth and seventeenth centuries. Where cruelty appears as a constant leitmotif and prevalent theme is in texts related to corsairs, slavery and captivity in the Mediterranean of this era. With few exceptions, *they* (the Muslims) are the cruel ones, not *us*, even though *we* also have our corsairs, our captives and slaves. *Our* prisons, say authors such as Jerónimo Gracián, Pierre Dan and Gabriel Gómez de Losada, are very humane compared to theirs, which are the stage for all kinds of cruelty.[8] I'm of course referring to texts written in Spanish, French, Italian, Portuguese, English and Dutch, but not in Arabic or Turkish, in which accounts of captivity are rare. As Nabil Matar explains, captivity was a source of shame for Muslims, and there was almost no justification for telling it (Matar, *Europe through Arab eyes*, 57, 62–3), while in Christian countries there was an enormous demand for any kind of literature on these topics, and stories of captivity in particular were written in the mould of an *imitatio Christi* where suffering ultimately dignified the sufferer when his or her captivity became spectacle or text.

Occasionally in Christian texts one finds stories of extreme cruelty committed by Christians. So *we* too can be cruel, although we rarely call our fellow Christians cruel. As he recounts in his autobiography, the young soldier Miguel de Castro, based in Otranto, Italy, participates in a razzia on the Albanian coast populated by Muslims under Ottoman rule. Up to this point, the author seems quite insensitive to the suffering of others, but in this exceptional passage he expresses horror at the abominable cruelties inflicted by his fellow soldiers on Muslim women and children and does all he can to save lives and discourage his companions from so gratuitously and viciously killing the innocent. He says there were 'some soldiers' who were 'so merciless' that they murdered women and children in cold blood, and that he would have liked some enemies to come to defend the women and rout these cowards. Ultimately it's Castro himself who emerges as compassionate in contrast to the other soldiers. He spares no detail in his narration of acts 'worthy of abomination' perpetrated against women and children begging for mercy, but the rhetorical effect is softened by the fact that cruelty here is individualised

---

[8] As Jerónimo Gracián says in his *Peregrinación de Anastasio*, 'Because the prison [*baño*] was so narrow and crammed with six hundred Christians, most of them in chains, there was so much noise and stench, such an infinity of pests that exasperated the human body, that I can only say that any Christian dungeon is a delightful garden compared to what goes on there' (100).

in 'some soldiers' and is characterised as a lack of pity (30–1). In any event, texts like this one confirm the obvious: that cruelty was practised all over the Mediterranean, probably in similar doses and by comparable methods.

To attribute cruelty to the antagonistic 'others' – including a collective cultural or religious or political 'other' – is, of course, a very common ploy. As we've seen, Protestants and Catholics had no qualms about labelling one another as cruel without recognising their own cruelty. Spain in particular was the target of the Calvinist wrath of the Low Countries, as can be seen in elaborations of the Black Legend that represented the Spaniards committing atrocities in various parts of the world.[9]

Likewise, for most Christian writers, Muslims had almost a monopoly on cruelty in the Mediterranean. In many European languages the adjective *cruel* stuck easily and almost naturally to the Turks and Moors or their actions, functioning not as a descriptive adjective but rather as an epithet. In texts such as Antonio de Sosa's *Diálogo de la captividad* (*Topografía* III), Pierre Dan's *Histoire de Barbarie et de ses corsaires* or Gabriel Gómez de Losada's *Escuela de trabajos* – fundamental works on Algiers – there was never a crueller captivity than that of Algiers, nor were there crueller masters than those of Algiers. The words *cruel* and *cruelty* strike the tonic note throughout these texts, which catalogue the types of cruelty practised and even invented by such inhuman masters. These three works were written by clerics – two of them priests of the Redemptive Order of the Trinitarians – and all manipulated the subject of cruelty for propagandistic (ideological and financial) purposes.

Cruelty, then, was often considered an almost essential quality of the Turkish masters. Here arises the problem that the vast majority of 'Turks' were not Turks but converts from Christianity to Islam, the renegades who had 'turned Turk', and this group included almost all civilian authorities in ports like Algiers and Tunis, as well as corsair captains, commanders of the Ottoman fleet and many thousands of other *new* Muslims, so to speak. These renegades were for the most part Italians, Spaniards, French, Greeks, Slavs and Portuguese, that is, ex-European ex-Christians. Almost all the texts emphasise that by far the cruellest *Turks* were renegades, that is, people like *us* from our countries, who spoke *our* languages, who had grown up in *our* religion, and so on. Of course, cruelty varies by degree and type, and not all renegades were considered equally cruel. One of the most well-known passages in this sense is that of the captive's tale in *Don Quixote* (I, 40, 461–2) that contrasts two historically eminent renegades, the Calabrian Uchalí (the renowned Uluç

---

[9] See the introduction by Antonio Cortijo Ocaña and Ángel Gómez Moreno, 'Bernardino de Mendoza (propaganda, contrapropaganda y leyenda negra)', to the volume *Comentarios de lo sucedido en las guerras de los Países Bajos*; Antonio Cortijo, *Don Carlos Coloma de Saa. Las guerras de los Estados Bajos*.

Ali) and the Venetian Azán Agá (or Hasan Pasha), principal figures of the Ottoman Empire: what distinguishes them is that one shows great humanity towards his slaves (he had up to three thousand) and the other has the cruellest disposition imaginable. Even so, very few renegades are characterised in European texts as benevolent, and many are branded as unspeakably cruel, especially to their slaves. Christian writers often find it very disturbing that the cruellest Turks of Barbary are a transfigured version of themselves, viewing them as a corruption and perversion of themselves, a version whose essential attribute, in addition to a betrayal of religion and country, is cruelty. Since renegades almost never wrote about themselves, we're left with anti-Muslim texts that describe and interpret their cruelties.

Muslim lands were almost a paradise for Christians who chose to be martyrs because they could often count on the collaboration of Muslims to achieve their goal. We should recall that the girl who would be the future St. Teresa of Ávila recounts with a touch of humour that she read saints' lives with her brother Rodrigo, and 'as I saw the martyrdom suffered for God by the saints, it seemed to me that they bought their passage to God's paradise very cheaply, and I much desired to die like that ... We decided to go to the land of the Moors and beg them for the love of God to cut off our heads' (*Libro de la vida*, ch. 1, 121). The 'land of the Moors' would refer to Morisco villages in the nearby Sierra de Guadarrama; as it happened, the two children had barely left Ávila when they were found by an uncle of theirs and brought home unmartyred. In that other 'land of the Moors', the Maghrib, those who wanted to become martyrs could usually manage to do so. A repentant renegade only had to proclaim he was a Christian to be declared an apostate, and if he persisted in spite of all attempts to dissuade him, he was likely to be executed. Clerics who tried to proselytise were subject to the same fate.[10]

---

[10] There were exceptions, of course. Diego de Torres tells of a friar who fled from Spain and 'went to turn Moor in Fez'; later, remorseful, he retracted in the presence of the king, 'who was so incensed that he commanded him to be dragged, and he would have been dragged if it had not been for certain caciques with whom he had made friends, who led the king to understand he was mad' (ch. 95, 254). The captive priest Jerónimo Gracián himself risked martyrdom for having persuaded a renegade named Mamí, alias Alonso de la Cruz, to return to Christianity and declare it publicly, but neither of them was martyred because the beylerbey, Mamí Baxá – more interested in material than spiritual matters, said when he heard about this: 'I wish many renegades like Alonso ... would become Christians, so I could use them on my galleys as I'll do with Mamí: it's plenty punishment to make him row the rest of his life. Let no one say anything about this to the mufti (who is like the bishop of the city) or to the qadi (who is like the magistrate) lest they burn our archpriest here, for I'll cut off the head of anyone who tells' (113). See also the study of martyrdom in the Alpujarras by Barrios Aguilera and Sánchez Ramos.

By most definitions, a martyr in one way or another chooses to die such a death. The *Diccionario de la Real Academia Española* (twenty-second ed.) defines *mártir* in the first place as a person who suffers death for the sake of Jesus Christ and in defence of the Christian religion, and secondly as a person who dies or suffers greatly in defence of his or her beliefs, convictions or causes, while the next edition adapts the latter as its primary definition: a person who suffers death in defence of his or her religion. The key here is always suffering *in defence of* one's religion, which implies that martyrs' function is to defend the religion of their own people against the religion of their adversaries; and *suffering* suggests submission to a death imposed by others. We'll see that this definition in both respects doesn't fit many cases of martyrdom narrated in texts of this period in the Mediterranean – including Cervantes' writings – because martyrs very often provoke their own martyrdom and don't exactly act *in defence of* their religion.

In its first definition of *martyr* with reference to Christianity, the *Oxford English Dictionary* places emphasis rather on *choosing* death *rather than renouncing* one's faith: 'A person who chooses to suffer death rather than renounce faith in Christ or obedience to his teachings, a Christian way of life, or adherence to a law or tenet of the Church; also a person who chooses to suffer death rather than renounce the beliefs or tenets of a particular Christian denomination, sect, etc.' This implies *choosing* death *instead of choosing* its alternative, i.e. renouncing Christianity and living. The texts discussed here don't fit this definition either, since Muslim adversaries seldom impose such a dilemma on *martyrs*. In his article on martyrdom in the context of religious struggles of Catholics against Protestants, Alfonso Rodríguez begins with this definition: 'Martyrdom must be considered as an act of extreme violence, extending from previous torture to death, coercing a person to give up his/her beliefs and opinions of whatever kind' (217). Here elements of the above-cited definitions are incorporated (death imposed on someone to try to force the renunciation of beliefs), but it also adds that there is a process of violence from torture to death: the notion of process is indeed important, but I think the term *cruelty* would be more appropriate than *violence*.

From early modern texts about Christian martyrdom in the Mediterranean, it is readily apparent that many were 'martyrs' against their will: their coreligionists interpreted their deaths as acts of martyrdom, acts of dying for their faith when evidently they did nothing of the sort. Antonio de Sosa's *Diálogo de los mártires de Argel* (*Topografía* IV), written towards the end of the sixteenth century, tells thirty stories of 'martyrdom' in Algiers from the reign of Hayreddin Barbarossa (as of 1518) to the years when Sosa himself was captive (1577–81). This work is very much in line with other Catholic martyrologies, narrating acts of extreme cruelty directed against Christians. Although Sosa recognises that, strictly speaking, perhaps not all the protagonists of these episodes are martyrs,[11] only a few seem to meet the official criteria of martyrdom because most of these stories recount cruel deaths, usually punishments for some crime. Captives devise plots against their masters who in turn retaliate with exemplary punishments, others instigate rioting, others try to escape, others are Christian corsairs captured and executed, and so on. Only a few deaths are attributed to religious motives as such.[12] Thus, what turns such deaths into martyrdom is the interpretation, usually *a posteriori*, and its adaptation to the narrative moulds of martyrdom. Few of these martyrs chose martyrdom, but they *were martyred*, that is, martyred *by* those who tortured and killed them, as well as by those who turned them into martyrs by recounting their deaths. Some resigned themselves to their fate and accepted martyrdom, but would have preferred to live. Sosa presents to his readers a deviation where martyrdom doesn't necessarily imply choosing death and where it's rarely required that those who die should renounce their religion. For Sosa, the essence of martyrdom is rather the suffering of cruelties and often death, in a context in which Christians are viewed as victims of Muslim hatred. Martyrdom without cruelty and death would make no sense, and the more cruelty there is, the better.

Faces of martyrdom

What do these tortures and deaths mean to those who inflicted them, to those who suffered them, and to the writer who narrated them as acts of martyrdom? The second of the stories of Sosa's *Diálogo de los mártires* tells of the uprising and escape planned by many of Hayreddin Barbarossa's captives – a conspiracy frustrated by the betrayal of a Christian captive who had twice been a renegade. Calling the seventeen leaders 'traitorous dogs', Barbarossa told them 'that they had wanted to lead an insurrection and would now receive the reward for such great audacity', and thus ordered that they be executed outside the city. The text says:

> They carried them outside the gate of Bab Al-Wad, which faces west. And when they came to the field there, the Turks grasped their scimitars and, as the seventeen Christians were tied up, tame as sheep or lambs, with

---

[11] The stories are collected in a document entitled 'Memory of some martyrs *and other cruel deaths*' (my emphasis), and Sosa himself as interlocutor of his dialogue admits: 'Also, for that matter, let's not quarrel for now over whether all those I've written about here ought to be deemed martyrs, although you'll find among them some so illustrious in the testimony they gave with their blood of the truth of our faith or Christian justice, that it would be rash for anyone not to judge them to be most excellent martyrs' (153r).

[12] See Emilio Sola's introductory essay to the *Diálogo de los mártires*, 33–5, for a classification of these punishable offences which are subsequently interpreted as martyrdom.

fierce strokes they cut them to pieces and severed their heads, and cut off their arms and slashed their legs and all other members of their bodies. This being done, and letting those cruel Turks and renegades satisfy their viciousness on those Christian bodies, Barbarossa ordered that on pain of death no one should dare to bury them or even cast them into the sea and that there on those dungheaps they be eaten by dogs or birds of the air. (*Topografía* IV, 155r)

This would have occurred in 1531, half a century before Sosa's captivity in Algiers. In Sosa's account the mention of weapons implies that the uprising of the captives would have been violent, and it's acknowledged that Barbarossa acts as a judge when he tells them that they will pay for what they've done. But apart from this the account minimises the magnitude of this insurrection and strives to represent the death of the Christians with the utmost pathos whereby, like defenceless lambs, they're sacrificed in the cruellest ways and their 'Christian bodies' are left without burial to be eaten by dogs and birds. We know that for Barbarossa, as he's represented here, it's an exemplary punishment, but Sosa manipulates his story so that those who are punished become innocent sacrificial victims. What tilts the balance here is cruelty, which involves an unjustified excess and turns what might have been seen as justice on the Muslim side into something that resembles martyrdom on the Christian side. It *resembles* martyrdom because martyrdom is more a rhetorical effect of representation on the part of the author than a logical expression derived from a concept: these executed men would have had no idea that they were martyrs, they would have understood their fate within the context of Mediterranean captivity as punishment for a legitimately motivated but failed uprising, they did not choose their death nor would they have accepted it with the resignation of martyrs, and were not given the option of renouncing Christianity.

There is another version of this episode, probably closer to the event itself, in a Turkish biography of Hayreddin Barbarossa. This narrative tells that the conspirators planned to kill the jailer, among others, and to leave Algiers with about seven thousand Christian captives. Barbarossa intuited this in a dream, discovered their conspiracy and even obtained evidence of the plot through signed letters. The death of the conspirators is told like this: 'And he commanded that they be slain and that their signed letters be sent to the land of Christians so that, upon recognition of their signatures, no harm be done to the Moorish slaves on account of this incident.'[13] In this version their death

---

[13] 'Y los mandó degollar y enviar las cartas firmadas de ellos a tierra de cristianos; porque conociendo las firmas de ellos no hiciesen daño por aquel caso a los moros que tenían esclavos' (Murād 114; this edition is based on a 1578 translation into Spanish of the Turkish manuscript).

was simple justice – a justice that would be recognised as such by Christians elsewhere who would thus not retaliate by harming their Muslim slaves – and, no matter how severe this death sentence may seem to us today, it lacked cruelty and could not be considered martyrdom.

To return to the range of martyrs in the texts of this epoch, some would indeed see themselves as martyrs, and among them there were, on the one hand, those who had no desire for martyrdom but accepted their death with resignation, and, on the other, those who actively embraced martyrdom. It seems to me that the dynamics of cruelty as well as the expected reaction to cruelty are very different in these two categories.

We now return to the case of the Valencian friar Miguel de Aranda, whose story is inextricably connected with the Morisco corsair Alicax, who, as we saw in the last chapter, was condemned by the Inquisition for being an apostate. Fray Miguel did everything he could to avoid martyrdom, and yet behaved like a martyr once his fate was sealed. In his longest story of martyrdom (Sosa IV, 179r–83r),[14] Sosa tells how fray Miguel is captured on the Catalan coast and taken in July of 1576 to Algeria, where, as we'll recall, relatives of the Morisco corsair Alicax buy him as currency of exchange, having learned that Alicax has been captured and imprisoned in Valencia but *not* that he is being tried by the Inquisition (a fact known but withheld by the Christian captives including fray Miguel). When these *andaluces* from Sargel (Cherchell, a port west of Algiers) finally learn in April of 1577 that Alicax was condemned by the Inquisition and publicly burned in Valencia back in November, they become furious and, desiring revenge, ask permission to burn Miguel de Aranda in Algiers. No amount of money will quench their 'thirst for Christian blood'. Some of the Muslim sectors of Algiers, including renegade corsairs no less, oppose this vehement *quid pro quo*, but the frenzy of the Moriscos (more precisely *ex*-Moriscos) intent on burning a priest incites popular anger in their favour. The last pages of this episode represent the masses in all their festive cruelty – and the word *fiesta* figures among so many images of collective cruelty – as they lead the holy *martyr*, as he is called time and again, to be insulted, tortured, stoned and burned. After he dies they keep stoning and burning him again until all that remains are ashes and bones that his Christian companions secretly gather as relics.

For the Moriscos, fray Miguel is not innocent, since as a Valencian priest – indeed a knight of the military order of Montesa, founded in the fourteenth century after the dissolution of the Templars to combat Muslims who attacked the Valencian coast – he partakes by association in the persecution of Muslims perpetrated by the Church, the Inquisition and the State. Even so, we don't see him playing any role within that order. For the Moriscos, *someone* has to

---

[14] In the edition of Sola and Parreño it is story no. 23 (162–73).

be tortured and killed to compensate for what was done to Alicax, and this priest fits the desired profile. From here on, all vengeful anger is channelled towards him, and it even seems irrelevant whether he does or does not feel pain since the ritualistic annihilation of his body continues after his death. As the Morisco exiles harbour an enormous resentment over the situation of Spanish Muslims in general and the fate of Alicax in particular, they undoubtedly see their cause as more than justified, and thus the killing of a priest would not be an act of cruelty but a collective cathartic event that for the time being provides recompense for many ills. This can be discerned in Sosa's account. From a Catholic Christian perspective, nothing could be crueller, and the pain inflicted by cruelty is what constitutes martyrdom and gives it meaning. The opposition between bad persecutors and innocent martyr couldn't be more marked. Here we have the story of an authentic martyr who never wanted to be one, a priest who was captured in his own country, used as a pawn and executed without any fault of his own, only as recompense for another ceremony of cruelty held in his native city. Each gesture of his turns out to be an *imitatio Christi*, according to the mould adopted by this story. No matter how sceptical we might be towards this textual manipulation, it's hard not to feel sympathy for this man entangled in such a strangely cruel fate, and perhaps also (despite all the propaganda against him) towards his counterpart Alicax in Valencia.

Most impressive with regard to our current theme is that despite the relentless use of inquisitorial techniques from torture to intimidation and possible reduction of Alicax's sentence if he were to renounce Islam, Alicax remains absolutely firm, or, as the trial record says, 'pertinacious' (*pertinaz*). Ironically, although Islam in the early modern period needed no new martyrs to defend the faith, Alicax does in effect choose death rather than renounce Islam, to paraphrase the OED definition, and he thus comes closer to martyrdom than any of the Christian 'martyrs' discussed here, but with one important difference: there is no hint that he assumes the role of a martyr, and martyrdom, as understood within Christianity of that time, was best when it was *performed* by the martyr.

By common Mediterranean practice, any other corsair captain would most likely have entered into an operation of prisoner exchange. The 'elephant in the room' in subsequent versions of fray Miguel de Aranda's martyrdom – the cause that sets in motion this *double* martyrdom that didn't have to happen – is the Inquisition's persecution of Moriscos, and of Alicax in particular. The deck is stacked against the Morisco Alicax, both because of the system of internal colonialism and, more importantly, inquisitorial zeal towards the Moriscos during these years. Sosa was told the entire story by Antonio Esteban, the Valencian captive who initially informed Alicax's brother Caxetta that Alicax was in prison, and knew both brothers. Only Sosa, then, with his characteristic attention to detail, clearly describes the dynamics of this situation and lets us see the 'elephant in the room' before he shifts into hagiographic mode.[15] In their plays that recount the martyrdom of fray Miguel, Cervantes and Lope de Vega go much further in villainising and obfuscating the character of the 'other' martyr.

This story as Sosa tells it emanates the palpable immediacy of a lived experience: he had just been brought as a captive to Algiers in April of 1577 when this happened (in May). Cervantes, who by that time had been there for a year and a half, puts this story in the mouth of a slave named Sebastián (no less) in a long passage at the end of the first act of his propagandist work *El trato de Argel* on slavery in Algiers, written around 1583 and never published by its author. The Cervantine version reduces the story almost to its most essential outline: there are only two individualised characters and they're not named (though there's no doubt about who they are), the Moriscos buy the priest only *after* knowing what happened to their relative, there's a horizontal geographic axis that locates at opposite poles Valencia (associated with justice, Inquisition, Christianity, charity, etc.) and Algiers (associated with injustice, angry mobs, Islam, cruelty, etc.), and another vertical axis that polarises *suelo* (ground, earth, the stage of martyrdom, dead body) and *cielo* (heaven, glory, living spirit). Practically all of Sebastian's uninterrupted speech is articulated along these two axes. This story is undoubtedly intended to pluck the audience's most affective strings with regard to the experience of Algerian captivity: Sebastián has just witnessed martyrdom, he's so distressed that he can hardly begin to communicate it to his companions, and his whole story is charged with the extreme emotions that this scene brought forth. Cervantes' poetic version thus produces a condensed account that will have its echoes and artistic counterpoints in the rest of this work, but which in itself becomes a propagandistic resource designed to galvanise the sensibility of the public. There's not the slightest ambiguity: the 'righteous inquisitors' *over there* are praised time and again whereas *here* the cruel rabble is cursed, everything is polarised in a manichean way, the martyr is glorified while those who want to stone this 'second St. Stephen' (v. 671) are dehumanised. Whether or not it's

---

[15] Sosa's text shows the complexity of the situation on the Algerian side, too, revealing, for example, the varied responses to the Moriscos on the part of a number of the leading figures of the city. Before he becomes a martyr as such, fray Miguel is represented as a character who tries to manage the shifting situations to his benefit, but to no avail. As mentioned, he knows from the start that Alicax is being tried by the Inquisition, but says nothing. When he's bought by Caxetta he makes weak promises to the effect that he'll try to intercede to save Alicax, but he knows it's quite out of his hands. His ineffectiveness in intervening results in the harsh treatment he receives. Later, when his death is imminent, he vigorously intervenes to try to save himself (a ransomer's ship has arrived), believing that since the Moriscos are poor and need cash, a bargain can be struck, but in this he completely misjudges the Moriscos and their vengefulness towards the Inquisition and everything and everyone associated with it.

justified by experience, a representation of martyrdom like this one in *El trato de Argel* marks a zealous rejection of *others* and a victimisation of *ourselves*. Its purpose is not so much to represent a reality as to influence the ideological and emotional reactions of an audience towards what's represented.

In his play *Los cautivos de Argel* (1599) – which has long been acknowledged as a *rifacimento* of this early unpublished work by Cervantes[16] – Lope de Vega rewrites this scene of the martyrdom of the priest/knight of the order of Montesa, economising even more on narrative detail and drenching the speech in more blood, tears and polarising sentiment, as well as with more reminiscences of Christ's martyrdom. Lope creates more dramatic immediacy as the scene moves towards the impaled martyr himself (named Felis in this play), who utters his last words to end the narrative. Like the Cervantine text, Lope's play appeals to charity to rescue the captives of Algiers. In fact, this whole scene of martyrdom begins with a none-too-subtle exhortation on the part of the character Sahavedra (Cervantes' adopted second surname) to make donations (vv. 1911–19).

Martyrdom in Muslim lands was very much on the periphery of those struggles over martyrdom between Protestants and Catholics, but it had its own more local circuit in the Mediterranean where ransoming orders (particularly Trinitarians and Mercedarians), together with ransomed captives, were the main protagonists and beneficiaries, since speech about martyrs was more effective than any other topic for collecting money. This Valencian priest lived his own drama which, like all Christian martyrdom, would recall the prototypical martyrdom of Christ, but martyrdoms like his were also very profitable for all human commerce in the *mare nostrum*.

This story of a martyr who didn't want to be one can be compared to that of someone who did want to be a martyr, another Valencian priest as it happens. I'm aware of three versions of this story, whose authors and works are these:

- William Okeley, captive in Algiers 1639–44, English Calvinist: *Ebenezer: A small monument of great mercy, appearing in the miraculous deliverance of William Okeley*, published in 1675.
- Emanuel d'Aranda, captive in Algiers 1640–42, Belgian Catholic of Spanish descent: *Les Captifs d'Alger*, published in 1656.
- Pierre Dan, a French Trinitarian priest who in 1634 spent months in Algiers rescuing captives: *Les Plus Illustres Captifs*, written *c.* 1649.

Later we'll look briefly at the similar fictitious case of Hazén in Cervantes' *Los baños de Argel*: this is such a recognisable type in texts of the period that we could call it 'the repentant renegade who provokes his own martyrdom'.

---

[16] See Canavaggio, *Cervantès dramaturge*, 64–76, and *Cervantes, entre vida y creación*, 110–12, 121; Case 117–21; Fernández 7–26; Márquez Villanueva, *Moros*, 39–44; Mas 2: 83, 120, 241–51, 409–10; and Ohanna in his introduction to Lope's play (31–49).

In 1636, while travelling by ship to Rome, the Dominican priest José Morano was captured by corsairs and taken to Algiers where, six years later in 1642, he converted to Islam, and some five months afterwards (in early 1643) declared he was a Christian, thus forcing the Muslim authorities to execute him for apostasy. Of the three authors mentioned, Okeley had briefly known the priest, d'Aranda knew him well, and Dan received the story second-hand.

Okeley's Calvinism predisposes how he tells the story: according to him, the priest feels offended that he has not been ransomed and impulsively renounces 'not only his popery but his Christianity'. But his conscience tortures him, as this passage indicates through language evocative of cruelty: 'His own conscience, which was a thousand witnesses against him, was a thousand tormentors to him. Long he bore its secret and stinging lashes, but when he could no longer stand under them, he goes to the viceroy's palace and there openly declares himself a Christian and protests against the superstition and idolatry of Mahomet.' After looking into other options, Okeley says, 'they proceeded to the last remedy and inexorably condemned him to the fire, a way of punishment which they learnt from the Spaniards themselves, who first set up the Inquisition against the Moors and have now turned the edge of it against the Protestants. And now they proceed to the execution of the sentence, which was performed with some pomp and state.' Okeley reverently describes the bonfire but mocks Catholic martyrdom by saying that at night a fervent Spaniard 'carried away some of his scorched flesh and bones as the holy relics of a martyr, saying, "I have now done enough to make satisfaction for all the sins that I have committed"' (161–2). For Okeley this is an example of how Muslims incoherently allow freedom of religious conscience at the same time as they condemn to death those who renounce Islam. In Okeley's account, the priest suffers two forms of martyrdom: the first is the torture to which his conscience subjects him, and the second is the burning of a Christian (even if he is Spanish and papist) by Muslims.

D'Aranda, with his wonderful capacity for observation, portrays padre José as a jovial man, a good drinker, who deceived his Morisco master to be well treated. Perhaps because he saw little chance of being ransomed, or perhaps because he felt drawn to the kind of life that the Quran allowed, says d'Aranda, he embraced Islam and took the name of Youcef, to the rejoicing of the Muslims who conveyed him ceremoniously around the city. When, after a time, two captive priests reproached him, Youcef 'was so moved that he promised the two priests that he would leave the Mohammedan religion and be reconciled with the Holy Church' (187). He dressed as a Christian and declared that he was prepared to die. The Muslims tried to dissuade him, but then condemned him to be burned at low heat. D'Aranda concludes: 'They lit a fire whose flame boosted the courage of this holy martyr who, stronger than ever, asked God for forgiveness for the scandal he had given to Christians, urging them to hold on to the Christian faith. In the end, suffocated by smoke, he fell to the ground, ending his life by giving all Christian slaves an example of true religion and of a very repentant Christian' (187–8). In this version, padre José is recognised as a good man who made an understandable mistake, and when he was led to see his error he chose martyrdom as a form of repentance and carried it out in an exemplary manner.[17] Cruelty is almost absent here: padre José accepts the rules of the game and chooses to die by them. The Muslims try to prevent his execution, but when he perseveres they're obliged to carry it out, although without any gratuitous sign of punishment other than the slow fire. The only cruelty we can point to is his cruelty towards himself.

Pierre Dan's version is the one that puts this story in the orthodox mould of martyrdom. This involves discarding all the superfluous details about padre José, showing him very cruelly treated by his Morisco master and representing his conversion to Islam as that of a sinner fallen into 'bankruptcy with God' (346) because of his debauched life devoted to food and drink. When his sense of shame brings him back to Christianity, he has the option of covering it up as a crypto-Christian and attempting to return to his homeland, but he does what he's obliged to do by deciding to atone for his crime 'with his own blood' in 'glorious martyrdom' because this is what he *owes* his fellow captives. The angry mufti wants to punish him exemplarily and orders him to be tortured and subjected to circumcision, but even so padre José refuses to renounce Christianity. The furious pasha puts chains on him and threatens him, but the priest is unshakeable. Many masses are said throughout the city asking for the grace of God in a saintly death. Pierre Dan recounts in great detail how he's taken to the bonfire and how, with the fire lit, the Muslims shout to him that he can still save his life but he exclaims that he is dying as a Christian. Pierre Dan brings this scene to a catharsis.

This version presents a very different martyrdom from that of the other two. There's something even orgiastic in this will to receive pain, in this supreme cruelty towards himself. There are two types of cruelty in evidence here, the cruelty of the martyr against himself and the cruelty of the Muslims towards him, and the first depends on the second for the act to be fully realised. As the repentant renegade Hazén says with shocking clarity in the *Los baños de Argel* when he is about to be martyred: 'Do not change his mind, / good Jesus; strengthen in him / his intent and my plea, / for my salvation depends / on the qadi's being cruel' (v. 852–6).[18] Martyrdom often involved a willingness to die, and a calculation of the sundry benefits that would result from such a death.

---

[17] As a headline of the parodic newspaper *The Onion* once put it: 'Cost of living now outweighs the benefits' (13 April 2005).

[18] 'No le mudes la intención, / buen Jesús; confirma en él / su intento y mi petición, / que en ser el cadí crüel / consiste mi salvación' (vv. 852–6).

Martyrdom in perspective

It's worth recalling a passage from Nietzsche's *Beyond good and evil* which proposes that a perverse cruelty underlies a great number of diverse cultural and social phenomena: 'Almost everything we call "higher culture" is based on the spiritualisation of *cruelty*, on its becoming more profound.' He offers examples that include tragedy, the Roman circus, the 'ecstasy of the cross', autos-da-fé and bullfights, submission to Wagnerian music, and much else:

> To see this we must, of course, chase away the clumsy psychology of bygone times which had nothing to teach about cruelty except that it came into being at the sight of the sufferings of *others*. There is also an abundant, over-abundant enjoyment at one's own suffering, at making oneself suffer – and wherever man allows himself to be persuaded to self-denial in the *religious* sense, or to self-mutilation ... or altogether to desensualization, decarnalization, contrition, Puritanical spasms of penitence, vivisection of the conscience, and *sacrifizio dell'intelletto* à la Pascal, he is secretly lured and pushed forward by his cruelty, by those dangerous thrills of cruelty turned *against oneself*. (#229, here and elsewhere in these passages the emphasis is his)

Other Nietzschean passages reflect on:

- the relationship between 'the pleasure of cruelty' and 'the idea of the meaning and higher value implied by voluntary suffering and freely accepted martyrdom' (*Daybreak*, #18);
- the victory of the martyr and ascetic over himself, directing his gaze inward and seeing an individual who at the same time suffers and observes that suffering, who no longer looks outward except to gather wood to feed his own bonfire, thus attaining an ineffable bliss in contemplating a tortured being (*Daybreak*, #113);
- the link between guilt and suffering, the pleasure that sometimes involves '*making* suffer', and the 'festival' that this can produce (*Genealogy of morals*, 2nd essay, #6; emphasis in the original);
- the meaning that is conferred (in Christianity, for example) on suffering (*Genealogy of morals*, 2nd essay, #7).

I believe that these hypotheses offer clues, so obfuscated in other sources, about the psychology and sociology of martyrdom: those who choose to be martyrs experience a victory over themselves, a desire to make themselves suffer and at the same time contemplate themselves as they suffer; they also feel a 'festive' pleasure and the certainty that all of this takes on enormous significance since salvation itself is obtained through maximum suffering. It seems to me that those who actively seek their own martyrdom – according to the texts and images of the sixteenth and seventeenth centuries – fit well within this mould of cruelty directed against oneself, a cruelty that passes for innocence or repentance or spiritual fortitude, and that disguises itself as cruelty of *others*, which is none other than the means of their martyrdom, not its cause.

Cervantes' play *Los baños de Argel* presents two main cases of martyrdom, one issuing from guilt and the other from innocence. The renegade Hazén is indignant at the behaviour of his fellow renegade Yzuf, who has just led a razzia in his Spanish homeland, capturing and selling his nephews and their father. Although the Christian captives try to dissuade Hazén from putting himself in mortal danger, he kills Yzuf and proclaims his Christian faith, ecstatically provoking his own martyrdom: 'I am indeed [Christian]; / and am so firm in being so, / that I desire, as you have seen, / to be undone and to be with Christ, / if possible, today.'[19] More emotive is the case of one of the captured children, Francisquito, whom the qadi wants to turn into a *garzón* of his. He is a tender and beautiful boy, very childish in his pastimes but loyal to his family and firm in his faith to the point of being ready very soon to suffer martyrdom: 'Father, my name is Francisco, / not Azán, Alí or Jaer; / I am and will be Christian, / even if they put to my neck / two garrottes and a knife.'[20] Unlike Hazén, Francisquito does not have to pay any debt of guilt because he's innocent, and thus creates a situation of pure sacrifice that not only demonises his persecutor but also transforms the little martyr into a Christ-child. Thus the frustrated qadi, after trying everything, 'affronted and ashamed, / today has vented on Francisco / his Luciferine rage. / He is tied to a column, / turned into an image of Christ, / from head to toe / in his own red blood. / I fear that he has perished, / because such a cruel martyrdom / would not have been resisted / by greater years and strength'.[21] A stage direction indicates: '*A curtain opens; Francisquito appears, tied to a column in such a way as to induce the greatest pity.*'[22] Shortly afterwards his father receives the child's soul in his mouth, and towards the end another stage direction reads: '*The father leaves with a bloody white cloth, as if bearing the bones of Francisquito.*'[23] As has been

---

[19] 'Sí soy [cristiano]; / y en serlo tan firme estoy / que deseo, como has visto, / deshacerme y ser con Cristo / si fuese posible, hoy' (vv. 827–31).

[20] 'Padre, Francisco me llamo, / no Hazán, Alí ni Jafer; / cristiano soy, y he de sello / aunque me pongan al cuello / dos garrotes y un cuchillo' (vv. 1360–4).

[21] 'como afrentado y corrido, / su luciferina rabia / hoy ha esfogado en Francisco. / Atado está a una coluna, / hecho retrato de Cristo, / de la cabeza a los pies / en su misma sangre tinto; / témome que habrá expirado, / porque tan crüel martirio / mayores años y fuerzas / no le hubieran resistido' (vv. 2357–67).

[22] '*Córrese una cortina; descúbrese* Francisquito *atado a una coluna, en la forma que pueda mover a más piedad*' (after v. 2541).

[23] '*Sale el* padre *con un paño blanco ensangrentado, como que lleva en él los huesos de* Francisquito' (after v. 2994). Moisés Castillo (233) comments insightfully on the father's intrusive intensification of Francisquito's martyrdom.

observed, this case recalls that of the Holy Child of La Guardia: devoid of any sociohistorical verisimilitude, it is a brazen manipulation of a public perhaps predisposed to swallow such falsehoods and to enjoy their perverse cruelty. Published in 1615 and probably written not long before as a *rifacimento* of both Cervantes' own *El trato de Argel* and Lope's *Los cautivos de Argel*, this martyrdom may be the most extreme in the Cervantine corpus, and the late date of the work prevents us from sketching a coherent evolution regarding the treatment of martyrdom in Cervantes' works. We should recall that the captive's tale in the first part of *Don Quixote* (1605) suppresses almost every suggestion of martyrdom and shares important plot elements with *Los baños de Argel*. But *Los baños* consists not only of these two stories of martyrdom but of an ensemble of different intrigues, and its *gracioso* figure, the sacristan Tristán, accused by an old man of having a 'wide conscience', says that 'it is foolish impertinence / to let oneself die'.[24] (vv. 1158–9).

The theme of martyrdom surfaces in Cervantes' play *La gran sultana*, from the same collection (1615), as of the moment that protagonist doña Catalina de Oviedo first appears. The theme also affects the eunuch Rustán and the couple Zelinda and Zaida (alias Lambert and Clara), all of whom are at some point ready to suffer a Christian death if necessary.[25] But it's doña Catalina who has a vocation for martyrdom and insists on it, especially in the second act when she resists marrying an infidel, the sultan himself. In a fascinating exchange with Rustán, we see that the eunuch rebuts doña Catalina:

> Sultana: I'll be martyr as long as I'm willing
> to die rather than sin.
> Rustán: Being a martyr requires
> a higher cause
> than losing one's life
> for confessing one's faith.
> Sultana: I'll take that opportunity.
> Rustán: Who is asking you to do so?
> The Sultan wants you as a Christian
> …
> Many saints wanted
> to be martyrs, and found
> the right means to become martyrs,
> but these were not enough:

---

[24] 'es necia impertinencia / dejarse morir' (vv. 1158–9).

[25] Rustán is ready to suffer 'any torture whatsoever' owing to his 'Christian conduct' for having protected and hidden the young captive doña Catalina (vv. 284–9). Zelinda and Zaida, afraid of being discovered in the harem because Zelinda is a man and Zaida is pregnant with his child, affirm their willingness to die as Christians if there's no solution (vv. 1454–61).

> for great virtue is needed
> to become a martyr,
> and this is a special gift
> that God gives to whom He wants.
> Sultana: I will ask heaven,
> since I don't deserve so much,
> to bestow its strength
> on my holy purpose.[26]

Leaving aside the inscrutable will of God, it's more than obvious that the legitimate circumstances for martyrdom are lacking here. The devout Catalina indeed finds herself in Muslim lands, captive in the imperial harem and trapped by her suitor the sultan, 'this infernal serpent' as she unfairly refers to him (v. 825). But otherwise everything plays against martyrdom: no one wants to kill her, there's no enraged enemy who tells her to change her religion but rather a lover who adores her, wants to marry her and insists that she remain Christian (and Spanish) and pray to the Virgin Mary, 'to your Lela Marïén, / who among us is holy'.[27] Lacking any motive for martyrdom, the absurdity of her wanting to be a martyr in such circumstances becomes evident. After perhaps the ugliest anagnorisis of the entire Cervantine *oeuvre* – when the sultana is reunited with her unpalatable father – the latter accuses her of living 'in mortal sin' (v. 2012) and encourages her to be a martyr (vv. 2057–8). For her part, she's tormented by the fact that she can't be a martyr: 'Is it fair for me to kill myself, / since they do not want to kill me?'[28] 'A martyr I am in desire' (v. 2037), she affirms, pointing once more to that troubling character trait, an unjustified desire to die as a Christian martyr. In sum, the father wants his daughter to die, and she would be thrilled to suffer a glorious death. Given the circumstances, none of this makes any sense whatsoever unless we consider the psychology of a female character who, from a young age until recently, never knew anything outside of captivity and confinement.

Perhaps this is the reverse of the mock martyrdom that Sancho Panza undergoes, where the unintentional martyr does not participate emotionally in his own 'martyrdom', while doña Catalina wants to be a martyr but can't, adopting an exaggeratedly tragic stance in her own *comedia*. In both cases

---

[26] '(Sultana) Mártir seré si consiento / antes morir que pecar. / (Rustán) Ser mártir se ha de causar / por más alto fundamento, / que es por el perder la vida / por confesión de la fe. / (Sultana) Esa ocasión tomaré. / (Rustán) ¿Quién a ella te convida? / Sultán te quiere cristiana, / … / Muchos santos desearon / ser mártires, y pusieron / los medios que convinieron / para serlo, y no bastaron: / que al ser mártir se requiere / virtud sobresingular, / y es merced particular / que Dios hace a quien Él quiere. / (Sultana) Al cielo le pediré, / ya que no merezco tanto, / que a mi propósito santo / de su firmeza le dé' (vv. 1130–53).

[27] 'a tu Lela Marïén, / que entre nosotros es santa' (vv. 1743–4).

[28] '¿será justo que me mate, / ya que no quieren matarme?' (vv. 2019–20).

the social context created by Cervantes trivialises martyrdom. Reflecting on the few cases of martyrdom in Cervantes' writings, we can appreciate how seldom Cervantes yields to the strong temptation during that epoch of turning his characters into martyrs. We could consider martyrdom in the work of his friend Antonio de Sosa, who doesn't miss the slightest chance of representing martyrs even when their profile is quite unmartyrly; or in Gonzalo de Céspedes y Meneses' *El español Gerardo*, which novelises and combines a couple of Sosa's stories to amplify the martyrdom of a Christian corsair in Algiers;[29] or in Lope's novel *La desdicha por la honra*, where the Morisco protagonist Felisardo dies emphatically Christian at the hands of the Turks; or in the works of other writers like Diego de Torres, Jerónimo Gracián, Jerónimo de Pasamonte, Otavio Sapiencia, Pierre Dan, Gabriel Gómez de Losada, or the many books on martyrs and martyrdom registered in the *Junta de libros* (1624) by Tomás Tamayo de Vargas. Christian texts related to the Mediterranean at this time are populated with martyrs, but in Cervantes' works the only true martyrs are those we've seen in the two Algerian plays. Apart from these cases, then, Cervantes avoids representing martyrdom or represents it irreverently or obliquely, making the character least prone to martyrdom (Sancho) suffer it in ludic mode and the character most anxious to be a martyr (doña Catalina) happily survive without being able to fulfil her desire. In Sancho's case, the text mockingly questions the efficacy of martyrdom (the beneficial consequences of pain inflicted through the cruelty of others), and in Catalina's case the text ironises about her eagerness to be a martyr (the desire to be cruel against oneself). In general, the Cervantine position regarding martyrdom seems unusual.[30]

The representation of martyrdom within the Mediterranean context implies characterising Muslims as martyrisers capable of maximum cruelty and intolerance towards Christians. Needless to say, my intention in this chapter is not to deny or minimise the kinds of cruelties that people of the Mediterranean evidently committed against one another during those centuries, but rather to study different manifestations and representations of

---

[29] I'm referring to the character Hernando Palomeque. See Teijeiro Fuentes 38.

[30] Rabelais exhibits an even less reverent attitude towards martyrdom in the Mediterranean. In chapter 14 of *Pantagruel* (1: 289–94), Panurge says that he rejects the religion of the Quran for its prohibition of wine, and tells of his escape from the Ottoman Turks. When he was a slave in Turkey, he was put to roast like a rabbit on a spit, but he provoked a fire and ended up roasting his own master the pasha. On the one hand, Panurge plays here with the stereotype of the Turks as supposed cannibals, but on the other he alludes to martyrdom by fire: he invokes St. Lawrence – who was martyred on the grill – and asks God for help because they are giving him this torment for being a Christian ('pour la maintenance de ta loy'). There's thus a comic inversion of martyrdom where the roaster ends up roasted, the martyriser martyred. Jamil Chaker offers interesting commentaries on this episode (181–3).

so-called 'martyrdom'. As we've seen, not every martyr knows that he or she is one, not every martyr wants to be one, not all who want to be martyrs are able to attain martyrdom, those who impose martyrdom on others almost always understand this act as something quite different, and martyrs' cruelty against themselves is typically obfuscated as innocence. The few examples of martyrdom in Cervantes' writings show a variety of attitudes and ways of understanding it, but perhaps what stands out most is how seldom martyrdom arises in Cervantes' narrative, or even in his theatrical works if we except the two plays set in Algiers. This is very consistent with the more complex and humane view of Muslim otherness that can most often be inferred from Cervantes' writings. Just as Cervantes exposes the internal reasoning of so many modalities of human relations,[31] he lays bare the suspicious logic of martyrdom so often shrouded in sanctity. In general, discourse on martyrdom not only represents hatred but generates hatred, creating an extreme situation that impedes any kind of mutual understanding.

---

[31] This theme is explored in the second part of my book *Economía ética en Cervantes*.

5

Counternarratives

Portraying the Moriscos

She knew, as well as he knew, that words themselves do not convey meaning, that they are but a gesture we make, a dumb show like any other.

D. H. Lawrence

There's an unnamed character in Vicente Espinel's novel *Vida del escudero Marcos de Obregón* (*Life of the squire Marcos de Obregón*) (1618) who is – or has been – a Morisco, a Christian, a Moor, a renegade, a Spaniard, a Turk, a Valencian and an Algerian. He is Marcos's slave-master, and this wide-ranging set of apparently contradictory epithets is resolved in a single character who once hailed from Valencia as a noble Morisco and a Christian from a lineage whose Christianity dated far back, clandestinely abandoned Spain because he couldn't tolerate the indignities he was subjected to by people of lesser status, settled in Algiers, converted to Islam and became a famous corsair. As we know, such terms as *Morisco*, *Moor*, *renegade* and *Turk* are charged with a complex history, alien values and semantic ambivalences. From a 'Spanish' viewpoint this character is a Morisco, although – as Míkel de Epalza reminds us – from the moment that the Moriscos emigrated from Spain they were no longer Moriscos (a term that only had currency in Spain, from the perspective of those who were not Moriscos). Being a Muslim and, moreover, of Muslim *caste*, as well as a resident of 'Barbary' (which corresponds roughly to the Maghrib), he can indeed be called a *Moor*. On the other hand, being a corsair *renegade*, he is a *turco de profesión* (i.e. someone who has 'turned Turk', converted to Islam), and he's even referred to as a *turco español* (Spanish Turk). It's of course the fictional author Marcos who calls him by all of these qualifying names, and does so without animosity, although his characterisation of his master shows some typical biases. For his part, this slave-master doesn't exactly refer to himself by any of these identifiers. According to the terms used in the Maghrib, he would be called a *balansi* for being from the realm of Valencia, or a *tagarino* for being from the Crown of Aragon, a word derived from the Arabic *thaghrī* meaning *fronterizo* (of the frontier with Islam). More generally, as explained previously, ex-Moriscos would often be referred to as *andaluces*, 'Andalusians', derived from the Arabic toponym al-Andalus, denoting the Iberian Peninsula. In the Maghrib they were foreigners and in many cases religiously suspect, partly from Christian influences and partly from the lack of adequate Islamic indoctrination. Yet they had a historical connection to the Maghrib, and were linguistically (to the extent that they still spoke dialects of Arabic), culturally and politically assimilable to Islamic societies.

From both sides of the politico-religious divide, this unnamed character is simultaneously one of 'us' and one of 'them'. This profoundly frontier character straddles cultures, religions, languages and Mediterranean shores. His past as a Morisco and his present as a Barbary corsair are only comprehensible as expressions of a consciousness of traversable frontiers that separate and unite the Mediterranean of that time. He's one example, fictional but in some ways emblematic, of hundreds of thousands of 'Andalusians' who emigrated from Spain to Muslim lands from at least the thirteenth to the seventeenth century.

As prominent studies by, among others, Míkel de Epalza, Luis Bernabé Pons, Mercedes García-Arenal and Miguel Ángel de Bunes have amply shown, apart from earlier emigrations, 'Andalusians' left the Iberian Peninsula after the fall of Granada and the first Morisco uprising in 1501, and continued to do so in significant numbers throughout the sixteenth century. They had various routes and strategies of escape as well as international networks which they later adapted to the circumstances of the expulsion itself. From eastern and southwestern France they had various options, some of them routes leading to Morocco, Algeria or Tunisia, another via Venice to Istanbul. They also settled in Libya, Egypt, the Levant and Anatolia, thus spreading themselves widely in the Mediterranean. Even by the sixteenth century they had repopulated or founded towns and seaports and integrated themselves into their host societies in remarkably diverse ways, often close to the centres of power and in communication with both the other allochthonous people such as Turks and renegades as well as with autochthonous populations. They joined the militias in Morocco and Algeria, became corsairs along the front line of hostile contact with Spain and Portugal – establishing the 'republics' of Salé-Rabat and Tetuan – engaged in commerce in the Moroccan capitals as well as Algiers and Tunis, developed new modes of agriculture on the urban fringes of Algiers and Tunis, introduced silk production and other artisanal activities, worked hydraulic and horticultural wonders in Algiers, took positions at the courts, and much else.

All of this is now quite well known, particularly with respect to the Maghrib, which was revitalised by these immigrants. What I want to emphasise here is that the former Moriscos became perhaps 'more Mediterranean' than they had ever been, on a par with Jews and renegades and perhaps no other major category. They were instrumental and resourceful, and bolstered the diverse regimes and economies especially of the Maghrib. For various rulers they were the ideal kind of foreigners: mobile, capable, adaptable, loyal, and predisposed to confront the Christian north and to fit in culturally and religiously in the Islamic south and east. Being positioned along the coastlines and in or around vital urban centres, they were largely frontier people and participated directly in the making of the early modern Mediterranean. At least for the first generation or two, they were mostly bilingual and bicultural, with a knowledge of life on the other side, and in their ways could bridge the kinds of gaps that existed between north and south. Their emigration, in all the forms it took, was what made them become *so* Mediterranean, as occurs with the nameless Protean ex-Morisco mentioned above.

Scholarship of extraordinary quality – only a fraction of it available in English – has burgeoned over the past half-century to reveal virtually every researchable aspect regarding the 'Moriscos', a questionable name for nominally Christian descendants of the Spanish Muslims (by decree in Castile and later Aragon) that gradually gained traction during the sixteenth century, well after the fall in 1492 of Granada, the last Islamic kingdom in Spain. Among much else, we know about the cultural, linguistic and religious diversity of Moriscos throughout the regions of Spain, their books including the remarkable forgeries of the lead books, their commerce, networks, historical shifts, uprisings, periods and places of relative coexistence, well-known personages, communications with Muslims from the Maghrib and Istanbul as well as with Christian realms in Europe, and so on. We also know much about what led up to the definitive expulsion of 1609–14, how this played itself out, and how the Moriscos integrated themselves mainly in the lands of the Maghrib and contributed enormously to them by revolutionising their agriculture and commerce and devoting themselves to the militia and corsairing, among other activities. We know, too, about the continued presence (legal or clandestine) of a small but significant proportion of Moriscos in Spain after the expulsion, as well as the emigration (mostly illegal) of Moors/Moriscos between 1492 and 1609.

Some of the most renowned scholars, far from limiting themselves to Moriscos in Spain, have also carried out innovative research on Moriscos from Istanbul to Morocco and have explored other aspects of the Mediterranean world. What seems to have been almost unthinkable for many other scholars is that the Moriscos were far more than a Spanish 'national problem', that they had an Islamic dimension and perennial communication that connected them particularly with the Maghribian lands of the other shore. East of the Strait of Gibraltar there stretched a long arm of the sea between Spain and the Maghrib – the Alboran Sea – that kept communication open between the two parallel shores, the *'idwatayn*; alternatively, from al-Andalus, the Maghribian coastline over these centuries was referred to as *al-'idwa*, 'the shore' (Lapiedra 19–24, 34). Despite the new geopolitical frontier that surfaced in the water between Spain and the Maghrib – between Europe and Africa – after the fall of Granada, there continued to be a great deal of traffic, including commerce, corsairing and southward migration between the shores, into the seventeenth century, owing in considerable part to the activities of Moriscos.

As indicated, the ex-Moriscos were among the 'most Mediterranean' of all the peoples of the *mare nostrum*, and in our own times the exile of these 'last Muslims' of Western Europe has in ideological terms come to transcend the contours of the Mediterranean. For centuries during the Middle Ages the internal frontiers between Christian and Muslim kingdoms kept changing until the kingdom of Granada more or less held its own for two and a half centuries, after which the internal frontier shifted to the North African shores and hinterlands, where most 'Andalusians' would sooner or later find themselves displaced, becoming more 'Mediterranean' than ever.

An overview, say, of Mercedes García-Arenal's now classic anthology of primary texts by and about Moriscos, *Los moriscos* (1975), reveals that Moriscos were more than capable of representing themselves in various ways, and yet that there was a compulsion on the part of non-Moriscos to represent them. They were a topic to be written about, a people to be estranged, homogenised and characterised, and they were fair game for anyone able to wield a pen. What's more, at the time of the expulsion there was a concerted effort on the part of a network of clerical and lay writers – in effect, a small minority close to the nexus of political power – to justify the expulsion itself, yet the monologic vacuum they tried to establish was never absolute.

In the first part of this chapter I'll briefly explore how discourse tends to be framed within the context of the Moriscos' expulsion, what rhetorical strategies are used, and how the diverse intonation of similar statements can produce radically different meanings.

Three years before the first edict of expulsion of the Moriscos, Pedro de Valencia, in his *Tratado de los moriscos* (*Treatise on the Moriscos*, written 1606) commissioned by Philip III's confessor, imagines the horrors, injustice and inhumanity that such a measure would bring about:

> how can it be justified with God or men, nor what Christian heart could bear to see in the country and the shores such a great multitude of baptised men and women shouting to God and the world that they were and wanted to be Christians, while their children and property were being taken from them out of greed and hate, without their being heard fairly, and they were being sent away to become Moors? ... Imagine what in all likelihood would happen there.[1]

---

[1] '¿cómo se puede justificar con Dios, ni con los hombres, ni qué corazón cristiano había de haber que sufriese ver en los campos y en las playas una tan grande muchedumbre de hombres y mugeres bauptizados y que diesen vozes a Dios y al mundo que eran Cristianos y lo querían ser, y les quitaban sus hijos, y haciendas por avaricia y por odio, sin oírlos ni estar con ellos a Juicio, y los enviaban a que se tornasen Moros? ... Represéntese lo que es verosímil que allí pasaría' (112).

If his sympathy connects above all with Christian Moriscos, since 'those who were Moors in their hearts would be joyful', this prestigious humanist argues vigourously in favour of various forms of assimilation of the entire Morisco people who, despite being enemies, 'with regard to their natural complexion and consequently in relation to their ways of thinking, their character and spirit, are Spaniards like everyone else who dwells in Spain, since for almost nine hundred years they have been born and brought up in this land'.[2] His premonitions visualise scenes similar to what other writers, even those most hostile to the Moriscos, later describe, and what much of the remaining population would witness during the years of exodus. Even the most hardline apologists of the expulsion can't refrain from offering images of Moriscos filled with anguish, no matter how these are framed with ideological antipathy and aligned with official propaganda. Despite their best attempts at falsifying this experience for those sent into exile as well as for the rest of the Spanish population, these writers allow us to see people wrenched from their homes, communities and the fabric of their lives, forced along the roads towards danger and uncertain exile, separated from loved ones, suffering hunger, thirst, disease, violence, confiscation and theft. Nor are we spared images such as those of women leaping from cliffs or drowning in the sea, nor details of abuse taking place in Spain, on the ships and Maghribian coasts.

The commissioned expulsion paintings of Pere Oromig, Vicent Mestre and Jerónimo Espinosa, rediscovered in the 1970s, mostly concur with the representations of the apologists, trivialising the human experience of the expulsion, relegating violence to rebellions in the sierras or attacks of local tribesmen on the North African coast and showing only a few details of suffering hidden among so much orderliness and folklore in the ports of departure (*La expulsión*). Where we see the human face of the expulsion represented in all its vividness is in the striking ink sketch by the royal painter Vicente Carducho, in which sorrowful Moriscos – adults and children, women and men – embark under the watchful gaze of soldiers. Velázquez, too, portrayed the theme in a large painting that won a contest called for by Philip IV in 1627 to commemorate this event. This work is thought to have been lost along with hundreds of other artworks in the Real Alcázar de Madrid in the fire of 1734. According to Antonio Palomino, Velázquez's earliest biographer,

> in the middle of this painting is king Philip III in armour, pointing with his staff at a throng of weeping men, women and children led by soldiers, and in the distance ... a shoreline with ships to take them away ... To the right of the king is Spain, shown as a majestic matron, seated at the foot of a

---

[2] 'en quanto al ingenio, condición y brío, son españoles como los demás que habitan en España, pues ha casi novecientos años que nacen y se crían en ella' (78).

building with a shield and some darts in her right hand and ears of corn in her left, armed in Roman style, and at her feet an inscription. (27)

The Latin inscription at Spain's feet glorifies Philip III's expulsion of the Moriscos. In a work by a young court painter vying for a prize on a theme whose protagonist was Philip IV's father, such glorification would have been *de rigueur*, and one wouldn't expect any ambivalence about this in Palomino's naive ekphrasis. Velázquez's depiction of the Moriscos themselves, however – men, women and children weeping – leaves some doubt as to how he might have viewed the expulsion, a harrowing event he would have seen as an eleven-year-old boy in Seville. Accounts written in Seville at that time by no means exulted in the expulsion. We may well have lost a crucial pictorial document in the fire, one that could easily have been misinterpreted, just as Cervantes' passages on the Moriscos and the expulsion were misread for centuries, appearing to celebrate the expulsion while, as is now more than evident, they operate under the radar of state ideology.

Towards the end of the nineteenth century the eminent scholar Menéndez Pelayo could still say that 'we will always judge the great enactment of expulsion with the same enthusiasm with which Lope de Vega, Cervantes and all of seventeenth-century Spain celebrated it: as a triumph of the unity of race,

5 *Vicente Carducho, ink drawing of the expulsion of the Moriscos, c. 1627*

6 *Diego Velázquez,* Juan de Pareja, *1650 (detail)*

of the unity of religion, language and customs' (336–7). Yet as of the watershed publication in 1925 of Américo Castro's *El pensamiento de Cervantes* (roughly, *Cervantes' modes of thought*), Cervantes has more often than not been erased from the list of enthusiasts, and, moreover, this supposed enthusiasm has often been questioned. Some sixty years later, the masterly essay by Francisco Márquez Villanueva titled 'El problema historiográfico de los moriscos' – a study that has marked the parameters of many others – analyses the *maurophilia* of early modern Spanish literature and situates the apologists of the expulsion within a minority alliance backed by royal power that allowed for no dissenting opinion. It's in this context that Cervantes composed the sublime episode of the encounter between Sancho Panza and the Morisco Ricote followed later by the no less audacious story of Ricote's daughter Ana Félix.

My aim here is to juxtapose different textual representations of the expulsion and comment on their affective orientation, their degrees of authenticity, their techniques for controlling such a volatile subject, and the tropes that give them meaning within this historical context. I'll outline some of the main lines of this discursive background – especially among those in favour of the expulsion – that contrast so sharply, for example, with Cervantes' treatment of the expulsion in *Don Quixote*, whose second part was written during the expulsion. Although it's impossible to maintain a neutral stance towards any of these texts and their authors, at this point it seems anachronistic to produce one more pro-Morisco harangue full of moral indignation, because the facts and texts speak for themselves. Instead, I'm interested in looking into the discursive strategies of intolerance concerning an event of such drastic consequences and into how Cervantes' passages on the Moriscos both mimic such rhetoric and undermine it.

Let's begin, however, with examples of how writers of radically diverse ideological positions appear to say more or less the same thing and yet mean something entirely different by it. What they say, *mutatis mutandis*, is that Philip III of Spain was divinely inspired to expel the Moriscos, or, with a shift of emphasis, that God used Philip III as his instrument for the expulsion. In each case the writer or character ostensibly invokes the idea of divine inspiration to confer an ultimate meaning on the expulsion as God's will. We start with the expulsion apologist Juan Ripol, then cite Cervantes' Morisco character Ricote in *Don Quixote*, then a letter by the licentiate Molina – an exiled Morisco from Granada – to his Christian gentleman friend in Extremadura, and finally the pre-expulsion Morisco fugitive Aḥmad ibn Qāsim al-Ḥajarī:

> And thus, Serapión, rest assured that *this was divine inspiration, admirable foresight, magnanimous resolution, and that kind of providence which the poets called the daughter of God*. (Ripol 19v; emphasis mine in this series of quotations)[3]
>
> *it seems to me it was divine inspiration that moved His Majesty to put into effect such a gallant resolution* … (Ricote in *Don Quixote* II, 54, 1072)[4]
>
> and thus all of us from Trujillo came to this city of Algiers, where most of those from Extremadura, La Mancha and Aragon went. And *don't imagine that it was in the power of the king of Spain to banish us from his land, because it was divine inspiration*. Here [in Algiers] I have seen prophecies from over a thousand years that tell us what has happened to us and what will happen, and that *God would take us out of that land, and would put this thought in the heart of the king and his advisers*. (letter from the Morisco Molina, in García-Arenal, *Los moriscos*, 264)[5]

---

[3] 'Y así, Serapión, creed que ha sido inspiración divina, prevención admirable, resolución magnánima, y aquella providencia que dijeron los poetas ser hija de Dios.'

[4] 'me parece que fue inspiración divina la que movió a Su Majestad a poner en efecto tan gallarda resolución'

[5] The letter, dated in July 1611, is here entitled 'Carta de un morisco granadino escrita desde Argel a un caballero de Trujillo'. The original passage reads: 'y así todos los de Truxillo venimos a esta ciudad de Argel, donde estavan los más de Estremadura, Mancha y Aragón. Y no piense V. Merced ha sido en mano del rey de España el avernos desterrado de su tierra, pues ha sido inspiración divina. Porque aquí he visto pronósticos de más de mil años, en que cuentan, lo que de nosotros ha sucedido, y ha de suceder. Y que nos sacaría Dios de esa tierra: y que para esto pondría Dios en el corazón al rey y a sus consejeros, el hazer esto.'

God had created in my heart a longing to leave the lands of Al-Andalus ... God realized this purpose and fulfilled this wish and brought me to the city of Marrakesh in Morocco [in 1007/1599]. Twelve years later *the exalted God released the Muslim Andalusians who were still living in Al-Andalus* under the oppression and injustice of the Christians *when the sultan of the country called Philip III ordered all of them to leave his country.* (al-Ḥajarī 61–2)

The first of these has variants throughout the works of other apologists of the expulsion and was no doubt the sanctioned interpretation. Within the context of Ripol's dialogue, the character Alberto – spokesman for the author – consoles his landowner friend by saying that the loss of his Morisco labourers is more than compensated for by the king's divinely guided act of extirpating them. The second statement, Ricote's encomium, saturated with authorial irony through his caricature of the apologists' rhetoric, contrasts with the heartrending catastrophe that the expulsion has wrought in his own family, as he recounts in these same paragraphs. In the third passage, the Morisco Molina writes to a Christian friend back in Spain of the hardships he and many others have suffered in France and Italy prior to their arrival in Algiers, but is ultimately grateful to be where 'no one has obliged us to do any spiritual or bodily act that makes us deny what we have been',[6] and he insists that he's not writing out of anger or resentment. He explains that this was God's will, of which the king and his counsellors were mere pawns. Having risked his life to escape to Morocco and practise Islam, Al-Ḥajarī in the fourth passage goes even further by stressing how God *released* Spanish Muslims from religious oppression by having Philip III prohibit Muslims from *staying* in the country rather than, as was previously the case, from *leaving*. The four statements reveal a spectrum of religious adherence and life circumstances in relation to the expulsion. The first is Christian and belligerently anti-Islamic, while Moriscos pronounce the other three, one (Ricote) describing himself as more Christian than Muslim, another being exiled but ultimately content to live as a Muslim, and the last being a militantly anti-Christian fugitive exile, although he enjoys friendship and conversation with both Protestants and Catholics. All four draw from the same kind of rhetoric, but with widely divergent ideas about how the expulsion was divinely inspired, produced by 'naked acts of God' ('obras desnudas suyas', 20r), as Ripol's text puts it.

One of the minor works of expulsion apologists is that of the court clerk from Zaragoza Juan Ripol, *Diálogo de consuelo por la expulsión de los moriscos de España* (*Dialogue of consolation for the expulsion of the Moors of Spain*) (1613). Ripol through his character Alberto takes distinct pleasure in describing the sufferings of the Moriscos during the expulsion and then saying

---

[6] 'no nos han obligado a ningún acto espiritual ni corporal que nos haga desdezir de lo que avemos sido' (265).

that they deserved it and were divinely punished. This is a habitual strategy in the apologists' writings. Throughout the *Dialogue*, Alberto assumes the role of a moral philosopher who guides his landowning interlocutor in questions of values and virtues, and despite such a moral aura he seems to be as incapable as Emmanuel Levinas – high priest of the ethics of alterity in our own time – of recognising the suffering of the 'other' if that other is of Arab or Muslim origin (or, for that matter, a woman). Alberto enumerates the worst imaginable afflictions of the Moriscos, alleging that three-quarters of them perished in their journey to exile, thanks to the mighty hand of God. Serapión should therefore be consoled and participate in the 'general joy' of the other Spaniards who have been dispossessed of their agricultural labour. What allows for this dehumanisation of the Moriscos are the same motives that are found in all the apologists' texts, although not only in these: the firm conviction that the Moriscos are 'as Muslim' ('tan moros') as the Moors of Africa, on the one hand, and that they're natural enemies of Spain. The Moriscos, because of their great guilt, deserve to suffer. Their pain is not our pain: on the contrary, their pain comforts us and gives us happiness (20r).

Probably the most well-known passage of this type is that of the *Expulsión justificada de los moriscos españoles* (*Rightful expulsion of the Spanish Moriscos*) (1612) by the Aragonese Pedro Aznar Cardona, which expressively evokes scenes of the expulsion and then takes pleasure in the very suffering it describes:

> So the hapless Moors left on the days appointed by the royal ministers, in disorderly procession, on foot and on horseback, in a motley mass, bursting with pain and tears, in a great rumble of confused voices, bearing their children and women as well as the sick and elderly, covered with dust ... all greeting those who looked on or whom they came upon, saying 'God be with you.'
>
> Among the carriages and those mounted on horseback ... there were rich women, agitated, with assorted medallions of silver on their bosoms and hanging from their necks, with necklaces, pendants, dangling earrings, corals and a thousand adornments and colours on their dresses and garments, with which they were able to conceal some of the pain in their hearts. The others, who were incomparably more numerous, went on foot, tired, in pain, lost, exhausted, sad, confused, ashamed, rabid, filthy, angry, hateful, thirsty and hungry; so much so that, with just punishment from heaven, they were never full or satisfied, for the bread of places along the way did not satiate them, nor did the water from the springs quench their thirst.[7]

---

[7] Salieron, pues, los desventurados moriscos por sus días señalados por los ministros reales, en orden de processión desordenada, mezclados los de pie con los de a caballo, yendo unos entre otros, reventando de dolor y de lágrimas, llevando grande estruendo y confusa vozería, cargados de sus hijos y mugeres, y de sus enfermos, y de sus viejos y niños, llenos de polvo ... todos saludando a los que miravan o encontravan, diziéndoles: –el

Curiously, this author who dehumanises the Moriscos throughout his book is by no means insensitive to their misfortune and imagines the pain behind so much colourful attire. He nonetheless shields himself against any sympathy by turning all that pain into 'just punishment from heaven' that condemns them to hunger and thirst that can't be satisfied even when there's no lack of bread or water or money to pay for it. It seems that God – with Dantesque inspiration – gives the Moriscos in advance an infernal punishment in the form of insatiable hunger and thirst. Aznar Cardona writes with the vitriol of an intolerant Old Christian, revealing throughout his work how viscerally anti-Morisco attitudes were codified in writing.

Gaspar Aguilar's epic poem *Expulsión de los moriscos de España* (*Expulsion of the Moriscos of Spain*) (1610) employs similar techniques of representation through a different genre, an epic poem of sorts. Although the work lacks artistic merit, some historians have pointed to passages in it as examples of pathos. Aguilar does offer a good number of vignettes that, viewed in isolation, might suggest some understanding of the tragedy of expulsion. Of course, not everything is sad on the part of the Moriscos since Aguilar, like other apologists, also insists on the great joy of the Moriscos induced by the edicts of expulsion. The poem refers to 'poor Moors' who 'embracing their tender children / leapt from the high mountains', or 'how many sold their beloved children / to our people, only / to get a piece of bread / sometimes black, tasteless and made with chaff' (348–50), or of little children hidden by Old Christians 'to let them deviate from treachery / and be nourished by the sweet breast of the Faith' (211). The images of tribulations only offer caricatures of false pathos. Indeed, as we've seen with other writers, before and after such vignettes we're told that the Moriscos are guilty of treason and apostasy so that any moment of feigned compassion is already framed in the logic of guilt. Aguilar introduces the last canto of his epic by saying that 'all misfortunes' are more than 'just reward', a 'punishment' much lighter than what their 'immense guilt' deserves (345). For the population that remains, there is something cathartic and edifying in the spectacle of the expulsion (353). Aguilar has all the rivers and nymphs of Spain celebrate the expulsion while it's happening in a fluvial festival to which he devotes hundreds of verses (318–43). The work ends like other apologetic texts with a panegyric at

---

Señor los ende guarde: –Señores, queden con Dios. Entre los sobredichos de los carros y cavalgaduras … yban de quando en quando (de algunos moros ricos) muchas mugeres hechas unas debanaderas, con diversas patenillas de plata en los pechos, colgadas de los cuellos, con gargantillas, collares, arracadas, corales, y con mil gayterías y colores en sus trages y ropas, con que disimulavan algo el dolor del coraçón. Los otros, que eran más sin comparación, yban a pie, cansados, doloridos, perdidos, fatigados, tristes, confusos, corridos, rabiosos, corrompidos, enojados, aburridos, sedientos y hambrientos, tanto que por justo castigo del cielo no se veýan hartos ni satisfechos, ni les bastava el pan de los lugares, ni la agua de las fuentes' (part 2, 5r–6r).

full volume to Philip III, defender of the faith and Spain and prime mover of the expulsion (359–66).

In his edition of Aguilar's poem, Manuel Ruiz Lagos associates this writer ideologically and textually with a network of figures called the Brotherhood of the Holy Cross (among other variants), founded thanks to the tireless work of Jaime Bleda in Rome and Madrid, fully supported by Philip III, comprising the key personages in the expulsion of the Moriscos of Valencia. It was headed by the highest authority for that expulsion, don Agustín Mexía of the order of Santiago, accompanied by members of the other military orders, and its intellectual circle revolved around the patriarch Juan de Ribera, archbishop of Valencia (33–55). The existence of this brotherhood helps to explain the strategic coordination of the expulsion and the connections between some of the apologists in addition to their commitment to publishing justifications for the expulsion *while* it was being carried out. As is well known, the figure of Bleda is crucial: his anti-Morisco zeal began many years before the expulsion, and in his *Corónica* he claims a primary role in it, for example in his efforts to convince the king to undertake it. As his *Corónica* begins with Muhammad followed by the Muslim invasion of Spain and concludes a thousand pages later with the restoration of Christian Spain thanks to the expulsion, Bleda sees himself as a kind of counterpart to the traitor don Julián, the (mostly legendary) figure who facilitated that invasion nine centuries earlier.

The fundamentalist Bleda's *Corónica* offers a series of images of Moriscos very happy to be expelled until they learn of the mistreatment of Moriscos by their coreligionists in North Africa, particularly Oran. 'The women dressed in their finest clothes to embark. There were some who left husbands and children on land to embark, and others forgot their brothers and sisters' (1001). A woman in labour, against the advice of others, 'as soon as she had given birth, as if she were a greyhound, went on foot to embark.' As Bleda explains: 'They gladly left their towns, houses and fields to be taken to Barbary, where they could freely live in the damned sect of Muhammad, and although they knew that there would be dangers in the voyage, they had little regard for this, thinking only of how to reach a goal so desired by all of them' (1002). He then tells the story of an eminent Morisco named Baltasar Saba Bayle de Alberique who, when arriving near Oran in the company of his wife and daughters, is attacked by Arabs who take away his family and possessions and kill the other men in the group:

> When other Moriscos there consoled him for such a great misfortune, he replied with a cheerful face that the pain of having lost the delight of his home, his wife, and so much property was far less than his joy in Allah's having given him a life long enough to see the expulsion, owing to which he had been able to die in the land of Barbary ... and he promised them that if

they bore their trials with patience they would enjoy the delights prepared for them in the paradise of Muhammad, who had delivered them from the oppression of the Christians, so that they could better serve him and freely profess. (1002)

This Morisco serves as a subhuman puppet for the ventriloquism of Bleda. The underlying message in all these anecdotes is that the Moriscos, neither Christian nor Spanish, are essentially Moors (Muslims). If the Moriscos themselves don't feel their losses and misfortunes, no one else should feel compassion for them. Bleda, like Aguilar, believes that God is eager to start punishing the Moriscos already in this world and this life (1020–1). Bleda goes on to list the ways in which many Moriscos have perished in private ships and Barbary 'in the hands of such ferocious, inhuman and barbarous people', with only a quarter of them surviving. He adds: 'And if they all had perished, it would have been better for Spain' (1021).

In Bleda we see the extreme anti-Morisco position, which in effect ended up imposing itself on all the others. Unlike archbishop Ribera, Bleda never wavered. Years before the expulsion, Bleda affirms that the king 'can lawfully take away the new converts' life, liberty and goods'; he opposes the baptism of Morisco children and marriages between Morisco men and Old Christian women, and contends 'that the bodies of these new converts should not appear in churches or sacred places' (Boronat 454–5). It would be interesting to know how his extreme positions found support as well as resistance in the circles and strata of religious and secular power. Many of these ideas are also exposed in his *Breve relación de la expulsión* (*Brief account of the expulsion*) (1610), where he can't contain his ecstasy over the expulsion (594). Although the Moriscos do suffer in this text – from aggressions perpetrated by Old Christians – Bleda goes out of his way to say that even they recognise the beneficent protection of the authorities and the hand of God in their expulsion.

Bleda believes he understands the historical sense of the present: 'With this the kingdom is now free of the infinite spiritual and temporal harm suffered by Christians for nine hundred years … in the company of the Moors. Therefore, recognising this great benefit, we give infinite thanks to God our Lord, who is the main author of this work' (*Breve relación*, 595). They deserve to be expelled not only because they're Muslims and therefore apostates (having been baptised), but also because they're enemies of Christians and of Christianity itself. The expulsion is thus to be understood as a victory over these enemies, and for this reason has been celebrated with great joy by the 'people' (587). Other Valencian and Aragonese apologists also refer to the alleged happiness of the 'people', a statement that may have held some truth with regard to the kingdom of Valencia but doesn't match reports from other parts of Spain, which mostly speak of attitudes that vary from bewilderment to compassion, without signs of joy.[8] God leaves unmistakable signs of this victory over the enemy, in the form of the cross:

> The Holy Cross, our only hope and protection, assisted with its invincible virtue in the expulsion of its self-declared enemies. And so that we could rejoice that the Holy Cross was now free of the calumny that those accursed people here uttered against it, it appeared on Thursday, September 17 [1610] at nine o'clock at night, very white and resplendent above the port of the Alfaques in the shape of a beautiful cross of Caravaca. And then on the following morning, the last Moriscos of Aragon and Catalonia embarked there. Till the last moment those dogs were hoping for the help of the Turk, as His Majesty warned in the edict of Catalonia, but it turned out the reverse for them, because the venerable Cross, which is their scourge, ended up expelling them from there. Other marvels have occurred with a Crucifix of Aragon, near Vililla, and in various ways it is known that this was the work of God our Lord. (*Breve relación*, 596)

This passage takes on even more meaning in light of the Brotherhood of the Holy Cross that Bleda founded.[9]

If perhaps no one else reached the extremes of Jaime Bleda, other authors such as Damián Fonseca (*Justa expulsión de los moriscos de España*) (*The legitimate expulsion of the Moors of Spain*) (1612) and Marco Guadalajara y Xavier and Xavier (*Memorable expulsión y justísimo destierro de los moriscos de España*) (*Memorable expulsion and most just exile of the Moriscos of Spain*) (1613), as their titles indicate, offer variants of what we've seen so far with regard to scenes of expulsion and, above all, the attempt to justify the expulsion. This is not surprising if we consider that most of the apologist authors belonged to the same circles and participated in the same mission, citing, praising and even reproaching one another. A telling example of this is Bleda's denunciation of the Portuguese Dominican Fonseca for plagiarism of his *Defensio fidei* (*Corónica* 946–50), all the more bitter because Fonseca attributes almost all the protagonism of the long process of expulsion to archbishop Ribera and not to Bleda: 'it was I', says Bleda, 'who brought to light and showed the errors of the Moriscos, I was the first one to do so, to the glory of God and honour

---

[8] See, for example, Caro Baroja, 'Los moriscos aragoneses', 94–8, and *Los moriscos del reino de Granada*, 233–8; Perry 180; Domínguez Ortiz and Vincent 253 and 281–2; and an interesting document cited by Guadalajara 126r–8v; cf. also Harvey, *Muslims in Spain*, 95–7.

[9] 'I wrote a memorandum with many ordinances for the foundation of a brotherhood of the most holy Cross, for the veneration throughout Spain of the Crosses and Mount Calvaries that are found along the roads and outlets of towns' (*Corónica* 961). With the support of prominent clergy, this memorandum led to a letter from the king to the pope endorsing the idea of such a brotherhood.

of my holy habit, which is denigrated by whoever denies my labours, which are mine' (950).[10] A rather different case is that of the Valencian chronicler Gaspar Escolano, who often adopts the same anti-Morisco rhetoric and ends his massive work with the conventional panegyric to Philip III but in several passages seems to distance himself from the official line.[11] Although he affirms on some occasions that the Moriscos deserve to suffer, especially after some of them profane the churches and many others rebel, Escolano is more of a chronicler than an apologist, and his sketches of horrors like this one are not frivolous:

> More than a thousand five hundred of the rebels died as the soldiers engaged in the kinds of cruelties that accompany such occasions. They snatched suckling children from their mothers' arms and smashed them against the rocks, and, so as not to linger in taking off their earrings they cut off their ears ... Many women covered their faces with their skirts and, embracing their children, threw themselves onto the rocks below, believing they would be better received there than by the soldiers, and all those who fell wounded before dying were stripped and left naked.[12]

Márquez Villanueva affirms that 'the apologists, in their attempt to influence public opinion largely hostile to the expulsion, falsify a reality that has not been taken into account until now'. For Bleda, says Márquez Villanueva – and this also applies to the other apologists – 'the absolute apostasy of the Moriscos is sufficient to deny them any right as Christians, Spaniards or mere human beings' ('El problema historiográfico', 105–6). In fact, the works of the apologists, and particularly the clergy among them, are not specific justifications but great panoramic histories in which the Moriscos already have their assigned role. The grandiosity of this worldview in defence of the faith admits no legitimate subjectivity on the part of the Moriscos. Guadalajara begins his work by explaining the 'means that Lucifer provided for the seven Ages of the world to pervert man and make him fall into errors and heresies'

---

[10] See the introduction by Bernard Vincent and Rafael Benítez Sánchez-Blanco to this facsimile edition of the *Corónica*, 32–4.

[11] Various passages are in fact tinged with satire, e.g. against none other than Philip III (792), the patriarch Ribera (834), and the highest authorities of the expulsion in Valencia (821).

[12] 'Murieron de los rebeldes más de mil y quinientos, usando los soldados de las crueldades que traen consigo semejantes ocasiones. Porque los niños de teta arrebataban de los brazos de las madres y los estrellaban en las peñas; y por no detenerse a quitarles los zarcillos a ellas, les cortaban las orejas ... Muchas mujeres se cubrían el rostro con las faldillas y abrazadas con sus hijos, se arrojaban por las peñas abajo pensando hallar mejor acogimiento que en los soldados; y todos los que caían heridos antes de ser muertos, eran luego despojados, y quedaban desnudos' (822).

(I, 1, 9), so that everything, including the rise of Islam and the expulsion of the Moriscos, has its place fixed within the grand scheme of things. Others start with Muhammad. Others begin with a defence of Christianity so as to contextualise the hostile presence of the Moors/Moriscos in Spain. Fonseca, perhaps the most moderate – if such a qualifier is warranted – of clergy apologists, limits himself to writing about Valencia and relatively immediate circumstances, and devotes one of the books of his work to responding to a range of doubts. However, there is a grandiose scheme implicit in his work too because it associates the Moriscos with the Biblical Ishmaelites and classical Saracens, and this enables him to use his telescopic sense of history and his capacity for allegorical thought to affirm that the Moriscos as a caste imbibe idolatry and rebellion in their mother's milk and have corrupted blood (e.g. 152–3). For him, then, it's not surprising that once expelled from Spain, the Moriscos were 'treated even by the Moors themselves like the dung that clings to their feet, and their dead bodies served as manure for the earth' (334–5).

While the grand religio-historical schemes reserve the role of antagonists for the Moriscos, an ensemble of metaphors and analogies also contributes to associating the Moriscos with disease, pestilence, poison, danger, etc. Briefly, one group of metaphors refers to Moriscos as weeds and other undesirable plants that must be 'extirpated'.[13] Another set identifies the Moriscos as a plague or tumour, as Guadalajara eloquently explains: 'Our monarch Felipus, seeing that the malice of the Moriscos spread the damage and that the body of the Republic was in spiritual and temporal danger, without being able to cure this illness through benign remedies of preaching, like an artful surgeon resolved to use the cautery of expulsion to heal the wound'.[14] Thus the body politic of Spain is polarised into the body (Old Christians) and a disease (Moriscos) that can only be cured by cautery. Another choice metaphor is that of Moriscos as snakes that are being raised in one's breast or one's home. Although variants of it are found in a good number of seventeenth-century texts, it doesn't appear to be of recent coinage: Guadalajara cites a letter from

---

[13] As Guadalajara, among others, often indicates, what has to be *extirpated* is apostasy, and this means expelling the apostates. Fonseca quotes a letter to Philip III of 1602 from archbishop Ribera: 'The remedy called forth by great spiritual and corporal evils is to uproot them so that they cannot do harm nor their roots give rise to new shoots, which in a short time grow into trees … God said to His people through a prophet (to teach them how to govern their houses): "Do not sow in fields that have weeds, but pull them out first and then sow"' (178–9).

[14] 'Viendo nuestro monarca Felipo que el daño cundía por la malicia de los moriscos y que estava en peligro el cuerpo de la República en lo espiritual y temporal, sin poder curar su enfermedad los remedios suaves de la predicación, como artificioso cirujano tomó el cauterio de su expulsión, con que remediava la llaga' (105r). Cf. Fonseca 173, Aguilar 354, Aznar Cardona 2:32r, Ripol 17r. Even Pedro de Valencia describes *Mahometismo* ('Muhammedanism') as 'cancer' (87).

Pope Clement III (1265–68) to King Jaume the Conqueror, where he warns that 'it is neither sane nor safe to have such treacherous and sinful enemies in your house, just as it is not sane or safe to have a snake or burning coals in one's breast' (45r). With great irony, Cervantes puts this trope in the mouth of the Old Christian dog Cipión by having him say that 'Spain breeds and has in its breast as many vipers as Moriscos',[15] and has the Morisco Ricote himself utter it: 'it is not wise to nurture a snake in your bosom, sheltering enemies in your household'.[16] There's no need here to analyse the snake within the collective imaginary to understand how this metaphor dehumanises the Moriscos and portrays them as dangerous natural enemies. Anti-Morisco discourse exhibits a select bestiary of metaphors, including that of the serpent, that alienate the Moriscos from the human species.[17]

Almost everything we've seen so far has been a few apologist strategies to dehumanise the Moriscos, de-Hispanicise them and turn them into enemies of the faith, strategies meant to antipathise them so as not to understand their drama and falsify the interethnic realities of diverse characteristics and intensities that were integral to Spain's social composition. Its primary intention seems to have been to break all ties between the expelled and the remaining population, thus validating a politically inspired action unapproved by Rome, advocated only by those who saw the Moriscos as religiously and culturally undifferentiated apostates entirely alien to the rest of the population.[18]

The jocose chapter title in *Don Quixote* that narrates the first encounter between the Morisco Ricote and Sancho announces that it 'deals with things concerning this history and none other' (II, 54). Considering the overwhelming silence of everything that was not applause for the expulsion, the title may ring true. This chapter and the others about Ricote and his daughter Ana Félix manifest strategies opposed to those used by apologists. As these characters have attracted much critical attention, I'll limit my comments to bringing into relief Cervantes' peculiar handling of the expulsion.

With profound sarcasm, Cervantes' only apologist for the expulsion in *Don Quixote* – which took place while he was writing the second part of the novel – is none other than his Morisco character Ricote, an innocent victim who speaks of the unspeakable pain that he and his family have suffered owing to that 'heroic' and 'gallant resolution'. Faced with this intense personal

---

[15] 'España cría y tiene en su seno tantas víboras como moriscos' (*Novelas ejemplares* 2: 350).

[16] 'no era bien criar la sierpe en el seno, teniendo los enemigos dentro de casa' (*Don Quixote* II, 54, 1072).

[17] Cf. Ripol 16r and 17r, Janer 267–8, Boronat 718–19.

[18] For a wide-ranging analysis of how Moriscos have been represented from the early modern period until now, as well as how they saw themselves prior to the expulsion, see Bernabé Pons, 'Musulmanes sin al-Andalus'.

and family drama, the repeated praise of Philip III and the state apparatus sounds entirely hollow. Mercedes Alcalá Galán has formulated the concept 'mirror characters' to refer to such characters as Ricote associated mainly with Islam issuing from a narrative technique that deliberately configures psychologically incoherent characters that 'absorb the stereotypes, contradictions, fabulations and doubts as well as a reflexion of the ideological debate that surrounds a particular historical process' ('Personajes espejo', 946–7). The long history of the analysis of characters such as Zoraida, Ana Félix and Ricote in *Don Quixote*, as well as other comparable characters in the Cervantine *oeuvre*, has nearly always assumed a logical or psychological coherence in them – in my view a false premise that leads to erroneous conclusions about what these characters are about, how their author might have understood them, and how they might relate to the polemical vortex that surrounds and even constitutes them. The concept of 'mirror characters', in contrast, allows for an understanding of the integral relations between such characters and their dense socio-religio-historical context, as is the case with Ricote. With minimal if any awareness of the rhetoric he's pronouncing, Ricote mimes in a single sentence many of the apologists' favourite clichés about the Moriscos:

> although it is true that [don Bernardino de Velasco, in charge of the expulsion in Castile] *mixes mercy with justice*, he sees that the *whole body of our nation is contaminated and rotten*, and *he burns it with a cautery* rather than soothing it with an ointment; and so, *with prudence, sagacity, diligence* and the fear he imposes, he has borne on his strong shoulders the weight of this great plan, and put it into effect, so that *our schemes, stratagems, pleas and deceptions* have not been able to dazzle his eyes of Argos, which are always alert so that none of our people can stay behind or be concealed, *like a hidden root that in times to come will send out shoots and bear poisonous fruits in Spain, which is clean now* and *rid of the fears caused by our great numbers*.[19]

Here we have a collage of images: of the ideal ruler (stern, merciful, prudent, shrewd, etc.); of the corrupt Morisco 'nation'; of the use of cautery to put an

---

[19] 'porque aunque es verdad que él mezcla la misericordia con la justicia, como él vee que todo el cuerpo de nuestra nación está contaminado y podrido, usa con él antes del cauterio que abrasa que del ungüento que molifica, y así, con prudencia, con sagacidad, con diligencia y con miedos que pone, ha llevado sobre sus fuertes hombros a debida ejecución el peso desta gran máquina, sin que nuestras industrias, estratagemas, solicitudes y fraudes hayan podido deslumbrar sus ojos de Argos, que contino tiene alerta porque no se le quede ni encubra ninguno de los nuestros, que como raíz escondida, que con el tiempo venga después a brotar y a echar frutos venenosos en España, ya limpia, ya desembarazada de los temores en que nuestra muchedumbre la tenía' (II, 65,1165–6; my emphasis in the translation).

end to the infection in the body politic; of the Moriscos as twisted and impertinent; of the Moriscos as plants with poisonous fruit and of Spain already cleansed of this plague; and of the Moriscos as a demographic threat owing to their ability to reproduce.[20] Ricote agrees with the 'resolution' because the vast majority of the Moriscos have not been 'firm and true Christians' and, as he has said earlier, because 'it is not wise to nurture a snake in your bosom, sheltering enemies in your household' (II, 54, 1072).

Ricote gets about this far in his mimicry of anti-Morisco rhetoric. He invokes no cosmic scheme that might assign a role to the Moriscos in God's divine comedy, nor any religio-historical or allegorical vision that identifies the Moriscos as natural heretics or descendants of Ishmael or eighth-century jihadist invaders. He doesn't speak of apostasy but simply of his own locus between Islam and Christianity. He emphasises the Moriscos' deep sense of belonging to Spain. Although he reproduces tropes like those of the diseased body, the snake or toxic plants, he doesn't dehumanise the Moriscos. In sum, all the fundamental elements of the apologist argument are lacking, leaving only the clichés devoid of any persuasive or expressive value. Above all, this intensely moving 'mirror character' is the prime victim before us of the anti-Morisco discourse he echoes.

No other character in *Don Quixote* speaks in favour of expulsion. On the contrary, the friendship between Sancho and Ricote stands out, as does how the viceroy don Antonio Moreno and his wife go out of their way to welcome Ricote and his daughter and try to help them resolve their plight. The departure of Ana Félix into exile is one of the moments of most intense pathos in the entire novel since she and her family belong to their community and she possesses beauty and virtues that transcend the differences between Moriscos and Old Christians. It's very significant that the character who tells Ricote about her departure is his friend Sancho, who witnessed it and wept (II, 54, 1075–6). While Ana Félix is entirely integrated into Old Christian culture, including its religious and linguistic modalities, her noble Old Christian suitor don Gaspar Gregorio offers us a sign of inverse flexibility: he knows Arabic, he mixes with the Moriscos as he accompanies them into exile, he becomes friends with Ana Félix's uncles – at least one of whom is Muslim, according to Sancho, and he is disguised as a woman in a harem to protect him from the sexual whims of the king of Algiers. Ana Félix and don Gaspar Gregorio are two sexually and culturally hermaphrodite beauties whose amorous pairing offers an alternative model of relations between the sexes, ethnic groups, social classes and languages.

---

[20] See Hutchinson, 'Arbitrating the national *oikos*' (70–7) and 'Poética de la emoción' (1379–81) regarding the Moriscos' alarming fertility and Cervantes' techniques for eliciting emotion in this episode, respectively.

Cervantes leaves God out of the expulsion. He individualises the collectivity of the Moriscos in two extremely endearing characters, father and daughter, to whom he grants the ability to express a subjectivity fully aware of the tragedy they are experiencing. He emphasises the Spanishness of his characters, their perfect mastery of Spanish and their partial or total assimilation to the life and religious practice of an Old Christian community in Castile – and not of Valencia or Aragon, for example, where tensions and differences were often more marked. He isolates them from all forms of guilt, reminding readers of the contemporary case of the Moriscos of the Ricote Valley in Murcia so that their innocence betrays the injustice of the 'gallant resolution' towards the Moriscos and the communities where they lived. He destabilises the use of shifters such as possessives and other expressions that demonstrate a split and a radical disorientation in the consciousness of the uprooted Moriscos (e.g. 'my dear friend', 'my good neighbour', 'our village', 'my nation [i.e. Moriscos]', 'our homeland [i.e. Spain]', 'all of us', 'enemies in your household'). And to this series of strategies could be added other techniques used by Cervantes to capture the human drama that was unleashed with the expulsion. Like three centuries of Cervantes' readers, a number of contemporary historians have been unable to grasp the subtlety and magnitude of what is going on here.

One typical posture regarding Cervantes, shared by both literary scholars and historians, is that he's indecipherable and enigmatically ironic so that we have no way of knowing what he thought about the expulsion of the Moriscos or anything else.[21] In my view such scholars are oblivious to the specificity of rhetorical techniques that are more than evident in Cervantes' texts, not to mention the historical contexts in which Cervantes creates his poetics. As we've seen, the apologists do everything possible to obfuscate interethnic relations, to misunderstand the Moriscos and end up distorting the emotional realities unrecognised both with regard to the expelled and the remaining population. Borrowing from the apologists' rhetoric but emptying it of meaning, Cervantes restores and accentuates the affective bonds with the two Morisco characters of *Don Quixote* who return to their homeland as de facto criminals but are welcomed with maximum hospitality and affection into the homes of the noble don Antonio and the viceroy himself. Their lamentable stories deeply move the other characters present, and this in turn channels and intensifies the affectivity that is expected from the novel's readers. Even the narrator participates in this wave of sympathy: 'Whose heart was so hard that these words would not soften it, at least enough to hear what the sad and sorrowful boy [Ana Félix, who has just declared that she's a Christian woman]

---

[21] An interesting interdisciplinary assortment of views about Cervantes' treatment of the expulsion of the Moriscos in *Don Quixote* can be found in the thirty brief scholarly reponses elicited by Luis F Bernabé Pons in *Áreas: Revista Internacional de Ciencias Sociales* 30 (2011): 149–57.

wished to say?'²² Indeed, everyone is moved by the pitiful story of the beautiful Ana Félix, including the vengeful general: 'Drop by drop, your tears will not let me fulfil my vow; live, beautiful Ana Félix, the years that heaven has in store for you.'²³ This solidary sympathy, this understanding that the apologists want to deny, constitutes an ethical position that annuls all the arguments in favour of expulsion. In *Don Quixote*, Cervantes persuades through the ethics of emotion, which affects above all the viceroy himself: 'so much was the benevolence and charity that the beauty of Ana Felix inspired in his heart'.²⁴

Thus far we've seen how similar language by or about Moriscos takes on very different meanings. When non-fictional authors write about this, we can take their utterances more or less at face value, give or take a modicum of irony, concealment or distortion. In the case of *Don Quixote*, that rhetoric passes through the prisms and folds of a fictional Moorish-Muslim author (Cide Hamete Benengeli), a fictional Morisco translator from Arabic to Spanish, a fictional Christian editor-composer, perhaps another narrator, and the Morisco character Ricote. Speaking and writing become enormously complex, by no means transparent. The passage about Moriscos in the *Colloquy of the dogs* comes up in a conversation between two dogs overheard by a mendacious soldier suffering from syphilis and delirium who then transcribes what he heard, according to him, as the main narrator lets all his unreliable characters speak (*Novelas ejemplares*, 2: 349–50; Hutchinson, 'Arbitrating the National *Oikos*', 71–7). The episode about the village of Moriscos in Cervantes' last novel, *Los trabajos de Persiles y Sigismunda*, presents us with its own complexities: this too is a novel supposedly translated from another language and has a highly bigoted, intrusive narrator of Counter-Reformational perspectives who misrepresents the story beyond recognition. Needless to say, this narrator is not Cervantes' mouthpiece, though nearly all of the most skilled readers and critics have fallen into the traps of obfuscation.²⁵ Cervantes is a profoundly unreliable author throughout his writings. With regard to certain topics such as the Moriscos, his unreliability encodes very complex games about human and historical truths.

The episode of the Moriscos villagers by the Valencian coast (*Persiles* III, 11) comes right after the tongue-in-cheek passage on history and fable

---

²² '¿Quién fuera el de corazón tan duro que con estas razones no se ablandara, o a lo menos hasta oír las que el triste y lastimado mancebo decir quería?' (II, 63, 1152).

²³ 'Una por una vuestras lágrimas no me dejarán cumplir mi juramento: vivid, hermosa Ana Félix, los años de vida que os tiene determinados el cielo' (II, 63, 1155).

²⁴ 'tanta fue la benevolencia y caridad que la hermosura de Ana Félix infundió en su pecho' (II, 63, 1156).

²⁵ The list would be long. One quite recent case is that of Antonio Feros's long article 'Rhetorics of the expulsion', which echoes the usual platitudes regarding Cervantes' passages on the Moriscos and sees the *xadraque* Xarife of the *Persiles* as the 'wise Morisco' of Cervantes' last work.

and the story of the false captives. This alone should be enough to put any reader on guard about this encounter, which reads from beginning to end like a game of 'what's wrong with this picture?' Nearly all of the surface detail is suspect if not absurd, and it is produced by the only two Christian Moriscos in the village, the lovely Rafala and her uncle Xarife, as well as the insufferable narrator. What substitutes for an elephant in the room is the corsair fleet offshore, invited by the crypto-Muslim villagers to take them to exile in Algiers. There in the distance is where the real story happens, not in the foreground with the naive misconceptions of Rafala, the aping of official anti-Morisco rhetoric by Xarife or the malevolent misrepresentations of the narrator. It's a deadly serious story that gets past the censors and resonates with clandestine Morisco migrations to Muslim lands throughout the sixteenth century, often with the help of 'Barbary' corsairs, mostly renegades, otherwise referred to as 'Turks'.

We have no testimonies as to how the Morisco episodes in *Don Quixote* and the *Persiles* (particularly in III, 11) were read by Cervantes' contemporaries. By placing anti-Morisco diatribes derived from official discourse in the mouths of Moriscos – and dogs – Cervantes gave the censors sufficient excuses not to expurgate these passages. More surprising is that the stories of Ricote and Ana Félix are still sometimes read according to the literal meanings of the words put in their mouths rather than the highly charged historical context and emotional rhetoric of these captivating characters, such that, for some, Cervantes remains an advocate for the expulsion of the Moriscos, or at best indecipherably ironic, adopting a transcendent neo-Kantian neutrality towards this issue. In my view such attitudes are as untenable as imagining Goya in his 'May 3rd executions' or Picasso in his 'Guernica' indifferently presenting a moral dilemma or dabbling dispassionately in forms and colours. Cervantes has produced a powerful counternarrative here. Márquez Villanueva demonstrated many years ago that the anti-Morisco harangues of Xarife are nothing more than a hollow echoing of official discourse ('El morisco Ricote', 285–95). Yet there are various other impediments to acknowledging the episode of the Morisco villagers in the *Persiles* as another formidable counternarrative to the prevailing policies and discourse about Moriscos: among others, the *Persiles* as Cervantes' last work is seen to have the aura of the author's last will; the fanatical anti-Morisco narrator is confused with the author; narrative minutiae imply that the Moriscos are naturally destructive and pernicious; foreground details distract readers from what's happening in the background; 'good' Moriscos are still seen as those who have 'sincerely' adopted Christianity while 'bad' ones are crypto-Muslims, as was very much the norm in the kingdom of Valencia; anyone associated with Barbary corsairs on their itinerary of razzias is an enemy; the Moriscos are seen as a national 'problem' and, as the narrator implies, will be much worse off on the North African shore, living in poverty and dishonour (III, 11, 551). All of this is readily refutable.²⁶ What we're left with is a disturbing counternarrative that can't be adequately contained within a Hispano-Christian perspective, an understanding of the Moriscos that acknowledges their Islamic and Mediterranean dimensions as they head towards the city where Cervantes spent five years as a slave.

Divergent accounts

As we've seen repeatedly, in many early modern texts of the Mediterranean, cruelty, intolerance and incomprehension across the lines of religious affiliation tend to set the dominant tone. Or at least that's what we expect to hear in the background, accompanied by dissonant notes in the foreground. Life in frontier zones – configured as it was by geopolitical alignments, corsairing, wide-scale captivity and slavery, religious tensions, and so on – undoubtedly allowed and even cultivated many kinds of cruelty and intolerance. The distribution of cruelty would have been geographically quite uneven throughout the *mare nostrum*, more in some places and less in others, but quite equitably divided between Christians and Muslims in their treatment of each other: as seen in previous chapters, despite the vehement rhetoric of many Christian treatises about Muslim cruelty, there's plenty of evidence from Christian sources demonstrating that Christians were no kinder, and that neither side had a monopoly on hostility or cruelty. Nonetheless, Christian (especially religious) writers and Muslim writers dealt with cruelty and suffering in entirely different ways, the latter refraining from describing acts of cruelty and humiliation (Matar, *Europe*, 40) while the former seem to revel in their hyperbolic accounts, as in Sosa's *Topografía de Argel* when he describes the sufferings of galley slaves:

> The torments with sticks, fists, kicks, whips, hunger, thirst, with endless inhuman cruelties they inflict on poor Christian galley slaves, without letting them rest for half an hour, split open the flesh on their backs, drain their blood, tear out their eyes, break their arms, crush their bones, cut off their ears, slash their noses, savagely slit their throats, and cut off their heads and throw them in the sea to get the others to row and make the ship fly. No human tongue can describe these sufferings, nor pen express them.²⁷

---

[26] I have examined the episode in much detail in 'The Morisco problem in its Mediterranean dimension: exile in Cervantes' *Persiles*'.

[27] 'El tratamiento de palos, puños, coces, azotes, hambre, sed, con una infinidad de crueldades inhumanas y continuas de que usan con los pobres cristianos que bogan, y como sin los dejar reposar media hora, les abren cruelmente las espaldas, sacan la sangre, arrancan los ojos, rompen los brazos, muelen los huesos, tajan las orejas, cortan las narices y aun los degüellan fieramente, y les cortan las cabezas y los echan a la mar, porque arranquen la boga y caminen más que volando. No basta lengua humana para decirlo, ni pluma para declararlo' (I, 22, 17r).

Muslim writers of the era offer nothing to compare with such graphic prose, but they often pepper their commentaries about war-like Christians (as opposed to more peaceful ones) with formulas like *dammarahum* ('may God destroy them'), as Nabil Matar points out (*Europe*, 30).

Yet here and there we've also seen what would appear to be exceptions to the rule in the form of more positive relations between those who were nominally adversaries. I'd like to question the rule itself by suggesting that, in various kinds of situations, exceptions were bound to happen – exceptions that sometimes set their own rules and often played themselves out in unpredictable ways. An ample bibliographical array of historical and religious treatises, geographies, autobiographies, tales of captivity, and the like, as well as Mediterranean frontier literature, points to a complex and nuanced mosaic of human relations.

Propagandistic texts by members of Catholic religious orders, as we know, tend to accentuate cruelties, real or alleged, against Christians in Muslim lands. A telling reminder of how genre affects content is the case of Jerónimo Gracián, whose treatise on captivity adopts a conventionally hostile approach while the autobiographical accounts of his captivity in Tunis nuance the relations between members of all religions, allowing for remarkable anecdotes about human interaction that contravene the official script. Modern historiographical trends sympathetic to the 'clash of civilisations' hypothesis likewise filter out 'positive' relations (if any were found at all in the sources used) and stress discord, difference and indifference.

Formulaic applications of alterity that brand Muslims as *the* 'other' – singular but collective, determinate, unconditional, ontologically opposed – also predispose scholars to maximise religious, social and cultural difference, thus impeding insight into how interactions between Christians and Muslims might at times have allowed for more fluid interactions than what such alterity would imply. Once again this raises the question of the modes of religious alterity between Christians and Muslims in the historically and geographically specific contexts relevant to this study. Since this complex issue has been addressed from different angles in the preceding chapters, let it suffice here to outline some of its salient aspects. Then as now, although with different accentuation, Muslims – particularly those more informed about religious differences – objected to the doctrine of the Trinity, God's paternity, Christ's divinity, the eucharist, the 'idolatrous' veneration of saints, and the use of sacred images, among other things. Christians, especially Catholic clergy, objected to these objections and scorned Muhammad, often wilfully obscuring the figure of the Prophet as a diabolical replacement for Christ and depicting Islam as a 'false sect' devised by him and founded on 'his' Quran. The expansion of the Ottoman Empire, as Miguel Ángel de Bunes Ibarra observes, was viewed as 'the second Muslim invasion of Europe', just as destructive as the first. In the early sixteenth century more texts were written in Europe about the Ottomans than about the newly discovered lands of America, remarks Bunes, and he adds: 'At no time was there produced a history intended to understand the [Turkish] adversary; instead, texts strove to create an image comprised of entirely contrary traits to enlarge the definition of Turks as the adversary.' From a Spanish-Catholic viewpoint, this definition would become supple enough to include European allies of the Ottomans such as the French as well as English and Dutch Protestants ('La llegada', 122, 124). Here again the perceptions of religion merge with politics. And what applies to the Turks also pertains, of course, to all other Muslims in the Mediterranean region, including 'Moors', 'Moriscos' and 'renegades', though with some qualitative differences.

Yet to return to religious issues as such, no one doubts the prime importance of religion and religious affiliation within the history of Mediterranean cultures, along with the prevalence of more or less unfavourable attitudes towards adherents of the other religions. This, however, doesn't necessarily translate into mutually hostile blocks in the early modern period or into a propensity towards adverse relations between Muslims, Jews and Christians. Religion as we've seen it was seldom a matter of theological belief, rarely a matter of 'faith' as such, much as this term was widely used in the early modern period and is still invoked by scholars as a synonym for religion. Mark Twain wryly remarks: 'Creeds mathematically precise and hair-splitting niceties of doctrine are absolutely necessary for the salvation of some kinds of souls' (196). Such souls, abundant in Protestant Europe, were a rarity in the early modern Mediterranean. At most, belief or 'faith' was a synecdoche, a minor part of a large whole that included practices, attitudes, valuations, orientations towards life, and so on. Regardless of how religion meshed with cultural practice, there was much in life that was religiously 'neutral', rather akin to those matters considered (since the Stoics) *adiaphora* that were indifferent to religious or moral judgement. Many of the day-to-day relations between people of different religions would have been configured by factors other than religious difference, and in various kinds of relations there would have been common ground for conversation and other flexible forms of interaction.

How much effort was exerted in converting religious others to Christianity or Islam? The Moriscos in Spain were a special case owing to their nominal conversion to Christianity by decree and mass baptism, as well as the mostly frustrated evangelical efforts to persuade them over decades. For many the suppression of Islam only fortified their religious allegiance and exacerbated their animosity towards Spain and Catholicism until well after their escape or expulsion. The Moriscos understandably brought these attitudes with them to the Maghrib and the eastern Mediterranean.

Otherwise, however, we should recall that there never was a war of religions as such in the Mediterranean during the early modern era, and that commerce and exchange, though they often issued from violent acts, channelled activities far more than religious or political ideologies did. Much less proselytising took place than is generally supposed. There was indeed sporadic effort by religious orders with little to show for it, there was some 'spontaneous' persuasion on both sides, and, to be sure, when someone of note converted to Islam or Christianity the event was publicly and defiantly celebrated. As we know, relatively few Muslims converted to Christianity, and although hundreds of thousands of Christians did convert to Islam, becoming 'renegades', many were denied the right to convert because, through their labour or ransom, they were more valuable to their masters as Christian captives than as Muslims. Not many of those who converted to Islam seem to have done so out of religious motives, even if an indeterminate proportion of them would undoubtedly have adopted Muslim beliefs and practices over time, thereby *becoming* Muslims in a process that most often would not have been defined by the initial act of converting. Even the question of religious sincerity on the part of renegades was secondary. According to the contemporary Portuguese writer Hyeronimo de Mendoça, the Moroccan sultan 'Abd al-Malik (husband of the historical figure whom Cervantes would transform into Zoraida and Zahara) would go into church in Marrakesh, throw holy water on his renegades and laugh at them if they showed any scruples. And he would sometimes tell them: 'lives and people serve me faithfully, souls are of no interest to me'. Mendoça adds that 'the kings of Barbary do indeed know that the renegades [*elches*] are not Moors' (Rodríguez Mediano 189). In his *Topografía de Argel*, Antonio de Sosa devotes an impressive chapter to commerce, showing Algiers as the hub of an intense traffic of goods and people to and from everywhere else in the Mediterranean, including enemy territories (I, 24). Commerce – or in the larger sense, economics – can tell us more than religion or politics about how the early modern Mediterranean world worked, though all aspects of life came into play and were often intertwined.

As Stuart Schwartz has demonstrated in his book *All can be saved*, there was an age-old though minority view, particularly in the Iberian Peninsula, that doubted the doctrine going back over a millennium and embraced by St. Augustine that no one outside the Church could be saved. Such scepticism was voiced both by theologically trained scholars and sectors of the populace at large. To some it made no sense that God would damn virtuous, right-living people who weren't Christians, and the more contact there was with other religions, chiefly Judaism and Islam but also a plethora of religions around the world that opened up as of the fifteenth century, the more doubts arose about there being just one way to live or to be saved. Many renegades with no formal education were struck by the resemblances between the Abrahamic religions such as their having the 'same God', comparable rituals and practices, and, specifically in the case of Islam, the significant presence of Jesus and Mary, as well as the existence of heaven and hell as the destiny of the saved and the damned, among many other correspondences.

Whereas religious authorities vehemently stress differences between Christianity and Islam that point to salvation or damnation, interrogations by the Inquisition as part of the required reconciliation of returning renegades reveal a wealth of spontaneous answers that express more similarity than difference between the two religions. Many of their remarks, undoubtedly prompted by the questions asked by inquisitors less prone to punish former renegades than to facilitate their reentry, reveal a tendency to make equivalences between the 'law' of Christ and that of Muhammad, as the two religions were most often referred to, and to regard them both as viable: the notion of different kinds of 'law' already invites comparison between religions. Taught more by experience than cultural tradition, renegades in effect tended to relativise religious alterity and minimise the switch from one religion to another. In their reconciliation sessions, numerous renegades found an equivalence between baptism and circumcision, considering them as equally valid for salvation. More generally, as we've seen, they associate virtually every aspect of one religion with the other, including the place of worship, forms of prayer and fasting, religious holidays, principles of morality, and the like, while also noting marked differences in some regards, e.g. sexuality. Unlike returning renegades who downplay the importance of *which* 'law' they were living under (as noted in chapter 3), Domenico Toppi di Udine's confession in 1766 is surprisingly forthright:

> My sin consists of voluntarily abandoning the Catholic Christian religion and voluntarily turning Turk, voluntarily letting myself be circumcised, take a wife, say prayers in the Turkish way the usual four times a day. I fasted in the Turkish way and did everything that the Turks do. In my heart I always felt remorse for having abandoned the Catholic law, but for all that I was voluntarily a Turk and in my heart I had at least some doubt that maybe the Turkish religion was good, though I've always believed that the Catholic religion was good. (Rostagno 65)

This statement again confirms the widespread notion among returning renegades that both religions were feasible. The curious variants of such testimonies likewise show how they correlate religions, as in this testimony by Giovanni Palusevich in 1666: 'I know nothing else except that they told me it should be believed that Muhammad is the first Prophet next to God and that the Madonna – whom they call Merima in their language, who never gave birth, and whom they hold in great veneration – turned Turk and went to heaven, not wanting to help Christians anymore but rather the Turks' (Rostagno 65).

Relative alterity with regard to religion extended to other facets of social and cultural life: there was no absolute 'other' in Mediterranean frontier relations. In this regard it should be recalled that the Ottoman Empire, which came to encompass most of the Mediterranean Sea, incorporated into its very core a great many people of Christian origin, including the elite women of the harem, talented young captives educated within the seraglio, renegades of many kinds, janissaries, courtiers, army leaders, admirals of the fleet, pashas, beylerbeys, and so on. Abdeljelil Temimi remarks that of the first forty-seven grand viziers from the conquest of Constantinople in 1453 until 1623, only five were Turkish as such, while 'the majority were from the Balkans and therefore Christian or of unknown origin' ('L'impact des racines chrétiennes', 513). The Islamic ideal of tolerance towards 'peoples of the book', despite moments of hostility or brutality, was most often observed in Ottoman lands, as Christian writers go out of their way to mention. As has always been acknowledged, the many communities of Jews throughout the empire were vitally important, especially in the eastern Mediterranean. Some of these modes of tolerant accommodation were no longer thinkable in Christian lands, particularly in the Iberian Peninsula, and some had *never* been thinkable in those countries. The very peculiar modus operandi of the Ottomans systematically dismantled any manichean dichotomies between those who were originally Muslims and non-Muslims, or between Europeans and non-Europeans, and affected the workings of all frontier zones under Ottoman control. This affected the modalities of relations within those heterotopias, and opened them up to somewhat unprescribed behaviours to which European diplomats, clerics, merchants, slaves and renegades were by no means unresponsive. Some of the above also applies to Morocco – which maintained its independence from the Ottoman Empire – though with less incorporation of Europeans and more local and tribal influence.

Despite manifold differences and adversarial modes of relations, or perhaps rather *because* of such circumstances, people in frontier zones generally had enough in common to understand each other, and behave and speak to each other 'like human beings', as it were, and would indeed have been impelled to do so. I'll be focusing here on stories of encounters across the religious and geopolitical divide that are characterised by distinct modes of reciprocity, including kindness, generosity, friendship, love, courtesy, sympathy or empathy, but also mutual interest. These counternarratives question the dominant stereotypes about human relations in the early modern Mediterranean, showing that these relations often worked themselves out in mutually beneficial ways rather than what anthropologist Gregory Bateson insightfully called schismogenesis, whereby differences or breaches tend to become successively more accentuated, often with destructive results. These stories serve as cases and as evidence, and as such can alter our views of how things worked in that time and region, but some of them serve almost as paradigms, as surprising narrative formulations that persist long after their epistemological use has been exhausted.

Some of these are fictional while others are presumably factual even if they're stranger than fiction. As Nietzsche puts it: '*Facta! Yes, facta ficta*: A historian has to do, not with what actually happened, but only with events supposed to have happened: for only the latter have *produced an effect*. [...] All historians speak of things which never existed' (*Daybreak*, #307, his emphasis). All of these stories are probably altered from the hypothetical events that gave rise to them. All of them, it seems to me, relate to certain kinds of truths based on experience and reflexion. Most of them take place in Muslim-controlled Mediterranean frontier zones, and although the specificity of place is important, they could have occurred in various other frontier zones, other places in the Mediterranean region where similar circumstances would have allowed similar events. All of them involve overcoming major barriers. As mentioned early in this book, Turkish and Arabic sources about 'crossover' encounters during these centuries remain all too scarce. After a lapse of years and sometimes decades that allowed for an evolution of oral versions, most of these stories were eventually written by Christian writers. This presupposes all the processes of distortion, suppression, elaboration and so on that go into formulating an effective story, be it autobiographical or not, fictional or not, processes that may disguise aspects of what supposedly happened but that in all probability convey that event or sequence of events as a narrative synthesis whose irreducibility allows us to reflect on characters and events within their context. In these particular stories I'll aim to tease out the situational logic as well as the ethical and emotional dimensions of each event or encounter as it's told, because the encounter itself may be irrecoverable, so that whatever truth there might be in it lies in the tale (and also *lies* in the tale).

Telling other stories

Early modern stories and accounts constantly remind us about the inadequacy of stereotypes regarding what people of the early modern Mediterranean supposedly thought and did. In a section titled 'The significance of anecdote', Braudel affirms: 'These apparently trivial details tell us more than any formal description about the life of Mediterranean man' (2: 758). I believe that the stories we'll be considering have this capacity. Drawing from a document called *Saco de Gibraltar* (*The sack of Gibraltar*), Braudel remarks on how circumstances often led warring adversaries to fraternise:

> During the unsuccessful attack on Gibraltar by the Algerians in 1540, eighty Christians were in the hands of the corsairs. After the alarm was over, there were as usual negotiations. A sort of armistice was agreed and bargaining began. The Algerian ships entered the port, their sailors went ashore and met old acquaintances, their former captives or masters, before going off to

eat in the *bodegones* [taverns]. Meanwhile the civilian population helped to transport casks of fresh water for the supply of the enemy fleet. There was an exchange of goodwill and a familiarity.

Braudel goes on to reflect more generally: 'Men passed to and fro, indifferent to frontiers, states and creeds' (2: 759). As noted earlier, he goes so far as to insist on what he calls 'the positive correlation between piracy [corsairing] and the economic health of the Mediterranean', positive because 'they rise and fall together' (2: 887).

We now turn to an array of positive encounters or relations that reveal quite different sides of life in Mediterranean frontier zones.

1. Predisposing kismet

Cervantes' novella *La española inglesa* begins with a troubling and, even by the standards of war, illegitimate kidnapping by Ricaredo's father Clotaldo of a seven-year-old girl from Cádiz, Isabela, who will eventually marry Ricaredo. Years after this kidnapping, the queen of England (Elizabeth, 'Isabel') puts one of our two protagonists, the crypto-Catholic Ricaredo, in a difficult bind by sending him as a corsair captain to intercept Portuguese ships returning from the East Indies. Fortune favours him: a storm blows the two ships to the Strait of Gibraltar, the death of his commanding officer leaves him in charge of both ships, and, best of all, two 'Turkish' galleys appear with a large Portuguese vessel they have captured. Thus, after a deadly sea battle, Ricaredo captures what the so-called Turks had already captured, sets the 300 Christian captives free along with twenty surviving Turks, and returns to London with the bounty, having found the ideal formula for doing good to Catholics, protecting himself from overt suspicion but satisfying the queen's desire for wealth at the expense of Spain and Portugal. As an English corsair combatting Barbary corsairs, he is a thief stealing stolen goods already alienated from their former owner, a captor who liberates other captors' captives, provides them with money and earns their profound gratitude even as he takes away the Portuguese ship laden with treasure. The Muslim adversary has done all the dirty work that he would otherwise have been obliged to do. Moreover, his good deeds with regard to freeing Christian and Turkish captives will be profoundly rewarded when, after being captured by Algerian corsairs much later, a Turk in Algiers gives him in return the two great gifts that Ricaredo had bestowed on his own captives: life and liberty. This is the only detail that Ricaredo tells of his year-long captivity in Algiers:

> I'll only say that I was recognised by one of the twenty Turks I set free along with the other Christians, and he was so thankful and such a good man that he didn't give me away. Because if the Turks had known that I had sunk their ships and taken out of their hands the great ship from the Indies,

they would either have given me over to the Grand Turk or taken my life. (*Novelas ejemplares* I, 282)

The Turk shows his extreme gratitude and goodness by *not* saying anything, by not exposing him, and, now that the former captor-captive relation is to some extent inverted, it's this act of generous silence that saves him, all by a chance encounter far removed in place and time. What's more, the kindness of this English corsair to the Spanish and Portuguese, among them his future parents-in-law, is his passport for acceptance into the society of his new home, Seville, as a man tells the crowd: 'This young man is a great English corsair, and I know him; he is the one who, just over two years ago, took from the Algerian corsairs the Portuguese galley that came from the East Indies. There's no doubt that it's him, I recognise him, because he gave me freedom and money to come to Spain, and not only to me but to three hundred other captives' (I, 278).

Ricaredo's good deeds thus come back to reward him in the most unexpected but opportune times and places, directly from one of the twenty Turks and one of the three hundred Spaniards. Generosity breeds gratitude which transforms into generosity, all of this across political and/or religious lines. We might attribute this to an ethical ideology in the novella which is realised through the fortuitous events that literature allows. There is this sense that *somehow*, in ways almost inconceivable, his charitable use of power will make others respond in kind towards him when he is powerless. I would note that these events occur in the most 'Mediterranean' part of this otherwise Atlantic novel, and that such notions of good *karma* (understood in a more colloquial than religious sense) can be found in other stories of the Mediterranean world. Corsairs in particular practised an accepted, even legitimated, line of work, so that there's no condemning of Ricaredo either in Algiers or in Seville for having been an English corsair, whose job it was to kill, capture and steal.

There were moments in Algiers when the corsairs saved the lives of captured Spanish corsairs from angry mobs because they recognised that the enemy corsair had merely been doing his job, and what's more, it was very much in the interests of corsairs to protect captured corsairs because the same thing might happen to them. This hints at rules of the game that the vast majority of corsairs accepted.

2. Freedom in exchange for a promise to free

The ethical logic in *La española inglesa* is comparable to a luminous moment in Diego Galán's captivity narrative, *Relación del cautiverio y libertad* (ch. 37, 214–18). Galán narrates his escape after many years as a slave, mostly in Istanbul, and his journey across Greece, where he's discovered and caught by two Turks, Mahamet Baxá and his friend Rugep. He's tied up, threatened and harshly interrogated, and admits he's a fugitive slave, though he alters the details about his master. Just when Mahamet wants to have him tortured, Rugep intervenes: 'For the love of God, let's free this man, because if he sees himself free he can do good to my brother, who's a captive in Malta.' As it's illegal to release a runaway captive, and several Greek labourers have witnessed the event, Mahamet threatens to kill anyone who reports it. Persuaded by Rugep, Mahamet declares: 'I want to free you for the love of my companion's brother who's captive in Malta, and another Turk from our village who's with him, on condition that you swear that if you reach Christian lands you'll go [to Malta[28]] and help them.' Diego of course swears and even seems to mean it ('in this case I wanted to fulfil the promise'); he writes down the names of his captors and of their people who are captive in Malta, and they set him free. Yet he never seems at all bound by his promise, even if it is made under duress. The Turks' generosity is extraordinary under the circumstances, and is predicated on a kind of quid pro quo where it's hoped that he will return the great favour that's being done to him by helping to free Rugep's brother and another Turk from their village. Here we have a karmic logic whereby *we* liberate *you* with the hope that you can help free two specific people who are dear to us, that is, a slightly deflected return of generosity. There seems to be a moment of empathy and a naive hope that one good turn will produce another that will come back to them. Such reasoning is not entirely unfounded.

3. Good karma across religions

Jerónimo Gracián, a disciple of Teresa de Ávila and the last of her confessors, was captive in Tunis from 1593 to 1595. In the tales of his captivity, particularly the autobiographical dialogue *Peregrinación de Anastasio* where he is Anastasio, he relates the complex circumstances of his ransoming in Tunis (68–81, 85–124). Years earlier in Lisbon he saved a Jew named Abraham Gebre from death at the hands of soldiers and also quelled revolts against the prince of Morocco. The grateful Jew offered him three hundred ducats, which Gracián refused but told him 'I hoped that God would pay me even better by the hand of another Jew' (120).

> It happened, then, that my rich Jew from Tunis, named Simón Escanasi, had gone with merchandise to Naples, and, upon arriving at the port of Gaeta, he was arrested and his goods were seized. Some relatives of mine from there, when they found out that the Jew was rich and powerful in Tunis, favoured him and had him freed and his goods released, begging him to ask for my ransom and giving him six hundred *escudos* to bring to me for that purpose, which were obtained in exchange with a Neapolitan Genoese banker named Damián Palavecino. The grateful Jew took the money to the

---

[28] This clarification is added in the later version of his captive's tale, in the composite edition prepared by Matías Barchino, 413.

Genoese who live on [the island of] Tabarca near Tunis, and who have an alliance and treaty with the Turks. (120)

Escanasi takes advantage of a moment when the pasha, fearing the wrath of the janissaries whose wages haven't been paid, is desperate for money. He offers Gracián's release for 1,300 escudos, much less than what the pasha had been asking. Escanasi explains this to Gracián, who is despondent because he can only count on the 600 escudos handed over to the Genoese in Tabarca. But Escanasi replies: 'Let's take the shackles off now, because afterwards, God great [Dios grande]. I said to myself: if the Jew says God great, am I going to say God little [Dios chico]? I begged him to do what he could' (121). Sure enough, the Jew manages to come up with cash lent by Moors and Jews, and furthermore saves him through legal means from the pasha's anger at having sold him so cheaply and takes him to the island of Tabarca, one of several islands in the Mediterranean with a long tradition of neutrality. At sea, a Muslim corsair generously refrains from recapturing him, though the rules would have allowed him to do so.

Essentially there seems to be a sequence of causality, sometimes tenuous, sometimes direct, within and between networks of Jews, Christians and Muslims. Gracián sees the origin of his release in his good deeds towards a Jew in Lisbon and Moors in Morocco years earlier, and more immediately, in the chain of events where the relatives of Gracián negotiate the release of Escanasi and his goods *so that* he will help Gracián by delivering part of the ransom to the Genoese in Tabarca and by using his diplomatic, legal and financial skills to negotiate the ransom. It seems to me that Escanasi goes well beyond the obligations of this quid pro quo, and that he earns Gracián's unequivocal gratitude and admiration. There's also a less traceable causality in this Mediterranean karma, where Gracián believes that his good deeds to a Jew in Lisbon and Moors in Morocco would be recompensed someday somewhere by the hand of another Jew and another Muslim. Ultimately, Dios grande, no chico. As in the two previous examples, all the participants know the rules of the game in the Mediterranean, they calculate what's best for themselves, they enter into mutually beneficial relations with different 'others' and have very positive feelings towards those 'others' – be it friendship, gratitude, respect, trust, or similar. In these cases at least, the protagonists resolve a complex situation by transcending the religious difference that allowed for the problems to arise in the first place. To put it otherwise, economy and ethical economy exploit religious difference but overcome it.

I should explain my use of the term *karma*, which of course originated far from the Mediterranean in India, with variations in five different religions. Setting aside the aspects involving rebirth, the ethical meaning of karma supposes that it's an act motivated by intention. Good intentions and good actions are believed to bring about good karma, future happiness, in a complex and rather indirect sequence of cause and effect. This of course is close enough to our colloquial use of the work *karma*, and the almost timeless and universal notions that 'you reap what you sow' and that 'what goes around comes around', but one particularly interesting aspect of *karma* understood as a kind of law of nature is that it's understood to be autonomous of any divine intervention as such. Regardless of how easily God is invoked in these last two stories, we see that karmic logic is shared across the religions, and doesn't belong exclusively to any one of them. The Turkish term *kismet*, derived through Persian from the Arabic *qisma* (portion, fate), would be an interesting 'Mediterranean' alternative, except that it's not always understood within an ethical dimension as something indirectly influenced by favourable conduct in a tenuous sequence of cause and effect. In any event, if Mediterranean peoples of this era lacked the *mot juste*, they understood the wordless principle.

4. Voluntary slavery, voluntary emancipation

A number of accounts of master-slave relations show affective bonds, as seen in chapter 4. The Belgian ex-captive Emmanuel d'Aranda, in his lucid account of captivity in Algiers, tells the story of a slave who offers to become a slave for a third time to the same master (143–5). Briefly, a successful Spanish renegade named Saban Galan Aga, a mariner's son from near the Portuguese border who was captured as a lad, passes by the slave market one day when he spots a fisherman from near his home country. He buys him for a modest price, takes him home and offers to free him if he promises to pay the same amount to a poor relative of his back home. The man, overjoyed, accepts and returns to Portugal, where he sells his boat and fishing supplies and takes the money to this relative, who sends Saban a letter of gratitude. Soon afterwards the fisherman is recaptured and taken to Algiers, where an astonished Saban buys him again and offers to free him under the same terms. The man promises, but says he needs more time since he has no fishing boat or supplies of his own. When the term of two years is almost up and the man has only been able to pay a third of the amount to the relative, he acquires a bale of tobacco and boards a Portuguese ship bound for Algiers in order to sell it there, where tobacco is expensive. Upon arriving he goes directly to Saban, who is again astonished to see him, and tells him that he intends to sell the tobacco, and if he's unable to do so, he says, 'I'd rather be your slave than have you, my lord, from whom I have received so many good deeds, accuse me of ingratitude'. Amazed by the man's faithfulness and gratitude, Saban pardons him of his debt and offers him hospitality until the ship returns. This story of generosity and gratitude became widely known in Algiers and in Portugal, says d'Aranda. It also shows genuine affection and compassion, and resonates with a familiar theme whereby renegades in North Africa would maintain contact with their people back home and help them out.

5. A bacchanal of largesse

If this could happen in master-slave relations, let's consider cases of relations between equals. In his autobiography, the Spanish corsair Alonso de Contreras tells of how he negotiates the release of a Turkish captive (I, 4, 36–9). In the midst of this process, while his ship is anchored in an inlet near Athens, the large galley of Morato Gancho, governor of Negroponte, suddenly enters and, much to Contreras' relief, hoists a white flag and casts anchor a short distance away. Morato disembarks and heads towards Contreras, who goes to meet him, 'and we greeted each other, he in his way and I in mine'. What follows is a remarkable sequence of gestures, courtesies and acts of generosity in which the Turkish captive is exchanged amidst lavish gifts on both sides:

> Asking permission, he went to see the slave I had. I ordered the man to be brought to shore with his tunic and knives just as I had captured him, which they much appreciated. We spoke for a good while and they asked me to go to the galley. We went and, as I entered, they greeted me with the music of shawms. After a short while we went to shore and spent the time in conversation until they came with the money, which took no more than two hours to go and come back; they brought it in gold sequins. (I, 4, 38)

Contreras mentions a series of sumptuous gifts passed in both directions, with expressions of magnanimity and appreciation, and continues:

> The night was coming on, and as I wanted to leave he begged me to have dinner with him and leave in the morning. I accepted, and he regaled me well. As we were dining my captive sent him a note asking that his two servants be ransomed and that he entreat me to allow this; he greatly urged me to do so; I sent for them right away and said to him: 'Here you have them at your disposal.' He deemed this very highly. He offered me two hundred sequins; I refused to accept them, so he told me: 'Well, take this Christian who serves me in the stern.' I said I'd accept him because he'd regain his freedom. I went to my frigate and in the morning sent to ask him permission to sail, and he told me I could whenever I wanted. I did so, and when passing near his galley I gave him a gun salute; he answered me with another cannon, and we both went on our way. (I, 4, 39)

Before this encounter Morato Gancho and Alonso de Contreras were enemies, and will again be enemies now that they're sailing away. The kind of enmity they have permits negotiations, agreements, courtesy, largesse, congeniality, a dinner invitation, hours of conversation, and respect from the initial greeting to the final gun salute. Battle and capture could have been an option, but at great risk. What actually happens here goes far beyond a peaceful handling of an important captive's recovery of freedom, and what interests me is precisely that excess, that amicable contest of good will, that disposition to excel each other in favours and to pass the time revelling in each other's company. The geopolitical and religious divide in the Mediterranean actually makes this extraordinary encounter possible, yet equally important is the fact that such differences are downplayed. In the kind of Mediterranean we've seen throughout this book, unscripted, improvised encounters like this one were bound to happen with some frequency.

Here we might recall, as recounted in chapter 3, the story of the renegade Cigala, who, as admiral of the Turkish fleet, wrote to the viceroy of Sicily in 1598 asking for permission to see his mother, whom he hadn't seen for some forty years. The viceroy responded with the utmost courtesy and arranged for the blissful visit to take place, with Cigala's promise not to raid the Sicilian coastline. This was a noble understanding between adversaries who negotiated to get what they wanted with nothing to lose, a 'win-win situation' brought about in a spirit of magnanimity.

6. Language, lactation and law

Let's consider a couple of cases where religion does play a stronger role and sets up a barrier as well as a bridge, particularly between Christians and Muslims. One rare and strange text is the *Relación del milagroso rescate del crucifixo de las monjas de San José de Valencia* (*Story of the miraculous ransom of the crucifix of the nuns of Saint Joseph of Valencia*, 1625) written by fray Antonio Juan Andreu de San José. The story begins with a raid in 1529 by Algerian corsairs of a village on the Valencian coast, where Úrsola de Medina and her two-year-old son Cristóbal are captured. She and her son remain in the power of her Moorish captor, a widower who also has a son of about the same age. While she wants her freedom, he is charmed by her, pressures her to convert to Islam and expresses his desire to marry her. She resists. But she gladly nurses his son with great affection, along with her own. A mother's milk, of course, is much more than sustenance: 'She also came to love the little Moor [morito] (a natural condition and effect of milk, which also is blood whitened by the natural warmth of the breast), greatly desiring, if she could, with the Christian milk that she was giving him, to give him at the same time faith in Jesus Christ and the other virtues he needed.' The author goes on to say: 'How concerted and like-minded were the thoughts of this Catholic slave woman and of this infidel Moor in their hidden breasts, and how contrary, on the other hand, were their very conflicting and divergent means and ends' (119–20). They do indeed understand each other. A silent domestic war begins, where he teaches her son to say (in Mediterranean lingua franca) 'Yo estar moro, moro, moro' ('I be Moor, Moor, Moor'), and when she finds out about this she firmly corrects her son, much to the Moor's chagrin. What's perhaps most interesting about this story is the strong affection she has for both children she's nursing, her own son and that of her Muslim master and suitor.

Children's innocence is preserved in this story, and their religion comes to them not through paternity or caste or doctrine but through a mother's milk, her bodily contact and affection. The two children virtually become twins loved by both adults. Recounted by a Spanish friar with no interest in religious tolerance, this story degenerates into a silent battle where the Moor strives in vain to convert Úrsola's lactating child and finally resolves to sell them both. Historical sources show, on the contrary, that most captive women converted to Islam and married.

7. Frontier enemies swap religions

The other example comes from the *Book of travels* by the witty Turkish traveller and statesman Evliya Çelebi, who, when narrating the gruesome frontier war between the Ottoman Turks and Christians in Bosnia, tells of the beheading of over a thousand Christian captives at the orders of the pasha. But one Turkish fighter throws his arms around an infidel soldier's neck to protect him and cries out: 'Mercy, noble vizier! During the battle I gave this infidel my religion, and I took his religion. We have claimed each other as brothers. If you kill him he will go to paradise with my religion … When I die, the religion of this infidel, whom I have claimed as my brother, will remain with me and I will go to hell, so again it will be too bad for me.' He burst out crying and would not be separated from the infidel. The frontier warriors explain this to the irritated pasha. 'When one of our [warriors] on these frontiers falls captive to the infidels, while eating and drinking with them, one infidel may pledge to save him from captivity, and the Muslim, too, promises to rescue him from the Turks if he falls captive to us. They make a pact, saying: "Your religion is mine and my religion is yours." They lick each other's blood, and the infidel and the Muslim become "brothers in religion".' This warrior is now obliged to save his 'brother in religion', and if he fails he will be condemned to go to hell with the infidel's religion. The story concludes: 'So [the pasha] gave the captive infidel to the renegade infidel, and they ran off like dogs in a field. We were all amazed at this discussion' (249–50). Frontier enmity creates this kind of frontier fraternisation, a pact made while eating and drinking together that involves licking each other's blood and exchanging each other's religion as a guarantee that the pact will be honoured: they have at the same time remained themselves, become one with the other by sharing blood, and become the other by switching religions.

8. Cultural and religious crossovers

Cervantes' play *El gallardo español* exemplifies a number of the tendencies noted previously in works of numerous authors with regard to seventeenth-century literary developments of the 'Moorish novel' such as the *Abencerraje* or Ginés Pérez de Hita's *Historia de los bandos de los zegríes y abencerrajes* (vol. 1 of *Guerras civiles de Granada*). This play, set in and around Oran, both acknowledges the harsh realities of what was then a dreadful *presidio* on the Algerian coast[29] and *also* transforms them into a fairly idealised setting reminiscent of frontier conditions within Spain as portrayed in the *Abencerraje*. We thus have a superimposition of one chronotope on another. The play is historically contextualised within the Turkish siege of Oran in 1563 as well as other local events, but as in the *Abencerraje* itself the action also evokes the modalities of medieval chivalry in war and love.

Cultural and even sexual cross-dressing occurs throughout, accompanied by a gamut of friendships, love, empathy, voluntary slavery, and so on, while differences are minimised. There's much play on personal, cultural and religious identity, all the way to the double betrothal at the end with two couples in Moorish garb, one Christian and the other Muslim. What I'd especially like to point out here is that, amidst the typical insults uttered by secondary characters (e.g. Muslims and Christians calling each other *dogs*), there are some highly remarkable lines in this play. The oft-cited parting of two characters, Guzmán and Alimuzel – where Guzmán says 'May your Muhammad keep you, Alí' and Alimuzel responds 'May your Christ go with you' (vv. 475–6) – reveals a crossover perspective and deference to the *others* that's emblematic of the entire play. Later on, Alimuzel goes even a step further when he wishes the Prophet's favours for his non-Muslim friend don Fernando: 'May Muhammad help you / and give you what he can' (vv. 1053–4). While in the *Abencerraje* there's no mention of converting to the other religion, in *El gallardo español* the idea of conversion to the other religion is twice explicitly rejected as unworthy of a noble, whether this noble be Christian or Muslim (vv. 1068–70, 2327–9) – a surprising assertion in the context of two ostensibly proselytising religions. As in the *Abencerraje*, various passages make it

---

[29] As a captive, Cervantes was well informed about Oran and Mers-el-Kebir (the nearby port *presidio*, 'Mazalquivir'), having written letters in 1578 to one of the characters in this play, don Martín de Córdoba, when preparing his third escape attempt from Algiers. In 1581 after he was ransomed, he was sent there on an official mission. While the *comedia* certainly downplays the bitter conditions of Oran and Mers-el-Kebir, which included hunger, lack of soldier's pay, dismal morale, and so on, it does allude to soldiers' frequent desertion and conversion to Islam. Oran was the destination for many banished people, both high and low on the social scale. It was a multi-ethnic and multi-religious mini-society with a long-standing Jewish community, numerous Muslims including merchants, as well as Christians from the religious orders, families of soldiers, and the like. Yet the primary purposes of Oran since 1509 were military: getting a foothold for what would be a failed colonial strategy in Africa, deterring Ottoman expansion in the Maghrib, restraining Muslim corsairs, and ultimately, engaging in continuous raids (*cabalgadas*) to take captives from local tribes.

clear that friendship transcends enmity: as Alimuzel puts it, 'The Christian is not an enemy / but an adversary' (vv. 1035–6), and don Fernando reaffirms his friendship over and above 'the law [i.e. religion] that divides us' (1045). Wielding a sword and wearing a turban, he will in fact defend his Muslim friends against his Christian companions from the *presidio*.

In this work and others, Cervantes pushes the limits of what can be said and done in such a religiously charged setting and in effect questions much of the conventional manichean discourse about Christian-Muslim relations. Like Góngora in his Maghribian *romances*, Cervantes ennobles and humanises a sordid frontier by using a model derived from the *Abencerraje* but now turned into a malleable kind of *abencerrajismo* highly refined through poetic sensibility and theatrical dialogue. Many other writers, including Lope in his novella *Guzmán el bueno*, Alonso Castillo Solórzano in *Historia de Xarife y Zoraida*, Juan Barrionuevo y Moya in *Soledad entretenida*, Mariana de Carvajal in *El esclavo de su esclavo*, to name a few, adopt variations of this formula by minimising religious and geopolitical difference and weaving stories of positive interaction because the characters are seen to respect each other, share the same values and speak the same 'language'. While *abencerrajismo* is only one of the pathways that Cervantes explores, it seems that in this too he takes the lead by developing the possibilities of a subgenre.

Boundary-crossing love, passion and friendship are present in the majority of these texts. One of Cervantes' favourite plot devices, used in both of his Algerian plays and in *El amante liberal*, consists of a four-way relationship between a Muslim (often renegade) husband and wife who fall passionately for a female and a male Christian captive in their household who in turn pretend to be intermediaries in their master's or mistress's passion for the other, and end up fleeing together. Another favourite storyline, equally fanciful, is that of Zoraida or Zahara, the crypto-Christian daughter of Agi Morato who abandons Algiers for Spain with a Christian captive. *La gran sultana* in particular destabilises stereotypes by greatly exaggerating them (as commented on earlier), upsets the harem with a cross-dressed man and his pregnant lover, brings Islam and Christianity close together, presents us with love relations across religious lines (from the sultan to the *gracioso* Madrigal), and celebrates the as yet unborn prince as a 'Spanish Ottoman'. While doña Catalina wants to remain Christian, the young sultan insists that she do so and won't have it any other way, saying that her soul has nothing to do with him, only her body (vv. 1238–47). A renegade in that play dangerously says that he doesn't believe in anything (vv. 190–1). Renegades – whether depicted favourably or not – tend to be key figures in nearly all of these stories, which as an ensemble go a long way to finding ways to novelise or dramatise the Mediterranean and prepare the way for many other writers in the seventeenth century. They also increase exponentially the importance of women, of female protagonists, and this would also be the case in all Mediterranean frontier literature that followed him. In such literature, widely read and translated in European countries, counternarratives aren't the exception but the prevailing tendency.

Throughout this book we've seen numerous other instances of positive events or relations in Mediterranean frontier zones, and many more could be summoned here. Nabil Matar, in his introduction to a collection of English captivity narratives in the Mediterranean, cites a series of such encounters in a paragraph, and adds: 'All these positive anecdotes explain why the Algerian scholar Moulay Belhamissi has urged that the study of captivity accounts should discriminate between what is "histoire" and what is "hysteric", between what actually happened and what captives, their relatives, and modern historians have projected' (20). In my view, the more we listen to early modern testimonies, including those of captives, the more insight we can gain into what the early modern Mediterranean world was about, how it worked, and how it was seen or imagined to be. While the Morisco episodes of Cervantes' last two novels have long been discussed though with no consensus, 'counternarratives' like those above have often been ignored or altogether unread. My aim has not been to gloss over the harsh realities of Mediterranean life on both sides of the Christian-Muslim divide in the early modern era but rather to insist on alternatives to the ways in which scholars have most often understood that world, and to question the reliability of the kinds of accounts that have tended to shape the prevalent narrative. This is especially the case with blatantly propagandistic works, which perpetuate the lie that there was a war of religions, or that the worst slavery in the history of humanity was that of Algiers, or that the so-called renegades were the most despicable people on earth, etc., thereby suppressing most of the positive forms of reciprocity and exchange.

In sum, counternarratives bring out an unmistakable counterpoint to what has most often been considered the dominant theme of cruelty and hostility in early modern texts. The cosmopolitanism and conviviality of Laurent d'Arvieux (among others), together with his Muslim hosts, could alone fill a chapter. The many kinds of alterity we find in the early modern Mediterranean are nearly all quite relative, where modes of human interaction often transcended barriers of religion, ethnicity, language, imperial conflict, master-slave relations, gender, and so on. According to Sosa, over half the population of Algiers consisted of renegades and their households. What's more, taking into account the renegades, Turkish nationals, the 'Moors' from outside Algiers including the Morisco immigrants, as well as Jews of diverse origins, an astonishing three-quarters of the permanent population of Algiers not counting the Christian captives would have been allochthonous, coming from elsewhere. These figures in the *Topografía* are approximations, and though Sosa's numbers are arguable, his meticulous demography can't readily be discarded. Such a confluence of peoples of diverse origin is unthinkable in the Algiers of today, in which the city's Ottoman past seems to remain a sensitive issue. This early modern cosmopolitanism – no doubt with institutionalised inequalities and abuse, yet cosmopolitanism nonetheless – was mirrored to some extent in several other Muslim cities, and superseded only by Istanbul in the Mediterranean and perhaps nowhere else.

Conclusion

Although a number of its themes will be familiar, I believe that this book presents a quite different Mediterranean from those seen before, one that adds new or lesser-known faces, writings and voices along with an ensemble of perhaps unsettling perspectives with regard to method, approach and conceptual topography. The book project could no doubt have been carried out in many other ways, focusing more on other places, other texts, other problems and questions. In fact, a fair number of related studies of my own in the form of presentations, essays, etc. were initially intended to be part of this project, but have become autonomous pieces, 'satellites' relative to the book's core, as can be seen in the bibliography and references to them in the text. Investigations regarding slavery and religious conversion – or more concretely slaves and 'renegades' – constitute the core of this study, not only in the two chapters directly devoted to them but for the most part in all five chapters, whose sequence is conditioned by these two intertwined subjects. In my view, these topics are crucial for understanding how the early modern Mediterranean worked, reaching into the highest and lowest levels of politics and society and the modus operandi of Mediterranean economy, culture, religion and ethos, directly affecting the lives of millions of people and indirectly a great many more. Without them the early modern Mediterranean world would be illegible, unthinkable. Needless to say, this book by no means aims to be comprehensive in its handling of these topics, though it does strive to treat them in novel ways conducive to insight.

Also present from beginning to end is an attention to how early modern writers characterised the Mediterranean world from the partialities of the genres they employed as well as their perspectives and 'situatedness' in every respect. This has involved intently reading and listening to a proliferation of early modern sources in an array of genres and languages, and drawing upon passages that looked promising for the purposes of this book. Rhetoric, poetics and discourse analysis (along with some common sense) have helped to decipher strategies of representation both factual and fictive and their relations to certain kinds of truths or modes of obfuscation, with the assumption that much can also be learned about that world from its misconceptions, biases and other forms of misrepresentation. The vast expanse of relevant textual sources from inquisitional records to literary genres, including so many other kinds of works from that era in various languages, allows for an understanding of the main topics of this book that would be hard to reach via more limited means.

Several methodological and theoretical threads of diverse origin pass through the entire book. One is the assumption that the whole Mediterranean – despite its great diversity of peoples and languages, its innumerable local and regional spheres, its seas and basins, its religious divide – did function indeed as a kind of system or 'world' because of the continual movement and contact of its peoples north and south, east and west. Economy and politics, slaves and renegades, all participated in this interaction. This is Braudel's thesis predicated mainly on the perpetual 'movements of men' and the responsiveness of the major political adversaries to each other in war and peace, and I believe it's clarified and reinforced by Georg Simmel's comprehensive concept of unity that depends not only on harmonious relations but also on divisions and conflict. Its functioning as a 'world' neither prevented any of the peoples in its periphery from participating in other major 'worlds' (e.g. engaging with Europe, America, Africa, the Near East) nor justifies the conception of a 'Muslim world' as opposed to a 'Christian world'.

This book by no means deals with the whole Mediterranean as such. Instead, it focuses primarily on 'frontier zones', i.e. places where there was sustained interaction of any kind among people of different religious, cultural and social categories, most particularly among adherents of the three major Abrahamic religions. Although there's a clear sense of what lands and islands of the Mediterranean were under Christian or Muslim dominion, there's no way to draw a frontier line: ships from Muslim and Christian lands prowled almost the entire Mediterranean, which was an expansive aqueous frontier. Many port cities around the Mediterranean – 'cities of the sea', as Leonardo da Vinci would call them – had slave markets and were populated with people of diverse origin whose interchange constituted dense frontier zones. These cities included Istanbul, Valetta, Venice, Naples, Genoa, Palermo, Marseille, Valencia, Algiers, Tunis and Alexandria, though several important cities somewhat inland also had these characteristics (e.g. Rome, Seville, Marrakesh, Fez, Cairo, Jerusalem). Apart from more or less random places where ships confronted each other at sea or along coastlines, it was primarily in these *urban* zones where frontier interaction was most intense. These were spaces that created frontier consciousness whereby people acted with an acute awareness of what others of different cultural and religious signs were thinking, saying and doing, and learned how to imitate them or negotiate with them.

I insist throughout on the *plural* nature of alterity, on the notion that within any category of otherness there are *others*, and that there's no such phenomenon as 'the other' or 'the Muslim other' and so on, nor are *we* a singular entity but rather a plurality. A quick overview of, say, Antonio de Sosa's *Topografía de Argel* reveals that there's a whole taxonomy of different cultural and religious 'kinds' of Muslims, Jews and Christians in Algiers, and to the classifications he specifies we could add other categories or subcategories based on various criteria of alterity or of so-called 'identity' or 'sameness'. With their long history of living in the proximity of Christians in different epochs and regions of Spain, the Moriscos were paradigmatic for the profound differences among them. Even more so perhaps were the converts to Islam, those most often designated as 'renegades' who populated the full gamut of alterities and shifting identities. The renegades throw into doubt practically all the problematics of alterity, including the entire, mostly 'one-on-one', phenomenological tradition regarding alterity from Hegel to Levinas, though some formulations in other disciplines (e.g. that of Johannes Fabian, Edward Said, among others) have in my view maintained their validity.

I also insist on the *relative* nature of alterities among cultures and religions of the early modern Mediterranean. The religions were significantly different but recognisably related and similar, as were so many other aspects of life during that epoch (e.g. social organisation, forms of interaction, festivities, commerce, many kinds of technology, horticulture, gardening, food, building, warfare, the layout of many towns and cities, and much else). This meant that anyone crossing over as a slave or diplomat or merchant would already dispose of ready means of comparison that would allow for some initial understanding of similarity and difference, and would enable one to adapt more easily to the way of life on the other side, at least to some degree. In the case of slaves this would facilitate switching religions or becoming integrated into local communities. Such relative alterities would have profoundly affected the mode of slavery practised among Mediterranean peoples, providing rudimentary bases of comprehension, facilitating communication, and so on, despite hostilities. Besides, it should be borne in mind that racial differences were minimal if at all existent in Mediterranean frontier slavery, and this accounts in part for the differences between this type of slavery and those undergone by sub-Saharan Africans in the Mediterranean region. Such was by no means the case with encounters between Mediterranean peoples and more distant peoples of Africa, Asia and America with whom there had been no long history of interaction.[1]

Nietzsche's mistrust of language, beginning with his mistrust of words as concepts, has long been instructive for me. The beginning of his analysis of revenge is one of the key passages:

---

[1] Gonzalo Guerrero, one of the first Europeans to 'go native' in the Americas, for example, would likely have had to start from much more bewilderment and overcome much greater differences to become integrated as one of 'them', and when he did so he apparently saw no viable return nor wanted one even when he was offered the chance to leave. His story is recounted in Bernal Díaz del Castillo's *Historia verdadera de la conquista de la Nueva España*, ch. 27, among other sources.

Elements of revenge.– The word 'revenge' is said so quickly it almost seems as if it could contain no more than one conceptual and perceptional root. And so one continues to strive to discover it: just as our economists have not yet wearied of scenting a similar unity in the word 'value' and of searching after the original root concept of the word. As if every word were not a pocket into which now this, now that, now several things at once have been put! Thus 'revenge', too, is now this, now that, now something more combined. (*Human, all too human*, vol. 2, part 2, #33)

The widespread faith in words and names (reinforced by Heidegger) as bearers and conveyors of unified essences continues to stifle thought, as though the most axiologically charged nouns referred to something homogeneous because a single word encompasses it. Much more open to enquiry is the suspicion that in many cases no such unity exists in a word, and the notion above that every such word is a 'pocket' into which quite different things have been put. For our purposes, consider 'slavery', for example: the word 'slave' is so highly charged that it has the effect of blurring the differences between one kind of slavery and another, not to mention differences in how, say, women and men experience slavery, or in countless particular conditions of slaves. Slaves of one kind and another do have things in common, enough to warrant using the same word for lack of any other (unity of the pocket), but the different modalities are often more revealing than the similarities. Some scholars have long been cognizant of this, and in one way or another have adumbrated a typology of slavery in the early modern Mediterranean or elsewhere. Chapter 2 of this book also does so, enquiring into how Mediterranean frontier slavery (as I call it) contrasts with the other kinds of slavery practised in the Mediterranean world during that era, particularly with regard to what this means for the slaves themselves.

So it is with many of the keywords in this study: we see, for example, that there are slaves and slaves, renegades and renegades, martyrs and martyrs, Moriscos and Moriscos,[2] and so on. The often misguided and outmoded search for the 'identity' of peoples or categories of people leads to articulations of oneness and sameness rather than disparities and dynamic shifts of ways of being. Much more of interest in this book are modes of becoming: the kinds of experience and contact of nearly all those mentioned required them to change in accordance with radical alterations in circumstance. Moreover,

---

[2] José María Perceval devoted an entire book, *Todos son uno: arquetipos, xenofobia y racismo*, as well as subsequent studies, to dismantling the strategies on the part of the Spanish monarchy and its ideologues to falsify the Moriscos as 'one' (hence the title *Todos son uno*, 'all are one', a widely used phrase that justified the expulsion of the Moriscos). All scholars of Morisco studies are keenly aware of crucial regional and other historical variations among Moriscos in the sixteenth and early seventeenth centuries.

the issue is not whether people changed, or that they changed, but *how* they changed and kept changing.

The renegades in all their variations perhaps embody these kinds of transfiguration where 'selves' and 'others' are confounded and notions of identity and alterity disoriented. In these crossover figures the Mediterranean frontier becomes interiorised as they adopt a frontier consciousness that takes into account the multilingual, multicultural and multireligious ambience they live within. To one extent or another they become more versatile than they were before, developing techniques of translation, negotiation, manoeuvring, improvised action, and looking out for themselves. Let's recall the renegade Leo Africanus's fable of the trickster bird with its motto: 'when a man sees his advantage, he always follows it'. Renegades would also be constantly mindful of their being branded by their former companions, religion and country as traitors and apostates at the same time as they would have newer communities of alliance and support. Janus-like, duplicitous and capable of dissembling, renegades are simultaneously *us* and *them*.

It requires no special insight to realise that the vast majority of converts to Islam or Christianity were by no means motivated by theological conviction. Religious polemics were alive and well, but neither Christians nor Muslims had many converts to show for all their efforts, no matter how pleased they might have been with themselves for the ingenuity of their arguments. Even after the Council of Trent (1545–63), testimonies abound about how little theological content there tended to be in Catholic religious practice, which was generally centred on habitual rites and the calendar of festivities. Religious painting of the early modern epoch is rarely guided by theological ideas, engaging onlookers emotionally with key moments in the life of Jesus, the Virgin Mary, the saints as well as other Biblical and traditional stories. Portraits of the Virgin almost invariably give the sense of artists having employed local young women to pose. As we've seen, renegades returning from Muslim lands reveal in inquisitional records not only how little they know about the tenets of Islam but also about those of Christianity. This is a major reason why I've emphasised 'popular religion' over dogmatic religion. With rare exceptions (leaving aside the issue of Moriscos' religiosity), it makes no sense to try to understand, as many still do, conversions from Christianity to Islam in terms of persuasive belief or 'faith'. I've also stressed how Judaism, Christianity (Catholic and Orthodox) and Islam as practised in the early modern period lay much more stress on what people *did* than on what they believed or thought they believed. Religious conversion most often had little to do with religion as such, at least initially. Let's also recall that, unlike Christian clerical writers' deep anxiety over endemic reneging to Islam, Ottoman officials 'were not concerned with the motivation of the convert and rarely recorded any of his or her intentions in changing religion, let alone the former religion or name' (Marc Baer, qtd in Graf 3). It seems that they showed remarkable wisdom.

One of the greatest clichés of our time and our disciplines is the botanical metaphor of 'hybridity', which has come to mean a mixture of anything with anything else, as though there were or had ever been anything chemically pure in the humanities and social sciences. Mixtures, amalgamation, miscellanies and motley medleys have always been the norm in what we deal with. The problem is not in the term hybridity (or hybrid) as such, which botanists understand very well, nor in the affirmation that something or someone is heterogeneous, but in the run-of-the-mill abandonment of all enquiry once something or someone is declared to be 'hybrid', as though that actually said anything and were an answer rather than an inverted question. If something is 'hybrid', what are the specific elements that have gone into it, what are the proportions, what are the dynamics of this combination of elements, what are the forces and determining factors, and so on? These and similar questions about 'hybridity', if the term is going to have any meaning at all, need to be asked and explored, as in fact the primary theorists of discursive or sociocultural hybridity have done (e.g. Bakhtin, Bhabha, García Canclini).

'Syncretism' has been in common use much longer, and has its usefulness mainly in religious studies, which does tend to analyse the specificity of any syncretic instance. The problem here is that the term has little to contribute when applied, for example, to renegades, who may have syncretised elements of Christianity and Islam, but who often had such a confused and idiosyncratic sense of *both* religions that they had little idea as to what they were combining with what. Another criticism of syncretism, e.g. in L. P. Harvey's analysis of the Moriscos' lead books, is that whereas the term assumes a fusion of religious elements, the lead books were of Muslim inspiration and they consciously integrated what resonated with Christian-sounding elements (e.g. Jesus is referred to as *ruḥ Allāh*, the 'spirit of God', a Quranic expression) that were consonant with Muslim doctrine (265–70). In any event, we should bear in mind that, unlike the vast majority of renegades, the counterfeiters of the lead books knew very well what they were doing and belonged to an educated elite.

The examples of renegades we've seen show an astonishing variety of human beings who nonetheless tend to be endowed with comparable capabilities and characteristics of doubleness or multiplicity. We've seen an exceptional case of one who writes about himself, and in so doing brazenly fictionalises himself beyond credibility, becoming not so much the image he projects as a character who can't help but project such an image of himself; he was diplomatically useful to powerful rulers even though (or perhaps because) they knew he was a fraud. We've seen renegades with lives on both shores who are adept at convincing whomever they're with that they belong there before they slip away to the other side. Renegades sometimes experience a *prise de conscience*, whether it be self-induced or provoked by others such as priests or former companions, leading them to believe that they're no longer what they've become and that they need to do something resolute such as enacting their own martyrdom, escaping or merely dissembling. A few have become renegades ostensibly because of some transformative experience, whether religious or not. Some were never renegades at all but branded as such and punished for apostasy. Apart from these, all have learned to be someone quite other than what they were. It's not that they've become 'the other' but rather that they're no longer quite who they were and now can perform this difference to everyone else's satisfaction and perhaps even their own. And once they've done this they can keep on inventing themselves in accordance with how they're regarded by others and the new roles they take on. They develop the uncanny ability to be either/or as well as neither/both or sometimes 'several'. This is why I suggested that renegades were double or multiple people who had the ability to switch between different heteronyms, *being* each heteronym and thinking in the mode of that heteronym. It's also why I compared renegades to unusual places capacious enough to harbour contrary sets of objects and modes of behaviour, analogous to the cave of Lampedusa.

Their host society has much to do with renegades' sense of who they now are and what possibilities open themselves up to them. The cities, provinces and regencies under Ottoman rule offered previously unimaginable life opportunities to some of the great renegades, men and women, including power, influence, prestige and wealth. The integration of renegade women into these societies radically altered their life possibilities and must have connected many of them positively to whatever kinds of relations and activities were appropriate within their immediate circles. Hürrem Sultan (aka Roxelana) and Nurbanu Sultan were exceptional, but they could become the extraordinary sultanas they were because of how the Ottoman court and harem worked, as Cervantes understood well when he rather playfully had a fictive captive girl from Asturias become *La gran sultana*.

Renegades were also connectors, agents who in effect helped bring the Mediterranean together and maintained its interconnectedness, not only because of the active or passive bonds they would have felt towards their places and cultures of origin but also in the gamut of roles they performed mainly in frontier zones, including some of the most highly ranked positions in the Ottoman Empire. They infused their own foreignness into their new societies at the same time as they adapted to those societies, became part of them and contributed enormously to them, particularly on the Muslim sides. Those who were well integrated were also loyal, without conflicting connections such as to families, clans or factions, and were unhampered by forms of local myopia. Whereas many of the lands surrounding the Mediterranean could also turn their backs on the Mediterranean to engage in endeavours elsewhere, the renegades in their sheer numbers and activities, not least of all were the continual capture of Christian slaves, were a constant if often disagreeable reminder for slaves to remain vigilant and do the same if they needed any prompting at all.

The arrival in the western Mediterranean of Aruch and Hayreddin Barbarossa around 1503 would significantly change the map of the Maghrib and the reach of the Ottoman Empire, and would also initiate early modern corsairing practices in the Mediterranean just when Spain had begun to attack ports on the Maghribian coast to establish presidios there. Raised as socially humble pot makers and sea traders, they weren't precisely renegades – their father of Albanian origin had converted to Islam and married an Orthodox woman in Lesbos who remained Christian – though, raised in their father's religion, they came to demonstrate all the talents and skills later revealed by other great renegade pashas and admirals. Curiously, what forced them into corsairing was the plundering and violence of the Knights Hospitaller of St. John, who imprisoned Aruch for three years until Hayreddin helped him escape. The young Barbarossas, especially these two of the four brothers, learned to confront the Knights at sea, and Hayreddin in particular ultimately helped to dislodge them from Rhodes after more than two centuries of their occupancy of the island. Their exploits were daring and typically successful: they challenged Christian fleets, raided coastlines and ports, captured innumerable ships, helped many Spanish Muslims ('Moriscos') emigrate to the other shore, conquered many ports along the Algerian coast, subdued several inland kingdoms, and ruthlessly seized and ruled Algiers which they established as a Mediterranean hub. Aruch set up Algiers as an Ottoman regency in 1516, relinquishing the title of sultan but remaining governor, beylerbey, and when in 1518 he died in battle, Hayreddin took over and pursued an even more illustrious career, humiliating and outwitting the emperor Charles V and other Christian rulers on several occasions, commanding the Ottoman fleet, and much more. In 1545, while Hayreddin was still alive, the Spanish humanist historian Francisco López de Gómara wrote biographies of both brothers in his *Crónica de los corsarios Barbarroja*, aware (in the case of Hayreddin) that 'it is hard to write the life of someone who is still not dead' (13). But his unbounded admiration for Hayreddin inspired him to write the work, despite Hayreddin being alive and having for decades been the scourge of the western Mediterranean, in effect the worst enemy of Christendom as well as of Islamic kingdoms in the interior. López de Gómara exalts him on a par with Hernán Cortés, whose great feats were on land, whereas Hayreddin 'is the greatest corsair and best sea captain there has ever been' (120). Over several pages he tells how 'our friend Barbarossa', en route to Istanbul after escaping from Charles V's imperial forces in Tunis and regrouping in Algiers, performed 'a great feat' by stealth and audacity. His disguised ships peacefully entered the port of Mahón in Menorca, pillaged everything down to doorknockers and locks and took captive virtually the entire population including women and children as a gift to the Grand Turk (104–6).

Without the aggressions of the Knights of St. John in the east and the incipient attempts on the part of Portugal and Spain at subjugating the Maghrib, Aruch and Hayreddin would most likely have remained anonymous local pot makers and traders. Their extraordinary accomplishments, at least partly in response to such hostile developments, turned much of the Mediterranean (the western basin, the Adriatic and Ionian) into a theatre of intensified conflict, and transfigured these contemporaries of Machiavelli into major players of the early modern Mediterranean world. Though mostly bellicose, their actions were transformative, associative, responsive and provocative, unifying (in Simmel's sense of 'unity') the Mediterranean in untold ways.

As we've seen throughout this book, all frontier figures were in fact 'connectors' in the Mediterranean. Besides renegades, these included slaves, particularly those associated with Mediterranean frontier slavery, as well as religiously affiliated ethnicities, most notably Moriscos and Jews. Turks (officials, janissaries) and all other mobile categories of people (e.g. merchants, ransomers, diplomats) likewise contributed to the makeup of many of the Mediterranean frontier zones, spaces that connected among each other and created the kinds of ambience that fomented the reflexive consciousness that we've witnessed in many historical and literary personages. I wouldn't hesitate to refer to an early modern cosmopolitanism, one that has virtually nothing to do with the (laudable) ethical premises of present-day cosmopolitanism or even those that have been a millennial legacy since stoicism, but which was predicated on the impelled convergence and contact of very different peoples often under duress who nonetheless, for the most part, shared the divergent manifestations of a nexus of social and cultural heritages that Mediterranean cultures produced. This book is primarily *about* frontier figures, people who *became* frontier figures and developed the skills to know how to interact in complex situations which their upbringing in most cases didn't prepare them for.

How we know about them owes much to what extant early modern writings tell us about them, and this is also what the present book is about. It's my hope that the proliferation of narratives, voices and commentaries about slavery, corsairing, religious conversion, alterities, cruelty, martyrdom, expulsion, exile, capabilities, mutual understanding, self-interest, empathy, courtesy, generosity and kindness discussed over the course of this book, partial as many of these are, has not only revealed many strategies of representation regarding the early modern Mediterranean but has also led to insights and an unexpected acquaintance with a wide range of interesting and sometimes extraordinary human beings, both factual and fictive. Obviously, much of that world from the Bosphorus to Gibraltar is lost, and its written works are perhaps too scarce, but the texts we do have, regardless of their tenor, in their own ways cast light on many moments and places of the early modern Mediterranean and bring us into earshot and eyeshot of what people real or imagined were doing, saying and thinking about things that mattered most to them. Moreover, many of the stories and anecdotes are more than just that, saying more than what they are: *mutatis mutandis,* by contrast or similitude they *speak for* other cases, taking on figurative, sometimes paradigmatic qualities that allow us to imagine faces or voices of the early modern Mediterranean and understand the peculiar modalities of events and relations of that world.

Bibliography

Abad, Camilo María. *Una misionera española en la Inglaterra del siglo XVII: Doña Luisa de Carvajal y Mendoza (1566–1614)*. Comillas (Santander): Universidad Pontificia, 1966.
Abulafia, David, ed. *The Mediterranean in history*. London: Thames & Hudson, 2003. [Editor's prologue, 9–10, introduction, 11–31]
—— *The Great Sea: A human history of the Mediterranean*. New York/London: Allen Lane/Oxford University Press, 2011.
Abu-Lughod, Janet L. *Before European hegemony: The world system A.D. 1250–1350*. New York: Oxford University Press, 1989.
Africanus, Leo [Ḥasan al-Wazzān al-Fāsī]. *Descripción general de África, y de las cosas peregrinas que allí hay* [1526]. Trans. (from the Italian ms.) and ed. Serafín Fanjul, with Nadia Consolani. Madrid: El Legado Andalusí, 1995.
Aguilar, Gaspar. *Expulsión de los moriscos de España* [1610]. Ed. Manuel Ruiz Lagos. Seville: Guadalmena, 1999.
Akbari, Suzanne Conklin, and Karla Mallette, eds. *A sea of languages: Rethinking the Arabic role in Medieval literary history*. Toronto: University of Toronto Press, 2013.
al-Ḥajarī, Aḥmad ibn Qāsim. *Kitāb nāṣir al-dīn 'ala'l-qawm al-kāfirīn (The supporter of religion against the infidels)*. Trans. and ed. P. S. Van Koningsveld, Q. Al-Samarrai and Gerard A. Wiegers. Madrid: CSIC, 1997.
Albera, Dionigi, and Maria Couroucli, eds. *Sharing sacred spaces in the Mediterranean: Christians, Muslims, and Jews at shrines and sanctuaries*. Bloomington: University of Indiana Press, 2012.
Alcalá Galán, Mercedes. *Escritura desatada: poéticas de la representación en Cervantes*. Alcalá de Henares: Centro de Estudios Cervantinos, 2009.
—— 'Erotics of the exotic: Orientalism and fictionalization of the Mooress in the early modern Mediterranean'. *Journal of Levantine Studies* 2.1 (2012): 11–40.
—— 'From Mooresses to odalisques: Representation of the *Mooress* in the discourse of the expulsion apologists'. *Converso and Morisco studies*, v. 3. Ed. Kevin Ingram and Juan Ignacio Pulido Serrano. Leiden/Boston: Brill, 2015. 197–217.
—— 'Personajes espejo en el ámbito del islam: la inverosimilitud como crítica ideológica'. *Comentarios a Cervantes: Actas selectas del VIII Congreso Internacional de la Asociación de Cervantistas*. Ed. Emilio Martínez Mata and María Fernández Ferreiro. Oviedo: Fundación María Cristina Masaveu Peterson, 2014. 946–57.
Alcalá y Herrera, Alonso de. *La peregrina ermitaña*. In *Varios effetos de amor en cinco novelas ejemplares, sin una de las letras vocales*. Lisbon: Manuel da Silva, 1641. 60r–99v.
Alcalá Yáñez y Rivera, Gerónimo. *El donado hablador. Vida y aventuras de Alonso, mozo de muchos amos* [1624, 1626]. Paris: Imprenta de Fain y Trunot, 1847.
Alemán, Mateo. *Guzmán de Alfarache*. Ed. Benito Brancaforte. Madrid: Akal, 1996.

Alonso Acero, Beatriz. *Orán-Mazalquivir 1589–1639. Una sociedad española en la frontera de Berbería*. Madrid: CSIC, 2000.

——*Cisneros y la conquista española del norte de África: cruzada, política y arte de la guerra*. Madrid: Ministerio de Defensa, 2005.

——*Sultanes de Berbería en tierras de la cristiandad: exilio musulmán, conversión y asimilación en la monarquía hispánica (siglos XVI y XVII)*. Barcelona: Bellaterra, 2006.

Álvarez Oquendo, Saylín. 'Salvar el alma, disfrazar la piel: la identidad como irreverencia en la España morisca y en la Cuba mulata'. Doctoral dissertation, University of Wisconsin–Madison, 2016.

Arbel, Benjamin. 'Nūr Bānū (c. 1530–1583): a Venetian sultana?' *Turcica* 24 (1992): 241–59.

Archivo Histórico Nacional (AHN). Inquisición, legajo 1748 (25A). Contra Margarita en Cristiano, Arabia en turquesco, esclava. (Palermo, 1613–16).

Archivo Histórico Nacional (AHN). Inquisición, legajo 1747 II, 22. Contra Catalina de Barón Morisca de las espulsas de España y en Morisco Zara. (Palermo, 1613–16).

Arnaldi, Ivan. *Nostra Signora di Lampedusa. Storia civile e materiale di un miracolo mediterraneo*. Milano: Leonardo Editore, 1990.

Avilés, Luis F. 'El lenguaje oculto de Zoraida: tensión histórica y revelación narrativa en Cervantes'. In *Morada de la palabra: homenaje a Luce y Mercedes López-Baralt*. Ed. William Mejías López. 2 vols. San Juan: Editorial de la Universidad de Puerto Rico, 2002. 180–9.

Aznar Cardona, Pedro, *Expulsión justificada de los moriscos españoles*. Huesca: Pedro Cabarte, 1612.

Baena, Julio. 'Sintaxis de la ética del texto: Ricote, en el *Quijote II*, la lengua de las mariposas'. *Bulletin of Spanish Studies* 83:4 (2006): 505–22.

Bakhtin, Mikhail. 'Forms of time and of the chronotope in the novel'. *The dialogic imagination: Four essays*. Trans. Caryl Emerson and Michael Holquist. Ed. Michael Holquist. Austin: University of Texas Press, 1981. 84–258.

Barrio Gozalo, Maximiliano. *Esclavos y cautivos. Conflicto entre la cristiandad y el islam en el siglo XVIII*. Valladolid: Junta de Castilla y León, 2006.

Barrionuevo y Moya, Juan. *Soledad entretenida, en que se da noticia de la historia de Ambrosio Calisandro*. Écija: Luis Estupiñán, 1638.

——*Segunda parte de la Soledad entretenida*. Valencia: Bernardo Nogues, 1644.

Barrios Aguilera, Manuel, and Valeriano Sánchez Ramos. *Martirios y mentalidad martirial en las Alpujarras*. Granada: Editorial Universidad de Granada, 2001.

Bataillon, Marcel. '*La desdicha por la honra*: génesis y sentido de una novela de Lope'. *Nueva Revista de Filología Hispánica* 1.1 (1947): 13–42.

Belhamissi, Moulay. *Les captifs algériens et l'Europe chrétienne (1518–1830)*. Algiers: Entreprise Nationale du Livre, 1988.

——'Captifs musulmans et chrétiens aux XVIe–XVIIIe siècles: le cas des femmes et des enfants'. *Chrétiens et Musulmans à l'époque de la Renaissance*. Ed. Abdeldjelil Temimi. Zaghouan: Fondation Temimi pour la Recherche Scientifique et l'Information, 1997. 53–63.

Benafri, Chakib. 'La posición de la Sublime Puerta y de la regencia de Argel ante la rebelión de los moriscos granadinos (1568–1570): entre esperanza y decepción'. *Áreas: Revista Internacional de Ciencias Sociales* 30 (2011): 141–6.

Benítez Sánchez-Blanco, Rafael. 'La expulsión de los moriscos: el triunfo de la razón de Estado'. *Refugiados, exiliados y retornados en los mundos ibéricos (siglos XVI-XX)*. Ed. José Javier Ruiz Ibáñez and Bernard Vincent. Madrid: Red Columnaria, 2018. 175–94.

—— 'La historia de los moriscos en la obra de Cervantes. Apología de la expulsión, crítica de la limpieza de sangre'. In *Il Mediterraneo di Cervantes 1571–1616*. Ed. Michele Maria Rabà. Cagliari: Istituto di Storia dell'Europa Mediterranea, 2018. 37–55.

Bennassar, Bartolomé. 'En guise de conclusions'. In *Chrétiens et musulmans à la Renaissance: actes du 37ᵉ colloque internacional du CESR*. Ed. Bartolomé Bennassar and Robert Sauzet. Paris: Honoré Champion Éditeur, 1998. 533–41.

Bennassar, Bartolomé, and Lucile Bennassar. *Los cristianos de Alá. La fascinante aventura de los renegados*. Trans. José Luis Gil Aristu. Madrid: Nerea, 1989. [*Les Chrétiens d'Allah. L'histoire extraordinaire des renégats*. Paris: Perrin, 1989.]

Bernabé Pons, Luis F. *El cántico islámico del morisco hispanotunecino Taybili*. Zaragoza: Institución Fernando el Católico, 1988.

—— 'Las emigraciones moriscas al Mágreb: balance bibliográfico y perspectivas'. In *Relaciones hispano-marroquíes: una vecindad en construcción*. Ed. Ana I. Contreras and Fernando Ramos. Madrid: Ediciones del Oriente y del Mediterráneo, 2006. 63–100.

—— 'Cervantes y el islam: una revisión historiográfica'. In *Cervantes entre las dos orillas*. Ed. María Jesús Rubiera Mata. Alicante: Universidad de Alicante, 2006. 21–58.

—— 'Notas sobre la cohesión de la comunidad morisca más allá de su expulsión de España'. *Al-Qantara* 39.2 (2008): 307–32.

—— 'El exilio morisco. Las líneas maestras de una diáspora'. *Revista de Historia Moderna* 27 (2009): 277–94.

—— *Los moriscos. Conflicto, expulsión y diáspora*. Madrid: Catarata, 2009.

—— 'De aljamía lejana: la literatura de los moriscos en el exilio'. *Aljamías (In memoriam: Álvaro Galmés de Fuentes y Iacob M. Hassán)*. Ed. Raquel Suárez García and Ignacio Ceballos Viro. Gijón: Ediciones Trea, 2012. 105–30.

—— 'Taqiyya, niyya, y el islam de los moriscos'. *Alqantara* 34.2 (2013): 491–527.

—— 'De los moriscos a Cervantes'. *Cervantes and the Mediterranean* (monographic issue). Ed. Steven Hutchinson and Antonio Cortijo Ocaña. *eHumanista/Cervantes* 2 (2013): 156–82.

—— 'The mufti of Oran: Abū l-'Abbās Aḥmad ibn Abī Jum'a l-Maghrāwī l-Wahrānī'. *Christian-Muslim relations: A bibliographical history*. Ed. David Thomas and John Chesworth. Leiden: Brill, 2014. 6: 67–72.

—— 'Musulmanes sin al-Andalus. ¿Musulmanes sin España? Los moriscos y su personalidad histórica'. *eHumanista* 37 (2017): 249–67.

—— and Jorge Gil Herrera. 'The Moriscos outside Spain: Routes and financing'. *The expulsion of the Moriscos from Spain: A Mediterranean diaspora*. Trans. Consuelo López-Morillas and Martin Beagles. Ed. Mercedes García-Arenal and Gerard Wiegers. Brill: Leiden, 2014. 219–38.

Bleda, Jaime. *Breve relación de la expulsión de los moriscos del reyno de Valencia*. Supplement to the *Defensio fidei in causa neophytorum siue Morischorum Regni Valentiae totiusque Hispaniae*. Valencia: Ioannem Chrysostomum Garriz, 1610. 581–618.

—— *Corónica de los moros de España* [facsimile of the original 1618 edition]. Introd. Bernard Vincent and Rafael Benítez Sánchez-Blanco. Valencia: Universitat de València, 2001.

Bono, Salvatore. *Corsari del Mediterraneo: cristiani e musulmani fra guerra, schiavitù e commercio*. Milan: Arnoldo Mondadori, 1993.

—— 'Conversioni di musulmani al cristianesimo'. In *Chrétiens et musulmans à la Renaissance: Actes du 37ᵉ colloque internacional du CESR*. Ed. Bartolomé Bennassar and Robert Sauzet. Paris: Honoré Champion Éditeur, 1998. 429–45.

—— *Schiavi musulmani nell'Italia moderna. Galeotti, vu' cumprà, domestici*. Napoli: Edizioni Scientifiche Italiane, 1999.

—— *Il Mediterraneo da Lepanto a Barcellona*. Perugia: Morlacchi Editori, 1999.

—— 'Récits d'esclaves au Maghreb: considérations générales'. *Récits d'Orient dans les littératures d'Europe (xvie-xviie siècles)*. Ed. Anne Duprat and Émilie Picherot. Paris: Presses de l'Université Paris-Sorbonne, 2008. 115–22.

—— 'Slave histories and memories in the Mediterranean world'. *Trade and cultural exchange in the early modern Mediterranean: Braudel's maritime legacy*. Ed. Maria Fusaro, Colin Heywood and Mohamed-Salah Omri. London: Taurus, 2010. 97–115.

Boronat y Barrachina, Pascual. *Los moriscos españoles y su expulsión*. 2 vols. Valencia: Imprenta de Francisco Vives y Mora, 1901.

Braga, Isabel M. R. Mendes Drumond. *Entre a Cristiandade e o Islão (séculos xv–xvii). Cativos e renegados nas franjas de duas sociedades em confronto*. Ceuta: Instituto de Estudios Ceuties, 1998.

Braudel, Fernand. *The Mediterranean and the Mediterranean world in the age of Philip II*. Trans. Siân Reynolds (from revised 2nd ed.). 2 vols. London: Harper & Row, 1972.

Brogini, Anne. *Malte, frontière de Chrétienté (1530–1670)*. Rome: École Française de Rome, 2006.

Broodbank, Cyprian. *The making of the Middle Sea: A history of the Mediterranean from the beginning to the emergence of the classical world*. Oxford: Oxford University Press, 2013.

Bunes Ibarra, Miguel Ángel de. 'Los otomanos y los moriscos en el universo mental de la España de la Edad Moderna'. In *Europa e islam tra i secoli xiv e xvi / Europe and Islam between 14th and 16th Centuries*. Ed. Michele Bernardini, Clara Borrelli, Anna Cerbo and Encarnación Sánchez García. 2 vols. Napoli: Istituto Universitario Orientale, 2002. 2: 685–708.

—— 'La llegada de los turcos al Mediterráneo'. In *El Mediterráneo plural en la Edad Moderna. Sujeto histórico y diversidad cultural*. Ed. José Antonio González Alcantud and André Stoll. Rubí (Barcelona): Anthropos Editorial, 2011. 115–31.

—— and Beatriz Alonso Acero. 'Estudio preliminar' to facsimile edition of *Vida de don Felipe de África, príncipe de Fez y Marruecos (1566–1621)*, by Jaime Oliver Asín. Granada: Universidad de Granada, 2008. vii–lxvii.

——and Beatriz Alonso Acero, eds. *Orán. Historia de la Corte Chica*. Madrid: Ediciones Polifemo, 2011.

Buttay-Jutier, Florence. 'Les captivités de Giorgio del Giglio "Pannilini", renégat italien'. In *captifs en Méditerranée (xvie–xviiie siècles): histoires, récits et légendes*. Ed. François Moureau. Paris: Presses de l'Université Paris-Sorbonne, 2008.

Calderón de la Barca, Pedro. *Amar después de la muerte*. Ed. Erik Coenen. Madrid: Cátedra, 2008.
Camamis, George. *Estudios sobre el cautiverio en el Siglo de Oro*. Madrid: Gredos, 1977.
Camerino, José. *Novelas amorosas* [1624]. Ed. Fernando Gutiérrez. Barcelona: Selecciones Bibliófilas, 1955.
Canavaggio, Jean. *Cervantès dramaturge. Un théâtre à naître*. Paris: Presses Universitaires de France, 1977.
——*Cervantès*. Paris: Mazarine, 1986.
—— *Cervantes, entre vida y creación*. Alcalá de Henares: Centro de Estudios Cervantinos, 2000.
Cardaillac, Louis. *La Polémique antichrétienne des Morisques, ou L'opposition de deux communautés (1412-1640)*. Lille: Université de Lille, 1973.
Caro Baroja, Julio. 'Los moriscos aragoneses según un autor de comienzos del siglo xvii'. In his *Razas, pueblos y linajes*. Madrid: Revista de Occidente, 1957. 81-98.
——*Los moriscos del reino de Granada*. Madrid: Instituto de Asuntos Políticos, 1957.
Carrasco Urgoiti, María Soledad. 'Musulmanes y moriscos en la obra de Cervantes: beligerancia y empatía'. *Fundamentos de Antropología* 6-7 (1997): 66-7.
—— 'Exilio y dualidad cultural en la experiencia de los moriscos españoles'. *Círculo: Revista de Cultura* 29 (2000): 89-96.
——*Vidas fronterizas en las letras españolas*. Barcelona: Edicions Bellaterra, 2005.
Carvajal y Mendoza, Luisa de. *This tight embrace* [bilingual anthology]. Trans. and ed. Elizabeth Rhodes. Milwaukee: Marquette University Press, 2000.
Carvajal y Saavedra, Mariana de. *El esclavo de su esclavo*. In *Navidades de Madrid y noches entretenidas*. Madrid: Domingo García Morrás, 1663. 58r-71r.
Case, Thomas E. *Lope and Islam: Islamic personnages in his 'comedias'*. Newark, Delaware: Juan de la Cuesta, 1993.
Castillo, Moisés R. '¿Ortodoxia cervantina? Un análisis de *La gran sultana, El trato de Argel* y *Los baños de Argel*'. *Bulletin of the Comediantes* 56.2 (2004): 219-40.
Castillo Solórzano, Alonso de. *La libertad merecida*. In *Jornadas alegres*. Madrid: Juan González, 1626. 192-240.
—— *Lisardo enamorado* [1628]. www.cervantesvirtual.com/FichaObra.html?Ref=1277
—— *La ingratitud castigada*. In *La quinta de Laura*. Zaragoza: Matías de Lizau, 1649. 6-70.
Castro, Américo. *La realidad histórica de España*. Mexico City: Editorial Porrúa, 1987.
Castro, Miguel de. *Vida del soldado español Miguel de Castro (1593-1612)* [c. 1617]. Ed. A. Paz y Meliá. Barcelona: Biblioteca Hispánica, 1900.
Cervantes Saavedra, Miguel de. *Don Quijote de la Mancha* [1605, 1615]. Ed. Francisco Rico. 2nd ed. Barcelona: Crítica, 1998.
——*Novelas ejemplares* [1613]. Ed. Harry Sieber. 2 vols. Madrid: Cátedra, 1980.
——*La Galatea* [1585]. Ed. Juan Bautista Avalle-Arce. Madrid: Espasa-Calpe, 1987.
——*Los trabajos de Persiles y Sigismunda* [1617]. Ed. Carlos Romero Muñoz. 2nd ed. Madrid: Cátedra, 2002.
—— *Comedias y tragedias* [1615 (8 *comedias*), and 3 earlier mss. from c. 1581-86 (*El trato de Argel, Tragedia de Numancia, La conquista de Jerusalén*)]. Ed. Luis Gómez Canseco et al. 2 vols. Madrid: Real Academia Española, 2015.
——*Entremeses* [1615]. Ed. Eugenio Asensio. Madrid: Castalia, 1970.

—— et al. *Información de Miguel de Cervantes de lo que ha servido a S. M. y de lo que ha hecho estando captivo en Argel*. Ed. Pedro Torres Lanzas. Madrid: José Esteban, 1981.

Céspedes y Meneses, Gonzalo de. *Poema trágico del español Gerardo, y desengaño del amor lascivo* [1615–17]. Madrid: Pedro Marín, 1788.

——*Historias peregrinas y exemplares*. Zaragoza: Juan de Larumbe, 1623.

—— *Varia fortuna del soldado Píndaro* [1626]. Madrid: Pedro José Alonso y Padilla, 1733.

Chaker, Jamil. 'L'Image de l'Islam dans la littérature française de la Renaissance'. *Chrétiens et Musulmans à l'époque de la Renaissance*. Ed. Abdeldjelil Temimi. Zaghouan: Fondation Temimi pour la Recherche Scientifique et l'Information, 1997. 175–84.

Chejne, Anwar G. *Muslim Spain*. Minneapolis: University of Minnesota Press, 1974.

Childers, William. *Transnational Cervantes*. Toronto: University of Toronto Press, 2006.

Contreras, Alonso de. *Discurso de mi vida* [c. 1633]. Ed. Enrique Suárez Figaredo. 2005. https://users.pfw.edu/jehle/CERVANTE/othertxts/Suarez_Figaredo_Vida Contreras.pdf

—— *Derrotero universal del Mediterráneo (manuscrito del siglo XVII)*. Ed. Ignacio Fernández Vial. Málaga: Editorial Algazara, 1996.

Cook, David. *Martyrdom in Islam*. New York: Cambridge University Press, 2007.

Cortijo Ocaña, Antonio, and Adelaida Cortijo Ocaña. 'Entre Luisa de Carvajal y el conde de Gondomar. Nuevos textos sobre la persecución anticatólica en Inglaterra (1612–1614)'. *Voz y letra* 13.2 (2002): 17–19.

—— and Ángel Gómez Moreno. 'Bernardino de Mendoza (propaganda, contrapropaganda y leyenda negra)'. Editors' introduction to *Comentarios de lo sucedido en las guerras de los Países Bajos*. Madrid: Ministerio de Defensa, 2008.

——*Don Carlos Coloma de Saa. Las guerras de los Estados Bajos*. Madrid: Ministerio de Defensa, 2010.

Courcelles, Dominique de. 'Un lieu pour la raison des "Lumières": la conversion à l'islam d'Adam Neuser au XVIe siècle'. In *Conversions islamiques: identités religieuses en Islam méditerranéen / Islamic conversions: religious identities in Mediterranean Islam*. Ed. Mercedes García-Arenal. Paris: Maisonneuve et Larose, 2001. 141–50.

Covarrubias Horozco, Sebastián de. *Tesoro de la lengua castellana o española* [1611]. Ed. Ignacio Arellano and Rafael Zafra. Madrid: Universidad de Navarra, Iberoamericana, Vervuert, Real Academia Española, 2006.

Cowan, Alexander, ed. *Mediterranean urban culture 1400–1700*. Exeter: University of Exeter Press, 2000.

d'Aranda, Emanuel. *Les Captifs d'Alger* [1656]. Ed. Latifa Z'rari. Paris: Éditions Jean-Paul Rocher, 1997.

d'Arvieux, Laurent. *Mémoires du chevalier d'Arvieux. Voyage à Tunis* [1666]. [Vols. 3 and 4 of *Mémoires du chevalier d'Arvieux, envoyé extraordinaire du Roy a la Porte, consul d'Alep, d'Alger, de Tripoli, et autres échelles du Levant.*] Ed. Jacques de Maussion de Favières. Paris: Éditions Kimé, 1994.

da Vinci, Leonardo. *Cuaderno de notas*. Trans. into Spanish José Luis Velaz. Madrid: Ediciones Felmar, 1982.

Dadson, Trevor J. 'Cervantes y los moriscos de la Mancha'. In *De Cervantes y el islam*. Ed. Nuria Martínez de Castilla and Rodolfo Gil Benumeya. Madrid: Sociedad Estatal de Conmemoraciones Culturales, 2006. 135–50.

——— *Los moriscos de Villarrubia de los Ojos (siglos xv–xviii). Historia de una minoría asimilada, expulsada y reintegrada*. Madrid: Iberoamericana/Vervuert, 2007.

Dakhlia, Jocelyne. '"Turcs de profession"? Réinscription lignagères et redéfinitions sexuelles des convertis dans les cours maghrébines (xvie–xixe siècles)'. In *Conversions islamiques: identités religieuses en Islam méditerranéen / Islamic conversions: Religious identities in Mediterranean Islam*. Ed. Mercedes García-Arenal. Paris: Maisonneuve et Larose, 2001. 151–71.

——— *Lingua franca*. Paris: Actes Sud, 2008.

——— and Bernard Vincent, eds. *Les Musulmans dans l'histoire d'Europe: I. Une intégración invisible*. Paris: Albin Michel, 2011.

——— and Wolfgang Kaiser, eds. *Les Musulmans dans l'histoire d'Europe: II. Passages et contacts en Méditerranée?* Paris: Albin Michel, 2013.

Dan, Pierre. *Histoire de Barbarie et de ses corsaires, des royaumes et des villes d'Alger, de Tunis et de Tripoli* [1637]. 2nd ed. Paris: Pierre Rocolet, 1646.

——— *Les Plus Illustres Captifs, ou Receuil des actions héroïques d'un gran nombre de guerriers et autres chrétiens réduits en esclavage par les mahométans* [c. 1649]. 2 vols. Ed. le R. P. Calixte de la Providence. Paris: Delhomme et Briguet, 1892.

Davis, Natalie Zemon. *Trickster travels: A sixteenth-century Muslim between worlds*. New York: Hill and Wang, 2006.

Davis, Robert C. *Christian slaves, Muslim masters: White slavery in the Mediterranean, the Barbary coast, and Italy, 1500–1800*. New York: Palgrave Macmillan, 2003.

de Armas, Frederick A. *Don Quixote among the Saracens: A clash of civilizations and literary genres*. Toronto: University of Toronto Press, 2011.

Díaz Migoyo, Gonzalo. 'Memoria y fama de Ramón Ramírez'. *Actas del VI Congreso de la Asociación Internacional del Siglo de Oro*. Ed. María Luisa Lobato and Francisco Domínguez Matito. Madrid/Frankfurt: Iberoamericana/Vervuert, 2004. 39–53.

Domínguez Ortiz, Antonio, and Bernard Vincent. *Historia de los moriscos. Vida y tragedia de una minoría*. Madrid: Alianza, 1985.

——— *La esclavitud en Castilla en la Edad Moderna, y otros estudios de marginados*. Granada: Editorial Comares, 2003.

Duprat, Anne. 'Introduction'. *Récits d'Orient dans les littératures d'Europe (xvie–xviie siècles)*. Ed. Anne Duprat and Émilie Picherot. Paris: Presses de l'Université Paris-Sorbonne, 2008. 7–12.

Dursteler, Eric R. *Venetians in Constantinople: Nation, identity, and coexistence in the early modern Mediterranean*. Baltimore: The Johns Hopkins University Press, 2007.

——— *Renegade women: Gender, identity, and boundaries in the early modern Mediterranean*. Baltimore: The Johns Hopkins University Press, 2011.

El Abencerraje. Ed. Francisco López Estrada. Madrid: Cátedra, 1980.

El Alaoui, Youssef. 'Ignacio de Las Casas, jesuita y morisco'. *Sharq al-Ándalus* 14–15 (1997–98): 317–39.

Epalza, Míkel de. *Los moriscos antes y después de la expulsión*. Madrid: Mapfre, 1992.

——— *Fray Anselm Turmeda ('Abdullāh al-Tarŷumān) y su polémica islamo-cristiana. Edición, traducción y estudio de la 'Tuḥfa'*. 2nd ed. Madrid: Hiperión, 1994.

—— 'La naturaleza de la lengua franca de Argel y Cervantes'. In *Cervantes entre las dos orillas*. Ed. María Jesús Rubiera Mata. Alicante: Universidad de Alicante, 2006. 85–116.
Escolano, Gaspar. *Décadas de la historia de la insigne y coronada ciudad y reino de Valencia* [1611]. Part 2 (vol. 2 of the *Décadas*). Ed. Juan B. Perales. Valencia: Terraza, Aliena y Compañía, 1879.
Eslava, Antonio de. *Noches de invierno*. Barcelona: Hieronymo Margarit, 1609.
Espinel, Vicente. *Vida del escudero Marcos de Obregón* [1618]. Ed. Mª Soledad Carrasco Urgoiti. 2 vols. Madrid: Castalia, 1980.
Evliya Çelebi. *The intimate life of an Ottoman statesman Melek Ahmed Pasha (1588–1662) as portrayed in Evliya Çelebi's 'Book of travels' (Seyahat-name)*. Trans. and ed. Robert Dankoff. New York: State University of New York Press, 1991.
La expulsión de los moriscos del reino de Valencia [catalogue of the exhibition of paintings on the expulsion of the Moriscos commissioned by Philip III]. (Several authors.) Valencia: Fundación Bancaja, 1997.
Feijoo, Ramiro. *Corsarios berberiscos. El reino corsario que provocó la guerra más larga de la historia de España*. Madrid: Belacqva/Carroggio, 2003.
Fernández, Enrique. 'Los *tratos de Argel*: obra testimonial, denuncia política y literatura terapéutica'. *Cervantes* 20.1 (2000): 7–26.
Feros, Antonio. 'Rhetorics of the expulsion'. *The expulsion of the Moriscos from Spain: A Mediterranean diaspora*. Ed. Mercedes García-Arenal and Gerard Wiegers. Brill: Leiden, 2014. 60–102.
Finkel, Caroline. *Osman's dream: The story of the Ottoman Empire 1300–1923*. New York: Basic Books, 2005.
Floresta española [published as *La península a principios del siglo XVII*]. *Revue Hispanique* 34 (1915): 300–565.
Fonseca, Damián. *Justa expulsión de los moriscos de España, con la instrucción, apostasía y trayción dellos*. Rome: Iacomo Mascardo, 1612.
Fontenay, Michel. 'Corsaires de la foi ou rentiers du sol? Les chevaliers de Malte dans le "corso" Méditerranéen au XVIIe siècle'. *Revue d'Histoire Moderne et Contemporaine* 35 (1988): 361–84.
—— 'Routes et modalités du commerce des esclaves dans la Méditerranée des temps modernes (XVIe, XVIIe et XVIIIe siècles)'. *Revue Historique* 308.4 (2006): 813–30.
Foucault, Michel. 'What is an author?' In *The critical tradition: Classic texts and contemporary trends*. Ed. D. H. Richter. New York: St. Martin's Press, 1989. 978–88.
—— 'Different spaces [Hétérotopies]'. *Aesthetics, method, and epistemology*. Ed. James D. Faubion. Trans. Robert Hurley. New York: The New Press, 1998. 175–85.
Foxe, John. *Actes and monuments of these latter and perilous dayes*. London: John Day, 1563.
Fuchs, Barbara. *Passing for Spain: Cervantes and the fictions of identity*. Urbana: University of Illinois Press, 2003.
—— *Exotic nation: Maurophilia and the construction of early modern Spain*. Philadelphia: University of Pennsylvania Press, 2009.
Fusaro, Maria. 'After Braudel: A reassessment of Mediterranean history between the Northern Invasion and the Caravane Maritime'. In *Trade and cultural exchange in the early modern Mediterranean: Braudel's maritime legacy*. Ed. Maria Fusaro, Colin Heywood and Mohamed-Salah Omri. London: Taurus, 2010. 1–22.

Galán, Diego. *Cautiverio y trabajos*. Ed. Matías Barchino. Cuenca: Ediciones Universidad de Castilla–La Mancha, 2001.

—— *Relación de cautiverio y libertad de Diego Galán*. Ed. Miguel Ángel de Bunes y Matías Barchino. Madrid: Espuela de Plata, 2011. (This edition is cited except when referring to Barchino's edition with both versions.)

Gallonio, Antonio. *Trattato degli instrumenti di martirio e delle varie maniere di martoriare usate da'gentili contro christani*. Roma: A. & G. Donangeli, 1591.

Garcés, María Antonia. *Cervantes in Algiers: A captive's tale*. Nashville: Vanderbilt University Press, 2002.

—— *Cervantes en Argel. Historia de un cautivo*. Madrid: Gredos, 2005.

—— '"Grande amigo mío": Cervantes y los renegados'. In *USA Cervantes: 39 cervantistas en Estados Unidos*. Ed. Georgina Dopico Black and Francisco Layna Ranz. Madrid: Polifemo/CSIC, 2009. 545–82.

—— Introduction to *An early modern dialogue with Islam: Antonio de Sosa's 'Topography of Algiers'* [1612]. Trans. Diana de Armas Wilson. Notre Dame (Indiana): University of Notre Dame Press, 2011. 1–78.

García-Arenal, Mercedes. *Los moriscos*. Madrid: Editora Nacional, 1975.

—— *Inquisición y moriscos. Los procesos del Tribunal de Cuenca*. 3rd ed. Madrid: Siglo XXI, 1987.

—— *Ahmad al-Mansur: The beginnings of modern Morocco*. Oxford: Oneworld, 2009.

—— 'Introduction'. *After conversion: Iberia and the emergence of modernity*. Ed. Mercedes García-Arenal. Leiden: Brill, 2016. 1–18.

—— '"Mi padre moro, yo moro": The inheritance of belief in early modern Iberia'. *After conversion: Iberia and the emergence of modernity*. Ed. Mercedes García-Arenal. Leiden: Brill, 2016. 304–35.

—— ed. *Conversions islamiques: identités religieuses en Islam méditerranéen / Islamic conversions: Religious identities in Mediterranean Islam*. Paris: Maisonneuve et Larose, 2001.

—— and Miguel Ángel de Bunes. *Los españoles en el norte de África. Siglos XV–XVII*. Madrid: Mapfre, 1992.

—— and Gerard Wiegers, eds. *Entre el Islam y Occidente. Vida de Samuel Pallache, judío de Fez*. Madrid: Siglo XXI, 1999.

García Cárcel, Ricardo. 'Las mujeres conversas en el siglo XVI'. In *Historia de las mujeres en Occidente*. Ed. Georges Duby and Michelle Perrot. 5 vols. Madrid: Grupo Santillana de Ediciones, 2000. 3: 626–47.

García Martín, Pedro, Emilio Sola Castaño and Germán Vázquez Chamorro. *Renegados, viajeros y tránsfugas. Comportamientos heterodoxos y de la frontera en el siglo XVI*. Torres de la Alameda: Fugaz Ediciones, 2000.

Gerli, E. Michael. *Refiguring authority: Reading, writing, and rewriting in Cervantes*. Lexington: University Press of Kentucky, 1995.

Gómez de Losada, fray Gabriel. *Escuela de trabajos*. Madrid: Julián de Paredes, 1670.

Góngora y Argote, Luis. *Romances*. Ed. Antonio Carreira. 4 vols. Barcelona: Quaderns Crema, 1998.

Gonzalez-Raymond, Anita. *La Croix et le croissant: les inquisiteurs des îles face à l'Islam 1550–1700*. Paris: Éditions du Centre Nationale de la Recherche Scientifique, 1992.

Gordon, Michael. 'The Jews of Cervantes' Mediterranean and their representations in Spanish *cautivo* literature'. Doctoral dissertation, University of Wisconsin–Madison, 2014.

Gracián Dantisco, Lucas. *Galateo español* [1582]. Ed. Enrique Suárez Figaredo. Barcelona, 2010. https://docplayer.es/4244164-Galateo-e-s-p-a-n-o-l-lucas-gracian-dantisco-texto-preparado-por-enrique-suarez-figaredo.html

Gracián de la Madre de Dios, Jerónimo. *Tratado de la redención de cautivos* [includes autobiographical pieces 'Del cautiverio del padre Gracián' and the *Peregrinación de Anastasio*]. Ed. Miguel Ángel de Bunes Ibarra and Beatriz Alonso Acero. Seville: Espuela de Plata, 2006.

Graf, Tobias P. *The sultan's renegades: Christian-European converts to Islam and the making of the Ottoman elite, 1575–1610*. Oxford: Oxford University Press, 2017.

Granada, fray Luis de. *Obras*. Madrid: D. M. Rivadeneyra, 1818.

Granja, Fernando de la. *Maqāmas y risālas andaluzas*. Madrid: Instituto Hispano-Árabe de Cultura, 1976.

Greene, Molly. *A shared world: Christians and Muslims in the early modern Mediterranean*. Princeton: Princeton University Press, 2000.

—— 'Resurgent Islam: 1500–1700'. *The Mediterranean in history*. Ed. David Abulafia. London: Thames & Hudson, 2003. 218–49

Guadalajara y Xavier, Marco. *Memorable expulsión y justísimo destierro de los moriscos de España*. Pamplona: Nicolás de Assiayn, 1613.

Haedo, fray Diego de. *See* Sosa, Antonio de.

Harvey, L. P. *Islamic Spain, 1250 to 1500*. Chicago: University of Chicago Press, 1990.

—— *Muslims in Spain 1500 to 1614*. Chicago: University of Chicago Press, 2005.

Hautcœur, Guiomar. 'Le Roman héroïque français (*Almahide*, *Le Tolédan*, *Zaïde*) face à Grenade: entre histoire et fiction'. *Récits d'Orient dans les littératures d'Europe (XVIe–XVIIe siècles)*. Ed. Anne Duprat and Émilie Picherot. Paris: Presses de l'Université Paris-Sorbonne, 2008. 67–79.

Hegyi, Ottmar. *Cervantes and the Turks: Historical reality versus literary fiction in 'La gran sultana' and 'El amante liberal'*. Newark, Delaware, Juan de la Cuesta, 1992.

Hershenzon, Daniel. 'The political economy of ransom in the early modern Mediterranean'. *Past and Present* 231 (May 2016): 61–95.

Hess, Andrew C. *The forgotten frontier: A history of the sixteenth-century Ibero-African frontier*. Chicago: University of Chicago Press, 1978.

Hitzel, Frédéric. 'Turcs et turqueries à la cour de Cathérine de Médicis'. In *Les Musulmans dans l'histoire d'Europe: I*. Ed. Jocelyne Dakhlia and Bernard Vincent. Paris: Albin Michel, 2011. 33–54.

Horden, Peregrine, and Nicholas Purcell. *The corrupting sea: A study of Mediterranean history*. Oxford: Blackwell, 2000.

Horden, Peregrine, and Sharon Kinoshita, eds. *A companion to Mediterranean history*. Chichester: Wiley Blackwell, 2014.

Hurtado de Mendoza, Diego. *Guerra de Granada*. Ed. B. Blanco-González. Madrid: Castalia, 1970.

Husain, Adnan A., and K. E. Fleming, eds. *A faithful sea: The religious cultures of the Mediterranean, 1200–1700*. Oxford: Oneworld Publications, 2007.

Hutchinson, Steven. *Cervantine journeys*. Madison: University of Wisconsin Press, 1992.

—— *Economía ética en Cervantes*. Alcalá: Centro de Estudios Cervantinos, 2001.

—— 'Arbitrating the national *oikos*'. *Journal of Spanish Cultural Studies* 2.1 (2001): 69–80.

—— 'Poética de la emoción: de la risa a la grandeza de Sancho'. *Peregrinamente peregrinos*. Ed. Alicia Villar Lecumberri. Madrid: Asociación de Cervantistas, 2004, 1373–84.

—— 'Anagnórisis en las novelas de Cervantes (*Don Quijote* I, 42)'. *Edad de Oro Cantabrigense. Actas del VII Congreso de la Asociación Internacional del Siglo de Oro*. Ed. Anthony Close. Madrid: Iberoamericana, 2006. 345–50.

—— 'La *Vida* de Jerónimo de Pasamonte: economía del extravío'. In *El ingenioso hidalgo (Estudios en homenaje a Anthony Close)*. Ed. Rodrigo Cacho Casal. Alcalá de Henares: Centro de Estudios Cervantinos, 2009. 135–51.

—— 'Escribir el Mediterráneo: Cervantes entre dos riberas'. In *USA Cervantes. 39 cervantistas en Estados Unidos*. Ed. Georgina Dopico Black and Francisco Layna Ranz. Madrid: Polifemo, 2009. 637–64.

—— 'Fronteras cervantinas: Zoraida en el exilio'. In *Variantes de la modernidad: estudios en honor de Ricardo Gullón*. Ed. Carlos Javier García and Christina Martínez-Carazo. Newark, Delaware: Juan de la Cuesta, 2011. 147–67.

—— 'The Morisco problem in its Mediterranean dimension: Exile in Cervantes' *Persiles*'. In *The Morisco Issue*, vol. 2 of *The Conversos and Moriscos in Late Medieval Spain and beyond*. Ed. Kevin Ingram. Leiden/ Boston: Brill, 2012. 187–202.

—— '*Renegadas* in early modern Spanish literature'. *Perspectives on early modern women in Iberia and the Americas: Studies in law, society, art and literature in honor of Anne J. Cruz*. Ed. María Cristina Quintero and Adrienne L. Martín. New York: Artepoética, 2015. 522–42.

—— 'Literatura fronteriza mediterránea: rasgos de un género literario'. *Antes se agotan la mano y la pluma que su historia / Magis deficit manus et calamus quam eius hystoria. Homenaje a Carlos Alvar*. Ed. Constance Carta, Sarah Finci and Dora Mancheva. San Millán de la Cogolla: Cilengua, 2016. 2: 1431–50.

—— 'Topografía de los caminos del islam en el Mediterráneo'. *Revista Internacional de Mudejarismo* 13 (2017): 5–18.

——and Antonio Cortijo Ocaña, eds. *Cervantes y el Mediterráneo / Cervantes and the Mediterranean*. *eHumanista/Cervantes* (fall 2013). Prologue i–ix

Ibn Khaldūn. *The Muqaddimah. An introduction to history*. Trans. Franz Rosenthal. 3 vols. New York: Pantheon Books, 1958.

Infante, Catherine. 'Images at the crossroads: Representing Christian-Muslim encounters in early modern Spain and the Mediterranean'. Doctoral dissertation, University of Wisconsin–Madison, 2014.

Isom-Verhaaren, Christine, and Kent F. Schull, eds. *Living in the Ottoman realm: Empire and identity, 13th to 20th centuries*. Bloomington: Indiana University Press, 2016.

Janer, Florencio. *Condición social de los moriscos de España. Causas de su expulsión, y consecuencias que ésta produjo en el orden económico y político*. Madrid: Real Academia de la Historia, 1857.

Johnson, Carroll B. *Cervantes and the material world*. Chicago: University of Illinois Press, 2000.

—— *Transliterating a culture: Cervantes and the Moriscos*. Ed. Mark Groundland. Newark (Delaware): Juan de la Cuesta, 2009.
Johnson, Paul Michael. 'A soldier's shame: The specter of captivity in "La historia del cautivo"'. *Cervantes* 31.2 (2011): 153–84.
—— 'Sentimental geographies: Cervantes and the cultural politics of affect in the early modern Mediterranean'. Doctoral dissertation, University of California, Irvine, 2014.
Kagan, Richard L., and Abigail Dyer, trans. and eds. *Inquisitorial inquiries: Brief lives of secret Jews and other heretics*. Baltimore: The Johns Hopkins University Press, 2004.
Kaiser, Wolfgang. 'Zones de transit. Lieux, temps, modalités du rachat de captifs en Méditerranée'. *Les Musulmans dans l'histoire d'Europe: II. Passages et contacts en Méditerranée?* Ed. Mercedes García-Arenal and Wolfgang Kaiser. Paris: Albin Michel, 2013. 251–72.
—— and Bernard Vincent. 'La centralité du rachat dans l'histoire de la captivité. Expérience et narration'. *Récits d'Orient dans les littératures d'Europe (XVIe–XVIIe siècles)*. Ed. Anne Duprat and Émilie Picherot. Paris: Presses de l'Université Paris-Sorbonne, 2008. 137–43.
Khaf, Mohja. *Western representations of the Muslim woman: From Termagant to Odalisque*. Austin: University of Texas Press, 1999.
Kinoshita, Sharon. 'Mediterranean literature'. *A companion to Mediterranean history*. Ed. Peregrine Horden and Sharon Kinoshita. Oxford: Wiley Blackwell, 2014. 314–29.
Knott, John R. *Discourses of martyrdom in English literature, 1563–1694*. Cambridge: Cambridge University Press, 1993.
Koloğlu, Orhan. 'Renegades and the case Uluç/Kiliç Ali'. *Mediterraneo in armi (secc. XV–XVIII). Quaderni-Mediterranea. Ricerche storiche*. Palermo: Associazione Mediterranea, 2007. 513–31.
Krstić, Tijana. *Contested conversions to Islam: Narratives of religious change in the early modern Ottoman Empire*. Stanford: Stanford University Press, 2011.
—— 'Moriscos in Ottoman Galata, 1609–1620s'. *The expulsion of the Moriscos from Spain: A Mediterranean diaspora*. Ed. Mercedes García-Arenal and Gerard Wiegers. Leiden: Brill, 2014. 269–85.
Laborie, Jean-Claude. 'Les ordres rédempteurs et l'instrumentalisation du récit de captivité: l'exemple des Trinitaires, entre 1630 et 1650'. In *Captifs en Méditerranée (XVIe–XVIIIe siècles): histoires, récits et légendes*. Ed. François Moureau. Paris: Presses de l'Université Paris-Sorbonne, 2008. 93–102.
Lafayette, Marie-Madeleine Pioche de La Vergne, Madame de. *Zayde. Histoire espagnole* [1669–71]. Ed. Janine Anseaume Kreiter. Paris: A.-G. Nizet, 1982.
Lapeyre, Henri. *Géographie de l'Espagne morisque*. Paris: S.E.V.P.E.N., 1959.
Lapiedra, Eva. 'Al-'Idwatayn: espacios y fronteras entre al-Andalus y el Magreb'. In *Relaciones hispano-marroquíes: una vecindad en construcción*. Ed. Ana I. Contreras and Fernando Ramos. Madrid: Ediciones del Oriente y del Mediterráneo, 2005. 19–34.
Laugier de Tassy, Jacques Philippe. *Histoire du royaume d'Alger*. Amsterdam: Henri du Sauzet, 1725.
Levisi, Margarita. *Autobiografías del Siglo de Oro. Jerónimo de Pasamonte, Alonso de Contreras, Miguel de Castro*. Madrid: Sociedad General Española de Librería, 1984.

Levy, Avigdor. *The Sephardim in the Ottoman Empire*. Princeton: Darwin Press, 1992.

López Baralt, Luce. 'El sabio encantador Cide Hamete Benengeli: ¿fue un musulmán de al-Ándalus o un morisco del siglo XVII?' *Cervantes y las religiones*. Ed. Ruth Fine and Santiago López Navia. Pamplona: Universidad de Navarra/Iberoamericana/Vervuert, 2008. 339–60.

López de Gómara, Francisco. *Crónica de los corsarios Barbarroja* [1545]. Madrid: Ediciones Polifemo, 1989.

Loualich, Fatiha. 'Emancipated female slaves in Algiers: Marriage, property and social advancement in the seventeenth and eighteenth centuries'. In *Subalterns and social protest: History from below in the Middle East and North Africa*. Ed. Stephanie Cronin. New York: Routledge, 2008. 200–9.

—— 'In the Regency of Algiers: The human side of the Algerine *corso*'. Trans. Anissa Daoudi. *Trade and cultural exchange in the early modern Mediterranean: Braudel's maritime legacy*. Ed. Maria Fusaro, Colin Heywood and Mohamed-Salah Omri. London: Taurus, 2010. 69–96.

Loukili, Hind. 'D'une captivité musulmane á l'autre: un lettré au XVIe siècle et une *hâjja* au XVIIIe siècle'. In *Captifs en Méditerranée (XVIe–XVIIIe siècles): histoires, récits et légendes*. Ed. François Moureau. Paris: Presses de l'Université Paris-Sorbonne, 2008. 39–46.

Lozano Reniebas, Isabel. 'Religión e ideología en el *Persiles* de Cervantes'. In *Cervantes y las religiones*. Ed. Ruth Fine and Santiago López Navia. Pamplona: Universidad de Navarra/Iberoamericana/Vervuert, 2008. 361–76.

Lugo y Dávila, Francisco de. *Premiado el amor constante*. In *Teatro popular (novelas) de Francisco Lugo y Dávila* [1622]. Ed. Emilio Cotarelo y Mori. Madrid: Real Academia Española, 1906. 73–105.

Luna, Miguel de. *Historia verdadera del rey don Rodrigo* [1592, 1600]. Facsimile ed. and introd. Luis F. Bernabé Pons. Granada: Universidad de Granada, 2001.

Mallette, Karla. 'Boustrophedon: Towards a literary theory of the Mediterranean'. *A sea of languages: Rethinking the Arabic role in medieval literary history*. Ed. Suzanne Conklin Akbari and Karla Mallette. Toronto: University of Toronto Press, 2013. 254–66.

Mármol, Andrés del. *Vida de Jerónimo Gracián*. Appendix 16 of *Escritos de Santa Teresa*, vol. 2. Ed. Vicente de la Fuente. Madrid: M. Rivadeneyra (Biblioteca de Autores Españoles), 1879. 452–85.

Mármol Carvajal, Luis del. *Historia del rebelión y castigo de los moriscos del reino de Granada*. In *Historiadores de sucesos particulares*. Ed. Cayetano Rosell. Madrid: Real Academia Española, 1946. 123–365.

—— *Descripción general de África*. [1573–99] [facsimile edition]. 3. vols. Ed. Agustín G. de Amezúa. Madrid: CSIC, 1953.

Márquez Villanueva, Francisco. *El problema morisco (desde otras laderas)*. Madrid: Libertarias, 1991.

—— 'El morisco Ricote o la hispana razón de Estado'. In *Personajes y temas del 'Quijote'*. Madrid: Taurus, 1975. 229–335.

—— *Moros, moriscos y turcos de Cervantes. Ensayos críticos*. Barcelona: Edicions Bellaterra, 2010.

Martin, Maria. *History of the captivity and sufferings of Mrs. Maria Martin, who was six years a slave in Algiers* [written 1807]. St. Clairsville, Ohio: John Berry, 1815.

Martín Morán, José Manuel. 'Identidad y alteridad en *Persiles y Sigismunda*'. In *Peregrinamente peregrinos*. 2 vols. Ed. Alicia Villar Lecumberri. Lisbon: Asociación de Cervantistas, 2004. 1: 561–91.

Martínez Bonati, Félix. *El 'Quijote' y la poética de la novela*. Alcalá de Henares: Centro de Estudios Cervantinos, 1995.

Martínez de Castilla Muñoz, Nuria, and Rodolfo Gil Benumeya Grimau, eds. *De Cervantes y el islam*. Madrid: Sociedad Estatal de Conmemoraciones Culturales, 2006.

Martínez Góngora, Mar. *Los espacios coloniales en las crónicas de Berbería*. Madrid/Frankfurt: Iberoamericana/Vervuert, 2013.

Martínez Torres, José Antonio. *Prisioneros de los infieles. Vida y rescate de los cautivos cristianos en el Mediterráneo musulmán (siglos XVI–XVII)*. Barcelona: Ediciones Bellaterra, 2004.

Mas, Albert. *Les Turcs dans la littérature espagnole du Siècle d'Or. (Recherches sur l'évolution d'un thème littéraire)*. 2 vols. Paris: Centre de Recherches Hispaniques, 1967.

Mascarenhas, João Carvalho. *Memoravel relaçam da perda da nao Conceiçam que os turcos queymáraõ à vista da barra de Lisboa; varios successos das pessoas que nella cativáraõ. E descripçaõ nova da cidade de Argel & de seu governo; & cousas muy notaveis acontecidas nestes ultimos annos de 1621 até 1626*. Lisbon: Antonio Alvares, 1627.

Matar, Nabil. 'England and Mediterranean captivity, 1577–1704'. Introduction to *Piracy, slavery and redemption: Barbary captivity narratives from early modern England*. Ed. Daniel J. Vitkus. New York: Columbia University Press, 2001. 1–52.

—— *Europe through Arab eyes, 1578–1727*. New York: Columbia University Press, 2009.

Menéndez Pelayo, Marcelino. 'Moriscos. Literatura aljamiada. Los plomos del Sacromonte'. In his *Historia de los heterodoxos españoles*. 7 vols. 2nd ed. Madrid: Librería Victoriano Suárez, 1911–32. 5: 319–48.

Monta, Susannah Brietz. *Martyrdom and literature in early modern England*. Cambridge: Cambridge University Press, 2005.

Montaigne, Michel de. *Journal de voyage en Italie, par la Suisse et l'Allemagne, en 1580 et 1581*. In *Oeuvres complètes*. Ed. Maurice Rat. Paris: Éditions Gallimard, 1962. 1099–342.

Montaner Frutos, Alberto. 'Zara/Zoraida y la Cava Rumía: historia, leyenda e invención'. In *De Cervantes y el islam*. Ed. Nuria Martínez de Castilla and Rodolfo Gil Benumeya. Madrid: Sociedad Estatal de Conmemoraciones Culturales, 2006. 247–80.

Morgan, Joseph. *A complete history of Algiers* [first ed. 1728–29 in 2 vols.]. London: J. Bettenham, 1731.

Moüette, Germain. *Relation de la captivité du Sieur Moüette dans les royaumes de Fez et de Maroc, où il est demeuré onze ans* [1670–81]. Paris: Jean Cochart, 1683.

Moureau, François, ed. *Captifs en Méditerranée (XVIe–XVIIIe siècles): histoires, récits et légendes*. Paris: Presses de l'Université Paris-Sorbonne, 2008.

Munari, Simona. 'Grenade dans la littérature européenne: fondements et avatars d'un mythe littéraire'. In *Récits d'Orient dans les littératures d'Europe (XVIe–XVIIe*

siècles). Ed. Anne Duprat and Émilie Picherot. Paris: Presses de l'Université Paris-Sorbonne, 2008. 15–22.

Murād, Seyyid. *La vida, y historia de Hayradin, llamado Barbarroja [Gazavāt-i Hayreddīn Paşa]*. Ed. Miguel Ángel de Bunes and Emilio Sola. [Based on 1578 translation by José Luis Alzamora and an anonymous Turk.] Granada: Universidad de Granada, 1997.

Nietzsche, Friedrich. *Human, all too human: A book for free spirits*. Trans. R. J. Hollingdale. New York: Cambridge University Press, 1986.

——*Daybreak*. Trans. R. J. Hollingdale. Cambridge: Cambridge University Press, 1997.

—— *Beyond good and evil*. In *Basic writings of Nietzsche*. Trans. and ed. Walter Kaufmann. New York: Random House, 1968. 192–435.

——*On the genealogy of morals*. In *Basic writings of Nietzsche*. Trans. and ed. Walter Kaufmann. New York: Random House, 1968. 439–599.

Núñez Muley, Francisco. 'Memorial'. In K. Garrad, 'The original memorial of don Francisco Núnez Muley'. *Atlante* 1.2 (1954): 199–226.

O'Connell, Monique, and Eric Dursteler. *The Mediterranean world from the fall of Rome to the rise of Napoleon*. Baltimore: The Johns Hopkins University Press, 2016.

Ohanna, Natalio. *Cautiverio y convivencia en la edad de Cervantes*. Alcalá de Henares: Centro de Estudios Cervantinos, 2011.

Okeley, William. *Ebenezer* or *A small monument of great mercy, appearing in the miraculous deliverance of William Okeley*. In *Piracy, slavery and redemption: Barbary captivity narratives from early modern England*. Ed. Daniel J. Vitkus. New York: Columbia University Press, 2001. 124–92.

Oliver Asín, Jaime. 'La hija de Agi Morato en la obra de Cervantes'. *Boletín de la Real Academia Española* 27 (1947–48): 245–339.

——*Vida de don Felipe de África, príncipe de Fez y Marruecos (1566–1621)*. (Facsimile edition with new introduction by Miguel Ángel de Bunes Ibarra and Beatriz Alonso Acero.) Granada: Universidad de Granada, 2008.

Omri, Mohamed-Salah. 'Representing the early modern Mediterranean in contemporary North Africa'. *Trade and cultural exchange in the early modern Mediterranean: Braudel's maritime legacy*. Ed. Maria Fusaro, Colin Heywood and Mohamed-Salah Omri. London: Taurus, 2010. 279–98.

Orsoni-Avila, Françoise. *Les esclaves de Lucena (1539–1700)*. Paris: Publications de la Sorbonne, 1997.

Ould Cadi Montebourg, Leïla. *Alger, une cité turque au temps de l'esclavage: À travers le Journal d'Alger du père Ximénez, 1718–1720*. Montpellier: Presses Universitaires de la Méditerranée, 2006.

Palomino, Antonio A. *Vida de don Diego Velázquez de Silva* [1724]. Ed. Miguel Morán Turina. Madrid: Akal, 2008.

Pamuk, Orhan. *The white castle*. Trans. Victoria Holbrook. New York: Vintage Books, 1998.

Pasamonte, Jerónimo de. *Vida y travajos de Gerónimo de Passamonte*. Ed. R. Foulché-Delbosc. *Revue Hispanique* 55 (1922): 311–446.

Pastore, Stefania. 'Doubt in fifteenth-century Iberia'. *After conversion: Iberia and the emergence of modernity*. Ed. Mercedes García-Arenal. Leiden: Brill, 2016. 283–304.

Perceval, José María. *Todos son uno: arquetipos, xenofobia y racismo. La imagen del morisco en la monarquía española durante los siglos XVI y XVII*. Almería: Instituto de Estudios Almerienses, 1997.
Pérez de Chinchón, Bernardo. *Antialcorano. Diálogos christianos*. Ed. Francisco Pons Fuster. Alicante: Universidad de Alicante, 2000.
Pérez de Hita, Ginés. *Historia de los bandos de los Zegríes y Abencerrajes, caballeros moros de Granada, de las guerras civiles que hubo en ella*. Zaragoza: Miguel Ximeno Sánchez, 1595.
Pérez de Hita, Ginés. *La guerra de los moriscos (segunda parte de las guerras civiles de Granada)* [1619]. Ed. Paula Blanchard-Demouge. Granada: Universidad de Granada, 1998.
Pérez de Montalbán, Juan. *La desgraciada amistad*. In *Sucesos y prodigios de amor* [1624]. Ed. Luigi Giuliani. Barcelona: Montesinos, 1992. 213–57.
Perry, Mary Elizabeth. *The handless maiden: Moriscos and the politics of religion in early modern Spain*. Princeton: Princeton University Press, 2005.
Pirenne, Henri. *Mohammed and Charlemagne*. Trans. Bernard Miall. London: G. Allen & Unwin, 1939.
Pope, Randolph D. *La autobiografía española hasta Torres Villarroel*. Frankfurt: Peter Lang, 1974.
Pratt, Mary Louise. 'Arts of the contact zone'. *Profession* (1991): 33–40.
Prothero, Stephen. *God is not one: The eight rival religions that run the world*. New York: HarperCollins, 2010.
Quevedo, Francisco de. *La Hora de todos y la Fortuna con seso* [1635]. Ed. Luisa López-Grigera. Madrid: Castalia, 1975.
Rabelais, François. *Oeuvres complètes*. 2 vols. Ed. Pierre Jourda. Paris: Garnier, 1962.
Ripol, Juan. *Diálogo de consuelo por la expulsión de los moriscos de España*. Pamplona: Nicolás de Assiayn, 1613.
Rodríguez G. de Ceballos, Alfonso. 'La representación del martirio en el Siglo de Oro español dentro del contexto de las luchas religiosas'. In *La violencia en el mundo hispánico en el Siglo de Oro*. Ed. Juan Manuel Escudero and Victoriano Roncero. Madrid: Visor, 2010.
Rodríguez Mediano, Fernando. 'Les Conversions de Sebastião Paes de Vega, un Portuguais au Maroc sa'dien'. In *Conversions islamiques: identités religieuses en Islam méditerranéen / Islamic conversions: Religious identities in Mediterranean Islam*. Ed. Mercedes García-Arenal. Paris: Maisonneuve et Larose, 2001. 173–92.
Rodríguez-Rodríguez, Ana Mª. *Letras liberadas: cautiverio, escritura y subjetividad en el Mediterráneo de la época imperial española*. Madrid: Visor Libros, 2013.
Romancero general (1600, 1604, 1605). Ed. Ángel González Palencia. Madrid: CSIC, 1947.
Rostagno, Lucia. *Mi faccio turco. Esperienze ed immagini dell'islam nell'Italia moderna*. Rome: Istituto per l'Oriente C. A. Nallino, 1983.
Roşu, Felicia. 'Muslim slaves in early modern Europe: A forgotten history of slavery'. www.leiden-islamblog.nl/articles/muslim-slaves-in-early-modern-europe-a-forgotten-history-of-slavery.
Rubiera Mata, María Jesús. 'Las dos orillas cervantinas. A modo de introducción con *addenda*'. In *Cervantes entre las dos orillas*. Ed. María Jesús Rubiera Mata. Alicante: Universidad de Alicante, 2006. 9–20.

Ruhe, Ernstpeter. 'Dire et ne pas dire: les récits de captifs germanophones et les cérémonies de retour'. In *Captifs en Méditerranée (XVIe–XVIIIe siècles): histoires, récits et légendes*. Ed. François Moureau. Paris: Presses de l'Université Paris-Sorbonne, 2008. 119–33.

San José, Antonio Juan Andreu de. *Relación del milagroso rescate del crucifixo de las monjas de San José de Valencia que está en Santa Tecla, y de otros*. Valencia: Juan Chrysóstomo Carriz, 1625.

Sapiencia, Otavio. *Nuevo tratado de Turquía*. Madrid: Viuda de Alonso Martín, 1622.

Scaraffia, Lucetta. *Rinnegati. Per una storia dell'identità occidentale*. Rome: Editori Laterza, 1993.

Schick, Irvin Cemil. *The erotic margin: Sexuality and spatiality in alteritist discourse*. New York: Verso, 1999.

Schwartz, Stuart B. *All can be saved: Religious tolerance and salvation in the Iberian Atlantic world*. New Haven: Yale University Press, 2008.

Simmel, Georg. 'Conflict and society'. *The sociology of Georg Simmel*. Trans. and ed. Kurt H. Wolff. Glencoe: The Free Press, 1950. 13–17.

Sola, Emilio, trans. and ed. 'Carta escrita por el Cigala …, al virrey de Sicilia' [1598]. *Revista de Historia y Arte* (spring 1994): 219–29.

—— 'Historias de la frontera y oralidad: una cautiva que llega a gran sultana'. In *Las 'Relaciones de sucesos' en España (1500–1750)*. Ed. Mª Cruz García de Enterría, Henry Ettinghausen, Víctor Infantes and Augustin Redondo. Alcalá de Henares: Universidad de Alcalá, 1996. 339–48.

—— 'Francos o libertos en el mundo turco berberisco'. In *Renegados, viajeros y tránsfugas. Comportamientos heterodoxos y de frontera en el siglo XVI*. Ed. Pedro García Martín, Emilio Sola Castaño and Germán Vázquez Chamorro. Torres de la Alameda: Fugaz Ediciones, 2000. 91–9.

—— *Uchali: el calabrés tiñoso, o el mito del corsario muladí en la frontera*. Introd. Miguel Ángel de Bunes Ibarra. Barcelona: Edicions Bellaterra, 2010.

—— and José F. de la Peña. *Cervantes y la Berbería. Cervantes, mundo turco-berberisco y servicios secretos en la época de Felipe II*. Madrid: Fondo de Cultura Económica, 1995.

Sosa, Antonio de. *Topografía e historia general de Argel, repartida en cinco tratados*. [Published under the editor's name, fray Diego de Haedo, the work includes five treatises (numbered here in Roman numerals): (I) *Topografía o descripción de Argel y sus habitadores y costumbres*, (II) *Epítome de los reyes de Argel*, (III) *Diálogo de la captividad de Argel*, (IV) *Diálogo de los mártires de Argel*, (V) *Diálogo de los morabutos de turcos y moros*]. Valladolid: Diego Fernández de Córdova y Oviedo, 1612.

—— *Diálogo de los mártires de Argel*. Ed. Emilio Sola and José María Parreño. Madrid: Hiperión, 1990.

Stella, Alessandro. *Histoires d'esclaves dans la Péninsule Ibérique*. Paris: Édition de l'École des Hautes Études en Sciences Sociales, 2000.

Suárez Montañés, Diego. *Historia del maestre último que fue de Montesa y de su hermano don Felipe de Borja. La manera como gobernaron las plazas de Orán y Mazalquivir, reinos de Tremecén y Ténez, en África, siendo allí capitanes generales*. Ed. Beatriz Alonso Acero and Miguel Ángel de Bunes Ibarra. Valencia: Institució Alfons el Magnànim, 2005.

Tamagrouti, Abu-'l-Ḥasan 'Ali ben Muhammad. *Relation d'une ambassade marocaine en Turquie (1589-91)*. Trans. and ed. Henry de Castries. Paris: Paul Geuthner, 1929.
Tamayo de Vargas, Tomás. *Junta de libros*. Madrid: Universidad de Navarra / Iberoamericana/Vervuert, 2007.
Teijeiro Fuentes, Miguel Ángel. *Moros y turcos en la narrativa áurea (el tema del cautiverio)*. Cáceres: Universidad de Extremadura, 1987.
Temimi, Abdeldjelil. 'L'Impact des racines chrétiennes de quelques savants musulmans et hauts responsables politiques ottomans'. In *Chrétiens et musulmans à la Renaissance: Actes du 37ᵉ colloque internacional du CESR*. Ed. Bartolomé Bennassar and Robert Sauzet. Paris: Honoré Champion Éditeur, 1998. 509-18.
Teresa de Jesús (Saint). *Libro de la vida*. Ed. Dámaso Chicharro. Madrid: Cátedra, 1984.
Torres, Diego de. *Relación del origen y suceso de los Xarifes y del estado de los reinos de Marruecos, Fez y Tarudante* [1586]. Ed. Mercedes García-Arenal. Madrid: Siglo xxi, 1980.
Torres Corominas, Eduardo. *Literatura y facciones cortesanas en la España del siglo* xvi. *Estudio y edición del Inventario de Antonio de Villegas*. Madrid: Polifemo, 2008.
Turbet-Delof, Guy. *L'Afrique barbaresque dans la littérature française aux xvIᵉ-xvIIᵉ siècles*. Geneva: Librairie Droz, 1973.
—— *Bibliographie critique du Maghreb dans la littérature française 1532-1715*. Algiers: Société Nationale d'Édition et de Diffusion, 1976.
Türkçelik, Evrim. *Un notable italiano en la corte otomana: Cigalazade y el Mediterráneo 1591-1606*. Valencia: Albatros, 2019.
Twain, Mark. *The wit and wisdom of Mark Twain*. Ed. Alex Ayres. New York: Meridian, 1987.
Valencia, Pedro de. *Tratado acerca de los moriscos de España* [1606]. Ed. Joaquín Gil Sanjuán. Málaga: Algazara, 1997.
Valera, Cipriano de. *Tratado para confirmar los pobres cautivos de Berbería en la católica y antigua fe y religión cristiana, y para los consolar* [London, 1594]. Ed. Miguel Ángel de Bunes Ibarra and Beatriz Alonso Acero. Seville: Espuela de Plata, 2004.
Vega, Lope de. *Novelas a Marcia Leonarda* [1624]. Ed. Julia Barella. Madrid: Ediciones Júcar, 1988. [*La desdicha por la honra*, 101-42; *La más prudente venganza*, 143-85; *Guzmán el Bueno*, 187-231]
—— *Los cautivos de Argel* [1599, pub. 1647]. Ed. Natalio Ohanna. Madrid: Castalia, 2017.
Verstegan (alias Rowlands), Richard. *Theatrum crudelitatum haereticorum nostri temporis*. Antwerp: apud Adrianum Humberti, 1587.
Viaje de Turquía. Ed. Fernando García Salinero. Madrid: Cátedra, 1986.
Vila, Juan Diego: 'Tráfico de higos, regalados garzones y contracultura: en torno a los silencios y mentiras del Capitán Cautivo'. In *Peregrinamente Peregrino. Actas del V Congreso de la Asociación de Cervantistas*. Ed. Alicia Villar Lecumberri. Madrid: Asociación de Cervantistas, 2004. 1833-64.
Villalmanzo Cameno, Jesús. 'La colección pictórica sobre la expulsión de los moriscos. Autoría y cronología'. *La expulsión de los moriscos del reino de Valencia*. Valencia: Fundación Bancaja, 1997. 35-107.
Vincent, Bernard. 'Musulmans et conversion en Espagne au xvIIᵉ siècle'. In *Conversions islamiques: identités religieuses en Islam méditerranéen / Islamic conversions:*

Religious identities in Mediterranean Islam. Ed. Mercedes García-Arenal. Paris: Maisonneuve et Larose, 2001. 193–205.

—— 'L'esclavage moderne en Péninsule Ibérique'. In *Balance de la historiografía modernista 1973-2001*. Ed. Roberto J. López y Domingo L. Gónzález Lopo. Santiago de Compostela: Xunta de Galicia, 2003. 445–52.

—— *El río morisco*. Trans. Antonio Luis Cortés Peña. Valencia: Universitat de València/Universidad de Granada/Universidad de Zaragoza, 2006.

Vitkus, Daniel J. 'Early modern orientalism: Representations of Islam in sixteenth- and seventeenth-century Europe'. *Western views of Islam in medieval and early modern Europe: Perception of Other*. Ed. David R. Blanks and Michael Frassetto. New York: St. Martin's Press, 1999. 207–30.

—— ed. *Three Turk plays from early modern England: Selimus, Emperor of the Turks* [Robert Greene, 1594]; *A Christian turned Turk* [Robert Daborne, 1612]; *and The renegado* [Philip Massinger, 1623]. New York: Columbia University Press, 2000.

—— ed. *Piracy, slavery and redemption: Barbary captivity narratives from early modern England*. Introd. Nabil Matar. New York: Columbia University Press, 2001.

Wettinger, Godfrey. *Slavery in the islands of Malta and Gozo c. 1000–1812*. Malta: Publishers Enterprises Group, 2002.

Wiegers, Gerard A. 'A life between Europe and the Maghrib: The writings and travels of Aḥmad b. Qāsim al-Ḥajarī al-Andalusī'. *The Middle East and Europe: Encounters and exchanges*. Ed. G. J. van Gelder and E. de Moor. Amsterdam: Rodopi, 1992. 87–115.

—— 'European converts to Islam in the Maghrib and the polemical writings of the Moriscos'. In *Conversions islamiques: identités religieuses en Islam méditerranéen / Islamic conversions: Religious identities in Mediterranean Islam*. Ed. Mercedes García-Arenal. Paris: Maisonneuve et Larose, 2001. 207–23.

Williams, Ann. '*Sacra Militia*, the Order of St. John: Crusade, corsairing and trade in Rhodes and Malta, 1460–1631'. *Trade and cultural exchange in the early modern Mediterranean: Braudel's maritime legacy*. Ed. Maria Fusaro, Colin Heywood and Mohamed-Salah Omri. London: Taurus, 2010. 139–56.

Ximénez, padre Francisco. *Viaje y diario de Argel* [1718–20]. Unpublished. Biblioteca de la Academia de la Historia.

Zagorin, Perez. *Ways of lying: Dissimulation, persecution, and conformity in early modern Europe*. Cambridge, Massachusetts: Harvard University Press, 1990.

Zarinebaf, Fariba. *Mediterranean encounters: Trade and pluralism in early modern Galata*. Oakland: University of California Press, 2018.

Zayas, María de. *Desengaños amorosos* [1647]. Ed. Alicia Yllera. Madrid: Cátedra, 1983.

Zonza, Christian. 'Le Récit de captivité entre fiction et histoire'. *Récits d'Orient dans les littératures d'Europe (XVIᵉ–XVIIᵉ siècles)*. Ed. Anne Duprat and Émilie Picherot. Paris: Presses de l'Université Paris-Sorbonne, 2008. 145–60.

Index

Note the following: literary works can be found under authors' names; page numbers in *italic* refer to illustrations.

'Abd al-Malik 28, 178
El Abencerraje 24, 38n.5, 189–91
Abulafia, David 3–4, 9, 13, 15
Africanus, Leo (alias Ḥasan al-Wazzān al-Fāsī) 75, 78–9, 111–12, 111n.44, 121, 198
Aguilar, Gaspar 34, 163–5, 168n.14
Aḥmad al-Manṣūr (king of Fez) 112
Alcalá Galán, Mercedes 17, 26n.11, 29n.13, 170–1
Alcazarquivir, battle of 44, 112, 122
Algiers
  chorography 7
  demography 6, 8, 12–13, 40, 45, 117, 154, 192–3
  economy 42, 47, 178
  external relations 12, 25, 122, 178
  governors, viceroys 73, 83–5, 116–21, 171, 201
  Jews in 73n.6, 117–21, 195
  martyrs in 102–5, 138–46
  Moriscos in 102–8, 154, 160–1
  as regency 10, 29n.13, 193, 201
  renegades in 29, 73, 94, 96–100, 101n.36, 102–5, 123, 127–8
  representation of 17, 20–1, 73–7, 136
  slaves in 31, 45–54 *passim*, 54, 75, 102–3, 105, 118, 123, 139–41, 143–4, 186, 188–9, 192
al-Ḥajarī, Aḥmad ibn Qāsim 79–81, 101n.35–6, 160–1
Alicax (Alicaxet) 102–5, 141–4
Alonso Acero, Beatriz 111n.44–5, 112–16
alterities
  attenuated 44, 57, 100, 179–80, 196
  manifestations 28–31, 40, 56n.26
  Muslim 27, 162, 176–7
  as plural 13, 24, 176, 192, 195, 197
  renegades 33, 198–9

Álvarez, Saylín 110n.43
Andalusians, *andaluces*
  term 101, 101n.35, 153–4, 156
Arabia (alias Margarita) 109–10
Aranda, Miguel de 102–5, 141–4
Arbel, Benjamin 88, 88n.23
Aristotle 16, 56
Arnaldi, Ivan 128
Atlantic Ocean 3, 12–13, 41, 46, 183
Aznar Cardona, Pedro 34, 162–3, 168n.14

Baer, Marc 121n.54, 199
Bakhtin, Mikhail 22n.5, 199
Barbarossa, Aruch 1, 74, 201–2
Barbarossa, Hayreddin 1, 67–8, 74, 84, 88, 95, 138–41, 201–2
  portrait *2*
Barrio Gozalo, Maximiliano 78n.12, 123
Barrionuevo y Moya, Juan 191
Barrios Aguilera, Manuel, and Valeriano Sánchez Ramos 137n.10
Bateson, Gregory 180
Belhamissi, Moulay 78n.12, 191
Benítez Sánchez-Blanco, Rafael 106, 106n.40, 167n.10
Bennassar, Bartolomé and Lucile 31n.15, 75–6, 78, 92n.27, 96–7, 101n.36, 125
Bernabé Pons, Luis 19, 101n.35, 134, 154, 169n.18, 172n.21
Bleda, Jaime 34, 164–7
Bono, Salvatore 41n.10, 78n.12–13, 84–6
Boronat y Barrachina, Pascual 165, 169n.17
Braga, Isabel 76
Braudel, Fernand
  concept of Mediterranean 3–9 *passim*, 3n.1, 6n.3, 181–2
  renegades 84, 96
Brémont, Gabriel de 26

Bunes Ibarra, Miguel Ángel 111n.44–5, 112–13, 154, 176
Buttay-Jutier, Florence 74n.7, 94–6

Cairo 12, 40
Canavaggio, Jean 144n.16
captivity, captives *see* slavery; slaves
Carducho, Vicente 157
    ink drawing *158*
Caro Baroja, Julio 166n.8
Carrasco Urgoiti, María Soledad 24, 56n.26
Carvajal, Mariana de 191
Carvajal y Mendoza, Luisa de 133–4
Case, Thomas 144n.16
caste 76–7n.10, 107, 153, 168, 189
Castillo, Moisés 148n.23
Castillo Solórzano, Alonso 191
Castro, Américo 159
Castro, Miguel de 57–63, 68, 135
Çelebi, Evliya 189
Cervantes, Miguel de
    El amante liberal 37, 63–6, 130, 191
    Los baños de Argel 66, 66n.38, 91, 131, 144, 146, 148–9, 191
    La conquista de Jerusalén 131
    Coloquio de los perros 169, 173
    Don Quixote 22, 26–8, 34, 37, 38n.5, 84n.18, 85, 126–31, 136–7, 149–51, 159–61, 169–74, 174
    La española inglesa 130, 182–3
    La Galatea 66
    El gallardo español 39, 189–91
    La gran sultana 17, 37, 66, 87, 131, 149–52, 191, 200
    Persiles 21, 24, 34, 98, 173–5
    El trato de Argel 38n.5, 57, 66, 102–5, 131, 143–4, 149, 191
    representation of Muslims 158–60
    as soldier and slave 10, 36, 54, 54n.21, 143
    as writer 20, 24, 69
Céspedes y Meneses, Gonzalo de 27n.12, 105, 151
Chaker, Jamil 151n.30
Charles V (Emperor) 65, 67–8, 122, 201
Chejne, Anwar 134n.7
Cheleby, Mehmed (alias don Felipe) 114–17
Cherchell (aka Sargel) 102–5, 141–4 *passim*

Christians *see* martyrs, martyrdom; religions, Abrahamic; renegades; slaves
chronotope 21–3, 22n.5, 25–8, 31, 190
Cigala (alias Cığalazade Yusuf Sinan Pasha) 91–2, 188
Contreras, Alonso de
    as corsair 10, 12, 45, 83, 128, 187–8
    Muslims and Christians 81–3
Cook, David 134n.7
corsairs
    in Algiers 45, 77, 96–100, 151, 183, 188–9
    frontier figures 23, 77, 102–5, 141–4
    and slavery 77, 87, 201
    term 44–5, 77
    see also Contreras, Alonso de; renegades; Turks
Cortijo Ocaña, Antonio, 133n.5, 136n.9
cosmopolitanism 117, 193, 202
Courcelles, Dominique de 74
Covarrubias, Sebastián de 19, 38
cruelty 33, 42n.10, 50–3, 104, 118, 123, 131–52 *passim*, 167, 175–6
Cyprus 1, 9, 63–6

Dadson, Trevor 106–7, 106n.39–40
Dan, Pierre 19–20, 26, 38n.4, 49, 50, 69, 124, 135–6, 144–6, 151
d'Aranda, Emanuel 38n.4, 48–50, 52, 54, 123, 144–6, 186
d'Arcos, Thomas 74–5
d'Arvieux, Laurent 38n.4, 45, 52–4, 114–17, 192
da Vinci, Leonardo 35–6, 195
Davis, Natalie Zemon 79n.14, 111–12, 111n.44, 121
Davis, Robert C. 42n.11
Díaz del Castillo, Bernal 196n.1
Díaz, Diego 106–9, 111
Domínguez Ortiz, Antonio 166n.8
Dragut (Turgut Reis) 84, 91
Drusiana (Greek renegade) 97
Duprat, Anne 25
Dursteler, Eric 30n.14, 83

Epalza, Míkel de 71n.2, 74n.9, 101n.36, 110n.43, 153
Escanasi, Simón 184–6
Escolano, Gaspar 167

Espinel, Vicente 37, 96–100, 153–4
Espinosa, Jerónimo 157

Felipe de África (Mawlāy Shaykh) 111–13
Fez 12–13, 35, 86, 111, 137n.10
Finkel, Caroline 89n.24, 92n.27
Fonseca, Damián 34, 166–8
Fontenay, Michel 40n.6, 40n.8
Foucault, Michel 17, 31n.16
Foxe, John 132
frontier
  chronotope 25, 28
  consciousness 13, 33, 83, 154, 195, 198–200, 202
  figures 33, 71–128 passim, 154, 180, 182–93, 202
  literature 22–34, 89–91, 96–100, 143–4, 148–54, 169–75, 182–3, 189–92
  shifting 156
  zones 4, 12–13, 23–4, 28–31, 175, 180–1, 190, 192, 195, 200–2
  see also Algiers; Cervantes, Miguel de; Muslim-Christian divide; Tunis
Fuchs, Barbara 65
Fusaro, Maria 6

Galan Aga, Saban 186
Galán, Diego 92n.27, 183–4
Gancho, Morato 187–8
Garcés, María Antonia 73n.5, 84n.20, 117, 117n.49, 119n.52
García-Arenal, Mercedes 101n.34, 106–8, 134n.7, 154, 156, 160
Genoa 12, 93, 119, 184–5, 195
Gibraltar, Strait of 4, 10, 90, 155, 181–2
Giuseppe (Italian renegade) 92–4
Gómez de Losada, Gabriel 19–20, 26, 49, 91, 123–6, 135–6, 151
Gómez, Pablo F. 41n.9
Góngora, Luis de 191
González de Torres, Antonio 118–19, 118n.50
Gonzalez-Raymond, Anita 76, 97, 123
Gracián, Jerónimo 20, 50, 54, 69, 123, 135, 135n.8, 137n.10, 151, 184–6
Graf, Tobias 84n.18, 92n.27, 121n.54, 198
Granada 13, 24–5, 72, 79, 111–12, 154–6, 160
Granada, Luis de 133–4

Greene, Molly 9–10
Guadalajara y Xavier, Marco 166–9, 168n.13

Hajji Murad (Agi Morato) 28, 191
Harvey, L. P. 71n.2, 166n.8, 199
Hasan Veneciano (Pasha) 28, 84–5, 118, 118n.50, 136–7
Hautcœur, Guiomar 25
Heidegger, Martin 197
Hess, Andrew 4–9 passim
heterotopias 13, 31, 180
Horden, Peregrine 6, 9, 15
Huntington, Samuel 4
Hutchinson, Steven 21–2, 24, 26n.11, 28, 31n.15, 63n.36, 171n.20, 173, 175n.26

Infante, Catherine 112n.46
Inquisition 31n.15, 69, 71–128 passim
  see also religions, Abrahamic; renegades; slaves
irenicism 125
Islam see religions, Abrahamic; renegades; slaves
Istanbul 1–13 passim, 25, 30n.14, 40, 86, 94, 119, 131, 183, 193
  see also Ottoman Empire; renegades; slaves

Janer, Florencio 169n.17
Jews 12, 19, 21, 23–4, 49, 53, 73n.6, 76, 77n.10, 104, 154, 180, 184–6, 190n.29, 202
  converts to Islam 117–21, 124–5
Johnson, Carroll 64, 84n.20

Kagan, Richard, and Abigail Dyer 106–8, 107n.41
Kaiser, Wolfgang 37n.3, 92n.27
karma 182–6
Kinoshita, Sharon 22n.6
Knights of St. John 77, 83, 201–2
Koloğlu, Orhan 84n.18
Krstić, Tijana 83n.17

Lampedusa 128, 200
Laugier de Tassy, Jacques Philippe 38n.4, 53–4
Lisbon 3, 12, 41, 45–8, 110n.43, 184–5
London 132–3, 182

López de Gómara, Francisco 201
Loualich, Fatiha 40–1, 40n.8, 55
Loukili, Hind 74n.8, 79
Lugo y Dávila, Francisco de 67–8

Madrid 3–4, 35, 157, 164
Maghrib 1, 5–6, 10, 18, 25–6, 40–3, 53, 55, 70, 86, 137, 153–7, 191, 201
  see also Algiers; Morocco; Tunis
Mahamet the Jew, Alcaide 117–21
Mallette, Karla 22n.6
Malta 12, 42, 45, 77, 82–4, 103, 115, 184
Mármol Carvajal, Luis del 26, 101n.35
Márquez Villanueva, Francisco 144n.16, 159, 167, 174
Marrakesh 8, 12, 35, 79–80, 178
Marseille 12, 195
Martínez Torres, José Antonio 78n.11, 96n.31, 123n.57
martyrs, martyrdom 104–5, 116, 131–52
  becoming apostates 49, 200
  Catholics and Protestants 129, 132–4, 138, 144–5
  in Cervantes' works 129–31, 148–52
  definitions 138–9
  in Muslim lands 131–2, 144, 151
  performance of 142
  types of 141, 152
Mas, Albert 6n.2, 25, 144n.16
Mascarenhas, João Carvalho 45–52, 54, 122
Matar, Nabil 6, 18, 74n.8, 75, 78n.12, 135, 175–6, 192
Medina, Úrsola de 188–9
Mediterranean
  chorography 10–11
  cruelty to others, oneself 129–52
  definitions and parameters 1–12, 195
  fiction and non-fiction 16–26, 69, 181, 202
  genres and truths 16–26, 25n.8, 194
  lingua franca 18, 127, 188
  map xii
  movement of people, 5, 181, 195
  sources on 13–15, 73–6, 192, 202–3
  writers and writing 18–20, 73–6, 194
  see also frontier; Muslim-Christian divide; renegades; slaves
Meknes 8
Mendoça, Hyeronimo 178
Menéndez Pelayo, Marcelino 158

Menorca 97, 201
Mercedarians 19, 50, 144
Mestre, Vicent 157
'mirror characters' 170
Molière 25
Molina, licentiate (Morisco) 160–1
Monta, Susannah Brietz 132, 132n.3
Montaigne, Michel de 92–4
Moors, term 24–5, 27, 102, 162
  see also Algiers; frontier; Moriscos; religions, Abrahamic; Tunis
Morano, José 144–6
Morat Raez Maltrapillo 118n.50
Moriscos
  diversity of 196–7
  frontier figures 153–6, 202
  in literature 24–5, 97–100, 153
  migration, expulsion 6, 28, 153–75, 201
  as 'renegades' 100–9
  slaves 43, 159
  slave-owners 102–5, 141–5
  in Spain 112, 137, 141–4, 199
  term 24, 102
  war of Granada 10, 133n.4, 134n.7
  as writers 20, 79–81, 160–1
Morocco 6, 112–13, 122, 154, 161, 180, 184–6
Moüette, Germain 89–90
Munari, Simona 25
Murad III, Sultan 86–9
Murād, Seyyid 140n.13
Muslim-Christian divide 4–9 passim, 12, 31, 70, 90, 121, 123, 154

Naples 10, 12, 40, 42n.10, 77–8, 195
'nation' (as ethnic group, 'caste') 82n.16, 106, 119n.53, 170, 172
Neuser, Adam 74
Nietzsche, Friedrich 16, 31–2, 147–8, 181, 196–7
Nurbanu (alias Cali) 87–9, 200

Ohanna, Natalio 102n.38, 104, 144n.16
Okeley, William 144–5
Oliver Asín, Jaime 113
Oran and Mazalquivir (Mers-el-Kebir) 103, 164, 190, 190n.29
orientalism 29, 29n.13, 48
Oromig, Pere 157
Orsoni-Avila, Françoise 56n.26

otherness, 'the other' *see* alterities
Ottoman Empire
   foreign relations 30, 44, 86, 176
   regencies 10, 193, 201
   renegades in 85, 94–5, 200
   territories 9, 189

Palermo 12, 114
Palomino, Antonio 157–8
Pannilini, Giorgio del Giglio 74, 94–6
Pantoja, Gutierre 92n.27
Pasamonte, Jerónimo de 151
Paz y Meliá, Antonio 59n.30
Perceval, José María 197n.2
Pérez de Hita, Ginés 25, 133n.4, 190
Pérez de Montalbán 28–31
Pérez, Francisco (alias Alí) 106
Perry, Mary Elizabeth 166n.8
Pessoa, Fernando 127
Philip II of Spain 112
Philip III of Spain 156–61, 164, 167n.11
Philip IV of Spain 114, 157–8
Piccinino, Ali 123–4
Pirenne, Henri 4, 6n.3
Pitts, Joseph 74
Portugal 41, 44–8, 70, 122, 182–3, 186, 202
Pratt, Mary Louise 12–13
Prothero, Stephen 124n.58
Purcell, Nicholas 6, 9, 15

Quartier, Antoine 25

Rabelais, François 24–5, 151n.30
race 42, 76, 77n.10, 158, 196
Racine, Jean 25
religions, Abrahamic
   belief, 'faith', praxis 81, 124–5, 124n.58, 177, 198
   relations among 79–83, 113, 117–28, 171, 176–9, 184–6, 188–9, 190–1, 195, 198
renegades
   alterity of 33, 136, 198
   conversion 53, 71, 73–4, 121–2, 178, 189–91
   frontier figures 33, 71–128 *passim*, 139, 154–5, 180, 186, 189, 199–202
   heteronyms 127, 200
   historical 31, 31n.15, 71–128, 136–7
   literary 28–31, 96–100, 127–8, 189–92
   and Moriscos 101n.34
   numbers 41–2
   patronage system 84
   performance of 127–8, 200
   profiles 28–31, 84–121, 136–7
   religion, belief, practice 31–3, 71–128 *passim*
   as slave owners 55, 66, 90–1, 186
   sources 71, 75–6, 192
   terms, definition 32, 71–3, 102
   women 28–31, 33, 63, 66, 69, 87–9, 96–100, 109–10
   as writers 19, 74, 94–6
Rhodes 201
Ribera, Juan de 164–7, 167n.11, 168n.13
Ripol, Juan 160–2, 168n.14, 169n.17
Rodríguez G. de Ceballos, Alfonso 132n.3, 133, 138
Rodríguez Mediano, Fernando 71n.2, 125, 178
Rome 12, 35, 40, 78, 114–15, 133, 164, 169
Rostagno, Lucia 76, 125–6, 179
Roșu, Felicia 42
Roxelana (Hürrem Sultan, Roxane) 95, 200
Ruiz Lagos, Manuel 164

Salé-Rabat 154
San José, Antonio Juan Andreu de 188–9
Sapiencia, Otavio 26, 151
Scaraffia, Lucetta 76, 89n.24, 92n.27
Schick, Irvin Cemil 56n.26
Schwartz, Stuart 178
Selim II, Sultan 87–9
Seville 12, 40, 183
Sicily 10, 114
Simmel, Georg 8, 8n.4, 195, 202
slavery 35–71
   Mediterranean frontier 32, 36, 43–4, 70, 196, 202
   and narrative 18–22, 25–6
   types of 19, 32, 36–45, 49–50, 69–70, 196–7
slaves
   becoming slaves 46–55
   literary 21–8, 31, 56–8, 63–9, 182–3
   numbers 40–2
   race 39–42, 42–3n.11, 196
   slave markets 77, 83, 186
   sources 136

slaves (*cont.*)
  term 37–8, 37n.3, 38n.5
  value of 39, 55
  women 19, 28, 32, 35–6, 41, 44–8, 51–2, 55–69, 188–9, 197
Sola, Emilio 56n.26, 72n.1–2, 84n.18, 89n.25, 92n.27
Sola, Emilio, and José F. de la Peña 84n.18, 84n.20, 86
Sola, Emilio, and José María Parreño 102n.37, 132n.3, 141n.14
Sosa, Antonio de 75, 178
  demography of Algiers 13, 101n.35, 192–3, 195
  history of governors 84n.18, 85–7
  martyrdom 138–44, 143n.15, 151
  portrayal of Algiers 17, 20, 24–6
  renegades 73–5, 91, 99n.33, 102–5, 114–20, 136
  representation of Muslims 52, 69
  slaves 41–2, 50, 175
Spain
  and the Maghrib 104, 155–6, 202
  and Moriscos 153–75 *passim*
  and Ottomans 8, 44, 70
  and Protestants 136
Stella, Alessandro 55
Suleiman the Magnificent 68

Tabarca (island near Tunis) 185
Tarifa 89–90
Teijeiro Fuentes, Miguel Ángel, 151n.29
Temimi, Abdeldjelil 73, 180
Teresa de Ávila, St. 137
Tetuan 89–90, 154
Tlemcen 101n.36, 113
Torres, Diego de 26, 151
Trinitarians 19, 50, 136, 144
Tunis
  diverse population 6, 8, 154
  history of 10, 67, 85, 113, 201
  in literature 28–31, 67
  renegades 48, 74–5, 114–17
  slaves 114, 184–6
Turbet-Delof, Guy 25, 25n.8, 89–90, 123n.57
Türkçelik, Evrim 92n.27
Turks 52, 101n.36, 124, 125, 154, 177, 180, 183–4, 187–8, 189, 192, 202
  as corsairs 99n.33, 100
  in literature 24–5, 63–5, 151n.30, 153, 182–3
  slaves 55, 91, 109–10
  term 24, 27, 50, 72, 92–3, 102, 136
  treatment of slaves 46–53, 136–7
Turmeda, Anselm (alias 'Abdullāh al-Tarjumān) 74
Twain, Mark 16, 177

Uluç Ali (Uchalí) 64, 84–7, 95, 136–7

Valencia 96–100, 102–5, 141–4, 153, 188–9
'valenciana' (renegade) 96–100
Valencia, Pedro de 156–7, 168n.14
Valetta 12, 77, 195
Vega, Lope de 102–5, 112n.46, 113, 143–4, 149, 151, 158, 191
Velázquez, Diego 157–8
  portrait of Juan de Pareja *159*
Venice 12, 30n.14, 119
Vincent, Bernard 37n.3, 41, 56n.26, 78, 134, 166n.8
Vitkus, Daniel 74n.7

White, Hayden 16
Wiegers, Gerard 101n.34

Ximénez, Francisco 101n.35

Zayas, María de 38n.5
Zonza, Christian 26, 26n.9–10

EU authorised representative for GPSR:
Easy Access System Europe, Mustamäe tee 50,
10621 Tallinn, Estonia
gpsr.requests@easproject.com

www.ingramcontent.com/pod-product-compliance
Lightning Source LLC
Chambersburg PA
CBHW070346240426
43671CB00013BA/2425